8080A Microcomputer Interfacing and Programming

Second Edition

by
Peter R. Rony
Department of Chemical Engineering
Virginia Polytechnic Institute & State University

A Revision of
THE 8080A BUGBOOK: MICROCOMPUTER
INTERFACING AND PROGRAMMING
By Peter R. Rony

Howard W. Sams & Co., Inc.
4300 WEST 62ND ST. INDIANAPOLIS, INDIANA 46268 USA

International Standard Book Number: 0-672-21933-6
Library of Congress Catalog Card Number: 82-50016

Edited by: *Lou Keglovits*
Illustrated by: *Christine Lixon*

Printed in the United States of America.

Preface

In 1971, the first microprocessor chip became commercially available. This was the Intel Corporation 4004 four-bit microprocessor chip, which, while somewhat difficult to use in real computer applications, nevertheless did lead the way in control applications where it still is used today. The Intel 8008 eight-bit microprocessor followed quickly, and permitted the user to configure a small general-purpose "computer." At the time, several companies started to offer standard logic cards that had the necessary central processing unit, control logic, memory, and input/output buffers so that real applications could be tackled.

After the announcement of the 8008 chip, many semiconductor companies scrambled to get on the microprocessor bandwagon. Intel followed with their powerful 8080, Motorola with the 6800, Fairchild with the F-8, National Semiconductor with the SC/MP and PACE, Texas Instruments with the 9900, Zilog with the Z80, and so on. Early in 1977, we witnessed a surge of "computer-on-a-chip" devices, such as the 8048, that contained in a single integrated circuit chip package all the necessary CPU, memory, and I/O capability to construct a small microcomputer.

Not only are microcomputers finding widespread use in control and instrumentation applications, they have also spawned the hobby computer market. Seven years ago, some hobbyists may have dreamed of having their own computer, but few had one. Now, hundreds of thousands of hobbyists and professionals have their own computers and are using them for general programming applications, playing computer games, handling business accounting and inventory functions, teaching children, and saving energy in the home. Of the early companies that started to market home computers during 1975-77, Apple® Computer,

Inc. is considered to be one of the American success stories, Cromemco, Inc. is thriving, MITS Inc. and IMSAI Manufacturing Corporation are gone, and what ever happened to Southwest Technical Products Corporation? The surprise is that Radio Shack, with its TRS-80® product line, has out-marketed Texas Instruments in the personal computer field.

This is just the beginning. We can safely predict that home entertainment/communication centers based upon the marriage of television, satellite communications, VLSI integrated circuits, and microcomputers will be sold by the millions as a major consumer product during this decade. As Congress and the FCC come to grips with the communications revolution spawned by microelectronics technology, communication satellites, and optical fibers, the next step will be expanded digital communications—the "network nation." In fact, the only limitation today seems to be the speed of such communications; the use of modems operating at 300 baud is unsatisfactory for the communication of data files between homes, offices, libraries, and vendors of data base services.

Inexpensive microcomputers are penetrating every facet of life. Today they can be found in automobiles, sewing machines, microwave ovens, washers, driers, television sets, vending machines, gasoline pumps, pinball machines, telephones, typewriters, elevators, heating and cooling systems, taxi meters, laboratory instruments, children's toys, and so on. New industries are being created, and some existing ones threatened. How about a moment of silence for the slide rule?

The objective of this book is to teach you the four fundamental tasks of microcomputer interfacing:

- Device select pulse generation
- Microcomputer output
- Microcomputer input
- Interrupt servicing

in the context of 8080A-based microcomputers. I hope to give you the basic concepts of microcomputer I/O programming so that you can develop your own interfaces to other digital devices, including personal computers, crt displays, line printers, character printers, analog-to-digital converters, digital-to-analog converters, laboratory instruments, and the like.

Chapter 1 discusses the future role of microcomputers (as viewed from the late 1970s), the four fundamental tasks of microcomputer interfacing, and summarizes the digital concepts that you will require to make proper use of this book. Chapter 2 describes a small 8080A-based microcomputer and discusses the concept of microcomputer input/output in greater detail, especially from the point of view of the use of device select pulses to strobe digital integrated circuit chips. Chapter 3 provides an introduction to 8080 microcomputer programming. The entire 8080 instruction set is discussed in some detail. Specific attention is focused on data transfer operations, arithmetic and logical operations, branch instructions, input and output instructions, and register decoding. The 8080 instruction set is summarized in a variety of ways.

Chapter 4 treats the very important topic of device select pulse generation. A variety of practical and experimental decoder circuits are provided that can generate one, sixteen, or as many as 256 different device select pulses. Chapter 5 describes an extremely useful technique for counting the number of clock cycles required for the execution of segments of microcomputer programs. The technique permits you to verify the theoretical number of clock cycles for every instruction in the 8080 instruction set. Standard programs are provided that generate time delays that are multiples of either 0.5 ms or 0.2 s.

Chapter 6, perhaps the most difficult one in this book, provides a description of the internal operations of the 8080 microprocessor chip. The timing behavior of the 8080 is discussed in terms of states, machine cycles, and instruction cycles. Circuits are provided to demonstrate how the $\overline{\text{IN}}$ and $\overline{\text{OUT}}$ control signals can be generated. Chapter 7 discusses the important topic of microcomputer input/output, both the latching of output data and the input of three-state buffered data into the 8080. Circuits and programs are provided that teach you how to detect a specific key on an ASCII keyboard, how to output data to a multiplexed display, and how to log digital data in the laboratory.

Chapter 8 discusses in considerable detail several modes of microcomputer operation, including polled operation and interrupt operation. The subjects of subroutines, interrupts, external flags, masking, the stack, and the strategy of interrupt servicing and priority interrupt software and hardware are all treated.

Chapter 9 is a new chapter in this second edition. It provides a treatment of advanced I/O techniques that was first published as a series of monthly columns on "Interfacing Fundamentals" in Computer Design magazine during 1980-1981. With the recent advances in LSI and VLSI integrated circuits, it is no longer sufficient to only know the simple input/output techniques discussed in Chapter 7. Parallel data communications between microcomputers and between a microcomputer and a sophisticated processor chip—such as a floating-point arithmetic chip or an I/O processor—are becoming common. Consequently, an understanding of conditional input/output, flags, semaphores, I/O handshake protocols, and the IEEE 488 bus is necessary. In Chapter 9, we have tried to provide a logical, stepwise approach to advanced I/O techniques.

The first eight chapters of this book comprise a revised and expanded version of an earlier book entitled, *Microcomputer Interfacing Experiments Using the Mark 80 Microcomputer, an 8080 System*, published in August 1975 and marketed by E&L Instruments, Inc., Derby, Connecticut. [Incidentally, E&L Instruments, Inc. was one of the manufacturers in the early home computer sweepstakes—it was the second U.S. company to introduce a microcomputer in 1975, only several months after MITS, Inc.] Experiments in the original book were either rewritten as examples, incorporated into the text material, or eliminated. The chapter on interrupts and external flags was expanded considerably over its previous length. Numerous editorial changes were made in 1977 to improve the clarity of the material. Now, in 1982, I have observed that almost all of this technical information is still applicable, and thus have made very few changes to it in this second edition.

In this book, I assume that you have a knowledge of the basic concepts of digital electronics, including gates, flip-flops, latches, decoders, multiplexers, three-state and open-collector busing, memories, shift registers, displays, counters, arithmetic/logic units, and the like. Many such concepts are used in our discussions of microcomputer interfacing. *Logic & Memory Experiments Using TTL Integrated Circuits*, a Howard W. Sams & Co., Inc. publication, provides such information. If you wish to interface a microcomputer serially to a crt terminal, printer, or microcomputer, you will need to know some of the basic principles of asynchronous serial digital data communications. One book that treats such material in a systematic fashion is *Interfacing & Scientific Data Communication Experiments Using the Universal Asynchronous Receiver/Transmitter (UART) and 20 mA Current Loops*, also a Howard W. Sams & Co., Inc. publication. Finally, if you wish to make the transition from 8080 code to Z80 code, you may wish to look at *Z80 Microprocessor Programming and Interfacing*, Howard W. Sams & Co., Inc.

I wish to thank Mr. Sydney Shapiro for giving me the opportunity to publish material on advanced I/O techniques in Computer Design magazine.

PETER R. RONY

Contents

Computer Know?—8080 Microprocessor Registers—What Types of Operations Does the 8080 Microprocessor Perform?—8080 Mnemonic Instructions—Octal/Hexadecimal Listing of the 8080 Instruction Set—An Example of Instruction Decoding—Register Decoding—Arithmetic and Logic Operation Decoding—Immediate Operation Decoding—Branch Operation Decoding—Conditional Branch Instructions—Condition Flag Decoding—Register Pair Decoding—Increment and Decrement Operation Decoding—Data and Memory Addressing Modes—Accumulator Instructions—8080 Instruction Group—8080 Instruction Summary—Assembly Language—Machine Language vs. Assembly Language Programs—Introduction to the Examples—Example No. 1—Example No. 2—Example No. 3—Example No. 4—Example No. 5—Example No. 6—Example No. 7—Example No. 8—Example No. 9—Example No. 10—Example No. 11—Example No. 12—Test—What Have You Accomplished in This Chapter?

CHAPTER 4

Objectives—Definitions—8080 Microprocessor I/O Instructions—Device Select Pulse Decoding—A Sample Microcomputer Program—Device Select Pulses as Control Pulses—Example—Test—What Have You Accomplished in This Chapter?

CHAPTER 5

Objectives—Definitions—Monostable Multivibrators—The Microcomputer as a Monostable Multivibrator—How Long Does It Take to Execute a Microcomputer Instruction?—Clock Cycle Listing for the 8080 Instruction Set—Counting Clock Cycles: Some Simple Microcomputer Programs—Timing Loops—Sequencing With a Microcomputer—Controlling Power With a Microcomputer—Test—What Have You Accomplished in This Chapter?

CHAPTER 6

Objectives—Definitions—The Bidirectional Data Bus—Instruction Cycles Machine Cycles—Machine Cycle Identification—Single Stepping an 8080 Microcomputer—The 8212 Eight-Bit Input/Output Port Chip—Test—What Have You Accomplished in This Chapter?

CHAPTER 7

CHAPTER 8

CHAPTER 9

APPENDIX 1

APPENDIX 2

APPENDIX 3

CHAPTER 1

What Is a Microcomputer?

In this book, you will study real examples that demonstrate the principles, concepts, and applications of an 8-bit *microcomputer* that is based upon the *8080 microprocessor* integrated-circuit chip. In doing so, you will be able to participate in a remarkable electronics revolution in which the *computer* will be transformed from a large, expensive, and rather esoteric machine into a compact, inexpensive, and common device that will be used by millions of individuals. Before very long, you will find small computers in your home, automobile, lawn mower, office, and perhaps even in some of your recreational equipment. These small computers are everywhere—millions of them! They are having a profound influence upon everyday life. Already, a cousin of the microprocessor chip, the calculator chip, has essentially made the slide rule obsolete. What has happened with the slide rule will happen with other mechanical devices.

Large computers will continue to perform complicated mathematical calculations, and small hand-held electronic calculators will perform the simpler ones. Since the common view of the computer is as a calculating machine, one might ask: Where does the microcomputer fit? After all, if the large computers do all of the more difficult calculations and the electronic calculators all of the simple ones, is there anything left for the microcomputer to do? The answer to this seeming dilemma resides in the fact that computers have at least two important functions:

1. As number- and information-crunching machines in which digitally coded information is manipulated at high speeds.

2. As *programmable digital controllers* that control machines and processes by passing digital signals to and from the computer.

The major use of microcomputers will be as controllers, not as information-crunching machines. We could estimate the possible market for microcomputers if we knew how many machines that could be controlled by a microcomputer exist per capita in the United States. The telephone could use a microcomputer, as could an electric typewriter, a television set, a sophisticated child's game, a stereo set, a dishwasher, an electric range, a clothes washer, etc. When one includes homes, offices, industry, and laboratories, there may be between three and ten machines or devices per capita that can be automated with the aid of microcomputers. With 200 million individuals in the U.S., this translates to 600 million to 2 billion microcomputers. The market for electronic calculators may be no more than 100 million, which is still a large number.

The subject of computers is vast, and a series of textbooks can be written to cover the general scope of computer architecture, operation, and applications. This is not the intention with this book, which differs from most texts written on computers in the respect that the primary emphasis will be on the use of a computer as a controller rather than as a number-crunching machine. You will learn how to *interface* a microcomputer, where the word "interface" means the joining of the microcomputer to an instrument, device, or machine in a way such that both operate in a compatible and coordinated fashion.[1]* You will focus your attention only on a computer built around an 8080 microprocessor chip. The reasons for doing so are as follows:

1. Based upon the number of manufacturers who employ the 8080 microprocessor chip or its 8085 and Z80 successors, it is likely that 8080-family based software is more widespread and available than software for other types of microprocessors.
2. By 1981, the 8080 microprocessor chip is sold at a price of $5 in quantities of one, and even less for considerably larger quantities. The 8085 microprocessor is also inexpensive.
3. The 8080 microprocessor instruction set is quite powerful. Programs are relatively easy to write.
4. The 8080 microprocessor is relatively fast. It can execute an arithmetic instruction such as add or subtract in only 2 μs. With improvements in the state of the art, even faster 8080 chips are now available.

*See Appendix 1 for references in the text denoted by superscripts.

5. An 8080 microcomputer can directly access up to 65,536 different 8-bit memory locations and can generate 256 different input strobe signals and 256 different output strobe signals.
6. More textbooks describe programming and interfacing of 8080-family chips than any other microprocessor chip.
7. The most popular personal computer, as of 1981, is the TRS-80, a Z80-based microcomputer. The Zenith Z-89 also uses a Z80, but provides an operating system, editor, assembler, peripheral interchange program, and debugger that are written in octal 8080 instructions and whose complete source listing can be purchased. Just announced are the following small business computers—Datapoint Corporation 1550, Hewlett-Packard HP 125, IBM System/23 Datamaster, and Xerox Corporation 820—all of which contain 8080-family microprocessor chips (*Electronics 54* (16), August 11, 1981, pp. 85-86).

Thus, I believe that your time is well spent learning the principles, concepts, and applications of the 8080. Do not underestimate the value of the Z-89 source listings. They permit you to extend this introduction to microcomputer programming to some fundamental principles of computer science.

This book is concerned with the four fundamental tasks of computer interfacing:

1. *The generation of device select signals.*
2. *The latching of output data.*
3. *The acquisition of input data.*
4. *The servicing of interrupt signals.*

An extensive series of examples will provide you with the concepts and techniques necessary for developing your own circuits and the writing of your own programs to accomplish one or more of the four fundamental tasks. Once you have mastered these tasks, the world of microcomputer controls will be yours.

INTRODUCTION TO THIS CHAPTER

In the chapters that follow this one, you will encounter a series of examples that will help you to develop competence in *microcomputer interfacing*. Before you do so, however, it would be useful for you to develop an understanding of what a *computer* is and what the distinctions are between *microcomputers, minicomputers, computers, controllers, data processors,* and *logic processors.*

Simple instructions can be performed in as little as 1.28 μs (0.8 μs for the 8085A-2 chip), which compares to the 1.2-μs instruction time for similar operations in the Digital Equipment Corp. PDP-8/E minicomputer. The 8080A chip is being "second sourced" by Texas Instruments, National Semiconductor, NEC, Siemens, and perhaps other chip manufacturers. Such actions signify that the semiconductor industry considers the 8080 to be an important force in the microprocessor market.

Any discussion of the 8080 can be subdivided into the following topics:

- The pin configuration and pin functions of the 8080 chip.
- The organization of a typical microcomputer that employs the 8080 chip.
- The internal operation of the 8080 microprocessor.
- The instruction set of the 8080 microprocessor.

Starting in this chapter and continuing in several chapters, we shall discuss each of these topics. The detail with which we shall do so will vary from topic to topic. The objective is not to bombard you with a fusillade of timing diagrams and *machine cycle* descriptions, but rather to help you develop the skills that you will need to use an 8080-based breadboard microcomputer system.

For the interested reader, I recommend the following sources for additional information on the hardware characteristics and operation of the 8080 chip and its successor, the 8085:

Intel Corp., *Intel 8080 Microcomputer Systems User's Manual*, Santa Clara, California, September 1975. (Presumably this manual has been updated.)

Adam Osborne and Jerry Kane, *An Introduction to Microcomputers. Volume 2. Some Real Microprocessors*, Osborne/McGraw Hill, Berkeley, California, 1978-9.

Intel Corp., *MCS-85 User's Manual*, Santa Clara, California, 1977.

Intel Corp., *Peripheral Design Handbook*, Santa Clara, California, 1980.

OBJECTIVES

At the end of this chapter, you will be able to do the following:

- Explain the difference between a microprocessor and a microcomputer.

Table 1-1. The Spectrum of Computer-Equipment Complexity, from Simple Hard-Wired Logic Systems to High-Performance General Data Processing Equipment. This Table Is Based on Pro-Log Corp. Material and Is Adapted From an Article by Wallace B. Riley in the October 17, 1974, Issue of *Electronics*.

Word Length (Bits)	1	2	4	8	16	32	64
Complexity	Hard-Wired Logic	Programmed Logic Array	Calculator	Microprocessor	Minicomputer	Large Computer	
Application		Control		Dedicated Computation		Low-Cost General Data-Processing	High-Performance General Data Processing
Cost	Under $100 (1974)			$1000 (1974)			$10,000 (1974)	$100,000 and Up (1974)
Memory Size	Very Small 0-4 Words	Small 2-10 Words		Medium 10-1000 Words	Large 1000-1 Million Words		Very large More Than 1 Million Words
Program	Read-Only							Reloadable
Speed Constraints	Real Time	Slow		Medium			Throughput-Oriented
Input-Output	Integrated	Few Simple Devices		Some Complex Devices			Roomful of Equipment
Design	Logic	Logic + Microprogram			Microprogram Macroprogram		Macroprogram High-Level Language Software System
Manufacturing Volume	Large						Small

- Define the terms: computer, digital computer, data processor, controller, hardware, software, memory, memory word, memory address, memory data, read, write, random access memory, read-only memory, interfacing, device select pulse, and interrupt.
- Describe different types of computers and controllers on the basis of the following characteristics: word length, complexity, application, cost, memory size, program, speed constraints, input/output, design, and manufacturing volume.
- Describe the operation of a typical 8080 microcomputer system.

MICROPROCESSORS AS MICROCONTROLLERS AND LOGIC PROCESSORS

Microprocessor applications tend to fall into the following categories:

- Controllers
- Consumer products
- Communications

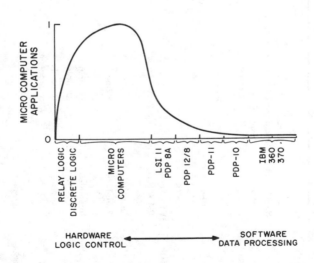

WHERE MICROCOMPUTERS FIT

Fig. 1-1. Applications foreseen for microcomputers. Microcomputers will carve out their own niche between discrete logic and inexpensive minicomputers.

- Terminals
- Microcomputers

Each of these categories is discussed in some detail in the *Microprocessor Handbook*.[3] As shown in Table 1-1 and Fig. 1-1, microprocessor applications fall between relay logic and discrete random logic (gates and flip-flops) on one hand and inexpensive minicomputers such as the LSI-11 and PDP-8/A on the other. By 1981, microcomputers fabricated from microprocessor chips and chip sets have exceeded the sophistication of the popular minicomputers and lack only the enormous software base of, for example, the PDP-11 series of minicomputers to become fully competitive. High-level languages have become common on most of the popular personal computers. For example, if you have a Zenith Z-89 equipped with two floppy disk drives, you can get Microsoft FORTRAN for $175, COBOL for $395, and UCSD P-System with PASCAL language for $295.

When it was first introduced, the Intel 8080 microprocessor chip sold for $360 in quantities of one. By 1981, you could get the same chip at your local Radio Shack for under $10. Increasingly, the price of a personal computer reflects the mechanical aspects of the equipment, i.e., the housing and electromechanical devices, and the software.

In this book the emphasis is on control and logic processing applications. We are using the 8080 microprocessor chip to teach you about microcomputer interfacing and programming. Although it is possible, and common, to tie a $3000 8-bit personal computer to $10,000 worth of input/output equipment and use it instead of PDP-11 type minicomputers, I would like to encourage you to consider the role of *computer networks* in which one to ten instruments and devices containing 8080 chips or other microprocessors are all tied to a single large computer, probably a minicomputer. An example of such a computer network is shown in Fig. 1-2. Instruments A through G all communicate directly to the much larger minicomputer through an 8080-based microcomputer contained within each instrument. The instruments are controlled by the 8080 computers, and the minicomputer oversees such control and logs important instrument parameters. The minicomputer might also provide the microcomputer control set points at the beginning of each day. Each microcomputer might contain only 16K of memory, whereas the minicomputer might have a minimum of 128K of memory to permit it to handle a group of high-level languages such as FORTRAN, PASCAL, and APL. Keep in mind that microcomputers can be quite inexpensive, perhaps no more than $300 for a personal computer that connects to a television set. It is becoming commonplace to purchase microcomputer systems that have several microprocessors or single-chip microcomputers within them, each controlling a single hardware function such as a keyboard/display, disk drive, etc. The more venturesome individuals in the electronics industry predict full microcomputer systems for a cost of $10 to $20 in quantities of 100.

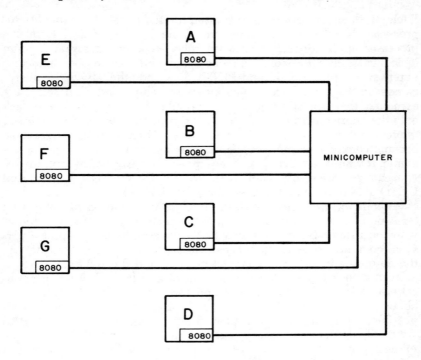

Fig. 1-2. An example of a computer network. The individual instruments or machines A through G are controlled by built-in 8080 microprocessors. These microprocessors also communicate back and forth with the minicomputer, which monitors the operation of the entire system.

Such microcomputers will be complete "systems on silicon," and will include 64K of memory, high-level software and communication protocols.

DEFINITIONS

accumulator—The register and associated digital electronic circuitry in the arithmetic unit of a computer in which arithmetic and logical operations are performed.

bidirectional—Responsive in opposite directions.[4]

bidirectional data bus—A data bus in which digital information can be transferred in either direction.

bus—A path over which digital information is transferred, from any of several sources to any of several destinations. Only one transfer of information can take place at any one time. While such transfer is taking place, all other sources that are tied to the bus must be disabled.

clock—(a) Any device that generates at least one clock pulse, or (b) a timing device in a system that provides a continuous series of timing pulses.[4]

computer—Any device, usually electronic, capable of accepting information, comparing, adding, subtracting, multiplying, dividing, and integrating this information, and then supplying the results of these processes in acceptable form. The major elements of a computer usually include memory, control, arithmetic, logical, and input and output facilities.[4]

computer interfacing—The synchronization of digital data transmission between a computer and one or more external input/output devices.

controller—An instrument that holds a process or condition at a desired level or status as determined by comparison of the actual value with the desired value.[4]

data processor—A digital device that processes data. It may be a computer, but in a larger sense it may gather, distribute, digest, analyze, and perform other organization or smoothing operations on data. These operations, then, are not necessarily computational. Data processor is a more inclusive term than computer.[2]

device select pulse—A synchronization pulse generated by a computer to synchronize the operation of a specific input or output device.

digital computer—An electronic instrument capable of accepting, storing and arithmetically manipulating information, which includes both data and the controlling program. The information is handled in the form of coded binary digits (0 and 1) represented by dual voltage levels.[6]

digital controller—A controller that acquires the actual value of the condition in digital form and compares it to the desired value contained within the controller. If there is any difference between the two, a digital signal is sent out by the controller to reduce this difference.

direct address—An address that specifies the location within memory of an instruction or data byte.

external device addressing—A device name, expressed as a digital code, that is generated by the CPU to address a specific external device. Both input and output devices can be addressed.

fixed-program computer—A computer in which the sequence of instructions is permanently stored or wired. The computer program is not subject to change either by the computer or the programmer except by rewiring or changing the storage input.[5]

general-purpose computer—A computer designed to solve a large variety of problems; a stored-program computer which may be adapted to any of a large class of operations.[5]

hardware—The mechanical, magnetic, electronic, and electrical devices from which a computer or computer system is fabricated; the assembly of material forming a computer system.[2]

input/output, input-output—General term for the equipment used to communicate with a computer and the data involved in the communication.[5]

interfacing—The joining of members of a group (such as people, instruments, etc.) in such a way that they are able to function in a compatible and coordinated fashion.[1]

interrupt—In a computer, a break in the normal execution of a computer program such that the program can be resumed from that point at a later time. The source of the interrupt can be external or internal.

memory—Any device that can store logic 1 and logic 0 bits in such a manner that a single bit or group of bits can be accessed and retrieved.[10]

memory address—The storage location of a memory word.

memory cell—A single storage element of memory, capable of storing one bit of digital information.

memory data—The memory word occupying a specific location in memory, or the memory words collectively located in memory.

memory word—A group of bits occupying one storage location in a computer. This group is treated by the computer circuits as an entity, by the control unit as an instruction, and by the arithmetic unit as a quantity. Each bit is stored in a single memory cell.

microcomputer—A fully operational computer system based upon a microprocessor chip.

microcontroller—A small controller, most likely one based upon a microprocessor chip.

microprocessor—A single integrated-circuit chip that contains at least 75 percent of the power of a very small computer.

monostable multivibrator—A circuit having only one stable state, from which it can be triggered to change the state, but only for a predetermined interval, after which it returns to the original state.

programmable read-only memory—A read-only memory that is field programmable by the user.[10]

pulser—A logic switch that generates a clock pulse.

random access memory—A semiconductor memory into which logic 0 and logic 1 states can be written (stored) and then read out again (retrieved).[10]

read—To transmit data from a memory to some other digital device.

read-only memory—A semiconductor memory from which digital data can be repeatedly read out, but cannot be written into, as is the case for a random access memory.[10]

software—The totality of programs and routines used to extend the capabilities of computers, such as compilers, assemblers, narrators, routines, and subroutines.[5]

special-purpose computer—A computer designed to solve a specific class or narrow range of problems.[5]

stored-program computer—A computer capable of performing sequences of internally stored instructions, usually capable of modifying those instructions as directed by the instructions.[5]

volatile memory—In computers, any memory which can return information only as long as power is applied to the memory. The opposite of nonvolatile memory.[4]

wired-program computer—A computer in which nearly all instructions are determined by the placement of interconnecting wires held in a removable plugboard. This arrangement allows for changes of operations by simply changing plugboards. If the wires are held in permanently soldered connections, the computer is called a fixed-program type.[4]

write—To transmit data into a memory from some other digital electronic device. A synonym is store.

REVIEW OF DIGITAL ELECTRONICS: WHAT IS USEFUL?

Two previous books, *Logic & Memory Experiments Using TTL Integrated Circuits, Books 1 and 2* provide the background that you will need to use for this book. Some of the more important chips and digital concepts that you should understand include the following:

- The logic operations AND, OR, NAND, NOR, and exclusive OR.
- The gating characteristics of the four basic logic gates: AND, NAND, OR, and NOR.
- The 7400, 7402, 7408, and 7432 integrated-circuit chips.
- Decoders, especially the 7442 four-line-to-ten-line and the 74154 four-line-to-sixteen-line integrated-circuit chips.
- Latches, including the 7474, 7475, 74100, 74175, 74192, 74193, and 74198 integrated-circuit chips. The 74192 and 74193 chips are counters, and the 74198 chip is an 8-bit shift register.
- J-K flip-flops, including the 7470, 7473, 7476, and 74106 integrated-circuit chips.
- Counters, including the 7490, 7493, 74192, and 74193 integrated-circuit chips.

- Three-state bussing.
- Input/output devices such as logic switches, pulsers, clocks, lamp monitors, and seven-segment LED displays.
- The terms *strobe, enable,* and *disable.*
- Monostable multivibrators, such as the 74121, 74122, 74123, and 555 integrated-circuit chips.
- Clocked logic.
- Registers, including the 74198 8-bit shift register.
- Arithmetic operations, such as addition and subtraction, and the use of carry bits in binary systems.
- Multiplexing, including the 74153 four-line-to-one-line multiplexer.
- The function of strobe or chip enable inputs on 7400-series integrated-circuit chips.
- Binary, binary-coded decimal, octal, hexadecimal, and ASCII codes.

SOME HELPFUL REFERENCES

While I would like to provide more introductory text on the subjects of computers, minicomputers, microcomputers, computer peripherals, and programming languages, I am not able to do so owing to the limitations of space in this chapter. For those readers who are interested, the following books are recommended. They approach the subject of computers in ways that are quite useful to the novice. I have updated the original listing provided in the 1977 edition of this book, and have focused on introductory books.

1. Robert Moody, *The First Book of Microcomputers*, Hayden Book Company, Rochelle Park, NJ, 1978.
   Easy reading. My son liked it.
2. Karen Billings and David Moursund, *Are You Computer Literate?*, dilithium Press, Beaverton, Oregon, 1979.
   Easy reading.
3. David Hagelbarger and Saul Fingerman, *CARDIAC: A Cardboard Illustrative Aid to Computation*, Bell Telephone Laboratories, Inc., Murray Hill, NJ, 1968.
   A 52-page Bell System Educational Aid that presents a simplified view of what a computer is. Very well written, and quite useful for teaching purposes.
4. Rodnay Zaks, *Your First Computer, A Guide to Business and Personal Computing*, Sybex, Berkeley, CA, 1978.
   More comprehensive introduction to computers than the first three books in this list. Nice chapter on peripherals.
5. Valdimir Zwass, *Introduction to Computer Science*, Barnes and Noble Books, New York, NY, 1981.
   More advanced treatment of programming and computer systems. Not for the novice.

6. Adam Osborne, *An Introduction to Microcomputers. Volume O. The Beginner's Book,* Osborne/McGraw Hill, Berkeley, CA, 1979.
   Pursues topics in greater detail than does reference 4 in this list.
7. Daniel R. McGlynn, *Personal Computing: Home, Professional, and Small Business Applications,* John Wiley & Sons, Inc., New York, NY, 1979.
   Very broad treatment at a level similar to reference 4.
8. Charles J. Sippl, *Microcomputer Handbook,* Petrocelli/Charter, New York, NY, 1977.
   Very broad treatment at a level similar to reference 4, but hardly any figures provided.
9. Louis E. Frenzel, Jr., *The Howard W. Sams Crash Course in Microcomputers,* Howard W. Sams & Co., Inc., Indianapolis, IN, 1980.
   More elementary treatment. A self-instructional course that requires the reader to provide answers and take review tests. Very well illustrated. Focuses on important words and concepts. One of the best introductory books available.

DATA PROCESSOR VS. MICROPROCESSOR VS. MICROCOMPUTER

It is difficult to find a good definition for the term *digital computer.* The perspective on what is a computer given by Donald Eadie in his book *Introduction to the Basic Computer* is quite appealing:

"This chapter serves as a general introduction to the field of digital devices, with particular emphasis on those devices called *computers,* or more properly, *data processors.* The name data processor is more inclusive because modern machines in this general classification not only compute in the usual sense, but also perform other functions with the data which flow to and from them. For example, data processors may gather data from various incoming sources, sort it, rearrange it, and then print it. None of these operations involves the arithmetic operations normally associated with a computing device, but the term computer is often applied anyway.

"Therefore, for our purpose a computer is really a data processor. Even such data processing operations as rearranging data may require simple arithmetic such as addition. This explains why a certain amount of imprecision has entered our language and why confusion exists between the terms *computer* and *data processor.* The two terms are so loosely used at present that often one has to inquire further to determine exactly what is meant."[2]

Eadie thus defined the term *data processor* as follows:

data processor—A digital device that processes data. It may be a computer, but in a larger sense it may gather, distribute, digest, analyze, and perform other organization or smoothing operations on data.

These operations, then, are not necessarily computational. Data processor is a more inclusive term than computer.

It is tempting to define the term *microprocessor* as follows:

microprocessor—An extremely small data processor.

We begin to have problems when we attempt to draw a distinction between a *microprocessor* and *microcomputer*. To quote the Texas Instruments, Inc., *Microprocessor Handbook:*

"This lesson begins with the word 'microprocessor.' To some people microprocessor means microcomputer. To other people the words microprocessor and microcomputer are different. To them, 'microprocessor' is a broader and more generic term which describes an extremely small electronic system capable of performing specific tasks. Thus, microcomputer is an application of microprocessors."[3]

The authors would include themselves among the "them" category in the quotation of Texas Instruments Inc. To them, a microprocessor is a single integrated-circuit chip that contains at least 75 percent of the power of a very small computer. It usually cannot do anything without the aid of support chips and memory. In contrast, a *microcomputer* is a fully operational computer system based on a microprocessor chip. Such a system contains memory, latches, counters, input/output devices, buffers, and a power supply, in addition to the microprocessor chip. It may be a black box with only a single switch: OPERATE/RESET.

Another "point on the curve" is from an article by Laurence Altman in the April 18, 1974, issue of *Electronics:*

"What a microprocessor is . . . but first, what it isn't. A microprocessor is not a computer but only part of one. To make a computer out of a microprocessor requires the addition of memory for its control program, plus input and output circuits to operate peripheral equipment. Also, the word is not short for microprogrammable central processing unit. For, though some microprocessors are controlled by a microprogram, most are not.

"What a microprocessor is, then, is the control and processing portion of a small computer or microcomputer. Moreover, it has come to mean the kind of processor that can be built with LSI MOS circuitry, usually on one chip. Like all computer processors, microprocessors can handle both arithmetic and logic data in bit-parallel fashion under control of a program. But they are distinguished both from a minicomputer processor by their use of LSI with its lower power and costs, and from other LSI devices (except calculator chips) by their programmable behavior.

"In short, if a minicomputer is a 1-horsepower unit, the microprocessor plus supporting circuitry is a ¼-hp unit. But as LSI technology improves, it will become more powerful. Already single-chip bipolar and CMOS-on-sapphire processors are being developed that have almost the capability of the minicomputer."

HARDWARE VS. SOFTWARE

Hardware and *software* are important terms that will be used repeatedly in this chapter. It is appropriate, therefore, to define them early.

hardware—The mechanical, magnetic, electronic, and electrical devices from which a computer is fabricated; the assembly of material forming a computer.[2]

software—The totality of programs and routines used to extend the capabilities of computers, such as compilers, assemblers, narrators, routines, and subroutines. Contrasted with hardware.[5]

The specific 8080-based microcomputer ssytem that you will use, along with any integrated-circuit chips, wire, breadboarding aids, and peripheral devices, are all considered to be the hardware. The programs and subroutines that you use and write are the software. In this book, you will first develop hardware skills in interfacing an 8080-based microcomputer. Once you acquire such skills, you will then develop software skills that will allow you to apply your hardware interfacing capability to a variety of instruments and machines. As you gain experience with microcomputers, you will learn that it can often take considerable amounts of time to write microcomputer programs that contain hundreds of program steps.

COMPUTER VS. DIGITAL COMPUTER

It is instructive to define the terms *computer* and *digital computer*. Good definitions are difficult to find, as was mentioned previously.

computer—Any device, usually electronic, capable of accepting information, comparing, adding, subtracting, multiplying, dividing, and integrating this information, and then supplying the results of these processes in acceptable form. The major elements of a computer usually include memory, control, arithmetic, logical, and input and output facilities.[4]

A device capable of accepting information, applying prescribed processes to that information, and supplying the results of these processes. It usually consists of input and output devices, storage, arithmetic and logical units, and a control unit.[5]

digital computer—An electronic instrument capable of accepting, storing, and arithmetically manipulating information, which includes both data and the controlling program. The information is handled in the form of coded binary digits (0 and 1), represented by dual voltage levels.[6]

A computer which processes information represented by combinations of discrete or discontinuous data as compared with an analog computer for continuous data. A device for performing sequences of arithmetic and logical operations, not only on data but its own program. A stored program digital computer capable of performing sequences of internally stored instructions, as opposed to such calculators as card-programmed calculators, on which the sequence is impressed manually.[5]

An electronic calculator that operates with numbers expressed directly as digits, as opposed to the directly measurable quantities (voltage, resistance, etc.) in an analog computer.[4]

Several subsidiary definitions include the following:

fixed-program computer—Computer in which the sequence of instructions are permanently stored or wired. The computer program is not subject to change either by the computer or the programmer except by rewiring or changing the storage input.[5]

general-purpose computer—Computer designed to solve a large variety of problems; a stored program computer which may be adapted to any of a very large class of operations.[5]

special-purpose computer—A computer designed to solve a specific class or narrow range of problems.[5]

stored-program computer—A computer capable of performing sequences of internally stored instructions, usually capable of modifying those instructions as directed by the instructions.[5]

wired-program computer—A computer in which instructions that specify the operations are specified by the placement and interconnection of wires. Wires are usually held by a removable control panel, allowing flexibility of operation, but the term is also applied to permanently wired machines which are then called fixed-program computers.[5]

A computer in which nearly all instructions are determined by the placement of interconnecting wires held in a removable plugboard. This arrangement allows for changes of operations by simply changing plugboards. If the wires are held in permanently soldered connections, the computer is called a fixed-program type.[4]

WHAT IS A CONTROLLER?

Graf has defined a *controller* as follows:

controller—An instrument that holds a process or condition at a desired level or status as determined by comparison of the actual value with the desired value.[4]

Controllers can be analog or digital, and can be electronic, mechanical, or even pneumatic, or perhaps some combination of these. A *digital controller* acquires the actual value of the condition in digital form and compares it to the desired value contained within the controller. If there is any difference between the two, a digital signal is sent out to the device, machine, or process to initiate actions to reduce this difference. The digital controller itself consists either of integrated-circuit chips and discrete components that are hard-wired to a printed-circuit board, or else a computer of any size with a limited number of chips to serve as an interface between the computer and the external world.

The question of cost becomes an important factor when one considers the use of computers as controllers. One would not control 100 devices, each with a value of $500, with a $1,000,000 computer; the use of such a large computer to control $50,000 worth of equipment is a form of overcontrol. On the other hand, such a computer would be useful in the control of a $20,000,000 chemical plant. It would appear that one could justify the cost of a computer controller if it represents only a modest percentage of the cost of operating a process or producing a product. The tradeoffs in costs constantly change as the prices of computers decrease. With the advent of microcomputers, the costs of controlling equipment should decrease.

A TYPICAL 8080 MICROCOMPUTER

A typical microcomputer constructed from the 8080 chip is shown in Fig. 1-3. This microcomputer processes all of the minimum requirements for a computer. For example:

- It can input and output data.
- It contains an arithmetic/logic unit (ALU), located within the 8080 chip, that performs arithmetic and logical operations.
- It contains "fast" memory (the authors believe that speed is an important requirement for a functional computer these days).
- It is programmable, with the data and program instructions capable of being arranged in any sequence desired.
- It is digital.

Fig. 1-3 shows the important data paths of the microcomputer. In the sections below, we shall dissect this diagram and discuss the individual paths.

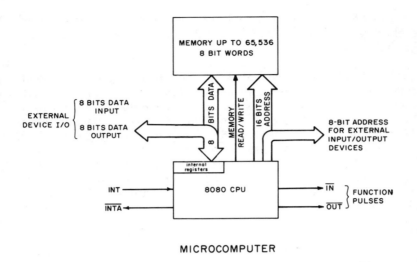

Fig. 1-3. A typical 8080 microcomputer system, in which the significant data paths are shown.

Memory

Consider first the data communication between the 8080 central processing unit (CPU) and memory. You will require some definitions, which will be useful in the ensuing discussion:

memory—Any device that can store logic 1 and logic 0 bits in such a manner that a single bit or group of bits can be accessed and retrieved.[10]

memory address—The storage location of a memory word.

memory cell—A single storage element of memory.

memory data—The memory word occupying a specific storage location in memory, or the memory words collectively located in memory.

memory word—A group of bits occupying one storage location in a computer. This group is treated by the computer circuits as an entity, by the control unit as an instruction, and by the arithmetic unit as a quantity. Each bit is stored in a single memory cell.

programmable read-only memory (PROM)—A read-only memory that is field programmable by the user.[10]

read/write memory—A semiconductor memory into which logic 0 and logic 1 states can be written (stored) and then read out again (retrieved).[10] Sometimes called RAM.

read-only memory (ROM)—A semiconductor memory from which digital data can be repeatedly read out, but cannot be written into, as in the case for read/write memory.[10]

read—To transmit data from a memory to some other digital electronic device.

volatile memory—In computers, any memory that can return information only as long as power is applied to the memory. The opposite of nonvolatile memory.[4]

write—To transmit data into a memory from some other digital electronic device. A synonym is *store*.

The 8080 microprocessor employs 8-bit words that are stored in memory and are addressed with a 16-bit memory address bus. With a quick calculation, we conclude that there exist $2^{16} = 65,536$ different memory locations that can be accessed by the microprocessor. This access to memory is direct, which means that you don't have to engage in any special tricks or digital electronic gimmicks to access any given memory location within the 65,536 possible locations. Forty-pin integrated-circuit chips do have their advantages, and having one pin for each of the sixteen address lines is one of them. The total memory capacity of the 8080 microprocessor is known in the trade as *64K*. This is far more memory than you will ever need for most applications, but it is nice to know that you have such power in reserve.

A given memory location is addressed with the aid of a 16-bit *memory address bus* that is shown in Fig. 1-3. It takes only 1 μs to accomplish such addressing. The memory address bus is shown in Fig. 1-4.

Data is transferred between the 8080 CPU and memory over 8-bit *data input* and *data output busses*, both of which are shown in Fig. 1-3 and Fig. 1-5. In most recent 8080 microcomputers, these two busses are combined into a single 8-bit *bidirectional data bus*. By *input*, we mean *input into the CPU*. By *output*, we mean *output from the CPU*. The point of reference is always the CPU. Data leaving the CPU is

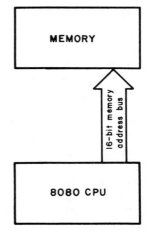

Fig. 1-4. The 16-bit memory address bus between the 8080 CPU and memory.

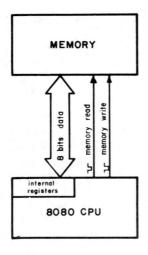

Fig. 1-5. Data transfer between the 8080 CPU and memory. In most 8080 systems there is a single bidirectional data bus.

always considered to be *output data;* data entering the CPU is always *input data.* In some cases, the input and output data are transferred between the *accumulator* and memory. The term *accumulator* is defined in the following way:

accumulator—The register and associated digital electronic circuitry in the arithmetic unit of a computer, in which arithmetic and logical operations are performed.

Data can also be transferred to other internal *registers* within the 8080 chip. A register is defined as:

register—A short-term digital electronic storage circuit, the capacity of which is usually one computer word.[4]

Other registers, besides the accumulator register, include the *instruction register,* from which the decoding of the instruction occurs; six *general-purpose registers,* which are classified by the letters B, C, D, E, H, and L; a *program counter register;* a *stack pointer register;* and at least three temporary registers to which you have no access. All of these registers are discussed in subsequent chapters. They are pointed out here so that you will not get the false impression that data from memory is only transferred to the accumulator register. The authors regard the accumulator register to be the heart of the entire microcomputer: Arithmetic and logic operations are always performed to or on the eight bits of data present within the accumulator. For extracted, ANDed, ORed, or compared to the contents of the accumulator register. It is not possible to add the contents of one memory location to the contents of another memory location. You must always proceed in such additions through the accumulator register. The accumulator register is also important because all input and output data passes through the accumulator whenever you use the two computer instructions IN and OUT.

Between the 8080 CPU and memory there exists a single output line, shown in Fig. 1-3, called *memory read/write*. When this line is at logic 1, you are able to *read* data into the CPU either from memory or from an external device. When this line is at logic 0, you are able to *write* data from the CPU into memory or an external output device. In some systems separate read and write lines are used.

As a final point, you can employ any type of "fast" digital electronic memory device, including read/write (R/W) memory, read-only memory (ROM), and programmable read-only memory (PROM). "Fast" memory means simply that the memory can perform either a read or a write operation during a single microcomputer instruction. A typical 8080 microcomputer system operates at a clock rate of 2 MHz, and a read or write operation takes only 650 ns. Thus, R/W memory, ROM, and PROM all need an access time of 650 nanoseconds to allow you to take full advantage of the maximum clock speed. Slower semiconductor memories can be employed, but the microcomputer will have to "wait" while a read or write operation takes place.

Data Output

The 8-bit *output data bus* between the 8080 CPU and memory also serves as the output data bus to an external output device. This is shown in Figs. 1-3 and 1-6.

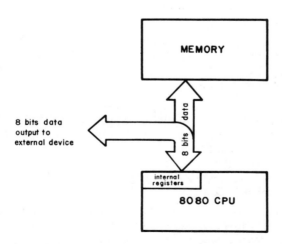

Fig. 1-6. Data transfer between the 8080 CPU and an output device.

When you output data to an external device, there are several important requirements that you must meet:

- You must select the specific output device that will receive eight bits of data from the accumulator register in the CPU.
- You must indicate to this device the precise instant of time when output data is available on the *output data bus.*
- The device must "capture" or "latch" this output data in a very short period, typically 500 ns.

All three of the preceding requirements are accomplished at the same time with a single output pulse, which is generated by the 8080 chip with the aid of some extra digital circuitry external to the 8080 chip. We call such a pulse a *device select pulse.* It synchronizes the 8080 CPU and the output device so that when the CPU is ready to provide output data, the output device is ready to receive it. Keep in mind that the microcomputer is operating at a clock rate of 2 MHz. Each computer instruction is executed in a very short period, which ranges from 2 μs to 9 μs. Thus, accumulator data designated as *data output* is not available for very long. *You must capture this data within 500 ns, or else it will disappear.* We cannot emphasize enough how important this rapid "capture" of output data is to the successful operation of a complete microcomputer system that includes input/output devices. We will consider these points in greater detail when we discuss the topic of microcomputer *interfacing* in this chapter. If you are interested in how the function pulse $\overline{\text{OUT}}$, which is used to generate device select pulses, is created by the 8080 microcomputer, please jump to the section titled "Machine Cycle Identification" in Chapter 6.

Data Input

The 8-bit *input data bus* between the 8080 CPU and memory also serves as the input data bus from an external input device. This is shown in Figs. 1-3 and 1-7. The basic considerations that apply to data output also apply to data input. Thus:

- You must select the specific input device that will transmit eight bits of data to the accumulator register within the CPU.
- You must indicate to this device the precise instant of time when the *input data bus* is ready to acquire the input data and transfer it to the accumulator register.
- The accumulator register must "capture" this data in a very short period, typically 500 ns.

All three of these tasks are accomplished at the same time with a single output pulse, which is generated by the 8080 chip with the aid of some extra digital circuitry external to the chip. Such a pulse is also called a *device select pulse.* It synchronizes the 8080 CPU and the input

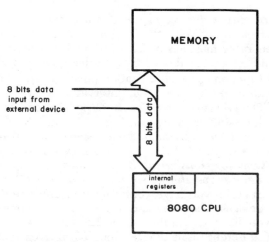

Fig. 1-7. Data transfer between an input device and the 8080 CPU.

device so that when the CPU is ready to receive input data, the input device is ready to transmit it.

Other Input/Output Techniques

There is an alternative and very exciting technique for transferring data *directionally between the microcomputer general-purpose registers B, C, D, E, H, and L and an input/output device*. The technique is called *memory mapped I/O* and the chips used are in a family of interface chips recently marketed by Intel Corporation and others. Included in this family is the 8255 programmable peripheral interface chip, which turns an input/output device into a pseudo-memory location that is addressed not with an IN or OUT instruction, but rather with memory instructions such as MOV, STA, LDA, and the like. The advantage of doing so is the savings of several microseconds per 8-bit data transfer. The computer programming may be easier as well. This technique is particularly well adapted for the acquisition or transfer of blocks of data in short intervals of time. We will not discuss the technique to any degree in this book.

External Device Addressing

External device addressing can be defined as the use of computer software to generate input/output synchronization pulses, called *device select pulses,* to synchronize the transfer of data between the CPU and an external input or output device. This is one of the most important tasks of microcomputer interfacing, and must be learned well.

The basic objective of external device addressing is *to generate a single unique clock pulse at a precise instant of time to a specific ex-*

ternal input or output device. The clock pulse can either be a positive or negative clock pulse. With the 8080 microcomputer, negative clock pulses are generated most easily. This is done by decoding an 8-bit *device code* that appears for about 1.5 μs on the memory address bus and using an I/O function or synchronization pulse, called $\overline{\text{IN}}$ or $\overline{\text{OUT}}$, that appears for 500 ns during the 1.5-μs interval associated with the 8-bit device code. The two function pulses and the 8-bit address for external I/O device addressing are shown in Figs. 1-3 and 1-8.

The details of how individual device select pulses are generated are provided in Chapter 4. Briefly, here is how this is done. *The computer instructions for transferring data between the accumulator and input/output devices specify the specific device desired.* For an output computer instruction, you have your choice of any one device among 256 different devices. The same is true for the input computer instruction. Thus, you have the ability to address, i.e., send device select pulses to, 256 different input devices and 256 different output devices. How is this done? Each input or output computer instruction contains an 8-bit *device code.* We can calculate that an 8-bit binary number can specify $2^8 = 256$ different devices. We use a pair of 4-line-to-16-line decoder chips, such as the 74154 decoder, to decode the 8-bit device code into a single output pulse. Seventeen 74154 decoders can generate 256 different pulses, as will be shown in Chapter 4. The remaining details can be discussed with the aid of Fig. 1-9.

Fig. 1-9 provides timing diagrams for the accumulator register contents, the memory address bus, and the $\overline{\text{OUT}}$ pulse that is generated

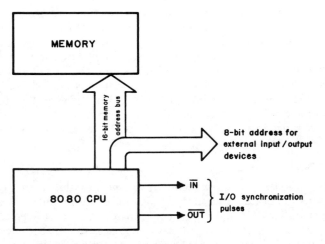

Fig. 1-8. During an 8080 input or output instruction, the 8-bit device code appears on the address bus, and an I/O synchronization pulse appears on the control bus. Such signals are used to gate the transfer of input/output data.

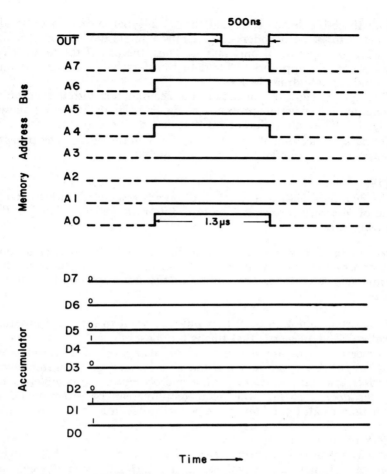

Fig. 1-9. Timing diagram indicating the logic states existing on the memory address bus, within the accumulator, and at the $\overline{\text{OUT}}$ signal line during an OUT instruction.

by the OUT computer instruction and some digital circuitry external to the 8080 chip. Note the following:

- The accumulator register contents are available for at least several microseconds, and perhaps much longer.
- The 8-bit device code appears at the eight least-significant bits of the 16-bit memory address bus for a period of 1.3 μs. In the figure, the device code is 11010001_2, or 321_8 in octal code.
- The $\overline{\text{OUT}}$ synchronization pulse lasts for only 500 ns. *It is during this 500 ns that data is transferred between the accumulator register and the output device.*

Both the 8-bit device code and the $\overline{\text{OUT}}$ synchronization pulse are connected to 74154 decoders to generate a single device code for device 321_8 for a period of only 500 ns. Thus, the use of the term, "capture," is entirely appropriate for data transfers between the accumulator and input/output devices.

The input of eight bits of data to the accumulator with the aid of an IN computer instruction proceeds along lines similar to those shown in Fig. 1-9. The only difference is that you should substitute the term *buffer data* for accumulator and $\overline{\text{IN}}$ for $\overline{\text{OUT}}$ in the figure. The transfer of data to the accumulator occurs in only 500 ns.

Interrupt Servicing

The final data path that we shall discuss is associated with the technique of *interrupt servicing*. The term *interrupt* can be defined in the following way:

interrupt—In a computer, a break in the normal execution of a computer program such that the program can be resumed from that point at a later time. The source of the interrupt can be internal or external.

The important question is: Why would we want to interrupt program execution? The answer is that this is the most efficient way to operate a microcomputer or, for that matter, any computer. *Until an external input/output device requests assistance, or "servicing," from the microcomputer, it is most efficient for the microcomputer to completely ignore the device.* In fact, the microcomputer can be programmed so that it ignores all input/output devices; it idles in a "wait loop" while it waits for an interrupt signal from one of the devices. If many I/O devices require servicing at essentially the same time, the microcomputer has a protocol in hardware or software and knows which device is the most important. It will assign a *priority* to each device, and will always service the higher-priority devices first.

When a program interrupt is generated, the following sequence of events usually occurs:

1. The computer stores the memory address of the instruction following the one that it is currently executing.
2. The computer stores any temporary information—flags, the contents of the accumulator register, and the contents of other registers—that may be important when the interrupted program resumes operation.
3. The computer goes to a well-defined location within memory and executes a series of program steps to "service" the interrupting device.

4. Once it has finished "servicing" the device, the computer recalls the temporary information and returns to the program step following that step at which the interrupt occurred.

This is similar to what you would do if you were interrupted while reading this book. You would mark your place, remember any special information, and then devote your attention to the "interrupt." After servicing the interrupt, you would restore the remembered information, locate the bookmark, and continue reading.

If more than one input/output device requires servicing, the microcomputer must make a decision which one to handle first. Once it has made this decision, it remembers which remaining devices have generated the interrupt requests, and then proceeds to the service subroutine.

In the 8080 microcomputer, an 8-bit instruction is jammed into the CPU at the time of the interrupt to tell the computer where to go in memory to "service" the interrupt. Only eight different memory addresses are provided for this purpose, certainly not a large number. There are a variety of tricks that can be employed to handle interrupts. The schematic diagram shown in Fig. 1-10 indicates the important signals during an interrupt request: an interrupt pulse, an interrupt acknowledge control signal, $\overline{\text{INTA}}$, and an 8-bit instruction that is jammed into the instruction register.

TEST

This test probes your understanding of the microcomputer and digital electronic concepts described in this chapter. Please write your answers on a separate piece of paper.

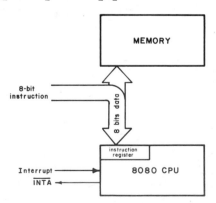

Fig. 1-10. On receiving an "interrupt" request, the 8080 CPU generates an "interrupt acknowledge" control signal, INTA, that is used to gate an 8-bit instruction into the instruction register within the CPU.

1-1. Explain the difference between a microprocessor and a microcomputer.

1-2. Draw a diagram and show the important data paths in a typical 8080-based microcomputer.

1-3. What are the minimum requirements for a computer *circa* 1977?

1-4. List and describe the four fundamental tasks of computer interfacing.

1-5. In your own words, define the following terms:

> data processor
> controller
> bus
> accumulator
> flag
> memory address
> memory cell
> memory word
> hardware
> software
> read
> write
> computer interfacing
> interrupt
> device select pulse
> clock
> bidirectional data bus
> read/write memory
> read-only memory (ROM)

Your performance on this test will be acceptable if you can answer all of the above questions correctly in a 90-minute closed-book examination. You will repeatedly encounter the above concepts in this book.

WHAT HAVE YOU ACCOMPLISHED IN THIS CHAPTER?

It was stated in the introduction to this chapter that at the end you would be able to do the following:

- Explain the difference between a microprocessor and a microcomputer.
  A microprocessor is a single IC chip, whereas a microcomputer is a fully operational computer system. This distinction has been discussed, with quotes from the literature, early in this chapter.

- Define the terms: computer, digital computer, data processor, controller, hardware, software, memory, memory word, memory address, memory data, read, write, read/write memory, read-only memory, interfacing, device select pulse, and interrupt.
  Definitions for these terms have been provided in this chapter.

- Describe the operation of a typical 8080 microcomputer system.
  This was done in modest detail. You should be able to do as well. Focus upon the signal lines and data paths within the system.

CHAPTER 2

A Small 8080 Microcomputer

In this chapter, you will see how an 8080 (or 8080A) microprocessor chip can be used to configure a small 8080-based microcomputer. We will examine the signals entering and leaving the 8080 chip, how auxiliary chips such as the 8224 are used to control the operation of the microcomputer, and the development of the address, data, and control buses, which are vital in interfacing applications. The microcomputer is known as the MMD-1, and is available from E&L Instruments, Inc., 61 First Street, Derby, Connecticut 06418. The advanced I/O experiments discussed in the new Chapter 9 were all performed on a pair of MMD-1 microcomputers. In my opinion, it still is one of the best student trainers available.

OBJECTIVES

At the end of this chapter, you will be able to do the following:

- Identify the memory address bus, data bus, control inputs, control outputs, and power inputs on the 40-pin 8080A microprocessor.
- Describe the function of each pin on the 8080A microprocessor.
- Describe in some detail the various component sections of a small 8080A microcomputer system.
- List the general principles of computer interfacing that apply to most digital computers.
- Explain what an I/O device is.
- List three important uses for device select pulses.

- List the inputs to the common 7400-series chips that can be strobed with device select pulses from a microcomputer.

DEFINITIONS

bit—Abbreviation for binary digit. A unit of information equal to one binary decision.

bootstrap—A technique or device designed to bring itself into a desired state by means of its own action, e.g., a machine routine whose first few instructions are sufficient to bring the rest of itself into the computer from an input device.[4]

bus driver—Generally refers to a specially designed integrated circuit that is added to the data bus system to facilitate proper drive from the CPU when several memories are tied to the data bus line. Any semiconductor device that improves the current sinking characteristics of each line on a bus.[14]

byte—A sequence of adjacent binary digits, which may be equal to or shorter than a word, operated on as a unit. For the 8080A a byte is a group of *eight* contiguous bits occupying a single memory location.

computer interfacing—The synchronization of digital data transmission between a computer and one or more external input/output devices.

flag—In a computer an indication that a particular operation has been completed.[4] A flag is typically a flip-flop that can be either set or cleared in response to operations occurring in the microcomputer or computer system.

HI memory address—For the 8080A microprocessor chip the eight most significant bits, which comprise a single byte, in the 16-bit memory address word. Abbreviated H or HI.

interfacing—The joining of members of a group (such as people, instruments, etc.) in such a way that they are able to function in a compatible and coordinated fashion.[1]

I/O—Abbreviation for input/output.[4]

I/O device—Input/output device. A card reader magnetic tape unit, printer, or similar device that transmits data to or receives data from a computer or secondary storage device.[4] Any digital device, including a single integrated-circuit chip, that transmits data to or receives data or strobe pulses from a computer.

latch—A simple logic storage element, such as a flip-flop, used to retain a logic state.

LO memory address—For the 8080A microprocessor chip, the eight least significant bits, which comprise a single byte, in the 16-bit memory address word. Abbreviated L or LO.

memory address—For the 8080A microprocessor, the 16-bit binary number that specifies the precise memory location of a memory word among the 65,536 different possible memory locations.

status bit—A single bit of output information that is placed on the external data bus early during the execution of a machine cycle and is latched by an integrated-circuit chip called a status latch. Since this bit is acquired early by the latch, it can be used to control external events that occur later in the machine cycle.

status byte—An 8-bit byte that contains eight different status bits.

status latch—An integrated-circuit chip, such as, for example, the 74174 6-bit latch, that latches status bits when they appear on the external data bus.

sync—Short for synchronous, synchronization, synchronizing, etc.[4]

synchronize—To lock one element of a system into step with another.[4]

synchronization pulses—Pulses originated by the transmitting equipment and introduced into the receiving equipment to keep the equipment at both locations operating in step.[4]

synchronous—In step or in phase, as applied to two devices or machines. A term applied to a computer, in which the performance of a sequence of operations is controlled by clock signals or pulses.[4]

synchronous computer—A digital computer in which all ordinary operations are controlled by signals from a master clock.[4]

synchronous inputs—Those inputs of a flip-flop that do not control the output directly, as do those of a gate, but only when the clock permits and commands.[4]

synchronous logic—The type of digital logic used in a system in which logical operations take place in synchronism with clock pulses.[4]

synchronous operation—Operation of a system under the control of clock pulses.[4]

three-state device—A semiconductor logic device in which there exist three possible output states: (1) a logic 0 state, (2) a logic 1 state, or (3) a high-impedance state in which the output is, in effect, disconnected from the rest of the circuit and consequently has no influence upon it.

two-phase clock—A two-output timing device that provides two continuous series of timing pulses that are synchronized together, with a single clock pulse from the second series always following a single clock pulse from the first series. Depending on the type of two-phase clock, the pulses in the first and second series may or may not overlap each other. The 8080A chip uses a nonoverlapping two-phase clock.

word—A group of contiguous bits occupying one or more storage locations in a computer. For the 8080A microprocessor chip, a word is defined as a group of eight contiguous bits occupying a single memory location.

word length—The number of contiguous bits that are handled as a unit and that normally can be stored in one or more locations in memory. A greater word length implies higher precision and more intricate instructions.[4]

THE 8080 MICROPROCESSOR CHIP

The 8080 microprocessor is a 40-pin LSI integrated-circuit chip that contains sixteen address lines, eight data lines, ten control lines, four power connections, and a pair of clock inputs. The pin configuration and the block diagram of the chip are shown in Figs. 2-1 and 2-2. If you are not familiar with reading pin numbers on integrated-circuit chips, the numbering always starts from pin 1 and proceeds counterclockwise from the notch or index mark on one end of the chip. Chips are always shown as top views.

Forty pins are quite a few with which to contend, so it would be useful to divide the pin functions into the following categories: power, memory address, data input/output, controls, and clocks.

Power

pin 28	+12 volts	(40 mA typical)
pin 20	+ 5 volts	(60 mA typical)
pin 2	ground	
pin 11	− 5 volts	(0.01 mA typical)

The voltage tolerances are ± 5 percent with respect to ground potential. Any popular power supply that provides voltages of ±15 and +5 volts and sufficient current can be adapted to the 8080 chip with the aid of suitable voltage regulators.

Clocks

The 8080 chip requires a *two-phase clock*. Recall that a *clock* is any device that generates at least one clock pulse, or is a timing device in a system that provides a continuous series of timing pulses. A *two-phase clock* is a two-output timing device that provides two continuous series

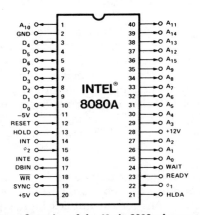

Fig. 2-1. Pin configuration of the 40-pin 8080 microprocessor chip.

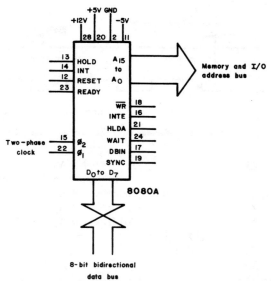

Fig. 2-2. Block diagram of the 8080 chip that clearly shows the 16-bit address bus and 8-bit bidirectional data bus. This is a more useful representation of the 8080 microprocessor chip.

of timing pulses that are synchronized together, with a single clock pulse from the second series always following a single clock pulse from the first series. The use of a timing diagram, shown in Fig. 2-3, is helpful in explaining how a two-phase clock operates. The frequency can vary from 500 kHz to 4 MHz depending upon the particular 8080 chip. The clock frequency cannot be reduced to zero owing to the fact that the internal operation of the chip is dynamic rather than static.

Note that the leading edge of the ϕ_2 series of clock pulse almost overlaps the trailing edge of the ϕ_1 series of pulses. In the 8080 specifications, it is stated that the minimum pulse width for the ϕ_1 clock phase is 60 ns, whereas for the ϕ_2 clock phase it is 220 ns. The pin locations for the two input clock signals are:

pin 22   clock phase ϕ_1
pin 15   clock phase ϕ_2

We call this type of clock device a *two-phase nonoverlapping clock.* This is not a TTL-level clock; rather, it swings from 0 volts to +12 volts. Such a clock can be easily generated with an 8224 clock generator chip, which is available from Intel and other manufacturers.

Memory Address

The 8080 microprocessor can directly address up to 65,536 eight-bit words of memory through the use of 16 three-state output address lines called the *address bus.* The pin locations can be summarized as follows:

43

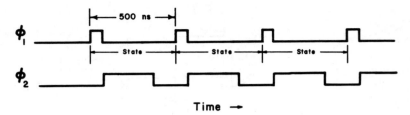

Fig. 2-3. Waveforms of the two-phase clock inputs.

pin 25		Address bit A_0, the least significant bit (LSB)
pin 26		Address bit A_1
pin 27		Address bit A_2
pin 29		Address bit A_3
	LO ADDRESS BYTE	
pin 30		Address bit A_4
pin 31		Address bit A_5
pin 32		Address bit A_6
pin 33		Address bit A_7, the MSB in the LO byte
pin 34		Address bit A_8, the LSB in the HI byte
pin 35		Address bit A_9
pin 1		Address bit A_{10}
pin 40		Address bit A_{11}
	HI ADDRESS BYTE	
pin 37		Address bit A_{12}
pin 38		Address bit A_{13}
pin 39		Address bit A_{14}
pin 36		Address bit A_{15}, the most significant bit (MSB)

Either address bits A_0 through A_7 or address bits A_8 through A_{15} can be used to provide the I/O device number for up to 256 input and 256 output devices. The address lines are fed into decoders, which provide one with the opportunity of selecting any single input or output device among 2^8 different ones.

Bidirectional Data Bus

The 8080 microprocessor chip is an 8-bit device, which means that there exist an 8-bit accumulator, several additional 8-bit registers, and an 8-bit input/output *data bus*. The data bus is *bidirectional,* so data can be both input into the chip and output from the chip. The data bus is the main communication bus between the central processing unit in the microprocessor, memory, and input/output devices. It is a three-state input/output bus. The pin locations are:

pin 10	Data bit D_0, the least significant data bus bit
pin 9	Data bit D_1
pin 8	Data bit D_2
pin 7	Data bit D_3
pin 3	Data bit D_4
pin 4	Data bit D_5
pin 5	Data bit D_6
pin 6	Data bit D_7, the most significant data bus bit

Controls

The control pins determine how the microprocessor functions in a microcomputer system. In discussing the functions of these pins, it is not possible to sidestep a variety of jargon, such as T_1, T_2, T_3, T_w, *fetch cycle*, M_1, and the like. The pin identifications and descriptions are provided below for future reference when you have a better understanding of the operation of the 8080 microcomputer system.

You will not see either an IN or OUT output control pin in the list below. The reason is that these two functions are generated as *status bits,* which are then externally latched and used to generate the $\overline{\text{IN}}$ and $\overline{\text{OUT}}$ synchronization pulses mentioned previously. If you are curious about how this is done, you can skip to Chapter 6.

The four control input pins on the 8080 microprocessor chip are:

pin 12 (input)	RESET. A logic 1 at this input will clear the program counter register and allow the program to start at memory location $HI = 000_8$ and $LO = 000_8$. The INTE and HLDA flags are also reset, but the condition flags, accumulator register, stack pointer register, and general-purpose registers are not cleared.
pin 14 (input)	INT, or interrupt request. A logic 1 at this input will generate an interrupt request that the CPU recognizes at the end of the current instruction or while halted. If the CPU is in the HOLD state or if the interrupt enable flip-flop is reset, i.e., at logic 0, the interrupt request will not be honored.
pin 23 (input)	READY. A logic 1 indicates to the 8080 that valid memory or input data is available on the data bus, D_0 through D_7. This signal, according to the Intel literature, is used to synchronize the CPU with slower memory or with I/O devices. If, after sending an address out on the address bus, the 8080 doesn't receive a logic 1 READY input, the micro-

	processor chip will enter a WAIT state for as long as the READY line is at logic 0. This input can also be used to single step the CPU.
pin 13 (input)	HOLD. This input pin requests the CPU to enter the HOLD state, which allows an external device to gain control of the 8080 address and data busses as soon as the 8080 has completed its use of these busses for the current machine cycle. Once the CPU enters the HOLD state, the address bus and the data bus will be in their high-impedance state. The CPU acknowledges the HOLD state with the HLDA, or HOLD ACKNOWLEDGE, output pin. HOLD is recognized under two conditions: (1) the CPU is in the HALT state, or (2) the CPU is in the T_2 or T_w state and the READY signal is at logic 1.

So much for the control inputs. Now the control outputs, many of which are flags. The term *flag* can be defined as follows:

flag—In a computer, an indication that a particular operation has been completed.[4] A flag is typically a flip-flop that can be either set or cleared in response to operations occurring in the microprocessor system.

The six control output pins on the 8080 microprocessor chip are:

pin 24 (output)	WAIT. The wait output signal acknowledges that the central processing unit is in a WAIT state. When in a WAIT state, this pin is at logic 1.
pin 18 (output)	$\overline{WR}$, or $\overline{WRITE}$. This output pin is used for memory Write and I/O control. When this pin is at logic 0, the data on the data bus is stable and can be written into a memory location or to an output device.
pin 21 (output)	HLDA, or HOLD ACKNOWLEDGE. This pin goes to a logic 1 state in response to a HOLD input signal. It indicates that the data and address busses are in their high-impedance states. The HLDA signal begins at either of two times: (1) at T_3 of read memory or input, or (2) the clock period following T_3 for write memory or output operations.
pin 16 (output)	INTE, or INTERRUPT ENABLE. This pin indicates the state of the interrupt enable flip-flop. This flip-flop may be set or cleared by the enable and disable interrupt instructions (373_8 and 363_8, respectively) and inhibits interrupts from being accepted by the CPU when the flip-flop is cleared. The flip-flop is automatically cleared (thus disabling

	further interrupts) when an interrupt is accepted. The flip-flop is also cleared by the RESET input signal.
pin 19 (output)	SYNC, or SYNCHRONIZING SIGNAL. The SYNC pin provides a logic 1 signal to indicate the beginning of each machine cycle.
pin 17 (output)	DBIN, or DATA BUS IN. When this pin goes to a logic 1, it indicates to external circuits that the data bus is in the input mode. This pin is used to enable the gating of data onto the 8080 data bus from memory and I/O devices.

Some of the preceding characteristics of the control pins will become clearer in Chapter 6, where the $\overline{\text{WR}}$, SYNC, DBIN, and READY control pins are discussed.

THE 8224 CLOCK GENERATOR/DRIVER CHIP

In early 8080 microcomputer systems, the clock inputs were provided by transistor driver circuits, MOS clock driver chips, or even open-collector TTL buffer chips. All worked reasonably well, but they complicated the design. A recent 8080A interface chip, the 8224 clock generator and driver, contains an internal oscillator and a clock generator/driver. All you need to provide is the appropriate crystal and power supply voltages of +5 and +12 volts. Since the 8224 will divide the crystal frequency by nine, you will require an 18-MHz crystal to produce a 2-MHz clock output from the clock generator. In the system described in this chapter, the microcomputer frequency is 750 kHz; a 6.750-MHz crystal is required.

The Intel specification sheets for the 8224 clock generator/driver are shown on the following pages. The functional description of the chip is excellent, so there is no need to repeat it here. Observe how the divide-by-nine counter circuit within the 8224 chip is used to generate the individual clock phases ϕ_1 and ϕ_2, which "swing" between +12 volts and ground.

The inputs to and outputs from the 8224 chip can be summarized as follows:

pin 15, pin 14	XTAL1 and XTAL2. The crystal is connected at these two pins.
pin 13	TANK. Used for overtone mode crystals, which have much lower gain than crystals that operate on the fundamental frequency.
pin 2 (input)	$\overline{\text{RESIN}}$. With the aid of a Schmitt trigger circuit, internal to the chip, and an external RC network, this input converts a slow transition in the power

Schottky Bipolar **8224**

THE CLOCK GENERATOR AND DRIVER
FOR 8080A CPU

- Single Chip Clock Generator/Driver for 8080A CPU
- Power-Up Reset for CPU
- Ready Synchronizing Flip-Flop
- Advanced Status Strobe
- Oscillator Output for External System Timing
- Crystal Controlled for Stable System Operation
- Reduces System Package Count

The 8224 is a single chip clock generator/driver for the 8080A CPU. It is controlled by a crystal, selected by the designer, to meet a variety of system speed requirements.

Also included are circuits to provide power-up reset, advance status strobe and synchronization of ready.

The 8224 provides the designer with a significant reduction of packages used to generate clocks and timing for 8080A.

PIN CONFIGURATION

BLOCK DIAGRAM

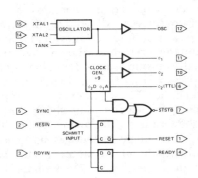

PIN NAMES

RESIN	RESET INPUT		XTAL 1	CONNECTIONS
RESET	RESET OUTPUT		XTAL 2	FOR CRYSTAL
RDYIN	READY INPUT		TANK	USED WITH OVERTONE XTAL
READY	READY OUTPUT		OSC	OSCILLATOR OUTPUT
SYNC	SYNC INPUT		ϕ_2 (TTL)	ϕ_2 CLK (TTL LEVEL)
STSTB	STATUS STB (ACTIVE LOW)		V_{CC}	+5V
ϕ_1	8080		V_{DD}	+12V
ϕ_2	CLOCKS		GND	0V

48

SCHOTTKY BIPOLAR 8224

FUNCTIONAL DESCRIPTION

General

The 8224 is a single chip Clock Generator/Driver for the 8080A CPU. It contains a crystal-controlled oscillator, a "divide by nine" counter, two high-level drivers and several auxiliary logic functions.

Oscillator

The oscillator circuit derives its basic operating frequency from an external, series resonant, fundamental mode crystal. Two inputs are provided for the crystal connections (XTAL1, XTAL2).

The selection of the external crystal frequency depends mainly on the speed at which the 8080A is to be run at. Basically, the oscillator operates at 9 times the desired processor speed.

A simple formula to guide the crystal selection is:

$$\text{Crystal Frequency} = \frac{1}{t_{CY}} \text{ times } 9$$

Example 1:   (500ns t_{CY})
              2mHz times 9 = 18mHz*

Example 2:   (800ns t_{CY})
              1.25mHz times 9 = 11.25mHz

Another input to the oscillator is TANK. This input allows the use overtone mode crystals. This type of crystal generally has much lower "gain" than the fundamental type so an external LC network is necessary to provide the additional "gain" for proper oscillator operation. The external LC network is connected to the TANK input and is AC coupled to ground. See Figure 4.

The formula for the LC network is:

$$F = \frac{1}{2\pi\sqrt{LC}}$$

The output of the oscillator is buffered and brought out on OSC (pin 12) so that other system timing signals can be derived from this stable, crystal-controlled source.

*When using crystals above 10mHz a small amount of frequency "trimming" may be necessary. The addition of a small capacitance (3pF - 10pF) in series with the crystal will accomplish this function.

Clock Generator

The Clock Generator consists of a synchronous "divide by nine" counter and the associated decode gating to create the waveforms of the two 8080A clocks and auxiliary timing signals.

The waveforms generated by the decode gating follow a simple 2-5-2 digital pattern. See Figure 2. The clocks generated; phase 1 and phase 2, can best be thought of as consisting of "units" based on the oscillator frequency. Assume that one "unit" equals the period of the oscillator frequency. By multiplying the number of "units" that are contained in a pulse width or delay, times the period of the oscillator frequency, the approximate time in nanoseconds can be derived.

The outputs of the clock generator are connected to two high level drivers for direct interface to the 8080A CPU. A TTL level phase 2 is also brought out ϕ_2 (TTL) for external timing purposes. It is especially useful in DMA dependant activities. This signal is used to gate the requesting device onto the bus once the 8080A CPU issues the Hold Acknowledgement (HLDA).

Several other signals are also generated internally so that optimum timing of the auxiliary flip-flops and status strobe ($\overline{STSTB}$) is achieved.

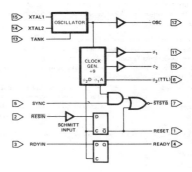

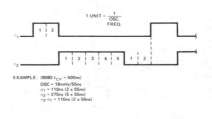

1 UNIT = $\frac{1}{\text{OSC. FREQ.}}$

EXAMPLE: (8080 t_{CY} = 500ns)
           OSC = 18mHz/55ns
           ϕ_1 = 110ns (2 x 55ns)
           ϕ_2 = 275ns (5 x 55ns)
           ϕ_2-ϕ_1 = 110ns (2 x 55ns)

STSTB (Status Strobe)

At the beginning of each machine cycle the 8080A CPU issues status information on its data bus. This information tells what type of action will take place during that machine cycle. By bringing in the SYNC signal from the CPU, and gating it with an internal timing signal (ϕ1A), an active low strobe can be derived that occurs at the start of each machine cycle at the earliest possible moment that status data is stable on the bus. The STSTB signal connects directly to the 8228 System Controller.

The power-on Reset also generates STSTB, but of course, for a longer period of time. This feature allows the 8228 to be automatically reset without additional pins devoted for this function.

Power-On Reset and Ready Flip-Flops

A common function in 8080A Microcomputer systems is the generation of an automatic system reset and start-up upon initial power-on. The 8224 has a built in feature to accomplish this feature.

An external RC network is connected to the RESIN input. The slow transition of the power supply rise is sensed by an internal Schmitt Trigger. This circuit converts the slow transition into a clean, fast edge when its input level reaches a predetermined value. The output of the Schmitt Trigger is connected to a "D" type flip-flop that is clocked with ϕ2D (an internal timing signal). The flip-flop is synchronously reset and an active high level that complies with the 8080A input spec is generated. For manual switch type system Reset circuits, an active low switch closing can be connected to the RESIN input in addition to the power-on RC net-network.

The READY input to the 8080A CPU has certain timing specifications such as "set-up and hold" thus, an external synchronizing flip-flop is required. The 8224 has this feature built-in. The RDYIN input presents the asynchronous "wait request" to the "D" type flip-flop. By clocking the flip-flop with ϕ2D, a synchronized READY signal at the correct input level, can be connected directly to the 8080A.

The reason for requiring an external flip-flop to synchronize the "wait request" rather than internally in the 8080 CPU is that due to the relatively long delays of MOS logic such an implementation would "rob" the designer of about 200ns during the time his logic is determining if a "wait" is necessary. An external bipolar circuit built into the clock generator eliminates most of this delay and has no effect on component count.

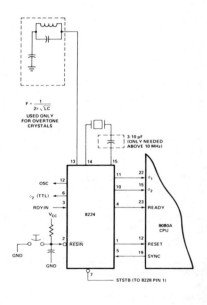

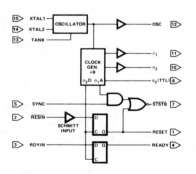

	supply to a clean, fast edge that resets the 8080A microprocessor chip when the RESET output signal is connected to the 8080A chip. A manual reset switch may also be connected to $\overline{\text{RESIN}}$.
pin 1 (output)	RESET. A logic 1 output that is applied at the RESET input of the 8080A chip to reset it.
pin 3 (input)	RDYIN. Accepts an asynchronous wait request and synchronizes it to produce a READY signal that is output to the 8080A chip.
pin 4 (output)	READY. A logic 1 indicates to the 8080A that valid memory or input data is available on the data bus.
pin 5 (input)	SYNC. The SYNC pin on the 8080A chip provides a synchronizing output to the 8224 chip to indicate the beginning of each machine cycle.
pin 11 (output), pin 10 (output)	ϕ_1 and ϕ_2. The two-phase clock that is output to the 8080A chip. Each of these two outputs swing between +12 volts and ground; they are not normal TTL outputs.
pin 6 (output)	$\phi_2(\text{TTL})$. This is a TTL clock output that has the same frequency and timing characteristics as does ϕ_2. It is used for external timing purposes, such as those described in Chapter 5.
pin 7 (output)	$\overline{\text{STSTB}}$. Status strobe output. This output is used to latch the status bits that appear on the bidirectional data bus.
pin 12 (output)	OSC. Buffered crystal oscillator output that can be used to generate other system timing signals.

It should be clear that the 8224 clock generator/driver chip is well designed for its particular function. Connections between it and the 8080A microprocessor chip are direct, and require no intermediate inverters, gates, or flip-flops. There is little incentive to use transistor driver circuits, MOS clock driver chips, or open-collector TTL buffer chips. The power to the 8224 chip is already available since both +5 volts and +12 volts are required by the 8080A.

AN 8080-BASED MICROCOMPUTER

Fig. 2-4 shows the central processor section of a small 8080A-based microcomputer. The figure is provided by *Radio-Electronics* magazine, which described the microcomputer in the May, June, and July, 1976, issues. We will now examine the component chips in the circuit as well as the signal flow between them. The objective here is to demonstrate that a microcomputer is a very straightforward and reasonable device, and that you should not feel intimidated by it.

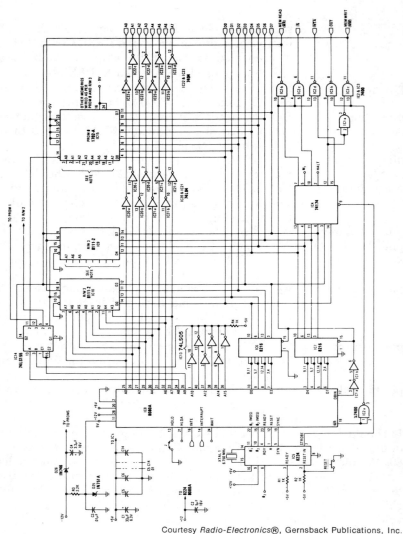

Courtesy *Radio-Electronics*®, Gernsback Publications, Inc.

Fig. 2-4. The processor, memory, and control sections of a small 8080A microcomputer system.

Power

It is assumed that power supplies for the required +5, −12, and +12 volts are available. They are common, and are relatively inexpensive. (However, be wary of the very cheap supplies.) The intermediate voltages of −5 and −9 volts required by our microcomputer are easily derived from voltage regulator integrated-circuit chips such as the LM320 series, or from zener diode shunts, as is shown in Fig. 2-5.

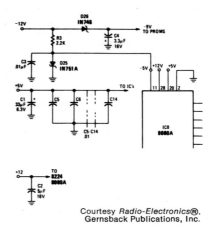

Fig. 2-5. The use of zener diodes provides the necessary −5 and −9 volts required by the microcomputer. It is assumed that +5, +12, and −12 volts are available from the power supply.

Courtesy *Radio-Electronics®*, Gernsback Publications, Inc.

8080A Microprocessor Chip

Individual output pins on the 8080 microprocessor chip have a fan-out of one low-power TTL input, or approximately 0.16 mA. The output pin specifications for the 8080A chip are 1.9 mA for each output pin, or a fan-out of a little greater than one standard TTL load. Neither of these fan-out capabilities are good, but clearly the 8080A is a superior chip that is easier to interface. For this reason, we use it in our microcomputer. Even a fan-out of one is insufficient to drive the required memory chips and output latches. Consequently, bus drivers are also required. These will be described in the following under the bus driver section.

Control Lines

The control section of the microcomputer is shown in Fig. 2-6. Included is the previously described 8224 clock generator/driver chip connected directly to the 8080A. The only additional electronic components required, besides the two chips, are a pair of 1-kilohm resistors, a reset switch, and a 6.750-MHz crystal.

The remaining control lines on the 8080A chip, those not connected to the 8224 chip, are HOLD, HLDA, INTE, INTERRUPT, WAIT, $\overline{\text{WR}}$, and DBIN. Five of these lines are not used in our small microcomputer, but are made available if you wish to experiment with them. The HOLD input permits you to drive the 8080A chip into the hold state and disable the address and data busses. The HLDA control output acknowledges the existence of a hold state. The INTERRUPT input permits you to interrupt the 8080A program execution, provided that the interrupt flip-flop within the 8080A chip is enabled. If it is enabled, the INTE output is at logic 1. Finally, the WAIT output permits the 8080A chip to signal that it is not ready or that it is wait-

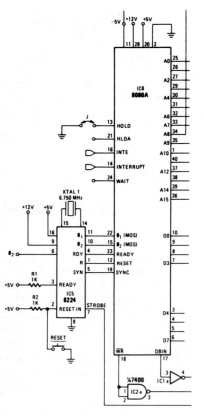

Fig. 2-6. The control of the 8080A chip is readily accomplished through the use of the 8224 clock generator/driver chip and a 6.750-MHz crystal.

Courtesy *Radio-Electronics®*,
Gernsback Publications, Inc.

ing for some external event. If the HOLD input to the 8080A input is not used, it must be grounded. This is easily done with the aid of a jumper, as shown in Fig. 2-6.

The final two control lines are both outputs. The WRITE ($\overline{WR}$) signal is active when at logic 0, and indicates that the 8080A chip is sending data out to some device. The remaining signal, data bus in (DBIN), indicates that the data bus is being used for the input of data. It is active in the logic 1 state. In the 8080A chip the data bus is bidirectional, i.e., data transfers into and out of the chip over the same wire connections. Careful management of this bus is necessary for the data to flow properly. This data bus management capability is built into the microprocessor chip itself, but we must be certain that our external devices do not attempt to place their data on the bus at the same time that some other device or the 8080A chip itself is trying to use it. Only one device should be transmitting data over the data bus at any given instant of time.

Bus Drivers

In order to drive the memory chips and output latches on our small 8080 microcomputer, a fan-out of at least ten is required for each output line on the data bus. In addition, the bidirectional character of the data must be maintained. The device that we use to accomplish such objectives is the Intel 8216 4-bit parallel bidirectional bus driver chip, the specifications of which are shown, courtesy of Intel Corporation, on the following pages. Consider output DB_0 in the 8216 logic diagram. The following truth table applies:

$\overline{DIEN}$	$\overline{CS}$	
0	0	$DI_0 \rightarrow DB_0$, i.e., data is output from the 8080 chip
1	0	$DB_0 \rightarrow DO_0$, i.e., data is input into the 8080 chip
0	1	high-impedance state; chip disabled
1	1	high-impedance state; chip disabled

In other words, when $\overline{DIEN}$ is at logic 0 and the chip is enabled, the 8216 chip acts as an input buffer. When $\overline{DIEN}$ is at logic 1 and the chip is enabled, the 8216 acts as an output buffer.

The bus driver section of our microcomputer is shown in Fig. 2-7. Observe that DBIN is connected to $\overline{DIEN}$ (pin 15 on the 8216 chip) and that each 8216 chip is permanently enabled. The truth table relating DBIN and $\overline{DIEN}$ is:

DBIN	$\overline{DIEN}$	
0	0	Data is output from the 8080 chip; DBIN = 0, and thus the data bus is in the output mode.
1	1	Data is input into the 8080 chip; DBIN = 1, and thus the data bus is in the input mode

According to the Intel specifications for the 8216, the absolute maximum output current at a logic 0 state is 125 mA, which is a substantial drive capability. Note that both DBIN and $\overline{WR}$ are buffered by a 7400 or 7404 chip to boost their fan-out from one to ten standard TTL loads.

Status Information

If you carefully study the Intel specifications for the 8080A microprocessor chip, you will observe that certain important control signals are not present on the chip itself. Included among these signals are memory read ($\overline{MR}$), memory write ($\overline{MW}$), input ($\overline{IN}$), output ($\overline{OUT}$), and interrupt knowledge ($\overline{INTA}$). To generate such control signals, the 8080A chip uses a "look ahead" technique: Since the data bus is not in use at all times for data transfer, the 8080A can use the bus to trans-

intel® Schottky Bipolar **8216/8226**

4 BIT PARALLEL BIDIRECTIONAL BUS DRIVER

- **Data Bus Buffer Driver for 8080 CPU**
- **Low Input Load Current — .25 mA Maximum**
- **High Output Drive Capability for Driving System Data Bus**

- **3.65V Output High Voltage for Direct Interface to 8080 CPU**
- **Three State Outputs**
- **Reduces System Package Count**

The 8216/8226 is a 4-bit bi-directional bus driver/receiver.

All inputs are low power TTL compatible. For driving MOS, the DO outputs provide a high 3.65V V_{OH}, and for high capacitance terminated bus structures, the DB outputs provide a high 50mA I_{OL} capability.

A non-inverting (8216) and an inverting (8226) are available to meet a wide variety of applications for buffering in microcomputer systems.

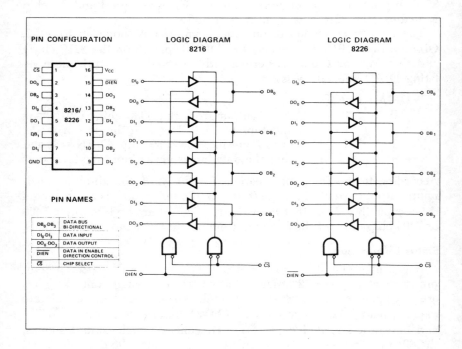

PIN CONFIGURATION

$\overline{CS}$	1	16	V_{CC}
DO_0	2	15	$\overline{DIEN}$
DB_0	3	14	DO_3
DI_0	4	13	DB_3
DO_1	5	12	DI_3
DB_1	6	11	DO_2
DI_1	7	10	DB_2
GND	8	9	DI_2

8216/8226

LOGIC DIAGRAM 8216

LOGIC DIAGRAM 8226

PIN NAMES

DB_0-DB_3	DATA BUS BI-DIRECTIONAL
DI_0-DI_3	DATA INPUT
DO_0-DO_3	DATA OUTPUT
$\overline{DIEN}$	DATA IN ENABLE DIRECTION CONTROL
$\overline{CS}$	CHIP SELECT

SCHOTTKY BIPOLAR 8216/8226

FUNCTIONAL DESCRIPTION

Microprocessors like the 8080 are MOS devices and are generally capable of driving a single TTL load. The same is true for MOS memory devices. While this type of drive is sufficient in small systems with few components, quite often it is necessary to buffer the microprocessor and memories when adding components or expanding to a multi-board system.

The 8216/8226 is a four bit bi-directional bus driver specifically designed to buffer microcomputer system components.

Bi-Directional Driver

Each buffered line of the four bit driver consists of two separate buffers that are tri-state in nature to achieve direct bus interface and bi-directional capability. On one side of the driver the output of one buffer and the input of another are tied together (DB), this side is used to interface to the system side components such as memories, I/O, etc., because its interface is direct TTL compatible and it has high drive (50mA). On the other side of the driver the inputs and outputs are separated to provide maximum flexibility. Of course, they can be tied together so that the driver can be used to buffer a true bi-directional bus such as the 8080 Data Bus. The DO outputs on this side of the driver have a special high voltage output drive capability (3.65V) so that direct interface to the 8080 and 8008 CPUs is achieved with an adequate amount of noise immunity (350mV worst case).

Control Gating $\overline{DIEN}$, $\overline{CS}$

The $\overline{CS}$ input is actually a device select. When it is "high" the output drivers are all forced to their high-impedance state. When it is at "zero" the device is selected (enabled) and the direction of the data flow is determined by the $\overline{DIEN}$ input.

The $\overline{DIEN}$ input controls the direction of data flow (see Figure 1) for complete truth table. This direction control is accomplished by forcing one of the pair of buffers into its high impedance state and allowing the other to transmit its data. A simple two gate circuit is used for this function.

The 8216/8226 is a device that will reduce component count in microcomputer systems and at the same time enhance noise immunity to assure reliable, high performance operation.

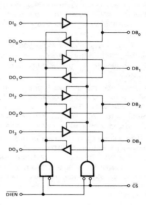

(a) 8216

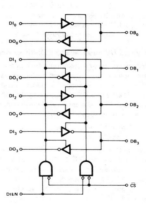

(b) 8226

DIEN	CS	
0	0	DI → DB
1	0	DB → DO
0	1	HIGH IMPEDANCE
1	1	

Figure 1. 8216/8226 Logic Diagrams

SCHOTTKY BIPOLAR 8216/8226

APPLICATIONS OF 8216/8226

8080 Data Bus Buffer

The 8080 CPU Data Bus is capable of driving a single TTL load and is more than adequate for small, single board systems. When expanding such a system to more than one board to increase I/O or Memory size, it is necessary to provide a buffer. The 8216/8226 is a device that is exactly fitted to this application.

Shown in Figure 2 are a pair of 8216/8226 connected directly to the 8080 Data Bus and associated control signals. The buffer is bi-directional in nature and serves to isolate the CPU data bus.

On the system side, the DB lines interface with standard semiconductor I/O and Memory components and are completely TTL compatible. The DB lines also provide a high drive capability (50mA) so that an extremely large system can be dirven along with possible bus termination networks.

On the 8080 side the DI and DO lines are tied together and are directly connected to the 8080 Data Bus for bi-directional operation. The DO outputs of the 8216/8226 have a high voltage output capability of 3.65 volts which allows direct connection to the 8080 whose minimum input voltage is 3.3 volts. It also gives a very adequate noise margin of 350mV (worst case).

The control inputs to 8216/8226 ($\overline{CS}$, $\overline{DIEN}$) are connected directly to the 8080. $\overline{DIEN}$ is tied to DBIN so that proper bus flow is maintained, and $\overline{CS}$ is tied to HLDA so that the system side Data Bus will be 3-stated when a Hold request has been acknowledged during a DMA activity.

Memory and I/O Interface to a Bi-directional Bus

In large microcomputer systems it is often necessary to provide Memory and I/O with their own buffers and at the same time maintain a direct, common interface to a bi-directional Data Bus. The 8216/8226 has separated data in and data out lines on one side and a common bi-directional set on the other to accomodate such a function.

Shown in Figure 3 is an example of how the 8216/8226 is used in this type of application.

The interface to Memory is simple and direct. The memories used are typically Intel® 8102, 8102A, 8101 or 8107A and have separate data inputs and outputs. The DI and DO lines of the 8216/8226 tie to them directly and under control of the $\overline{MEMR}$ signal, which is connected to the $\overline{DIEN}$ input, an interface to the bi-directional Data Bus is maintained.

The interface to I/O is similar to Memory. The I/O devices used are typically Intel® 8255s, and can be used for both input and output ports. The I/O R signal is connected directly to the $\overline{DIEN}$ input so that proper data flow from the I/O device to the Data Bus is maintained.

The 8216/8226 can be used in a wide variety of other buffering functions in microcomputer systems such as Address Bus Drivers, Drivers to peripheral devices such as printers, and as Drivers for long length cables to other peripherals or systems.

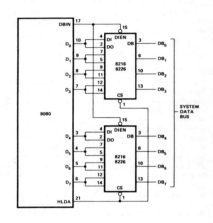

Figure 2. 8080 Data Bus Buffer.

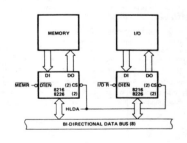

Figure 3. Memory and I/O Interface to a Bi-Directional Bus.

58

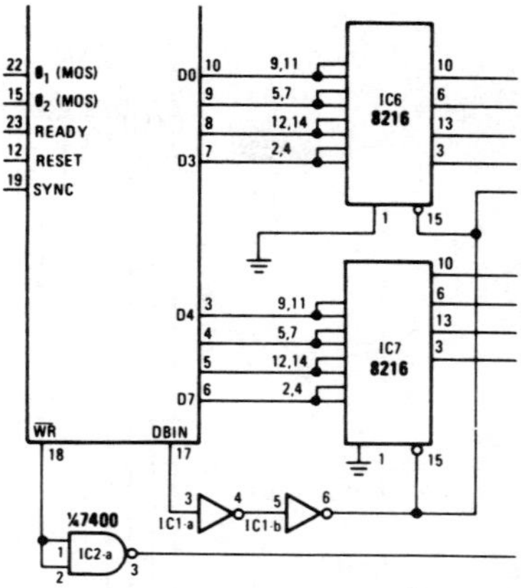

Courtesy *Radio-Electronics*®,
Gernsback Publications, Inc.

Fig. 2-7. Bus driver section of the small 8080-based microcomputer.

fer additional control information. *Such information is output very early in the machine cycle* (see Chapter 6) *to generate control signals used to control the transfer of data to or from input/output devices and memory.*

The status information appears on the data bus for a very short period, approximately 500 ns for an 8080 system operating at a 2-MHz clock rate. Since the information is to be used at a later time, it must be latched. The SYSTEM STROBE ($\overline{\text{STSTB}}$) is generated at pin 7 on the 8224 chip at the correct time to latch, or capture, the status information. Note that $\overline{\text{STSTB}}$ signal is generated from the system clock signal ϕ_1 and the SYNC signal from the 8080A. Any type of latch chip may be used. In Chapter 6, the use of an 8212 buffer/latch chip is described. In Fig. 2-8, a 74174 6-bit positive-edge–triggered latch chip is employed. The 74174 chip is clocked at pin 9.

All eight bits on the data bus provide some sort of status information, but not all eight may be needed. The information provided by Intel Corporation on the status bits is reproduced on page 61.

In our small 8080 system, the $\overline{\text{WO}}$ and STACK status signals are ignored since they are not very useful to us. HLTA and M1 are latched but are not used. The important status signals are INTA (interrupt acknowledge), INP (input), OUT (output), and MEMR (memory read). Together with the DBIN and $\overline{\text{WR}}$ outputs from the 8080A chip, these four signals provide five very important control signals, which basically constitute the control bus in our microcomputer:

- $\overline{\text{MR}}$. Memory read. Used to strobe data from a memory chip into the 8080A microprocessor chip.
- $\overline{\text{MW}}$. Memory write. Used to strobe data output from the 8080A chip into read/write memory.

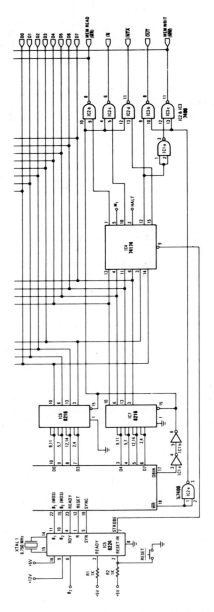

Courtesy *Radio-Electronics*®, Gernsback Publications, Inc.

Fig. 2-8. The status information and control section of the small 8080 microcomputer system. The status latch is the 74174 chip, which is a 6-bit latch.

8080 STATUS LATCH

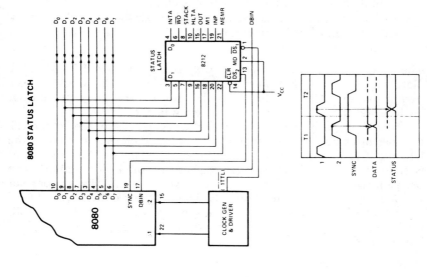

Instructions for the 8080 require from one to five machine cycles for complete execution. The 8080 sends out 8 bit of status information on the data bus at the beginning of each machine cycle (during SYNC time). The following table defines the status information.

STATUS INFORMATION DEFINITION

Symbols	Data Bus Bit	Definition
INTA*	D_0	Acknowledge signal for INTERRUPT request. Signal should be used to gate a restart instruction onto the data bus when DBIN is active.
$\overline{WO}$	D_1	Indicates that the operation in the current machine cycle will be a WRITE memory or OUTPUT function ($\overline{WO} = 0$). Otherwise, a READ memory or INPUT operation will be executed.
STACK	D_2	Indicates that the address bus holds the pushdown stack address from the Stack Pointer.
HLTA	D_3	Acknowledge signal for HALT instruction.
OUT	D_4	Indicates that the address bus contains the address of an output device and the data bus will contain the output data when $\overline{WR}$ is active.
M_1	D_5	Provides a signal to indicate that the CPU is in the fetch cycle for the first byte of an instruction.
INP*	D_6	Indicates that the address bus contains the address of an input device and the input data should be placed on the data bus when DBIN is active.
MEMR*	D_7	Designates that the data bus will be used for memory read data.

- $\overline{\text{IN}}$. Input. Used to strobe data from an input device into the accumulator within the 8080A chip.
- $\overline{\text{OUT}}$. Output. Used to strobe data from the accumulator into an output device external to the 8080A chip.
- $\overline{\text{INTA}}$. Interrupt Acknowledge. Used to strobe a single-byte instruction into the instruction register within the 8080A chip during an interrupt.

The other signals associated with the control bus are RESET, INT (interrupt), and INTE (interrupt enable). These eight control signals permit us to read and write into and from memory and input/output devices and they also allow us to process interrupts.

There is now a system controller and bus driver chip, the Intel 8228, that performs both the bidirectional data bus buffering as well as the latching and gating of the status signals. A typical interface circuit is shown on the following page, courtesy of Intel Corporation. The problem with the 8228 chip is that it is expensive and that it does not provide access to all eight status bits. The data bus buffering is limited to a standard fan-out of ten TTL loads, or 16-mA current sink capability. The authors prefer the simplicity of the individual 8216, 7400, and 74174 chips.

Memory

The necessary control section for the 8080A chip is in place and the status bits are latched. We are now ready to add external devices to our microcomputer. The first devices that will be needed are semiconductor memory chips. Memory comes in various forms and types, but we will only consider two, both of which are random access memories. "Random access" means that any single memory location may be accessed after any other location. We need not be concerned about the memory region between the two locations of interest.

As subgroups of semiconductor devices, we have read/write (R/W) memory and read-only memory (ROM). We will choose the 2111 read/write memory chip since it is easy to interface to the 8080A. It is organized as 256 memory locations with four bits per location, i.e., it is a 1024-bit, or one-kilobit, memory chip. The Intel Corporation specification for the 8111-2 chip, which is pin compatible and electrically similar to the 2111 memory chip, is shown on page 64. The 8111-2 has common input and output lines (I/O) over which data is transferred to and from the 8080A microprocessor chip. Clearly, these I/O lines are bidirectional. Each 8111-2 memory chip has eight address inputs (A_0 through A_7) to uniquely define a single memory location among the 256 possible locations. The control inputs to the 8111-12 include the read/write input (R/W), two chip enable inputs ($\overline{\text{CE}}_1$ and $\overline{\text{CE}}_2$), and an output disable input (OD).

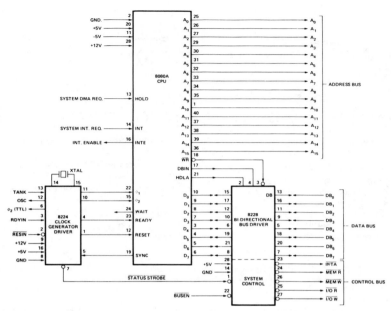

Since the word length in each 8111-2 chip is only four bits, **pairs** of such chips must be enabled and disabled simultaneously in order to provide the 8-bit word required by the 8080A microprocessor chip. Fig. 2-4 shows that $\overline{MW}$ (memory write) is connected to R/W (pin 16) on the 8111-2 chip, and that $\overline{MR}$ (memory read) is connected to pin 9 (OD) on the read/write chip. Assuming that the chip is enabled, the applicable truth table is as follows:

$\overline{MW}$	$\overline{MR}$	R/W	OD	
0	0	[NOTE: Input condition not possible]		
0	1	0	1	Memory write; disable memory output
1	0	1	0	Memory read
1	1	1	1	Disable memory output

The decoding of the address bus is depicted in Fig. 2-9. The desired truth table is:

A15	A14	A13	A12	A11	A10	A9	A8	A7 . . . A0	Memory	Use
0	0	0	0	0	0	0	0	X . . . X	Block 0	Reserved for EPROM
0	0	0	0	0	0	0	1	X . . . X	Block 1	Reserved for EPROM
0	0	0	0	0	0	1	0	X . . . X	Block 2	8111 read/write memory
0	0	0	0	0	0	1	1	X . . . X	Block 3	8111 read/write memory

intel® Silicon Gate MOS **8111-2**

1024 BIT (256 x 4) STATIC MOS RAM
WITH COMMON I/O AND OUTPUT DISABLE

- Organization 256 Words by 4 Bits
- Access Time — 850 nsec Max.
- Common Data Input and Output
- Single +5V Supply Voltage
- Directly TTL Compatible — All Inputs and Output
- Static MOS — No Clocks or Refreshing Required
- Simple Memory Expansion — Chip Enable Input

- Fully Decoded — On Chip Address Decode
- Inputs Protected — All Inputs Have Protection Against Static Charge
- Low Cost Packaging — 18 Pin Plastic Dual-In-Line Configuration
- Low Power — Typically 150 mW
- Three-State Output — OR-Tie Capability

The Intel®8111-2 is a 256 word by 4 bit static random access memory element using normally off N-channel MOS devices integrated on a monolithic array. It uses fully DC stable (static) circuitry and therefore requires no clocks or refreshing to operate. The data is read out nondestructively and has the same polarity as the input data. Common input/output pins are provided.

The 8111-2 is designed for memory applications in small systems where high performance, low cost, large bit storage, and simple interfacing are important design objectives.

It is directly TTL compatible in all respects: inputs, outputs, and a single +5V supply. Separate chip enable ($\overline{CE}$) leads allow easy selection of an individual package when outputs are OR-tied.

The Intel®8111-2 is fabricated with N-channel silicon gate technology. This technology allows the design and production of high performance, easy-to-use MOS circuits and provides a higher functional density on a monolithic chip than either conventional MOS technology or P-channel silicon gate technology.

Intel's silicon gate technology also provides excellent protection against contamination. This permits the use of low cost silicone packaging.

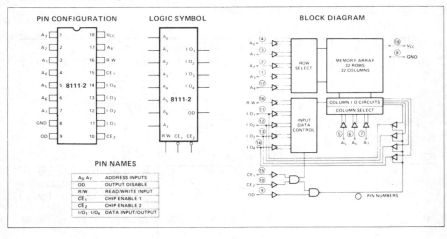

Here an X indicates that either a logic 0 or a logic 1 is permitted. A0 through A7 can be any combination of logic 0 and logic 1 states, a total of 256 different combinations. Observe that only address bits A8 and A9 change, giving all four possible combinations for the two bits. Address bits A10 through A15 remain at logic 0 for all of our selected addresses in our small 8080 microcomputer system.

It is customary practice to absolutely decode memory locations, that is, to ensure that all sixteen address bits participate in the decoding of a memory location by providing the chip enable ($\overline{CE}$) input as well as the eight address inputs A0 through A7. Fig. 2-9 demonstrates how this is done. Since the address bits A10 through A15 remain at logic 0, we use 74LS05 open-collector inverters in a "wired-or" configuration to provide a uniquely decoded logic condition. Observe the presence of a 1-kilohm pull-up resistor, R4. The truth table for the wired-or circuit is as follows:

A15	A14	A13	A12	A11	A10	Q
0	0	0	0	0	0	1
X	X	X	X	X	1	0
X	X	X	X	1	X	0
X	X	X	1	X	X	0
X	X	1	X	X	X	0
X	1	X	X	X	X	0
1	X	X	X	X	X	0

NOTE: X = either logic 0 or logic 1

Observe that this truth table, though implemented with open-collector inverters, is identical to that for a six-input NOR gate; the unique logic state is Q = 1, and this output condition occurs only when all inputs are at logic 0.

Whenever the output of the wired-or, or six-input NOR, circuit is at logic 1, we know that A10 through A15 are at logic 0 and that we are within one of the four selected 256-byte blocks of memory. We must further narrow our memory selection process to a specific memory block. This is done with the aid of a 74LS155 decoder chip, the block diagram and pin configuration both of which are given in Figs. 2-9 and 2-10. The 74LS155 chip is enabled and disabled using the output from the wired-or circuit, where disabled corresponds to logic 0 (no blocks selected) and enabled corresponds to logic 1 (one and only one memory block selected). The truth table for the 74LS155 chip is shown on page 67.

The outputs to blocks 2 and 3 go to the $\overline{CE}_1$ inputs (pin 15) of the respective pairs of 8111-2 read/write memory chips, as can be seen

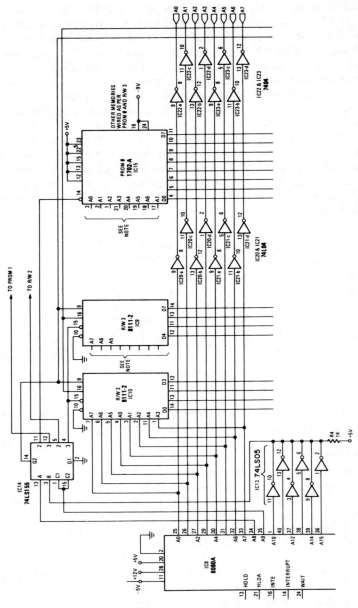

Courtesy *Radio-Electronics*®, Gernsback Publications, Inc.

Fig. 2-9. The address bus, address decoder, and memory section of the small 8080 microcomputer system. For simplicity, the IC9 and IC15 address lines have been omitted; they are in parallel with those of IC10.

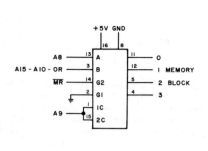

(A) 74LS155 memory decoder.

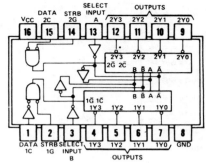

(B) 74LS155 chip.

Fig. 2-10. The 74LS155 chips.

G2 ($\overline{MR}$)	G1	C2 + C1 (A9)		B (HI)	A (A8)	Memory Selected
0	X	0	0	0	0	None
0	X	0	0	0	1	None
0	X	0	0	1	0	PROM Block 0
0	X	0	0	1	1	PROM Block 1
X	0	1	1	0	0	None
X	0	1	1	0	1	None
X	0	1	1	1	0	R/W Block 2
X	0	1	1	1	1	R/W Block 3

NOTE: The HI address represents A15-A10 all = logic 0.

for block 3 in Fig. 2-9. When pin 15 of the 8111-2 chip is at logic 0, the chip is enabled since $\overline{CE}_2$ (pin 10) is wired to logic 0.

In addition to read/write memory, our small microcomputer also contains some read-only memory. The reasons for providing such memory will be discussed later. Suffice it to say here that read-only memory is not destroyed when we shut the power off, as is the case with read/write memory. We say that read-only memory is *nonvolatile*. The type of read-only memory that we employ is actually a special type of read-only memory called *electrically programmable read-only memory*. Such a memory, which is abbreviated by the initials EPROM, is widely used for one-of-a-kind–type applications. You can purchase a special electronic device called an EPROM Programmer and program the EPROMs for your special applications rather than rely upon the chip manufacturer to do the job for you.

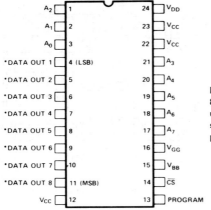

A₂	1		24	V_DD
A₁	2		23	V_CC
A₀	3		22	V_CC
*DATA OUT 1	4 (LSB)		21	A₃
*DATA OUT 2	5		20	A₄
*DATA OUT 3	6		19	A₅
*DATA OUT 4	7		18	A₆
*DATA OUT 5	8		17	A₇
*DATA OUT 6	9		16	V_GG
*DATA OUT 7	10		15	V_BB
*DATA OUT 8	11 (MSB)		14	$\overline{CS}$
V_CC	12		13	PROGRAM

Fig. 2-11. Pin configuration of the 1702A/8702A chip. Some of the power input pins are used only during programming. We shall assume here that the chip has been properly programmed prior to its inclusion in our 8080 microcomputer system.

*THIS PIN IS THE DATA INPUT LEAD DURING PROGRAMMING.

We employ the Intel Corp. 1702A (or 8702A) EPROM chips, which can be erased through the use of ultraviolet light and reprogrammed over one-hundred times. The pin configuration of the 1702A/8702A chip is shown in Fig. 2-11. Observe that there are eight address inputs, A_0 through A_7, and eight data output pins, DATA OUT 1 through DATA OUT 8, a chip select input (pin 14), and several power input pins. Fig. 2-9 shows this chip incorporated into the 8080 microcomputer system. Pins 12, 13, 15, 22, and 23 are all tied to +5 volts. Pins 16 and 24 are connected to −9 volts. The block 0 output from the 74LS155 decoder chip is connected to the $\overline{CS}$ input of the 1702A (pin 14). Observe that you can only read the 1702A chip; it is a read-only memory, not a read/write memory.

Microcomputer Bus

The "microcomputer bus" for our small 8080 microcomputer system consists of the address, data, and control busses. The address bus consists of sixteen buffered address lines. In Fig. 2-9, the buffering of address bits A0 through A7 is shown. A pair of inverters, first the 74L04 and then the 7404, are used for each address line. The 74L04 chip has a fan-in of 0.1, or 0.16 mA, and is well suited for use with the 8080A microprocessor chip. The 8216 chips (Fig. 2-4) provide sufficient buffering for the eight data bus lines, D0 through D7. The 7400 NAND gates each have a fan-out of ten, more than enough for each control bus signal line. RESET and INTERRUPT are inputs to the 8080A chip. The INTE output might require a buffer.

Input/Output

The input/output section of our 8080 microcomputer is shown in Fig. 2-12. In subsequent chapters in this book, you will become quite

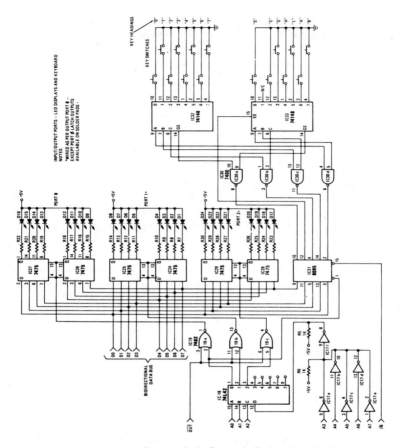

Courtesy *Radio-Electronics®*, Gernsback Publications, Inc.

Fig. 2-12. The input/output section of the small 8080A microcomputer system.

familiar with I/O decoding, the use of 7475 latch chips, and the use of 8095 three-state buffer chips. Consequently, we will discuss the I/O section only briefly here.

In order to transfer eight bits of data between the accumulator within the 8080A chip and an I/O device, an 8-bit device code is provided on the address bus at bits A0 through A7. To select a unique device among the 256 possible devices, a decoder is required. In Fig. 2-12, the decoder consists of the 74L42 chip and six 74LS05 open-collector inverters present at address lines A3 through A7. Five of the inverters serve as a wired-OR, or five-point NOR, circuit to decode address bits A3 through A7 into a unique logic state when the five lines are all at logic 0. The principle used is identical with that used for address bits A10 through A15 in the memory section of our micro-computer. Here, the truth table is as follows:

A7	A6	A5	A4	A3	Q
0	0	0	0	0	1
X	X	X	X	1	0
X	X	X	1	X	0
X	X	1	X	X	0
X	1	X	X	X	0
1	X	X	X	X	0

NOTE: X = either logic 0 or logic 1

The remaining 74LS05 open-collector inverter is used to invert Q to a logic 0 state when the five address bits are all at logic 0. This logic 0 condition is applied at the D input of the 74L42 chip.

Chip 74L42 is wired as a three-line-to-eight-line decoder that has the following truth table:

D	A2	A1	A0	0	1	2	3	4	5	6	7	Channel Selected
1	X	X	X	1	1	1	1	1	1	1	1	No channel selected
0	0	0	0	0	1	1	1	1	1	1	1	Channel 0
0	0	0	1	1	0	1	1	1	1	1	1	Channel 1
0	0	1	0	1	1	0	1	1	1	1	1	Channel 2
0	0	1	1	1	1	1	0	1	1	1	1	Channel 3
0	1	0	0	1	1	1	1	0	1	1	1	Channel 4
0	1	0	1	1	1	1	1	1	0	1	1	Channel 5
0	1	1	0	1	1	1	1	1	1	0	1	Channel 6
0	1	1	1	1	1	1	1	1	1	1	0	Channel 7

Channels 0, 1, and 2 are gated with the $\overline{OUT}$ control signal and used to strobe information from the bidirectional data bus into the latch chips for ports 0, 1, and 2, respectively. Channel 0 is gated with the $\overline{IN}$ control signal and used to strobe input data present at the 8095 three-state buffer chip into the 8080A microprocessor chip.

Finally, a pair of 74148 three-line-to-eight-line priority encoder chips are used to encode the fifteen-key keyboard, which consists of keys 0 through 7, the SEE/STORE key (S), the GO key (G), the HI address byte key (H), the LO address byte key (L), and three additional keys that have no specific defined use (A, B, and C).

Operation of the Microcomputer

You may refer to the previously mentioned articles in *Radio-Electronics* for a description of how the small microcomputer operates. Briefly, you can enter programs via the keyboard, inspect memory contents, execute 8080 programs that are within the memory capability of the microcomputer, and output information to the three output ports. To do all this requires a program stored in one of the 1702A EPROM chips, in block 0 to be specific. This preprogrammed chip is called the *Keyboard EXecutive*, or KEX. When you start the 8080 microcomputer, you first press the RESET button and the microcomputer goes to memory location 0000000000000000_2 (otherwise known as $HI = 000_8$ and $LO = 000_8$, where the HI and LO address bytes are given in octal code). At this memory location, the 8080A chip finds the first instruction that it must execute. From this point forward, there exists a series of instructions that function as a *bootstrap program* to permit you to operate the microcomputer. The bootstrap program described in the *Radio-Electronics* article is only one possible program. Depending upon the use of your microcomputer, you can write bootstrap programs to input data from an ASCII keyboard, a teletypewriter, a crt terminal, or a tape cassette and store the information in read/write memory. The bootstrap program might also contain subroutines to get data from and output data to magnetic tape cassettes, paper-tape punches and readers, and floppy disks. It is beyond the scope of this chapter to describe such software here. Suffice to say that you will be able to develop such software when you complete this book.

Once your 8080 microcomputer system is operational, you will want to *interface* it to external devices, be they integrated-circuit chips or larger electromechanical devices. Before we leave this chapter, it would be appropriate to define interfacing and to summarize how a microcomputer can be used to control the operation of other digital integrated-circuit chips, especially those in the 7400 series of chips. Since larger electromechanical devices contain 7400-series chips, once you understand how to interface such chips you will also understand how to interface the devices themselves.

WHAT IS INTERFACING?

Interfacing can be defined as the joining of members of a group (such as people, instruments, etc.) in such a way that they are able to function in a compatible and coordinated fashion.[1] By "compatible and coordinated fashion," we usually mean synchronized. Some important definitions include the following:

sync—Short for synchronous, synchronization, synchronizing, etc.[4]

synchronization pulses—Pulses originated by the transmitting equipment and introduced into the receiving equipment to keep the equipment at both locations operating in step.[4]

synchronize—To lock one element of a system into step with another.[4]

synchronous—In step or in phase, as applied to two devices or machines. A term applied to a computer, in which the performance of a sequence of operations is controlled by clock signals or pulses.[4] At the same time.

synchronous computer—A digital computer in which all ordinary operations are controlled by signals from a master clock.[4]

synchronous inputs—Those inputs of a flip-flop that do not control the output directly, as do those of a gate, but only when the clock permits and commands.[4]

synchronous logic—The type of digital logic used in a system in which logical operations take place in synchronism with clock pulses.[4]

synchronous operation—Operation of a system under the control of clock pulses.[4]

We can thus define *computer interfacing* as:

computer interfacing—The synchronization of digital data transmission between a computer and one or more external input/output devices.

Although the details of computer interfacing vary with the type of computer employed, the general principles of interfacing apply to a wide variety of computers. Some common characteristics include the following:

- The digital data that are transmitted between a computer and an I/O device are either individual clock pulses or full data words.
- The computer and the input/output device are both clocked or strobed devices.
- The computer sends synchronization pulses, called *device select pulses,* to the I/O device. They synchronize and select at the same instant of time.
- These device select pulses are generated by the computer program and interfacing hardware, *i.e.,* they are software controlled.
- The device select pulses are usually quite short. For an 8080 microcomputer operating at 2 MHz, they last only 500 ns.
- Individual device select pulses can be sent to individual input or output devices. This is called *external device addressing.*
- External device addressing is software generated and decoded externally.
- Computer program execution can be interrupted by the transmission of a clock pulse from an I/O device to a special input line to the computer.
- Upon being interrupted by an external I/O device, the computer goes to a computer subroutine that responds to, or *services,* the interrupt.
- Full data words can be output from, or input into, the accumulator register. For the 8080 microcomputer, a full data word contains eight bits.
- All data transmission operations are synchronized to the internal clock of the computer.

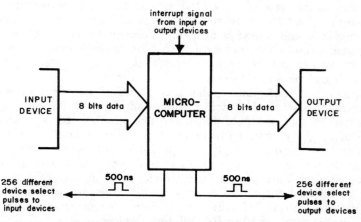

Fig. 2-13. The four fundamental tasks of interfacing: (1) external device addressing, (2) latching of output data, (3) strobing of input data, and (4) servicing of interrupts.

- Output data from the accumulator is available for only a very short period, and usually must be *latched*.
- Input data into the accumulator can be acquired over a very short period, and usually must be *strobed* into the accumulator.
- Device select pulses are used for latching data output and strobing data input.

As can be seen from Fig. 2-13 and the preceding comments, the *four fundamental tasks of computer interfacing are:*

- External device addressing through the generation of device select pulses.
- The latching of output data.
- The strobing of input data.
- The servicing of interrupts.

If you can master these four tasks, you will know how to interface a computer.

WHAT IS AN I/O DEVICE?

Some useful definitions include the following:

input-output, input/output—General term for the equipment used to communicate with a computer and the data involved in the communication.[5]

I/O—Abbreviation for input/output.[4]

I/O device—Input/output device. Any digital device, including a single integrated-circuit chip, that transmits data or receives data or strobe pulses from a computer.

The traditional view of an I/O device is that it is somewhat large or complex. Certainly card readers, magnetic tape units, cathode-ray tube displays, and teletypes fit such a description. However, *a single integrated-circuit chip, such as a latch, shift register, counter, or small memory, can be considered to be an I/O device to a computer.* If it is digital, it can be an I/O device.

Another important point is that *several device select pulses may be required for a single I/O device.* For example, a 74198 shift register has a pair of control inputs that determine whether the register shifts left, shifts right, or parallel loads eight bits of data. It also has a clock input and a clear input. So, this single 74198 chip, when serving as an output device, may require up to four device select lines from the microcomputer. Thus, the fact that we can generate 256 different input and 256 different output device select pulses does not necessarily mean that we can address 512 different "devices." A more reasonable number is on the order of 50 to 100 different devices.

Device select pulses are easy to implement and inexpensive. You should use them frequently in an attempt to *substitute computer software for integrated-circuit chip hardware.* Remember this theme: software vs hardware. There exists a tradeoff between the two, but your main objective in using microcomputers is to substitute software for hardware. When you substitute software for hardware, the only penalty that you may pay is time, i.e., it takes time to execute computer instructions. If you can accept the delays inherent in computer programs, then you can vastly simplify the circuitry required to accomplish a specific task.

USES FOR DEVICE SELECT PULSES

We have previously defined a *clock* as either (a) any device that generates at least one clock pulse, or (b) a timing device in a system that provides a continuous series of timing pulses. A *pulser* is a logic switch that can generate a single clock pulse. A *monostable multivibrator* is a circuit having only one stable state, from which it can be triggered to change the state, but only for a predetermined interval, after which it returns to the original state. With these three definitions in mind, we can consider a microcomputer to be, among other things, *a sophisticated electronic circuit that can act as a clock, a pulser, or a monostable multivibrator.* For example, an 8080 microcomputer operating at 2 MHz can:

- Generate individual clock pulses, of 500-ns pulse width, at any time, thus acting as a pulser or electronic strobe device.
- Generate a train of clock pulses in which the frequency is given by the formula, $\nu = 2/n$ MHz, where n is almost any integer that is greater than or equal to 20.

- Generate single monostable pulses, in which the pulse width is given by the formula $\tau = n/2$ μs, where n is almost any integer that is greater than or equal to 10. An external flip-flop is required to generate such monostable pulses.

The microcomputer does all of the above with the aid of device select pulses whose frequency, but not pulse width, is determined by the microcomputer program. As mentioned previously, such pulses are said to be *software generated,* where the software is the microcomputer program. Thus:

- If an isolated clock pulse is generated by the program, then the microcomputer is acting as a pulser or electronic strobe device.
- If the program contains a *timing loop* such that a series of clock pulses are generated at repetitive time intervals, then the microcomputer is acting as a clock.
- If a pair of clock pulses are generated to preset and clear a flip-flop, then the microcomputer/flip-flop combination is acting as a monostable multivibrator.

In this manner, *we are substituting software for hardware, i.e.,* we are eliminating the need to supply a mechanical or electronic pulser, a clock, or a monostable multivibrator.

The 8080 microcomputer can generate 256 different 500-ns output clock pulses and 256 different 500-ns input clock pulses with the aid of decoder circuits. In essence, the microcomputer has the capability to act as:

512 different pulser or electronic strobe devices, or
512 different clocks, or
512 different monostable multivibrators,

or any combination of pulsers, electronic strobe devices, clocks, and monostable multivibrators whose total is 512. It is difficult to conceive of a single digital circuit that would require so many devices.

USE OF A MICROCOMPUTER TO STROBE INTEGRATED-CIRCUIT CHIPS

Perhaps the most important application for microcomputers is to strobe the operation of instruments, electronic devices, and integrated-circuit chips. Chips are inexpensive, and with them we can demonstrate the entire range of applications for computer-generated device select pulses. Such pulses can, for example,

- Clear counters, shift registers, flip-flops, and latches.
- Load counters, latches, and shift registers.

- Enable multiplexers, demultiplexers, decoders, counters, latches, shift registers, memories, priority encoders, and a variety of other chips.
- Inhibit clock inputs to counters and shift registers.
- Set, clear, toggle, and clock flip-flops.
- Select shift left, shift right, load, and inhibit functions in shift registers.

By using device select pulses to generate clear, load, enable, inhibit, set, toggle, and select pulses and logic states, *we are substituting software for hardware.* This is the second time that we have observed this; it won't be the last. *Our fundamental objective with microcomputers and microprocessor chips is to substitute software for hardware!* This book thus has a dual purpose: (1) to teach you how to interface microcomputers, and (b) to show you how to substitute microcomputer software for integrated-circuit chip hardware.

To emphasize the above message, we will summarize the strobe characteristics of some of the common 7400-series integrated-circuit chips. We will group chips by function, and then identify pin numbers associated with strobing operations. For each pin listed, we will indicate the logic state required to accomplish the strobing function.

Counters

The popular counters are the 7490, 7493, 74192, and 74193. Not quite so popular are the 74160, 74161, 74162, 74163, 74190, and 74191 counters.

7490	pins 2 and 3: logic 1 at both pins clears counter
	pins 6 and 7: logic 1 at both pins sets counter to 9
	pin 14: clock input
7493	pins 2 and 3: logic 1 at both inputs clears counter
	pin 14: clock input
74163	pin 1: logic 0 clears counter
74160 to	pin 2: clock input
	pin 7: logic 0 inhibits counter
	pin 9: logic 0 enables flip-flops and allows counter to be loaded
	pin 10: logic 0 inhibits counter and ripple carry
74190,	pin 4: logic 1 inhibits counter
74191	pin 5: logic 0 for up counter and logic 1 for down counter
	pin 11: logic 0 enables flip-flops and allows counter to be loaded
	pin 14: clock input
74192,	pin 4: clock input for down counter; logic 1 disables
74193	pin 5: clock input for up counter; logic 1 disables

pin 11: logic 0 enables flip-flops and allows counter to be loaded

pin 14: logic 1 clears counter

Decoders

Enable inputs are provided on the 74LS1389, 74LS139, 74154, and 74155 decoders. bcd-to-decimal decoders can be converted to strobed octal decoders if the D input is used as the strobe input.

7442, 7445	pin 12: logic 0 enables octal decoder
7446, 7447, 7448	pin 3: lamp test; logic 0 lights all seven segments
74LS138	pins 4, 5, and 6: logic 0 at both pins 4 and 5 and logic 1 at pin 6 enable decoder
74LS139	pin 1: logic 0 enables first decoder
	pin 15: logic 0 enables second decoder
74154	pins 18 and 19: logic 0 at both pins enables decoder
74155	pin 1: logic 1 enables first two-line-to-four-line decoder
	pin 2: logic 0 enables first two-line-to-four-line decoder
	pin 13: logic 1 enables second two-line-to-four-line decoder
	pin 14: logic 0 enables second two-line-to-four-line decoder
	pins 2 and 14 (connected together): logic 0 enables three-line-to-eight-line decoder

Demultiplexers

A decoder can be wired as a demultiplexer. The 74LS138, 74154, and 74155 decoder/demultiplexers each have enable inputs.

74LS138	pins 4 and 5: logic 0 at both inputs enables demultiplexer
74154	pin 19: logic 0 enables demultiplexer
74155	pin 2: logic 0 enables first demultiplexer
	pin 14: logic 0 enables second demultiplexer

Data Selectors/Multiplexers

Enable inputs are provided on each of the three popular 7400-series data selectors/multiplexers, 74150, 74151, and 74153, as well as on the 74156, 74157, and 74158 multiplexers.

74150	pin 9: logic 0 enables data selector/multiplexer
74151	pin 7: logic 0 enables data selector/multiplexer
74153	pin 1: logic 0 enables first data selector/multiplexer
	pin 15: logic 0 enables second data selector/multiplexer
74156–58	pin 1: logic 0 selects A inputs; logic 1 selects B inputs
	pin 15: logic 0 enables data selectors/multiplexers

Shift Registers

Only the newer 7400-series shift registers will be described. These include the 74164, 75165, 74166, 74194, 74198, and 74199 integrated-circuit chips.

74164	pin 8: logic 0 clears register
	pin 9: clock input
74165	pin 1: logic 0 loads register; logic 1 shifts data
	pin 2: clock input
	pin 15: logic 1 inhibits clock
74166	pin 6: logic 1 inhibits clock
	pin 7: clock input
	pin 9: logic 0 clears register
	pin 15: logic 0 loads register; logic 1 shifts data
74194	pin 1: logic 0 clears register
	pins 9 and 10: mode select inputs; pin 9 is S0 and pin 10 is S1; S0 = 0 and S1 = 0 inhibits clock; S0 = 1 and S1 = 0 shifts data right; S0 = 0 and S1 = 1 shifts data left; and S0 = 1 and S1 = 1 parallel loads register
	pin 11: clock input
74198	pins 1 and 23: mode select inputs; pin 1 is S0 and pin 23 is S1; S0 = 0 and S1 = 0 inhibits clock; S0 = 1 and S1 = 0 shifts data right; S0 = 0 and S1 = 1 shifts data left; and S0 = 1 and S1 = 1 parallel loads register
	pin 13: logic 0 clears register
	pin 11: clock input
74199	pin 11: logic 1 inhibits clock
	pin 13: clock input
	pin 14: logic 0 clears register
	pin 23: logic 0 parallel loads register; logic 1 shifts data right

Priority Encoder

The 74148 *priority encoder* encodes eight data lines to three-line binary.

74148	pin 5: logic 0 enables priority encoder

Latches and Flip-Flops

Latch chips contain four or more D-type flip-flops on a single integrated-circuit chip. The common 7400-series latches include the 7475, 74100, 74116, 74173, 74174, and 74175 latches.

7475	pin 3: logic 1 enables first two latches
	pin 13: logic 1 enables second two latches

74100	pin 23: logic 1 enables first four latches
	pin 12: logic 1 enables second four latches
74116	pin 1: logic 0 clears first four latches
	pins 2 and 3: logic 0 at both pins enables first four latches
	pin 13: logic 0 clears second four latches
	pins 14 and 15: logic 0 at both pins enables second four latches
74173	pins 1 and 2: logic 0 at both pins enables three-state outputs
	pin 7: clock input
	pins 9 and 10: logic 0 at both pins enables registers
	pin 15: logic 1 clears registers
74174,	pin 9: clock input
74175	pin 1: logic 0 clears latches

The 7400-series flip-flops such as the 7470, 7473, 7474, 7476, 74106, etc., have too many different inputs to merit individual listing. The types of inputs found on these chips include: preset, clear, clock, R, S, J, and K. Several typical chips are described below.

7470	pin 2: logic 0 clears flip-flop
	pins 3, 4, and 5: J inputs
	pins 9, 10, and 11: K inputs
	pin 12: clock input
	pin 13: logic 0 sets flip-flop
7473	pin 1: clock input to first flip-flop
	pin 2: logic 0 clears first flip-flop
	pin 3: K input to first flip-flop
	pin 14: J input to first flip-flop
	pin 5: clock input to second flip-flop
	pin 6: logic 0 clears second flip-flop
	pin 7: J input to second flip-flop
	pin 10: K input to second flip-flop
7474	pin 1: logic 0 clears first flip-flop
	pin 2: D input to first flip-flop
	pin 3: clock input to first flip-flop
	pin 4: logic 0 sets first flip-flop
	pin 10: logic 0 sets second flip-flop
	pin 11: clock input to second flip-flop
	pin 12: D input to second flip-flop
	pin 13: logic 0 clears second flip-flop

Memories

The characteristics of a variety of memories, not just those found in the 7400 series of integrated-circuit chips, are summarized below.

7488	pin 15: logic 0 enables memory
7489,	pin 2: logic 0 enables memory
8225	pin 3: logic 0 writes; logic 1 reads
74200,	pins 3, 4, and 5: logic 0 at all three pins enables memory
74206	pin 12: logic 0 writes; logic 1 reads
2102,	pin 3: logic 0 writes; logic 1 reads
8102	pin 13: logic 0 enables memory
1602A,	pin 14: logic 0 enables memory
1702A,	
8702A,	
1302,	
8302	

Other Chips

Given below are the characteristics of several three-state integrated-circuit chips that support the 8080 microprocessor chip.

8212	pins 1 and 13: logic 0 at pin 1 and logic 1 at pin 13 select this device
	pin 2: logic 1 latches data and enables three-state outputs
	pin 11: logic 1
	pin 14: logic 0 clears latches
8255	pin 5: logic 0 reads input data
	pin 6: logic 0 enables chip
	pin 36: logic 0 writes input data

Pin Configurations

The pin configurations of 72 different integrated-circuit chips are provided on the following pages to assist you with your interfacing activities. The following pages are courtesy of Texas Instruments, Inc., and Intel Corp.

WHAT HAVE YOU ACCOMPLISHED IN THIS CHAPTER?

In the first part of this chapter it was stated that at the end you would be able to do the following:

- Identify the memory address bus, data bus, control inputs, control outputs, and power inputs on the 40-pin 8080A microprocessor chip.

  A description of the 8080A microprocessor chip has been given at the beginning of this chapter. Although you may not understand some of the control input and output pins, you certainly should be able to identify all of them.

- Describe the function of each pin on the 8080A microprocessor chip.

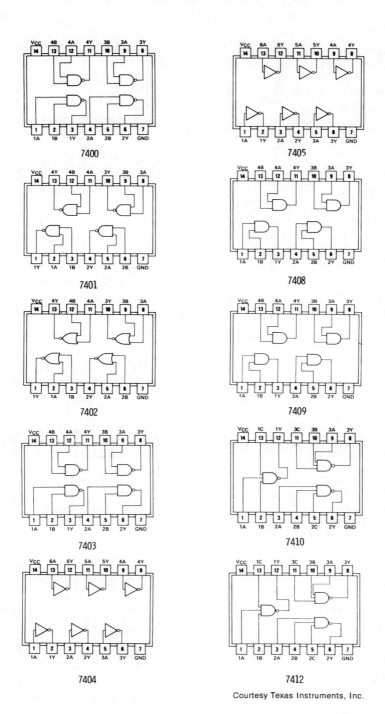

7400

7405

7401

7408

7402

7409

7403

7410

7404

7412

Courtesy Texas Instruments, Inc.

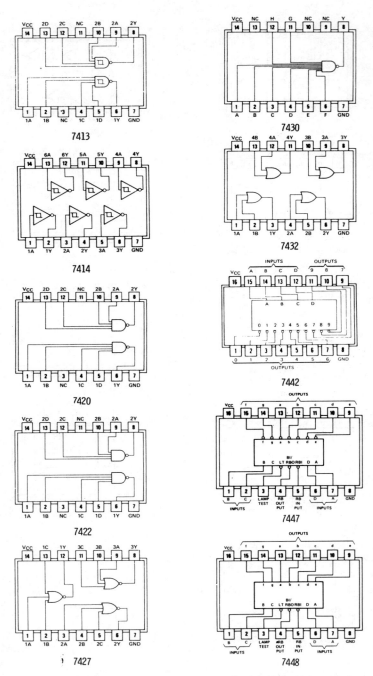

7413

7430

7414

7432

7420

7442

7422

7447

7427

7448

Courtesy Texas Instruments, Inc.

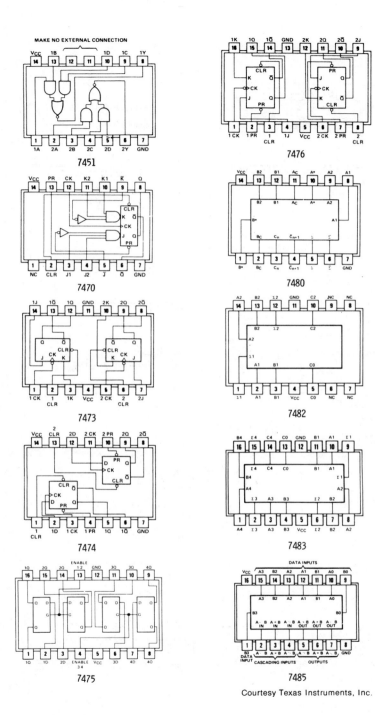

7451

7476

7470

7480

7473

7482

7474

7483

7475

7485

Courtesy Texas Instruments, Inc.

83

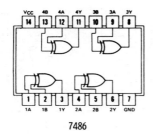

7486

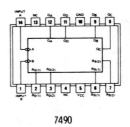

7490

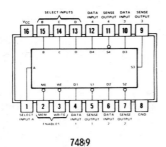

7489

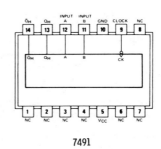

7491

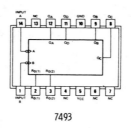

7493

RESULTANT DISPLAYS USING '46A, '47A, '48, '49, 'L46, 'L47

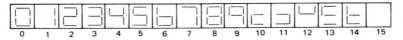

Courtesy Texas Instruments, Inc.

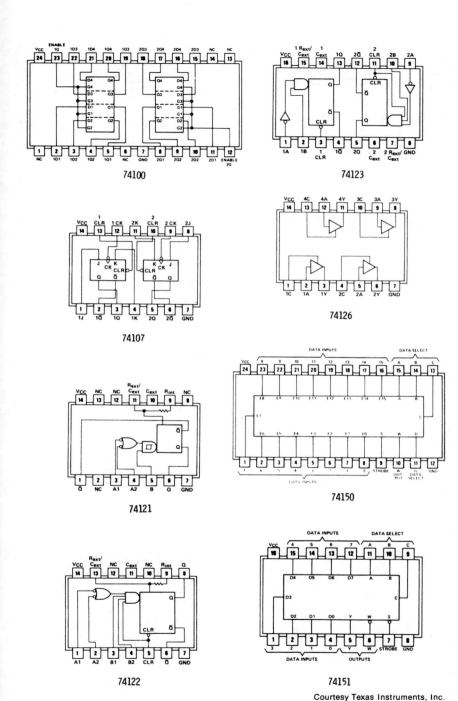

74100

74123

74107

74126

74121

74150

74122

74151

Courtesy Texas Instruments, Inc.

85

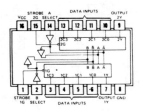

74153

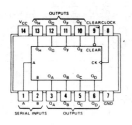

74164

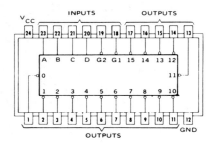

74154

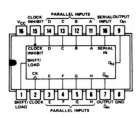

74165

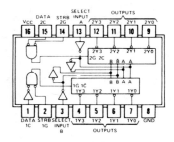

74155

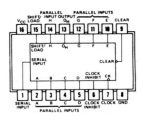

74166

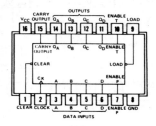

74160 to 74163

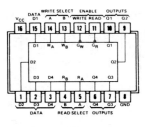

74170

Courtesy Texas Instruments, Inc.

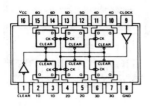

74174

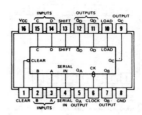

74179

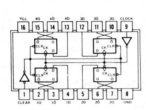

74175

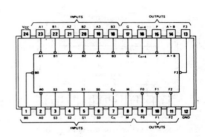

74181

74181

	TABLE 1		
		ACTIVE HIGH DATA	
SELECTION	M = H	M = L: ARITHMETIC OPERATIONS	
	LOGIC	C_n = H	C_n = L
S3 S2 S1 S0	FUNCTIONS	(no carry)	(with carry)
L L L L	$F = \overline{A}$	$F = A$	$F = A$ PLUS 1
L L L H	$F = \overline{A \cdot B}$	$F = A + B$	$F = (A + B)$ PLUS 1
L L H L	$F = \overline{A} + B$	$F = A + \overline{B}$	$F = (A + \overline{B})$ PLUS 1
L L H H	$F = 0$	$F = $ MINUS 1 (2's COMPL)	$F = $ ZERO
L H L L	$F = \overline{AB}$	$F = A$ PLUS $A\overline{B}$	$F = A$ PLUS $A\overline{B}$ PLUS 1
L H L H	$F = \overline{B}$	$F = (A + B)$ PLUS $A\overline{B}$	$F = (A + B)$ PLUS $A\overline{B}$ PLUS 1
L H H L	$F = A \odot B$	$F = A$ MINUS B MINUS 1	$F = A$ MINUS B
L H H H	$F = A\overline{B}$	$F = A\overline{B}$ MINUS 1	$F = A\overline{B}$
H L L L	$F = \overline{A} \cdot B$	$F = A$ PLUS AB	$F = A$ PLUS AB PLUS 1
H L L H	$F = A \oplus B$	$F = A$ PLUS B	$F = A$ PLUS B PLUS 1
H L H L	$F = B$	$F = (A + \overline{B})$ PLUS AB	$F = (A + \overline{B})$ PLUS AB PLUS 1
H L H H	$F = AB$	$F = AB$ MINUS 1	$F = AB$
H H L L	$F = 1$	$F = A$ PLUS A *	$F = A$ PLUS A PLUS 1
H H L H	$F = A + \overline{B}$	$F = (A + B)$ PLUS A	$F = (A + B)$ PLUS A PLUS 1
H H H L	$F = A + B$	$F = (A + \overline{B})$ PLUS A	$F = (A + \overline{B})$ PLUS A PLUS 1
H H H H	$F = A$	$F = A$ MINUS 1	$F = A$

*Each bit is shifted to the next more significant position.

	TABLE 2		
		ACTIVE LOW DATA	
SELECTION	M = H	M = L: ARITHMETIC OPERATIONS	
	LOGIC	C_n = L	C_n = H
S3 S2 S1 S0	FUNCTIONS	(no carry)	(with carry)
L L L L	$F = \overline{A}$	$F = A$ MINUS 1	$F = A$
L L L H	$F = \overline{AB}$	$F = AB$ MINUS 1	$F = AB$
L L H L	$F = \overline{A} + B$	$F = A\overline{B}$ MINUS 1	$F = A\overline{B}$
L L H H	$F = 1$	$F = $ MINUS 1 (2's COMPL)	$F = $ ZERO
L H L L	$F = \overline{A + B}$	$F = A$ PLUS $(A + \overline{B})$	$F = A$ PLUS $(A + \overline{B})$ PLUS 1
L H L H	$F = \overline{B}$	$F = AB$ PLUS $(A + \overline{B})$	$F = AB$ PLUS $(A + \overline{B})$ PLUS 1
L H H L	$F = A \odot B$	$F = A$ MINUS B MINUS 1	$F = A$ MINUS B
L H H H	$F = A + \overline{B}$	$F = A + \overline{B}$	$F = (A + \overline{B})$ PLUS 1
H L L L	$F = \overline{A}B$	$F = A$ PLUS $(A + B)$	$F = A$ PLUS $(A + B)$ PLUS 1
H L L H	$F = A \odot B$	$F = A$ PLUS B	$F = A$ PLUS B PLUS 1
H L H L	$F = B$	$F = A\overline{B}$ PLUS $(A + B)$	$F = A\overline{B}$ PLUS $(A + B)$ PLUS 1
H L H H	$F = A + B$	$F = A + B$	$F = (A + B)$ PLUS 1
H H L L	$F = 0$	$F = A$ PLUS A *	$F = A$ PLUS A PLUS 1
H H L H	$F = A\overline{B}$	$F = AB$ PLUS A	$F = AB$ PLUS A PLUS 1
H H H L	$F = AB$	$F = A\overline{B}$ PLUS A	$F = A\overline{B}$ PLUS A PLUS 1
H H H H	$F = A$	$F = A$	$F = A$ PLUS 1

Courtesy Texas Instruments, Inc.

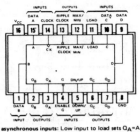

asynchronous inputs: Low input to load sets Q_A=A, Q_B = B, Q_C = C, and Q_D = D

74190

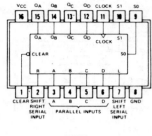

74194

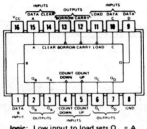

logic: Low input to load sets Q_A = A, Q_B = B, Q_C = C, and Q_D = D

74192, 74193

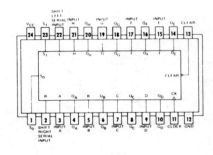

74198

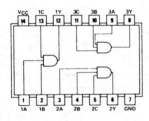

74H11

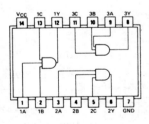

74H15

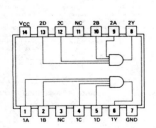

74H21

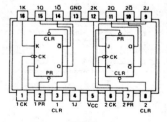

74H106

Courtesy Texas Instruments, Inc.

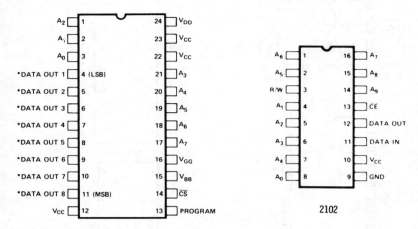

*THIS PIN IS THE DATA INPUT LEAD DURING PROGRAMMING.

1702A

2102

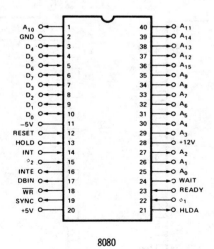

8080

Courtesy Intel Corp.

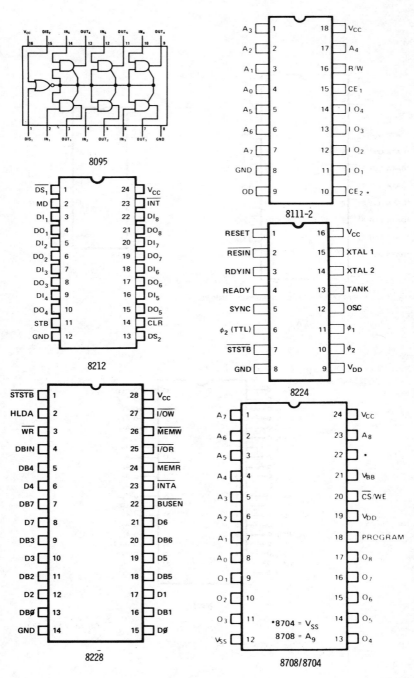

8095

8111-2

8212

8224

8228

8708/8704

Courtesy Intel Corp.

The proper description has been provided for each of the 40 pins. You may have trouble with this objective. Once you have read Chapter 6, you will better understand the control input and output pins on the chip.

● Describe in some detail the various component sections of a small 8080A microcomputer system.

The microcomputer system shown in Figs. 2-4 and 2-12 has been described in considerable detail. You should be able to explain the functions of the following chips: 8224, 8216, 74174, 8111-2, and 1702-A.

● List the general principles of computer interfacing that apply to most digital computers.

This was done later in the chapter, and the four fundamental tasks of computer interfacing also were listed. Know them well.

● Explain what an I/O device is.

It can be any digital device, including a single integrated-circuit chip, that transmits data to or receives data and strobe pulses from a digital computer.

● List three important uses for device select pulses.

They can serve as a source of clock or monostable multivibrator pulses. They can be used to enable latches, multiplexers, decoders, and shift registers. They can clear counters and registers, and set, clear, or toggle flip-flops.

● List the inputs to the common 7400-series integrated-circuit chips that can be strobed with device select pulses from a microcomputer.

This has been done in considerable detail in this chapter.

CHAPTER 3

An Introduction to Microcomputer Programming

In this chapter, you will learn the characteristics of the 8080 microprocessor instruction set, including the 78 basic instructions and the 244 instructions (twelve are not used) that are derived from this basic set. You will not have to write programs in this chapter, but examples of programs that you can study will be provided. It is the authors' opinion that microcomputer programming, though tedious, is somewhat easier to master than microcomputer interfacing. There are many books and manuals on microprocessors available, and most seem preoccupied with the subtleties of programming. You should study such books for the values which they provide. We will focus on interfacing, and limit our attention to those instructions that are most useful in interfacing.

OBJECTIVES

At the end of this chapter, you will be able to do the following:

- Explain what the difference is between an instruction, operation, program, machine code instruction, assembly language instruction, and mnemonic instruction.
- Define the terms: assemble, bit, byte, flag, mnemonic symbol, device code, HI address byte, LO address byte, increment, decrement, label, jump, call, return, label, operand, carry flag, parity flag, zero flag, sign flag, register, register pair, subroutine, two-byte instruction, three-byte instruction, unconditional operation,

conditional operation, branch instruction, stack, stack pointer, program counter, accumulator, ALU, data byte, and instruction register.

- Classify the 8080 instructions into five groups.
- Explain how an 8-bit instruction can be written in both octal code and hexadecimal code.
- List the mnemonic codes, following the Intel Corporation recommendations, for at least ten different 8080 instructions.
- Explain the difference between machine language and assembly language.
- Identify the HI address byte and the LO address byte in a 16-bit memory address word.
- Explain what the differences are between a bit, a byte, a word, and an address.
- List at least ten different registers that can be found in the 8080 microprocessor chip.
- Explain how the microprocessor knows what to do for a given instruction.
- Explain how the microprocessor decodes:

  instruction classes
  registers
  register pairs
  immediate operations
  branch operations
  condition flags
  increment operations
  decrement operations

DEFINITIONS

accumulator—The register and associated digital electronic circuitry in the arithmetic unit of a computer in which arithmetic and logical operations are performed.

address—In the 8080 microprocessor, a 16-bit number which identifies a memory location.

ALU—Abbreviation for arithmetic/logic unit. A computational subsystem that performs the mathematical and logical operations of a digital system.[3]

arithmetic operations—Addition, subtraction, multiplication, division and comparison.

assemble—To translate from a symbolic program to a binary program by substituting binary operation codes for symbolic operation codes and replacing symbolic addresses with absolute or relocatable addresses.[4]

assembler—A program that prepares a program in machine language from a program in symbolic language by substituting absolute operation codes for symbolic operation codes and absolute or relocatable addresses for symbolic addresses.[4]

assembly—A process whereby instructions written in symbolic form by the programmer are changed to machine language by the computer.

assembly language—A computer language that has one-to-one correspondence with an assembly program. The assembly program directs a computer to operate on a program in symbolic language to produce a program in machine language.[4]

assembly language programming—The writing of program instructions in a language that facilitates the translation of programs into binary code through the use of mnemonic symbols.[4]

assembly program—A program that enables a computer to assemble mnemonic language into machine language. Also called assembly routine.[4]

auxiliary carry flag—A flip-flop which goes to logic 1 when there is a carry from bit 3 into bit 4 in the 8080 microprocessor during operations such as addition, subtraction, and comparison. Used principally with additions preceding a Decimal Adjust Accumulator instruction.

bit—The smallest unit of information which can be represented. A bit may be in one of two states, represented by the binary digits 0 and 1.[7]

branch instruction—An instruction that causes a program jump to a specified address and execution of the instruction at that address. During the execution of a branch instruction, the central processor replaces the contents of the program counter with the specified address.

branch operation—See *branch instruction*.

byte—A group of eight contiguous bits occupying a single memory location in the 8080 microprocessor.

call—A special type of jump in which the central processor is logically required to "remember" the contents of the program counter at the time that the jump occurs. This allows the processor later to resume execution of the main program, when it is finished with the last instruction of the subroutine.[8]

call subroutine—See *call*.

carry flag—A flip-flop that goes to logic 1 when there is a carry or a borrow out of the high-order bit during an arithmetic operation. Otherwise it is cleared to logic 0.

computer instruction—A set of characters which defines an operation, together with one or more addresses, or no address, and which, as a unit, causes the computer to perform the operation on the indicated quantities.[5]

computer program—A sequence of instructions which, taken as a group, allow the computer to accomplish a desired task.[7]

conditional—In a computer, subject to the result of a comparison made during computation.[4]

conditional breakpoint instruction—A conditional jump instruction that causes a computer to stop if a specified switch is set. The routine then may be allowed to proceed as coded, or a jump may be forced.[4]

conditional jump—Also called conditional transfer of control. An instruction to a computer which will cause the proper one of two (or more) addresses to be used in obtaining the next instruction, depending on some property of one or more numerical expressions or other conditions.[4]

condition flag—See *flag*.

data byte—The 8-bit binary number that the 8080 microprocessor will use in an arithmetic or logical operation or store in memory.

decrement—To decrease the value of a binary word. Typically, to decrease the value by one.

destination register—The register that receives a transferring 8-bit data word.

device code—The 8-bit code for a specific input or output device. This code is decoded by external decoders which, together with an $\overline{\text{IN}}$ or $\overline{\text{OUT}}$ pulse from the 8080 microprocessor, generate a single *device select pulse*.

direct addressing—An 8-bit data byte is acquired via a three-byte instruction that contains the 16-bit memory address at which the data byte is located.

field—A group of bits in a byte or word that is treated as a single unit of information. Usually the number of bits in the field is specified as, for example, a three-bit field.[7]

flag—A single flip-flop that indicates that a certain condition has arisen during the course of arithmetic or logical manipulations or data transmission between a pair of digital electronic devices such as a computer and an instrument. For example, a flag may be a circuit that provides a signal which indicates that an input/output device is ready to receive or transmit data from/to a computer.

flag register—A register consisting of the flag flip-flops.

general-purpose registers—In the 8080 microprocessor, the B, C, D, E, H, and L registers.

hexadecimal code—A digital code based upon the radix 16, in which the decimal numbers 0 through 9 and the letters A through F represent the sixteen distinct states in the code.

HI address byte—The eight most significant bits in the 16-bit memory address word for the 8080 microprocessor. Abbreviated H or HI.

immediate addressing—Data bytes that are contained in a multibyte instruction.

increment—To increase the value of a binary word. Typically, to increase the value by one.

instruction—A set of characters which defines an operation, together with one or more addresses, or no address, and which, as a unit, causes the computer to perform the operation on the indicated quantities. The smallest single operation that the computer can be directed to execute.[7]

instruction code—A unique binary number that encodes an operation that a computer can perform.

instruction decoder—A decoder within a CPU that decodes the *instruction code* into a series of actions that the computer performs.

instruction register—The register that contains the instruction code.

jump—1. To cause the next instruction to be selected from a specified storage location in a computer. 2. A deviation from the normal sequence of execution of instructions in a computer.

label—One or more characters that serve to define an item of data or the location of an instruction or subroutine. A character is one symbol of a set of elementary symbols, such as those corresponding to typewriter keys.

LO address byte—The eight least significant bits in the 16-bit memory address word for the 8080 microprocessor. Abbreviated L or LO.

machine code—A computer instruction that is written as a sequence of 0 and 1 binary digits and that specifically characterizes the instruction and no other. A binary representation of a computer instruction.

machine instruction—See *machine code*.

machine language—See *machine code*.

mnemonic—Something used to assist the human memory.[4]

mnemonic code—Computer instructions written in a form that the programmer can remember easily, but which must be converted into machine language later.[4]

mnemonic instructions—Computer instructions that are written in a meaningful notation, such as, for example, ADD, MPY, and STO.[4]

mnemonic language—A programming language that is based on easily remembered symbols and that can be assembled into machine language by the computer.[4]

mnemonic operation code—See *mnemonic instructions*.

mnemonic symbol—A symbol chosen so that it assists the human memory; for example, the abbreviation MPY used for "multiply."[4]

octal code—A digital code based upon the radix 8, in which the decimal numbers 0 through 7 represent the eight distinct states in the code.

operand—The quantity that is affected, manipulated, or operated upon.

operation—A specific action that a computer will perform whenever an instruction calls for it (e.g., addition, division).[4]

operation code—See *instruction code*.

parity—A method of checking the accuracy of binary numbers. An extra bit, called a parity bit, is added to a number. If even parity is used, the sum of all 1's in the number and its corresponding parity bit is always even. If odd parity is used, the sum of the 1's and the parity bit is always odd.[4]

parity flag—A flip-flop such that if the modulo 2 sum of the bits of the result of a computer operation is logic 0, this flip-flop is set to logic 1.

pop—Retrieving data from a stack.

program—See *computer program*.

program counter—The 16-bit register that contains the memory address of the next instruction byte that must be executed in a computer program.

push—Placing data on a stack.

register—A short-term digital electronic storage circuit the capacity of which is usually one computer word.[4]

register pair—In the 8080 microprocessor, a pair of general-purpose registers that together make up a 16-bit word that is treated as a unit. The three register pairs are B and C, D and E, and H and L.

register pair addressing—An 8-bit data byte is acquired via a one-byte instruction that employs a register pair, usually H and L, to generate the 16-bit memory address.

return—A special type of jump in which the central processor resumes execution of the main program at the contents of the program counter at the time that the jump occurred.

return from subroutine—See *return*.

routine—Set of instruction codes arranged in proper sequence to direct the computer to perform a desired operation or sequence of operations. Alternatively, a subdivision of a program consisting of two or more instructions that are functionally related.[5]

sign flag—A flip-flop that goes to logic 1 if the most significant bit of the result of an operation has the value of logic 1.

single-byte instruction—An 8080 instruction consisting of eight contiguous bits occupying a single memory location.

source register—The register that contains an 8-bit word that is being transferred.

stack—An area in memory that stores temporary register information and the return addresses of subroutines.

stack pointer—A 16-bit register that provides the current location of the stack.

stack pointer addressing—Two 8-bit data bytes are acquired via a 1-byte instruction that transfers the data from a memory area called a stack to a register pair or the program counter.

subroutine—A small subprogram not stored in the main path of the routine. Such a subroutine is entered by a call operation; provision is made to return control to the main program at the end of the subroutine.

symbolic address—Also called floating address. In digital computer programming, a label chosen to identify a particular word, function, or other information that is independent of the location of the information within the routine.

symbolic code—A code by which programs are expressed in source language; that is, storage locations and machine operations are referred to by symbolic names and addresses that do not depend upon their hardware-determined names and addresses.[4]

symbolic coding—In digital computer programming, any coding system using symbolic rather than actual computer addresses.[4]

symbolic language programming—See *assembly language programming*.

symbolic programming—A program using symbols instead of numbers for the operations and locations in a computer. Although the writing of the program is easier and faster, an assembly program must be used to decode the symbol into machine language and to assign instruction locations.[4]

three-byte instruction—An instruction that consists of 24 contiguous bits occupying three successive memory locations.

two-byte instruction—An instruction that consists of 16 contiguous bits occupying two successive memory locations.

unconditional—Not subject to conditions external to the specific computer instruction.[4]

unconditional return—A return instruction that is unconditional.

unconditional jump—A computer instruction that interrupts the normal process of obtaining the instructions in an ordered sequence and specifies the address from which the next instruction must be taken.[4]

unconditional return—A return instruction that is unconditional.

word—A group of sixteen contiguous bits occupying two successive memory locations. (This definition is given by Intel for its 8080 microprocessor.)

zero flag—A flip-flop that goes to logic 1 if the result of an instruction has the value 000_8.

WHAT IS A COMPUTER PROGRAM?

Graf has defined a *computer program* as:[4]

A series of instructions or statements prepared in a form acceptable to the computer, the purpose of which is to achieve a certain result.

This is an acceptable definition, for it doesn't imply what the desired result is. In some cases, we may seek to evaluate a mathematical equation, whereas in others we may simply seek to rearrange input data into a more convenient form, which either is stored or else provided as output. With microprocessors, we will increasingly be interested in writing computer programs that will control the operation of a device or group of devices. In a home clothes washer, for example, we may wish to control the amount of water used, the temperature of the water at different washing cycles, the number and types of cycles employed to wash a particular type of fabric, and the time duration of each cycle. Finally, we may ask the microprocessor to sound a bell or buzzer when the washing cycle has been completed.

WHAT IS AN INSTRUCTION?

A computer *instruction* can be defined as:[5]

A set of characters which define an operation together with one or more addresses, or no address, and which, as a unit, causes the computer to perform the operation on the indicated quantities.

We will discuss the concept of an *operation* in a subsequent section.

A *character* is:[5]

One symbol of a set of elementary symbols such as those corresponding to typewriter keys. Symbols usually include the decimal digits 0 through 9, the letters A through Z, punctuation marks, dollar signs, commas, operation symbols, and any other single symbols which a computer may read, store, or write.

In computer programming, it is not uncommon for one to use the entire typewriter keyboard, including symbols such as @, #, $, %, ¢, &, *, (,), ?, /, and !.

Computer instructions come in a variety of forms. They can be *binary numbers:*

$$10110001_2$$
$$00011100_2$$
$$11101001_2$$

octal numbers:

$$027_8$$
$$353_8$$
$$124_8$$
$$001_8$$

hexadecimal numbers:

$$OA_{16}$$
$$79_{16}$$
$$FF_{16}$$
$$D3_{16}$$
$$BE_{16}$$

decimal numbers:

$$10$$
$$35$$
$$26$$
$$05$$

mnemonic code:

> NOP
> MOV B, C
> INR H
> ADD D
> SUB L
> OUT
> HLT
> JMP

full words:

> ADD
> SUBTRACT
> COMPARE
> NO OPERATION
> HALT
> JUMP
> CALL SUBROUTINE
> RETURN FROM SUBROUTINE
> EXCLUSIVE-OR

or full mathematical expressions:

$$X = A**2 + B*Y + C$$
$$X = SQRT(B**2 - 4*A*C)$$

to mention but a few commonly encountered types.

WHAT IS AN OPERATION?

We return to Graf for a simple definition for the term *operation:*[4]

A specific action which a computer will perform whenever an instruction calls for it (e.g., addition, division).

The number of different operations that a computer can perform and the speed with which it can perform such operations provide a measure of how "powerful" the computer is. The operations associated with the Intel 8080 microprocessor include:

INFORMATION TRANSFER OPERATIONS:	Move information from accumulator to memory
	Move information from accumulator to register
	Move information from memory to accumulator
	Move information from register to accumulator

	Move information to stack
	Move information from stack
	Move information to stack pointer
	Move information to program counter
ARITHMETIC OPERATIONS:	Add to accumulator
	Subtract from accumulator
	Compare with accumulator
	Rotate accumulator left
	Rotate accumulator right
LOGICAL OPERATIONS:	AND with accumulator
	OR with accumulator
	Exclusive-OR with accumulator
SUBROUTINE OPERATIONS:	Call subroutine
	Call subroutine if flag is at logic 0
	Call subroutine if flag is at logic 1
	Return from subroutine
	Return from subroutine if flag is at logic 0
	Return from subroutine if flag is at logic 1
	Restart at specified subroutine location
INPUT/OUTPUT OPERATIONS:	Input data from device into accumulator
	Output data from accumulator into device
INCREMENT/DECREMENT OPERATIONS:	Increment contents of accumulator
	Decrement contents of accumulator
	Increment contents of register
	Decrement contents of register
	Increment contents of memory
	Decrement contents of memory
JUMP OPERATIONS:	Jump unconditionally
	Jump to memory location if flag is at logic 0
	Jump to memory location if flag is at logic 1
OTHER OPERATIONS:	Complement accumulator
	Complement carry flip-flop
	Set carry flip-flop
	Decimal adjust the accumulator
	Enable interrupts
	Disable interrupts

No operation
Halt

MACHINE LANGUAGE

The modern electronic digital computer is capable of performing manipulations using binary electronic signals only, typically 0 volts (logic 0) and +5 volts (logic 1). Thus, *each computer instruction is written as a sequence of 1's and 0's that specifically characterize that instruction and no other.* Such a binary representation of a computer instruction is called *machine language* or *machine code.* For example, the machine language instruction 00000111_2 rotates the contents of the accumulator one bit to the left in the 8080 microprocessor. The instruction 00001111_2 rotates the contents of the accumulator one bit to the right. Altogether, it is possible to create $2^8 = 256$ different 8-bit binary machine language instructions for an 8-bit microprocessor such as the 8080. Of these 256 possible instructions, a total of 244 actually exist.

Some other examples of machine language instructions for the 8080 include the following:

00000000	No operation
00000100	Increment contents of register B by one
00000101	Decrement contents of register B by one
00001100	Increment contents of register C by one
00010100	Increment contents of register D by one
00011100	Increment contents of register E by one
00110111	Set carry flip-flop to logic 1
00111111	Complement carry flip-flop
01000111	Move contents of accumulator to register B
01011000	Move contents of register B to register E
10000000	Add contents of register B to contents of accumulator
10010000	Subtract contents of register B from accumulator
10110000	OR contents of register B with contents of accumulator
11001001	Return from subroutine
11010111	Call subroutine at memory address $H = 000_8$ and $L = 020_8$
11111011	Enable interrupt

All of the machine codes listed above are in binary.

OCTAL AND HEXADECIMAL MACHINE CODES

It can be difficult to remember 8-bit binary machine code instructions, so individuals who perform machine language programming frequently convert such instructions into either *octal code* or *hexadecimal code*. Such codes were discussed in Chapter 5 of *Bugbook I*, but we will repeat them here for convenience.

The octal digits for the eight 3-bit binary numbers ranging between 000 and 111 are:

Octal Digit	Binary Number
0	000
1	001
2	010
3	011
4	100
5	101
6	110
7	111

The Intel 8080 microprocessor generates 8-bit binary machine code instructions, so we must be able to convert an 8-bit binary word into octal code. The process whereby we accomplish this requires three steps:

1. Write down the full 8-bit binary word: XXXXXXXX.
2. Split the 8-bit binary word into groups of three, starting from the least significant bit. Two groups of three and one group of two are created, as in XX XXX XXX.
3. Substitute 0 through 7 for each of the groups to obtain the final octal coded word.

As an example, let us assume that we have the binary word 10011011. We first split it into groups:

$$10011011_2 = 10\ 011\ 011$$

Next, we write the equivalent octal word for each of these groups:

$$10\ 011\ 011 = 233_8$$

to produce 233_8, the octal equivalent of the binary word 10011011. Note that the most significant octal number has only two binary bits, and cannot be larger than octal 3. In summary, the conversion of an 8-bit binary word into its octal equivalent proceeds as follows:

$$XXXXXXXX_2 = XX\ XXX\ XXX$$

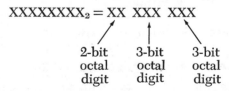

| 2-bit octal digit | 3-bit octal digit | 3-bit octal digit |

The hexadecimal code for the sixteen 4-bit binary numbers is as follows:

Hexadecimal Digit	Binary Number
0	0000
1	0001
2	0010
3	0011
4	0100
5	0101
6	0110
7	0111
8	1000
9	1001
A	1010
B	1011
C	1100
D	1101
E	1110
F	1111

To convert an 8-bit binary word into hexadecimal, we do the following:

1. Write down the full 8-bit binary word, XXXXXXXX.
2. Split the 8-bit binary word into two groups of four bits, as in XXXX XXXX.
3. Substitute 0 through F for each of the groups to obtain the final hexadecimal coded word.

We can, as an example, convert 10011011 to hexadecimal. We first split it into two groups of four bits:

$$10011011_2 = 1001\ 1011$$

Next, we write the equivalent hexadecimal word for each of these groups:

$$1001\ 1011 = 9B_{16}$$

to produce $9B_{16}$, the hexadecimal equivalent of the original binary word. In summary, the conversion of an 8-bit binary word into its hexadecimal equivalent proceeds as follows:

$$XXXXXXXX_2 = XXXX\quad XXXX$$

4-bit	4-bit
hex	hex
digit	digit

With the 8080 microprocessor, the memory address contains 16 bits. Such a word can also be converted into either octal or hexadecimal code. For example, memory location 1001100111000101_2 can be written as:

$$1001100111000101_2 = 1\ 001\ 100\ 111\ 000\ 101_2 = 114705_8$$
$$= 1001\ 1001\ 1100\ 0101_2 = 99C5_{16}$$

However, when we program in octal for the 8080, we will often see a 16-bit address that is subdivided into two eight-bit *bytes*. In this case, the eight most significant bits are the *HI address byte* and the eight least significant bits are the *LO address byte*. When split like this, each byte is treated as a separate octal number that ranges from 000 to 377. Therefore, our address can be written as:

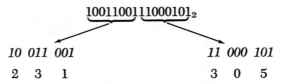

Such an address has a HI address byte of 231_8 and a LO address byte of 305_8.

Table 3-1 gives some useful conversions between binary, octal, and hexadecimal numbers.

The machine language instructions listed in the "Machine Language" section can therefore be rewritten in the following manner:

Binary Machine Code	Octal Machine Code	Hexadecimal Machine Code
00000000	000	00
00000100	004	04
00000101	005	05
00001100	014	0C
00010100	024	14
00011100	034	1C
00110111	067	37
00111111	077	3F
01000111	107	47
01011000	130	58
10000000	200	80
10010000	220	90
10110000	260	B0
11001001	311	C9
11010111	327	D7
11111011	373	FB

In this book, *we shall write machine instructions in octal code*. There are several reasons for doing so:

- It is easier to convert from an octal number to a binary number than from a hexadecimal number to a binary number. The hexa-

Table 3-1. Binary-Octal-Hexadecimal-Decimal Conversions

Binary Number	Octal Number	Hexadecimal Number	Decimal Number
00000000	000	00	0
00000001	001	01	1
00000010	002	02	2
00000011	003	03	3
00000100	004	04	4
00000101	005	05	5
00000110	006	06	6
00000111	007	07	7
00001000	010	08	8
00001001	011	09	9
00001010	012	0A	10
00001011	013	0B	11
00001100	014	0C	12
00001101	015	0D	13
00001110	016	0E	14
00001111	017	0F	15
00010000	020	10	16
00011000	030	18	24
00100000	040	20	32
00101000	050	28	40
00110000	060	30	48
00111000	070	38	56
01000000	100	40	64
01001000	110	48	72
01010000	120	50	80
01011000	130	58	88
01100000	140	60	96
01101000	150	68	104
01110000	160	70	112
01111000	170	78	120
10000000	200	80	128
10001000	210	88	136
10010000	220	90	144
10011000	230	98	152
10100000	240	A0	160
10101000	250	A8	168
10110000	260	B0	176
10111000	270	B8	184
11000000	300	C0	192
11001000	310	C8	200
11010000	320	D0	208
11011000	330	D8	216
11100000	340	E0	224
11101000	350	E8	232
11110000	360	F0	240
11111000	370	F8	248
11111001	371	F9	249
11111010	372	FA	250
11111011	373	FB	251
11111100	374	FC	252
11111101	375	FD	253
11111110	376	FE	254
11111111	377	FF	255

decimal symbols A, B, C, D, E, and F can occasionally be confusing.

- Seven-segment LED displays are more common and less expensive than hexadecimal LED displays.
- *The origins of specific Intel 8080 microprocessor instructions are easier to understand if such instructions are written in octal rather than in hexadecimal code.*

These three advantages outweigh the fact that there are only two digits in the hexadecimal instruction versus three digits in the octal one.

MNEMONIC CODE

Mnemonic is a term describing something used to assist the human memory.[4] With this in mind, we have the following definitions:

mnemonic code—Computer instructions written in a form the programmer can remember easily, but which must be converted into machine language later by a computer.[4]

mnemonic language—A programming language that is based on easily remembered symbols and that can be assembled into machine language by a computer.[4]

mnemonic operation code; mnemonic instructions—Computer instructions that are written in a meaningful notation, for example, ADD, MPY, STO.[4]

mnemonic symbol—A symbol chosen so that it assists the human memory; for example, the abbreviation MPY used for "multiply."[4]

A variety of different mnemonic instructions can be written for the 244 different 8080 machine language instructions. Since we believe in standardization, *we shall employ those mnemonic instructions suggested by the Intel Corporation.* Such mnemonic instructions are provided in a variety of Intel literature,[12] including:

- *Intel 8080 Microcomputer System Manual,* September, 1975.
- *Intel Assembly Language Programming Manual,* 1976 (Revision C).
- Intel Assembly Language Reference Card, 1974.

The mnemonics for the 8085 microprocessor chip are identical to those for the 8080. The mnemonics for the Z-80 microprocessor chip, which includes all of the 8080 instructions, are quite different. Though they use Z-80 chips in their personal computer, some companies—the Zenith Corporation, for example—still provide most of their literature in 8080 mnemonics because of the popularity of the 8080 microprocessor chip and the fact that it preceded the use of the Z-80. Once you know the 8080 mnemonics, it is not difficult to learn the Z-80 mnemonics.

The machine language instructions listed in both the "Machine Language" and the "Octal and Hexadecimal Machine Codes" sections can therefore be written in the following manner:

Octal Machine Code	Mnemonic Code
000	NOP
004	INR B
005	DCR B
014	INR C
024	INR D
034	INR E
067	STC
077	CMC
107	MOV B,A
130	MOV E,B
200	ADD B
220	SUB B
260	ORA B
311	RET
327	RST 2
373	EI

HOW DO I GO ABOUT THE TASK
OF LEARNING COMPUTER PROGRAMMING?

Some of you who will read this chapter already know how to do *machine language programming* and perhaps only desire to brush up on the 8080 microprocessor instruction set. Many more of you will be programming and interfacing a microcomputer for the first time. An important question in your mind might be: *How do I go about the task of learning computer programming?* In the paragraphs below, some suggestions are offered concerning how to proceed. These comments are provided at the beginning of this chapter, rather than at the end, because it is useful for you to have a "road map" of where you are going in this Bugbook. You may not be initially familiar with some of the terms and concepts that we will use in this section. Don't worry. Just read this material quickly the first time, then refer back to it.

Where Am I Going?

In this book, you will learn how to interface microcomputers to simple digital circuits typically consisting of 7400-series chips and a few specialized Intel 8000-series chips. You will have to learn how to transfer information between the microcomputer and external input/output devices, including integrated-circuit chips. Thus, two of the most important instructions that you should learn are the following, which generate device select pulses:

323
<B2>   Generate a device select pulse to synchronize the output of eight bits of accumulator data to the device with the device code given in the second byte of the instruction.

and

333
<B2>   Generate a device select pulse to synchronize the input of eight bits of data into the accumulator from the device with the device code given in the second byte of the instruction.

These are the *Out* and *In* instructions, respectively. You will certainly use the Out instruction frequently in later chapters.

In a following chapter, you will learn how to write *computer subroutines*. With such subroutines, the computer jumps from a main program to some other memory location, where it begins execution of the subroutine. Once it has finished with the subroutine, it returns to the main program. Thus the computer must know the location in the main program to which it should return. It does this with the aid of a group of memory locations known as a *stack*, which store returning memory locations for subroutines. *You will not be able to use any subroutine, including those on a preprogrammed PROM chip, unless you locate the stack within the read/write memory that you actually have in your microcomputer.* How do you relocate the stack? You employ the following three-byte instruction:

061   Relocate the stack pointer at the 16-bit memory address given by the following two bytes of this instruction.
<B2>   LO memory address byte
<B3>   HI memory address byte

One of the authors wasted several hours one evening trying to write a subroutine before he realized the need to relocate the stack from where it was initially (which was, in case you are interested, at $HI = 377_8$ and $LO = 377_8$). Subroutines are very important programming gimmicks, so important that it is a good idea to mention the stack right at the beginning of this chapter.

In general, you will not start program execution at memory location $HI = 000_8$ and $LO = 000_8$ and run sequentially through your available memory. You will jump around, sometimes ahead, usually back. So, you will need to know how to jump from one point in your program to another, where execution continues. The instruction that you will require is the *Unconditional Jump*, a three-byte instruction:

303   Jump unconditionally to the 16-bit memory location given by the following two bytes of this instruction.
<B2>   LO memory address byte
<B3>   HI memory address byte

It is a great instruction. You can do wonders with it.

You may want to call a subroutine, which simply means that you are asking the microcomputer to store the memory address of the next instruction in the main program, and then jump to some other memory address where the execution of the subroutine commences. To do this, you will require the *Unconditional Call* instruction, also a three-byte instruction:

315 Call unconditionally the subroutine at the 16-bit memory location given by the following two bytes of this instruction.

    \<B2>   LO memory address byte

    \<B3>   HI memory address byte

This instruction is not sufficient, however. Once you have executed the subroutine, you will need an instruction that will get you back to the main program. This is the *Unconditional Return* instruction, a one-byte instruction:

311 Return unconditionally to the main program. The specific address in the main program is contained in two memory locations in the stack.

We have used the term *unconditional* in each of the above three instructions on this page. There also exist a number of *conditional* jump, call, and return instructions that perform their indicated actions only if a flag has a certain specified logic state. This book won't use many of them, so you will be required to learn them on your own. Probably the only conditional instruction that you will use frequently in this book is one associated with the programming of *timing loops:*

302 Jump to the 16-bit memory location given by the following two bytes of this instruction if the *zero flag* is at logic 0.

    \<B2>   LO memory address byte

    \<B3>   HI memory address byte

You may ask: What is a *zero flag?* It is simply a single flip-flop that goes to a logic 1 state only if the content of the register or memory operated upon in the preceding instruction goes to 000_8. This is an important instruction and one that you will use frequently in Chapter 5.

Observe that we haven't yet discussed an Add, Subtract, And, Or, or other type of arithmetic/logical instruction. The fact of the matter is that you won't use many of these instructions in this Bugbook. You may be much too busy and interested in outputting and inputting data to worry much about adding a pair of numbers. There is one subtract instruction that the authors are rather fond of:

227 Subtract the contents of the accumulator from the contents of the accumulator, i.e., clear the accumulator.

With this instruction, you set the value of the accumulator to 000_8. It is very useful.

When you make timing loops, you may desire to *increment* the B and C general-purpose registers. The instructions that you will require are:

004   Increment B register by one.
014   Increment C register by one.

You will also want to *decrement* these two registers:

005   Decrement B register by one.
015   Decrement C register by one.

You will certainly want to halt the computer after it has executed a program. To do this, you will employ the popular and highly regarded *Halt* instruction:

166   Halt the microcomputer

If you are lazy, you can program the computer to do nothing:

000   No operation

This instruction does absolutely nothing. In its spot in the program, it simply consumes time, 2 μs to be exact. You can use it to provide spaces in your program that you may fill at a later time.

You may want to clear a register, as would be the case with a long timing loop. First, you can clear the accumulator. Then you move the contents of the accumulator to the desired register, as in the following instructions:

107   Move contents of accumulator to register B.
117   Move contents of accumulator to register C.
127   Move contents of accumulator to register D.

You may wish to load a specific 8-bit binary number into the accumulator or a register. The following two-byte *immediate* instructions will do the job:

006   Move the data in the second byte of this instruction into
<B2>   register B.
026   Move the data in the second byte of this instruction into
<B2>   register D.
076   Move the data in the second byte of this instruction into the
<B2>   accumulator.

You may wish to load a pair of 8-bit binary numbers into two registers with the same instruction. One example of such an instruction is:

041   Move the data in the second and third bytes of this instruction into register pair H.

<B2>   This byte goes into register L.
<B3>   This byte goes into register H.

Along about Chapter 8, you will need to enable the *interrupt flag* so that you can interrupt the microcomputer from the front panel. You do this with the following instruction:

373   Enable the interrupt system following the execution of the next instruction.

In Chapter 8, you will "jam" a one-byte instruction during the interrupt. This is an instruction that calls a subroutine at one of the following memory addresses (all with HI = 000_8): 000_8, 010_8, 020_8, 030_8, 040_8, 050_8, 060_8, or 070_8. These are the *Restart* instructions, an example of which is given below:

317   Call the subroutine at the memory address given by H = 000_8 and L = 010_8.

You can have fun and play games with the accumulator and carry flag. For example, you can:

007   Rotate the contents of the accumulator left one position.
017   Rotate the contents of the accumulator right one position.
047   Decimal adjust the accumulator.
057   Complement the accumulator.
067   Set the carry flag to logic 1.
077   Complement the carry flag.

And, finally, you can move the contents of a specified memory location to the accumulator, as in the following instruction:

176   Move contents of the memory location addressed by the register pair H,L to the accumulator.

Now we come to the point of this section: *The above instructions are almost all that you will need for this book!* The emphasis has been on computer interfacing, not programming. Just enough program steps have been provided to allow you to make your interfaced integrated-circuit chip to do something useful.

How Do I Learn Microcomputer Programming?

You can learn computer programming with the aid of this Bugbook and some hands-on experience with an 8080-based microcomputer. It is possible to "dry lab" this book, but having a microcomputer before you would make your learning much more interesting. Here are some suggestions:

- As your first step in learning how to program a microcomputer, survey the microcomputer instruction set and try to learn what you can from it.

   In this book the 8080 microprocessor instruction set has been organized in a variety of ways to help you: (1) an octal/hexadecimal/ mnemonic listing of all 256 instructions, from 000_8 to 377_8; (2) an alphabetic listing of the mnemonic instructions; (3) a group listing of the instructions, including the data transfer group, arithmetic group, logical group, branch group, and stack/input/output/machine control group; (4) an instruction summary on a single sheet of paper; and (5) detailed written descriptions of different classes of instructions, in which each class or group is described in terms of how it is decoded by the *instruction decoder* within the 8080 chip.

- Study the numerous examples of computer programming given in this book.

   We haven't used all of the 8080 instructions, but we have used many of the more important ones. You should learn from this book that a computer program doesn't have to be long and involved in order to be useful. You will observe how to generate device select pulses and latch accumulator data with only a few instructions. With several additional instructions, you can generate a timing loop.

- Practice computer programming by writing many simple programs, each of which illustrate the characteristics of a different 8080 instruction.

   The authors have followed this rule in this book. They have tried to highlight the behavior of a limited number of useful instructions. They hope they have done so in sufficient depth and with sufficient clarity that you are able to master them. They would encourage you to follow the same procedure as you learn the characteristics of other instructions, such as DAD, ANA, XRA, ORA, CMP; the conditional jumps, calls, and returns; and such interesting instructions as PCHL, XTHL, XCHG, SPHL, POP, and PUSH.

- Do all of the above with an 8080 microcomputer system in front of you.

   A microcomputer system is a lot of fun. You will not do justice to this exciting new technology simply by reading this book. Hands-on experience with a microcomputer will give you the depth of experience that you require.

BIT, BYTE, WORD, AND ADDRESS

The terms *bit, byte, word,* and *address* are so important that, though we have defined them in the preceding chapter, we shall define them again here. The definitions given below are from the Intel 8080 Assembly Language Programming Manual (Reference 7).

bit—The smallest unit of information which can be represented. A bit may be in one of two states, represented by the binary digits 0 or 1.[7]

byte—A group of eight contiguous bits occupying a single memory location.[7]

A representation of a byte in memory. Bits which are fixed as 0 or 1 are indicated by 0 or 1; bits which may be either 0 or 1 in different circumstances are represented by letters; thus rp represents a 3-bit field which contains one of the eight possible combinations of zeros and ones.[7]

word—A group of 16 contiguous bits occupying two successive memory locations.[7]

address—A 16-bit number assigned to a memory location corresponding to its sequential position.[7]

instruction—The smallest single operation that the computer can be directed to execute.[7]

program—A sequence of instructions which, taken as a group, allow the computer to accomplish a desired task.[7]

field—A group of bits in a byte or word which is treated as a single unit of information. Usually the number of bits in the field is specified as, for example, a three-bit field.

Keep in mind that the definitions here for byte, word, and address refer specifically to the 8080 microprocessor. Other computers may have smaller or larger bytes, words, and addresses.

MULTIBYTE INSTRUCTIONS

The 8080 microprocessor can execute 244 different instructions. Many of the instructions are similar, and it has been said that the 8080 has only 78 truly different instructions. We are not prepared to quibble on this matter. The point is that, of the 244 instructions, 200 are *single-byte* instructions, 18 are *two-byte* instructions, and 26 are *three-byte* instructions. These three terms can be defined as follows:

single-byte instruction—An instruction consisting of eight contiguous bits occupying a single memory location.

three-byte instruction—An instruction consisting of 24 contiguous bits occupying three successive memory locations.

two-byte instruction—An instruction consisting of 16 contiguous bits occupying two successive memory locations.

The first byte of a multibyte instruction is called the *operation code*. The remaining one or two bytes are either an 8-bit *data byte*, two 8-bit *data bytes*, an 8-bit *device code*, or a 16-bit memory address consisting of two 8-bit *address bytes*. Definitions for these new terms are as follows:

operation code, instruction code—The 8-bit code for the specific action that the 8080 microprocessor will perform.

data byte—The 8-bit binary number that the 8080 microprocessor will use in an arithmetic or logical operation or store in memory or a register.

device code—The 8-bit code for a specific input or output device. This code is decoded by external decoders which, together with an $\overline{\text{IN}}$ or $\overline{\text{OUT}}$ pulse from the 8080 microprocessor, generate a single *device select pulse*.

HI address byte—The eight most significant bits in the 16-bit memory address word for the 8080 microprocessor. Abbreviated H or HI.

LO address byte—The eight least significant bits in the 16-bit memory address word for the 8080 microprocessor. Abbreviated L or LO.

Clearly, an 8-bit word stored in memory can be an operation code, data byte, device code, HI address byte, or LO address byte. How do you tell? You examine each 8-bit byte in the context of the actual microcomputer program. Unless there is a mistake in the program, the computer can readily distinguish between the various types of bytes. There will be no ambiguities. We will continue our discussion of this topic in the following section.

The first, second, and third bytes in a multibyte instruction are represented by the symbols <B1>, <B2>, and <B3>, respectively. This is the Intel Corporation notation, one which we will follow.

The eighteen two-byte instructions for the 8080 microprocessor have the following mnemonic codes:

> eight MVI instructions: MVI B, MVI C, etc.
> ADI
> ACI
> OUT
> SUI
> IN
> SBI
> ANI
> XRI
> ORI
> CPI

The 26 three-byte instructions for the 8080 have the following mnemonic codes:

four LXI instructions
nine JUMP instructions
nine CALL SUBROUTINE instructions
SHLD
LHLD
STA
LDA

We will stick to the Intel Corporation mnemonic code throughout this Bugbook.

Simple representations for single-byte, two-byte, and three-byte instructions are shown in Fig. 3-1.

INSTRUCTION VS. DATA: HOW DOES THE COMPUTER KNOW?

With the 8080 microcomputer system, we store both instructions and "data," such as that from a laboratory instrument, in the same memory. Instructions and data can almost exist side by side. It is thus reasonable to inquire, how does the microcomputer know the difference between the two?

The basic answer is that instructions in memory are stored as a block, or perhaps as a group of blocks scattered throughout memory, and the same is true with data from an instrument. Except for the immediate-type instructions, you rarely, if ever, have both instructions and data

(A) A single-byte instruction, which consists only of an 8-bit operation code.

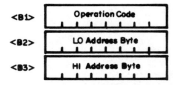

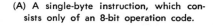

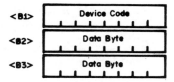

(B) A two-byte instruction that consists of an 8-bit operation code and an 8-bit data byte.

(C) A two-byte input or output instruction that consists of an 8-bit operation code and an 8-bit device code.

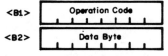

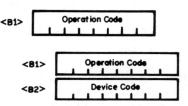

(D) A three-byte instruction that consists of an 8-bit operation code and two 8-bit data bytes.

(E) A three-byte instruction that consists of an 8-bit operation code and a 16-bit address word that is subdivided into a LO address byte and a HI address byte.

Fig. 3-1. Representations of instructions.

commingled. Such mixing is bad programming and memory organization if it occurs. Therefore, the computer will always know that it is operating on instructions as long as it starts in the correct location in memory and the program is properly written. The instructions will usually exist as a cohesive block in memory. If spread out in memory, there will be well-defined jump, call, return, and restart instructions to tie the subroutines and subsidiary programs together with the main program.

With regard to data in memory, the following is suggested: *Unless indicated otherwise, such as by proper programming, the computer will treat data in memory as computer instructions and will go wild trying to execute them.* In other words, a properly written program will access and store data via selected memory addressing commands such as MOV. However, if for any reason the microcomputer finds itself operating in a data block during the execution of a program, it will treat the data bytes as instruction bytes.

How does the computer know the difference between an instruction and data? You write the program in such a manner that it knows the difference. Carelessness on your part will cause the microcomputer to "go bananas." Computer programs must always start with a valid computer operation, not data!

8080 MICROPROCESSOR REGISTERS

The term *register* can be defined as follows:

register—A short-term digital electronic storage circuit the capacity of which usually is one computer word.[15]

Single registers in the 8080 microprocessor chip store a single byte, *i.e.*, eight contiguous bits.

There are two different sets of registers in the 8080 chip: those that we can address from a program and those that we cannot. The program addressable registers are shown in Fig. 3-2 and include the following:

- six 8-bit general-purpose registers addressed singly or in pairs:
  B register
  C register
  D register
  E register
  H register
  L register
- the 8-bit *accumulator*, also known as *register A*
- the 16-bit *stack pointer register*
- the 16-bit *program counter register*

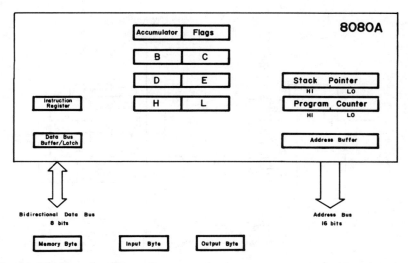

Fig. 3-2. The internal register architecture within an 8080 microprocessor chip. Temporary registers over which you have no direct control are omitted. The data bus buffer/latch and the address buffer provide the interface between the circuitry within the chip and the external busses.

Two other registers over which, in special cases, you have some control include:

- the 8-bit *instruction register*
- a 5-bit *flag register* in the arithmetic/logic unit (ALU)

Additional registers (see Fig. 3-3) that are required to allow the 8080 microprocessor chip to perform its internal operations include two 8-bit temporary registers used singly or as a pair, *W temporary register* and *Z temporary register;* an 8-bit *temporary accumulator* in the arithmetic/logic unit; and an 8-bit *temporary register* in the arithmetic/logic unit. You cannot address or control the contents of these temporary registers from a program and will not know when the 8080 uses them.

Some useful definitions include the following:

accumulator—The register and associated digital electronic circuitry in the arithmetic/logic unit (ALU) of a computer in which arithmetic and logical operations are performed.

general-purpose registers—In the 8080 microprocessor chip, 8-bit registers that can participate in arithmetic and logical operations with the contents of the accumulator.

instruction code—A unique 8-bit binary number that encodes an operation that the 8080 microprocessor chip can perform.

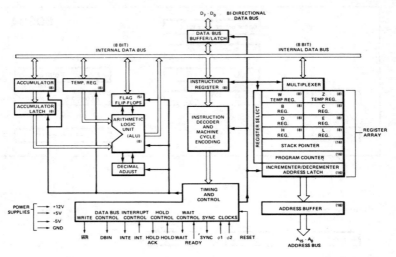

Courtesy Intel Corp.

Fig. 3-3. Functional block diagram of the 8080 central processing unit (CPU). Note the internal data bus, which communicates with the external bidirectional data bus through a data bus buffer/latch located within the 8080 chip.

instruction decoder—A decoder within the 8080 microprocessor chip that decodes the instruction code into a series of actions that the microprocessor performs.

instruction register—The 8-bit register in the 8080 microprocessor chip that stores the instruction code of the instruction being executed.

program counter—The 16-bit register in the 8080 microprocessor chip that contains the memory address of the next instruction byte that will be executed in a computer program.

stack pointer—The 16-bit register in the 8080 microprocessor chip that stores the memory address of the stack, which is a region of memory that stores temporary information.

The Intel Corporation *Intellec 8/Mod 80 Microcomputer Development System Reference Manual* provides several well-written paragraphs that summarize the concepts of instruction code, instruction register, and instruction decoder. These paragraphs are quoted below. (See Fig. 3-4 also.)

"Every computer has a *word length* that is characteristic of that machine. In most eight-bit systems, it is most efficient to deal with eight-bit binary fields, and the memory associated with such a processor is therefore organized to store eight bits in each addressable memory location. Data and instructions are stored in memory as eight-bit binary numbers, or as numbers that are integral multiples of eight bits:

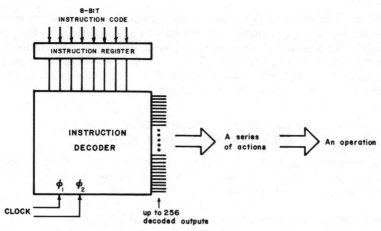

Fig. 3-4. The 8-bit instruction code is first stored in the instruction register, from where it is decoded into a series of clocked actions by the instruction decoder within the 8080 microprocessor chip.

16 bits, 24 bits, and so on. This characteristic eight-bit field is sometimes referred to as a *byte*.

"Each operation that the processor can perform is identified by a unique binary number known as an *instruction code.* An eight-bit word used as an instruction code can distinguish among 256 alternative actions, more than adequate for most processors.

"The processor *fetches* an instruction in two distinct operations. In the first, it transmits the address in its program counter to the memory. In the second, the memory returns the addressed byte to the processor. The CPU stores this instruction byte in a register known as the *instruction register,* and uses it to direct activities during the remainder of the instruction cycle.

"The mechanism by which the processor translates an instruction code into specific processing actions requires more elaboration than we can here afford. The concept, however, will be intuitively clear to an experienced logic designer. The eight bits stored in the instruction register can be decoded and used to activate selectively one of a number of output lines, in this case up to 256 lines. Each line represents a set of activities associated with execution of a particular instruction code. The enabled line can be combined coincidentally with selected timing pulses, to develop electrically sequential signals that can be used to initiate specific actions. This translation of code into action is performed by the *instruction decoder* and by the associated control circuitry."

The important point here is that the instruction code is translated into a sequence of specific actions. The two-phase clock is vital to this

121

process. The actions may result in the moving of data from memory to the accumulator, or adding the contents of register B to register A, or complementing the accumulator, or any of the specific operations contained in the 8080 instruction set. Nevertheless, *each specific operation performed by an 8080 instruction is the result of one or more specific actions caused by the instruction decoder.*

WHAT TYPES OF OPERATIONS DOES THE 8080 MICROPROCESSOR PERFORM?

The purpose of this section is not to subdivide the 8080 instruction set into categories, but rather to identify the basic types of operations that the chip actually performs.

- MOVE A BYTE FROM ONE LOCATION TO ANOTHER
  From one general-purpose register to another
  From a general-purpose register to memory, and vice versa
  From the accumulator to memory, and vice versa
  From the accumulator to a general-purpose register, and vice versa
  From memory to the instruction register
  From memory to the program counter, and vice versa
  From memory to the stack pointer
  From the accumulator to an output latch
  From an input device to the accumulator
  From an external three-state buffer to the instruction register
  From the flag register to memory, and vice versa
  From a general-purpose register to the stack pointer
  From the program counter to the stack, and vice versa
  From the general-purpose registers to the stack, and vice versa
  From the accumulator to the stack, and vice versa
  From the flag register to the stack, and vice versa
  From an input device to a general-purpose register
  From a general-purpose register to an output device
  From a general-purpose register to the program counter

- ARITHMETIC AND LOGICAL OPERATIONS
  AND contents of register or memory with accumulator
  OR contents of register or memory with accumulator
  Exclusive-OR contents of register or memory with accumulator
  Compare contents of register or memory with accumulator
  Add contents of register or memory to accumulator (with or without carry)
  Subtract contents of register or memory from accumulator (with or without borrow)
  Rotate contents of accumulator

Increment contents of general-purpose register, register pair, accumulator, memory, or stack pointer

Decrement contents of general-purpose register, register pair, accumulator, memory, or stack pointer

Add contents of register pair to contents of register pair or stack pointer

Decimal adjust the contents of the accumulator

- MISCELLANEOUS OPERATIONS
No operation
Halt
Enable the interrupt system
Disable the interrupt system
Complement the accumulator
Set the carry flag
Complement the carry flag

Most of the time, all that the 8080 microprocessor chip does is to move a byte from one location to another or perform an arithmetic or logical operation. Rarely does it perform one of the miscellaneous operations. In other words, the chip does not just compute it; it moves bytes around.

8080 MNEMONIC INSTRUCTIONS

You should learn as soon as possible the 8080 mnemonics so that you can do assembly language programming, read other assembly language programs for the 8080, and improve your capability to understand the instruction sets for other microprocessor chips. The 8080 mnemonics are listed by groups in the *Intel 8080 Microcomputer Systems User's Manual,* which you should obtain. Here, the mnemonics are listed in alphabetic order, and then described in detail. There are two reference sources for this material:

Intel 8080 Microcomputer Systems User's Manual, Intel Corporation, 3065 Bowers Avenue, Santa Clara, California 95051, 1975. $5.00.
μCOM-8 Software Manual, NEC Microcomputers, Inc., Five Militia Drive, Lexington, Massachusetts 02173, 1975. $7.50.

The authors gratefully acknowledge permission to use the above reference sources.

Mnemonic	Octal	Hexa-decimal	Description
ACI <B2>	316	CE	Add immediate byte to accumulator (with carry)
ADC M	216	8E	Add memory contents to accumulator (with carry)

Mnemonic	Octal	Hexa-decimal	Description
ADC r	21S	†	Add register contents to accumulator (with carry)
ADD M	206	86	Add memory contents to accumulator
ADD r	20S	†	Add register contents to accumulator
ADI <B2>	306	C6	Add immediate byte to accumulator
ANA M	246	A6	AND memory contents with accumulator
ANA r	26S	†	AND register contents with accumulator
ANI <B2>	346	E6	AND immediate byte with accumulator
CALL <B2> <B3>	315	CD	Call subroutine unconditionally
CC <B2> <B3>	334	DC	Call subroutine if carry flag is set
CM <B2> <B3>	374	FC	Call subroutine if sign flag is set
CMA	057	2F	Complement contents of accumulator
CMC	077	3F	Complement carry flag
CMP M	276	BE	Compare memory contents with accumulator
CMP r	27S	†	Compare register contents with accumulator
CNC <B2> <B3>	324	D4	Call subroutine if carry flag is reset
CNZ <B2> <B3>	304	C4	Call subroutine if zero flag is reset
CP <B2> <B3>	364	F4	Call subroutine if sign flag is reset
CPE <B2> <B3>	354	EC	Call subroutine if parity flag is set
CPI <B2>	376	FE	Compare immediate byte with accumulator
CPO <B2> <B3>	344	E4	Call subroutine if parity flag is reset
CZ <B2> <B3>	314	CC	Call subroutine if zero flag is set
DAA	047	27	Decimal adjust the accumulator contents
DAD B	011	09	Add register pair B to register pair H
DAD D	031	19	Add register pair D to register pair H
DAD H	051	29	Add register pair H to register pair H
DAD SP	071	39	Add stack pointer to register pair H
DCR M	065	35	Decrement memory contents
DCR r	0D5	†	Decrement register contents
DCX B	013	0B	Decrement contents of register pair B
DCX D	033	1B	Decrement contents of register pair D
DCX H	053	2B	Decrement contents of register pair H
DCX SP	073	3B	Decrement stack pointer
DI	363	F3	Disable interrupt system
EI	373	FB	Enable interrupt system
HLT	166	76	Halt unconditionally
IN <B2>	333	DB	Input data into accumulator
INR M	064	34	Increment memory contents
INR r	0D4	†	Increment register contents
INX B	003	03	Increment contents of register pair B
INX D	023	13	Increment contents of register pair D
INX H	043	23	Increment contents of register pair H
INX SP	063	33	Increment stack pointer
JC <B2> <B3>	332	DA	Jump if carry flag is set
JM <B2> <B3>	372	FA	Jump if sign flag is set
JMP <B2> <B3>	303	C3	Jump unconditionally
JNC <B2> <B3>	322	D2	Jump if carry flag is reset
JNZ <B2> <B3>	302	C2	Jump if zero flag is reset

Mnemonic	Octal	Hexa-decimal	Description
JP <B2> <B3>	362	F2	Jump if sign flag is reset
JPE <B2> <B3>	352	EA	Jump if parity flag is set
JPO <B2> <B3>	342	E2	Jump if parity flag is reset
JZ <B2> <B3>	312	CA	Jump if zero flag is set
LDA <B2> <B3>	072	3A	Load accumulator direct with contents of memory addressed by <B2> <B3>
LDAX B	012	0A	Load accumulator indirect with contents of memory addressed by register pair B
LDAX D	032	1A	Load accumulator indirect with contents of memory addressed by register pair D
LHLD <B2> <B3>	052	2A	Load L and H with contents of M and M+1, respectively, where M = <B2> <B3>
LXI B <B2> <B3>	001	01	Load immediate bytes into register pair B
LXI D <B2> <B3>	021	11	Load immediate bytes into register pair D
LXI H <B2> <B3>	041	21	Load immediate bytes into register pair H
LXI SP <B2> <B3>	061	31	Load immediate bytes into stack pointer
MVI M <B2>	066	36	Move immediate byte into memory
MVI r <B2>	0D6	†	Move immediate byte into register
MOV, M,r	16S	†	Move register contents to memory
MOV r,M	1D6	†	Move memory contents to register
MOV r1,r2	1DS	†	Move register 2 contents to register 1
NOP	000	00	No operation
ORA M	266	B6	OR memory contents with accumulator
ORA r	26S	†	OR register contents with accumulator
ORI <B2>	366	F6	OR immediate byte with accumulator
OUT <B2>	323	D3	Output accumulator contents
PCHL	351	E9	Load program counter with contents of register pair H (indirect jump)
POP B	301	C1	Pop register pair B off stack
POP D	321	D1	Pop register pair D off stack
POP H	341	E1	Pop register pair H off stack
POP PSW	361	F1	Pop program status word (accumulator and flags) off stack
PUSH B	305	C5	Push register pair B contents on stack
PUSH D	325	D5	Push register pair D contents on stack
PUSH H	345	E5	Push register pair H contents on stack
PUSH PSW	365	F5	Push program status word (accumulator and flags) on stack
RAL	027	17	Rotate accumulator contents left through carry
RAR	037	1F	Rotate accumulator contents right through carry
RC	330	D8	Return if carry flag is set
RET	311	C9	Return unconditionally
RLC	007	07	Rotate accumulator contents left
RM	370	F8	Return if sign flag is set
RNC	320	D0	Return if carry flag is reset
RNZ	300	C0	Return if zero flag is reset
RP	360	F0	Return if sign flag is reset

Mnemonic	Octal	Hexa-decimal	Description
RPE	350	E8	Return if parity flag is set
RPO	340	E0	Return if parity flag is reset
RRC	017	0F	Rotate accumulator contents right
RST n	3N7	†	Call subroutine at location HI = 000 and LO = 0N0
RZ	310	C8	Return if zero flag is set
SBB M	236	9E	Subtract memory contents from accumulator (with borrow)
SBB r	23S	†	Subtract register contents from accumulator (with borrow)
SBI <B2>	336	DE	Subtract immediate byte from accumulator (with borrow)
SHLD <B2> <B3>	042	22	Store contents of register pair H into M and M+1, respectively, where M = <B2> <B3>
SPHL	371	F9	Move register pair H contents to stack pointer
STA <B2> <B3>	062	32	Store accumulator contents direct into memory location address <B2> <B3>
STAX B	002	02	Store accumulator contents indirect into memory location addressed by register pair B
STAX D	012	0A	Store accumulator contents indirect into memory location addressed by register pair D
STC	067	37	Set carry flag
SUB M	226	96	Subtract memory contents from accumulator
SUB r	22S	†	Subtract register contents from accumulator
SUI <B2>	326	D6	Subtract immediate byte from accumulator
XCHG	353	EB	Exchange contents of register pair D with contents of register pair H
XRA M	256	AE	Exclusive-OR memory contents with accumulator
XRA r	25S	†	Exclusive-OR register contents with accumulator
XRI <B2>	356	EE	Exclusive-OR immediate byte with accumulator
XTHL	343	E3	Exchange top of stack with contents of register pair H

Not all possible 256 instruction codes are employed by the 8080 micro-processor chip. Missing codes include the following:

---

†These instructions are not easily translated into hexadecimal notation without register or other information. This is one reason why we have chosen to work with octal numbers.

Octal	Hexadecimal
010	08
020	10
030	18
040	20
050	28
060	30
070	38
313	CB
331	D9
335	DD
355	ED
375	FD

OCTAL/HEXADECIMAL LISTING OF THE 8080 INSTRUCTION SET

In addition to listing the 8080 instruction set alphabetically according to the mnemonic code, it is also useful to list the instructions in octal code. Such a list is provided below. You may wish to make a copy of it and keep it handy. The authors have found it to be quite useful when they are developing short programs in machine code. The indication --- indicates that the instruction byte has no influence on the 8080; it is not a valid instruction.

Octal	Hexa-decimal	Mnemonic	Description
000	00	NOP	No operation
001	01	LXI B <B2> <B3>	Load immediate into register pair B and C
002	02	STAX B	Store A indirect into M addressed by B and C
003	03	INX B	Increment contents of register pair B and C by one
004	04	INR B	Increment register B by one
005	05	DCR B	Decrement register B by one
006	06	MVI B <B2>	Move immediate into register B
007	07	RLC	Rotate A left
010	08	---	---
011	09	DAD B	Add contents of B,C to H,L and store in H,L
012	0A	LDAX B	Load A indirect from M addressed by B and C
013	0B	DCX B	Decrement contents of register pair B and C by one
014	0C	INR C	Increment register C by one
015	0D	DCR C	Decrement register C by one
016	0E	MVI C <B2>	Move immediate into register C
017	0F	RRC	Rotate A right
020	10	---	---

| | Hexa- | | |
Octal	decimal	Mnemonic	Description
021	11	LXI D \<B2> \<B3>	Load immediate into register pair D and E
022	12	STAX D	Store A indirect into M addressed by D and E
023	13	INX D	Increment contents of register pair D and E by one
024	14	INR D	Increment register D by one
025	15	DCR D	Decrement register D by one
026	16	MVI D \<B2>	Move immediate into register D
027	17	RAL	Rotate A left through carry
030	18	---	---
031	19	DAD D	Add contents of D,E to H,L and store in H,L
032	1A	LDAX D	Load A indirect from M addressed by D and E
033	1B	DCX D	Decrement contents of register pair D and E by one
034	1C	INR E	Increment register E by one
035	1D	DCR E	Decrement register E by one
036	1E	MVI E \<B2>	Move immediate into register E
037	1F	RAR	Rotate A right through carry
040	20	---	---
041	21	LXI H \<B2> \<B3>	Load immediate into register pair H and L
042	22	SHLD \<B2> \<B3>	Store L and H into M and M+1, where M = \<B2> \<B3>
043	23	INX H	Increment contents of register pair H and L by one
044	24	INR H	Increment register H by one
045	25	DCR H	Decrement register H by one
046	26	MVI H \<B2>	Move immediate into register H
047	27	DAA	Decimal adjust A
050	28	---	---
051	29	DAD H	Add contents of H,L to H,L and store in H,L
052	2A	LHLD \<B2> \<B3>	Load L and H with contents of M and M+1, where M = \<B2> \<B3>
053	2B	DCX H	Decrement contents of register pair H and L by one
054	2C	INR L	Increment register L by one
055	2D	DCR L	Decrement register L by one
056	2E	MVI L \<B2>	Move immediate into register L
057	2F	CMA	Complement A
060	30	---	---
061	31	LXI SP \<B2> \<B3>	Load immediate into stack pointer
062	32	STA \<B2> \<B3>	Store A direct into M addressed by \<B2> \<B3>
063	33	INX SP	Increment register SP by one
064	34	INR M	Increment contents of M by one
065	35	DCR M	Decrement contents of M by one
066	36	MVI M \<B2>	Move immediate into M addressed by H and L
067	37	STC	Set carry flip-flop to logic one

070	38	---	---
071	39	DAD SP	Add stack pointer contents to H,L and store in H,L
072	3A	LDA <B2> <B3>	Load A direct with contents of M addressed by <B2> <B3>
073	3B	DCX SP	Decrement register SP by one
074	3C	INR A	Increment register A by one
075	3D	DCR A	Decrement register A by one
076	3E	MVI A <B2>	Move immediate into register A
077	3F	CMC	Complement carry flip-flop
100	40	MOV B,B	Move contents of register B to register B
101	41	MOV B,C	Move contents of register C to register B
102	42	MOV B,D	Move contents of register D to register B
103	43	MOV B,E	Move contents of register E to register B
104	44	MOV B,H	Move contents of register H to register B
105	45	MOV B,L	Move contents to register L to register B
106	46	MOV B,M	Move contents of M to register B
107	47	MOV B,A	Move contents of register A to register B
110	48	MOV C,B	Move contents of register B to register C
111	49	MOV C,C	Move contents of register C to register C
112	4A	MOV C,D	Move contents of register D to register C
113	4B	MOV C,E	Move contents of register E to register C
114	4C	MOV C,H	Move contents of register H to register C
115	4D	MOV C,L	Move contents of register L to register C
116	4E	MOV C,M	Move contents of M to register C
117	4F	MOV C,A	Move contents of register A to register C
120	50	MOV D,B	Move contents of register B to register D
121	51	MOV D,C	Move contents of register C to register D
122	52	MOV D,D	Move contents of register D to register D
123	53	MOV D,E	Move contents of register E to register D
124	54	MOV D,H	Move contents of register H to register D
125	55	MOV D,L	Move contents of register L to register D
126	56	MOV D,M	Move contents of M to register D
127	57	MOV D,A	Move contents of register A to register D
130	58	MOV E,B	Move contents of register B to register E
131	59	MOV E,C	Move contents of register C to register E
132	5A	MOV E,D	Move contents of register D to register E
133	5B	MOV E,E	Move contents of register E to register E
134	5C	MOV E,H	Move contents of register H to register E
135	5D	MOV E,L	Move contents of register L to register E
136	5E	MOV E,M	Move contents of M to register E
137	5F	MOV E,A	Move contents of register A to register E
140	60	MOV H,B	Move contents of register B to register H
141	61	MOV H.C	Move contents of register C to register H
142	62	MOV H,D	Move contents of register D to register H
143	63	MOV H,E	Move contents of register E to register H
144	64	MOV H,H	Move contents of register H to register H
145	65	MOV H,L	Move contents of register L to register H
146	66	MOV H,M	Move contents of M to register H
147	67	MOV H,A	Move contents of register A to register H
150	68	MOV L,B	Move contents of register B to register L
151	69	MOV L,C	Move contents of register C to register L
152	6A	MOV L,D	Move contents of register D to register L
153	6B	MOV L,E	Move contents of register E to register L
154	6C	MOV L,H	Move contents of register H to register L

Octal	Hexa-decimal	Mnemonic	Description
155	6D	MOV L,L	Move contents of register L to register L
156	6E	MOV L,M	Move contents of M to register L
157	6F	MOV L,A	Move contents of register A to register L
160	70	MOV M,B	Move contents of register B to M
161	71	MOV M,C	Move contents of register C to M
162	72	MOV M,D	Move contents of register D to M
163	73	MOV M,E	Move contents of register E to M
164	74	MOV M,H	Move contents of register H to M
165	75	MOV M,L	Move contents of register L to M
166	76	HLT	Halt
167	77	MOV M,A	Move contents of register A to M
170	78	MOV A,B	Move contents of register B to register A
171	79	MOV A,C	Move contents of register C to register A
172	7A	MOV A,D	Move contents of register D to register A
173	7B	MOV A,E	Move contents of register E to register A
174	7C	MOV A,H	Move contents of register H to register A
175	7D	MOV A,L	Move contents of register L to register A
176	7E	MOV A,M	Move contents of M to register A
177	7F	MOV A,A	Move contents of register A to register A
200	80	ADD B	Add contents of register B to register A
201	81	ADD C	Add contents of register C to register A
202	82	ADD D	Add contents of register D to register A
203	83	ADD E	Add contents of register E to register A
204	84	ADD H	Add contents of register H to register A
205	85	ADD L	Add contents of register L to register A
206	86	ADD M	Add contents of M to register A
207	87	ADD A	Add contents of register A to register A
210	88	ADC B	Add carry and contents of register B to register A
211	89	ADC C	Add carry and contents of register C to register A
212	8A	ADC D	Add carry and contents of register D to register A
213	8B	ADC E	Add carry and contents of register E to register A
214	8C	ADC H	Add carry and contents of register H to register A
215	8D	ADC L	Add carry and contents of register L to register A
216	8E	ADC M	Add carry and contents of M to register A
217	8F	ADC A	Add carry and contents of register A to register A
220	90	SUB B	Subtract contents of register B from register A
221	91	SUB C	Subtract contents of register C from register A
222	92	SUB D	Subtract contents of register D from register A
223	93	SUB E	Subtract contents of register E from register A
224	94	SUB H	Subtract contents of register H from register A

225	95	SUB L	Subtract contents of register L from register A
226	96	SUB M	Subtract contents of M from register A
227	97	SUB A	Clear register A
230	98	SBB B	Subtract carry and contents of register B from register A
231	99	SBB C	Subtract carry and contents of register C from register A
232	9A	SBB D	Subtract carry and contents of register D from register A
233	9B	SBB E	Subtract carry and contents of register E from register A
234	9C	SBB H	Subtract carry and contents of register H from register A
235	9D	SBB L	Subtract carry and contents of register L from register A
236	9E	SBB M	Subtract carry and contents of M from register A
237	9F	SBB A	Subtract carry and contents of register A from register A
240	A0	ANA B	AND contents of register B with register A
241	A1	ANA C	AND contents of register C with register A
242	A2	ANA D	AND contents of register D with register A
243	A3	ANA E	AND contents of register E with register A
244	A4	ANA H	AND contents of register H with register A
245	A5	ANA L	AND contents of register L with register A
246	A6	ANA M	AND contents of M with register A
247	A7	ANA A	AND contents of register A with register A
250	A8	XRA B	Exclusive-OR contents of register B with register A
251	A9	XRA C	Exclusive-OR contents of register C with register A
252	AA	XRA D	Exclusive-OR contents of register D with register A
253	AB	XRA E	Exclusive-OR contents of register E with register A
254	AC	XRA H	Exclusive-OR contents of register H with register A
255	AD	XRA L	Exclusive-OR contents of register L with register A
256	AE	XRA M	Exclusive-OR contents of M with register A
257	AF	XRA A	Exclusive-OR contents of register A with register A
260	B0	ORA B	OR contents of register B with register A
261	B1	ORA C	OR contents of register C with register A
262	B2	ORA D	OR contents of register D with register A
263	B3	ORA E	OR contents of register E with register A
264	B4	ORA H	OR contents of register H with register A
265	B5	ORA L	OR contents of register L with register A
266	B6	ORA M	OR contents of M with register A
267	B7	ORA A	OR contents of register A with register A
270	B8	CMP B	Compare contents of register B with register A

Octal	Hexa-decimal	Mnemonic	Description
271	B9	CMP C	Compare contents of register C with register A
272	BA	CMP D	Compare contents of register D with register A
273	BB	CMP E	Compare contents of register E with register A
274	BC	CMP H	Compare contents of register H with register A
275	BD	CMP L	Compare contents of register L with register A
276	BE	CMP M	Compare contents of M with register A
277	BF	CMP A	Compare contents of register A with register A
300	C0	RNZ	Return from subroutine of zero flip-flop = logic 0
301	C1	POP B	Pop stack and store in register pair B and C
302	C2	JNZ <B2> <B3>	Jump if zero flip-flop = logic 0
303	C3	JMP <B2> <B3>	Jump unconditionally to M addressed by <B2> <B3>
304	C4	CNZ <B2> <B3>	Call subroutine if zero flip-flop = logic 0
305	C5	PUSH B	Push contents of register pair B and C on stack
306	C6	ADI <B2>	Add immediate to register A
307	C7	RST 0	Call subroutine at address 000$_8$
310	C8	RZ	Return from subroutine if zero flip-flop = logic 1
311	C9	RET	Return from subroutine
312	CA	JZ <B2> <B3>	Jump if zero flip-flop = logic 1
313	CB	---	---
314	CC	CZ <B2> <B3>	Call subroutine if zero flip-flop = logic 1
315	CD	CALL <B2> <B3>	Call subroutine located at M = <B2> <B3>
316	CE	ACI <B2>	Add immediate and carry flip-flop to register A
317	CF	RST 1	Call subroutine at address 010$_8$
320	D0	RNC	Return from subroutine if carry flip-flop = logic 0
321	D1	POP D	Pop stack and store in register pair D and E
322	D2	JNC <B2> <B3>	Jump if carry flip-flop = logic 0
323	D3	OUT <B2>	Output to device addressed by <B2>
324	D4	CNC <B2> <B3>	Call subroutine if carry flip-flop = logic 0
325	D5	PUSH D	Push contents of register pair D and E on stack
326	D6	SUI <B2>	Subtract immediate from register A
327	D7	RST 2	Call subroutine at address 020$_8$
330	D8	RC	Return from subroutine if carry flip-flop = logic 1
331	D9	---	---
332	DA	JC <B2> <B3>	Jump if carry flip-flop = logic 1
333	DB	IN <B2>	Input from device addressed by <B2>
334	DC	CC <B2> <B3>	Call subroutine if carry flip-flop = logic 1

335	DD	---	---
336	DE	SBI <B2>	Subtract immediate and carry flip-flop from register A
337	DF	RST 3	Call subroutine at address 030$_8$
340	E0	RPO	Return from subroutine if parity flip-flop = logic 0
341	E1	POP H	Pop stack and store in register pair H and L
342	E2	JPO <B2> <B3>	Jump if parity flip-flop = logic 0
343	E3	XTHL	Exchange top of stack with contents of H and L
344	E4	CPO <B2> <B3>	Call subroutine if parity flip-flop = logic 0
345	E5	PUSH H	Push contents of register pair H and L on stack
346	F6	ANI <B2>	AND immediate with contents of register A
347	E7	RST 4	Call subroutine at address 040$_8$
350	E8	RPE	Return from subroutine if parity flip-flop = logic 1
351	E9	PCHL	Jump indirect to M addressed by register pair H and L
352	EA	JPE <B2> <B3>	Jump if parity flip-flop = logic 1
353	EB	XCHG	Exchange contents of registers H,L with registers D,E
354	EC	CPE <B2> <B3>	Call subroutine if parity flip-flop = logic 1
355	ED	---	---
356	EE	XRI <B2>	Exclusive-OR immediate with contents of register A
357	EF	RST 5	Call subroutine at address 050$_8$
360	F0	RP	Return from subroutine if sign flip-flop = logic 0
361	F1	POP PSW	Pop stack and store in register A and flag flip-flops
362	F2	JP <B2> <B3>	Jump if sign flip-flop = logic 0 [positive sign]
363	F3	DI	Disable interrupt
364	F4	CP <B2> <B3>	Call subroutine if sign flip-flop = logic 0
365	F5	PUSH PSW	Push contents of register A and flags on stack
366	F6	ORI <B2>	OR immediate with contents of register A
367	F7	RST 6	Call subroutine at address 060$_8$
370	F8	RM	Return from subroutine if sign flip-flop = logic 1
371	F9	SPHL	Transfer contents of registers H,L to stack pointer
372	FA	JM <B2> <B3>	Jump if sign flip-flop = logic 1 [minus sign]
373	FB	EI	Enable interrupt
374	FC	CM <B2> <B3>	Call subroutine if sign flip-flop = logic 1
375	FD	---	---
376	FE	CPI <B2>	Compare immediate with contents of register A
377	FF	RST 7	Call subroutine at address 070$_8$

AN EXAMPLE OF INSTRUCTION DECODING

We have previously defined the *operation code,* also known as the *instruction code,* as the 8-bit code for the specific operation that the 8080 microprocessor will perform. Study the octal/hexadecimal listing of the 8080 instruction set given on the preceding pages. You will observe that the first octal digit can be a 0, 1, 2, or 3 and that *specific classes of operations correspond to the digits 0, 1, 2, and 3.* Thus we can write the following:

First Octal Digit	Class of Operation
0	Data operations only, with the possible exception of octal instructions 067 and 077
1	Data transfer operations only, all of which have the common Intel mnemonic MOV
2	Arithmetic and logic operations only, including add, subtract, AND, exclusive OR, OR, and compare
3	Miscellaneous operations, including all conditional operations such as jump, call subroutine, and return from subroutine

We have just decoded the 244-instruction set of the 8080 microprocessor into four classes of operations, each class containing related operations (perhaps with the exception of the final class, within which the operations are not all closely related). We have done the exact same thing on paper that the *instruction decoder* within the microprocessor does electronically.

REGISTER DECODING

Since we succeeded so well in decoding the set of 244 instructions into four distinct classes, let us examine the octal/hexadecimal instruction set listing for other coding patterns. We are told by Intel Corporation that the accumulator, the six general-purpose registers (B, C, D, E, H, and L), and memory M correspond to the following 3-bit binary codes:

Register Name	3-Bit Code	Octal Code
B	000	0
C	001	1
D	010	2
E	011	3
H	100	4
L	101	5
memory	110	6
accumulator (A)	111	7

Let us examine the 64 MOV instructions that begin with the octal digit 1. These instructions cause eight bits of data to be transferred between (a) the accumulator and a general-purpose register, (b) the accumulator and memory, (c) a general-purpose register and memory, or (d) two different registers. There is a consistent coding pattern, which is described in the following paragraph.

The three-octal-digit instruction, in which the first digit is 1, can be represented as follows:

1   **D**   **S**

instruction   *destination*   *source*
class   *register*   *register*
         (in octal)   *(in octal)*

The *source register* is the one that contains the 8-bit data byte that is being transferred. The *destination register* is the one that receives the transferring 8-bit data byte. Thus, in the octal/hexadecimal listing, we "move contents of [source register] to the [destination register]." The mnemonic is:

MOV [destination register], [source register]

Examine the 8080 instruction listing and verify the conclusions given above. Octal instruction 141 must mean "move contents of register C to register H," and sure enough it does. In these operations, the source register will still contain the transferred data since the MOV operation is simply a copy operation.

ARITHMETIC AND LOGIC OPERATION DECODING

We are also told by Intel Corporation that arithmetic and logic operations correspond to the following 3-bit binary codes:

Arithmetic or Logic Operation	3-Bit Code	Octal Code
add	000	0
add with carry	001	1
subtract	010	2
subtract with borrow	011	3
AND	100	4
exclusive-OR	101	5
OR	110	6
compare	111	7

If we examine the 64 arithmetic and logic operations that begin with the octal digit 2, we can spot yet another consistent coding pattern shown below.

The three-octal-digit instruction, in which the first octal digit is 2, can be represented as follows:

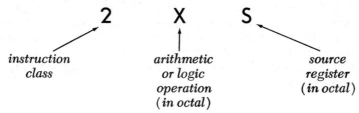

In the octal/hexadecimal listing, we perform an arithmetic or logic operation using a source register [with, to, or from] the accumulator. The mnemonic is:

[arithmetic or logic operation] [source register]

Examine the 8080 instruction listing and verify these additional conclusions. Note again that we are doing on paper what the instruction decoder does electronically.

So far, we have decoded 128 of the 244 microprocessor instructions. We are doing well, so let us continue. We note eight additional arithmetic/logical instructions:

306	ADI	\<B2\>
316	ACI	\<B2\>
326	SUI	\<B2\>
336	SBI	\<B2\>
346	ANI	\<B2\>
356	XRI	\<B2\>
366	ORI	\<B2\>
376	CPI	\<B2\>

The coding pattern is simply the following: *the three-octal-digit instruction, in which the first octal digit is 3 and the last octal digit is 6, can be represented as follows:*

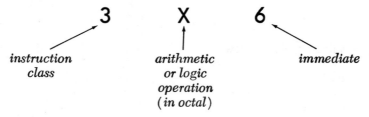

According to the octal/hexadecimal listing, we perform an arithmetic or logic operation using the immediate 8-bit byte [with, to, or from] the accumulator. The mnemonic is:

[arithmetic or logic operation] I

where the mnemonics for the arithmetic or logic operations are:

Arithmetic or Logic Operation	Immediate Instruction Mnemonic
add	ADI
add with carry	ACI
subtract	SUI
subtract with borrow	SBI
AND	ANI
exclusive OR	XRI
OR	ORI
compare	CPI

IMMEDIATE OPERATION DECODING

The term *immediate addressing* is defined as follows:

immediate addressing—The instruction contains the data itself. This data is either a single 8-bit data byte or two 8-bit data bytes. The least significant byte is first and the most significant byte is second when there are two 8-bit data bytes.

Immediate instructions can be represented as shown in Fig. 3-5. Eight immediate instructions were given in the preceding section. The remaining twelve such instructions are:

```
006    MVI B   <B2>
016    MVI C   <B2>
026    MVI D   <B2>
036    MVI E   <B2>
046    MVI H   <B2>
056    MVI L   <B2>
066    MVI M   <B2>
076    MVI A   <B2>
001    LXI  B  <B2> <B3>
021    LXI  D  <B2> <B3>
041    LXI  H  <B2> <B3>
061    LXI  SP <B2> <B3>
```

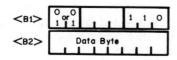

(A) Two-byte immediate instruction.

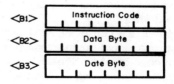

(B) Three-byte immediate instruction.

Fig. 3-5. Immediate instructions.

We can conclude that *all immediate instructions that have a single data byte have either a 0 or 3 octal digit as the instruction class and 6 as the third octal digit.* The mnemonic code, MVI [destination register] means "move the following 8-bit data byte to the [destination register]." The memory location M is really not a register, but let us not quibble over this minor detail.

BRANCH OPERATION DECODING

To quote the *Intellec 8/Mod 80 Microcomputer Development System Reference Manual* once again:

"The instructions that make up a program are stored in the system's memory. The central processor examines the contents of the memory, in order to determine what action is appropriate. This means that the processor must know which location contains the next instruction.

"Each of the locations in memory is numbered, to distinguish it from all other locations in memory. The number which identifies a memory location is called its *address.*

"The processor maintains a counter which contains the address of the next program instruction. This register is called the *program counter.* The processor updates the program counter by adding '1' to the counter each time it fetches an instruction, so that the program counter is always current.

"The programmer therefore stores his instructions in numerically adjacent addresses, so that the lower addresses contain the first instructions to be executed and the higher addresses contain later instructions. The only time the programmer may violate this sequential rule is . . ." with a *branch instruction* such as *jump, call, subroutine,* or *return from subroutine.*

Thus, we can define the following terms:

address—The 16-bit binary number which identifies a memory location.

program counter—The register that contains the address of the next instruction *byte* that must be executed in a computer program.

branch instruction, branch operation—An instruction that causes a program jump to a specified address and execution of the instruction at that address. During the execution of a branch instruction, the central processor replaces the contents of the program counter with the specified address.

jump—1. To cause the next instruction to be selected from a specified storage location in a computer. 2. A deviation from the normal sequence of execution of instructions in a computer.[4]

call subroutine, call—1. To transfer control to a specified closed subroutine. 2. A special type of jump in which the central processor is logically required to "remember" the contents of the program counter at the time that the jump occurs. This allows the processor later to resume execution of the main program, when it is finished with the last instruction of the subroutine.[8]

return from subroutine, return—A special type of jump in which the central processor resumes execution of the main program at the value of the program counter at the time that the call occurred.

subroutine—1. In computer technology, the portion of a program that causes a computer to carry out a well-defined mathematical or logical operation. 2. Usually called a closed subroutine. A small subprogram to which control may be transferred from a main program, and returned to the main program at the conclusion of the subroutine.

closed subroutine—Subroutine not stored in the main path of the *routine*. Such a subroutine is entered by a jump operation; provision is made to return control to the main *program* at the end of the operation.[5]

routine—Set of instruction codes arranged in proper sequence to direct the computer to perform a desired operation or sequence of operations. Alternatively, a subdivision of a program consisting of two or more instructions that are functionally related.[5]

program—Complete plan for the solution of a problem. More specifically, the complete sequence of machine instructions and routines necessary to solve a problem.[5]

With the 8080 microprocessor, branch instructions, except for the *unconditional* ones, correspond to the following 3-bit code for the least significant three bits:

Branch Instruction	3-Bit Code	Octal Code
return	000	0
jump	010	2
call	100	4

The instruction class for a branch instruction is always 3; this is the first octal digit of the three-digit instruction.

Branch instructions can be either *conditional* or *unconditional*:

conditional instruction—In the 8080 microprocessor, an instruction that is subject to a condition, viz., the logic state of a specified flag.

unconditional instruction—In the 8080 microprocessor, an instruction that is not subject to any condition, such as the logic state of a specified flag.

We shall now discuss the unconditional jump, call, and return instructions, which have the following instruction codes:

303 <B2> <B3>   unconditional jump (JMP)
315 <B2> <B3>   unconditional call (CALL)
311   unconditional return (RET)

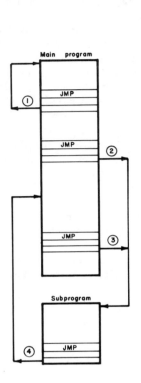

(A) Program with jump instructions.

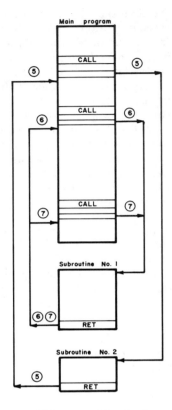

(B) Program with call and return instructions.

Fig. 3-6. Diagrams illustrating the differences between the unconditional jump, call, and return instructions. A call instruction always requires a return instruction in the subroutine.

Note that the unconditional return instruction is one-byte, whereas the other two are three-byte instructions.

The differences between unconditional jump, call, and return instructions can be seen with the aid of Fig. 3-6. The jump instruction ① creates a *loop* in the main program in Fig. 3-6A. If one would start at the beginning of this program, there would be no way in which one could get past this jump instruction. Let us assume that we can get past it and proceed to jump instructions ② and ③, which both jump to the same location, a subprogram. Unfortunately, from this subprogram the jump instruction ④ forces a return to a single point in the main program. A second loop is thus created as a consequence of jump instructions ③ and ④.

Let us now discuss the main program and two subroutines in Fig. 3-6B. This program flows smoothly and there are no problems with it. Thus:

- Call instruction ⑤ calls Subroutine No. 2. When this subroutine is finished, program control returns to the *instruction immediately following call instruction* ⑤.
- Call instruction ⑥ calls Subroutine No. 1. When this subroutine is finished, program control returns to the instruction immediately following call instruction ⑥.
- Finally, call instruction ⑦ calls Subroutine No. 1 also. However, the second time that Subroutine No. 1 finishes, program control returns to the instruction immediately following call instruction ⑦.

Clearly, the call instruction is a "smart" instruction, since it remembers where in the main program the call instruction occurred. In contrast, the jump instruction in the program on the left is a "dumb" instruction; it does not remember where it jumped from. Jump instructions are rarely used for the transfer of control to subprograms. Call instructions are used instead, and return instructions are added to convert the subprograms into subroutines.

CONDITIONAL BRANCH INSTRUCTIONS

The three conditional branch instructions can be stated as follows:

conditional jump   "Jump if [condition flag] is at [logic state] to memory location addressed by bytes B2 and B3. Otherwise, continue to the next sequential instruction."

conditional call: "Call subroutine if [condition flag] is at [logic state] at memory location addressed by bytes B2 and B3. Otherwise, continue to the next sequential instruction."

conditional return: "Return from subroutine to main program if [condition flag] is at [logic state]. Otherwise, continue to the next sequential instruction."

The jump and call conditional instructions are three-byte instructions, which can be represented by:

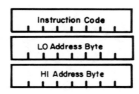

whereas the return conditional instructions are single-byte:

```
┌─────────────────────────────┐
│      Instruction Code        │
└─────────────────────────────┘
```

A popular technique in developing computer programs is *flow-charting*.

flowchart, flow diagram—A chart showing all the logical steps of a computer program. A program is coded by writing down the successive instructions that will cause the computer to perform the logical operations necessary for solving the problem, as represented on a flowchart.[4]

flowchart symbol—A symbol used on a flowchart to represent data, flow, equipment, or an operation.[4]

decision—In a computer, the process of determining further action on the basis of the relationship of two similar items of data.[4]

decision symbol—On a flowchart, a symbol used to mark a choice or branching in the sequence of programming of a digital computer.[4]

We have digressed here because we shall use the symbol for *decision* commonly found in flowcharts (see Fig. 3-7), and Figs. 3-8 through 3-10 will aid our discussion of the three conditional instructions. The symbol in Fig. 3-7 represents the following decisions: If the flag is at logic 0, go to the indicated instruction; if the flag is at logic 1, go to the alternative instruction.

The JZ instruction shown in Fig. 3-8A requires the following decision: If the *zero flag* is at logic 0, the program executes the next sequential instruction after the JZ instruction; if the *zero flag* is at logic 1, the program jumps to the memory address contained within the second and third bytes of the instruction. The JNZ instruction (Fig. 3-8B) behaves similarly, but the flag conditions are reversed.

The CZ instruction shown in Fig. 3-9A is similar to the JZ instruction but better: If the *zero flag* is at logic 0, the program executes the next sequential instruction after the CZ instruction; if the *zero flag* is at logic 1, the address of the following instruction is stored in the *stack*, and the program jumps to the subroutine given by the memory address contained within the second and third bytes of the instruction. With the

Fig. 3-7. Decision symbol used in flowcharts.

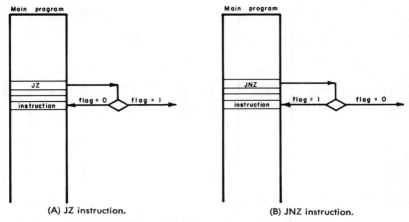

(A) JZ instruction. (B) JNZ instruction.

Fig. 3-8. The conditional instructions JNZ and JZ.

CNZ instruction, the flag conditions are reversed (Fig. 3-9B). These instructions are quite popular.

With the RZ instruction shown in Fig. 3-10A, the following decision is made: If the *zero flag* is at logic 0, the subroutine executes the next sequential instruction after the RZ instruction; if the *zero flag* is at logic 1, a 16-bit address is retrieved from the *stack* and the program control returns to the main program at the instruction immediately following

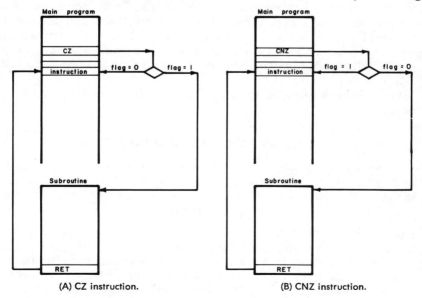

(A) CZ instruction. (B) CNZ instruction.

Fig. 3-9. The conditional instructions CZ and CNZ.

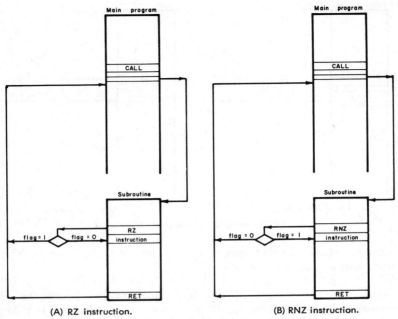

(A) RZ instruction. (B) RNZ instruction.

Fig. 3-10. Diagrams illustrating conditional instructions RZ and RNZ.

the three-byte call subroutine instruction. The figure points out that a return instruction must be executed during any pass through the subroutine. If the RZ instruction is skipped, some other return instruction, such as RET, must be present to transfer control back to the main program. With the RNZ instruction, the flag conditions are reversed (Fig. 3-10B).

In the following section, we shall discuss the condition flags in greater detail.

CONDITION FLAG DECODING

A flag is an ubiquitous digital electronic device that is widely used in machine language programming and in computer/instrument interfacing. Unfortunately, it is not easy to find a suitable definition for this term. The best seems to be the following:

flag, condition flag—A single flip-flop that indicates that a certain condition has arisen during the course of (a) arithmetic or logical manipulations in a computer program, or (b) data transmission between a pair of digital electronic devices such as a computer and an instrument. For example, a flag indicates when the accumulator has a value of 000_8. As another example, a flag can be a circuit that provides a signal which indicates that an input device is ready to transmit data to a computer.

The important point is that a flag is a flip-flop that provides a 1-bit piece of information about a condition that exists.

According to the Intellec 8/Mod 80 Reference Manual, there are five condition flags associated with the execution of instructions in the 8080 microprocessor. These flags are:

zero
carry
sign
parity
auxiliary carry

and are each represented by a one-bit register, or flip-flop, contained within the microprocessor chip. When you read the Intel literature, keep in mind the following:

> *When a flag is "set," the flag bit is at logic 1;*
> *when a flag is "reset," the flag bit is at logic 0.*

A synonym for "reset" is "cleared." Arithmetic or logical instructions performed on either the accumulator contents, the contents of one of the six general-purpose registers, or the contents of memory, influence the flags in the following ways:

zero flag—If the result of an instruction has the value 000_8, this flag is set to logic 1; otherwise, it is reset to logic 0.

carry flag—If the result of an instruction produces a carry (from addition or rotation) or a borrow (from subtraction or comparison) out of the MSB of the 8-bit data byte, the carry flag is set to logic 1; otherwise, it is reset to logic 0.

sign flag—If the result of an instruction produces a logic 1 in the MSB of the 8-bit data byte, this flag is set to logic 1 (indicating a negative result); otherwise, it is reset to logic 0 (indicating a positive result).[8]

parity flag—If the result of an instruction produces an 8-bit data byte the modulo 2 sum of the bits of which is logic 0 (indicating even parity), this flag is set to logic 1; otherwise, it is reset to logic 0 (indicating odd parity).[8]

auxiliary carry flag—If the result of an instruction causes a carry out of bit 3 into bit 4 of the resulting 8-bit data byte, the auxiliary carry flag is set to logic 1; otherwise, it is reset to logic 0. This flag is affected by single-precision additions, subtractions, increments, decrements, comparisons, and logical operations, but it is principally used with addition instructions preceding a DAA (*D*ecimal *A*djust Accumulator) instruction.[8]

Four of the five condition flags correspond to the following 3-bit binary code, which is contained within all conditional jump, call, and return instructions. This section is shown in the representation for byte B1 of all three instructions:

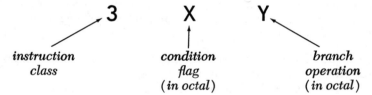

Condition Flag	Mnemonic	Flag Logic State	3-Bit Code	Octal Code
Result is not zero	NZ	0	000	0
Result is zero	Z	1	001	1
Result has no carry	NC	0	010	2
Result has a carry	C	1	011	3
Result has odd parity	PO	0	100	4
Result has even parity	PE	1	101	5
Result is positive	P	0	110	6
Result is negative (minus)	M	1	111	7

The consistent coding pattern for all conditional branch instructions is therefore:

$$\nearrow 3 \qquad X \qquad Y \nwarrow$$

instruction class	condition flag (in octal)	branch operation (in octal)

The 24 different conditional instructions are summarized in Table 3-2. (The auxiliary carry flag is not a valid condition flag; it has limited use in conjunction with the DAA instruction.) Table 3-2 can be best understood by reference to Figs. 3-8 to 3-10A. Though these three figures have been drawn with reference to the condition of the zero flag, it should be clear that they apply, with the appropriate changes, to the remaining three condition flags as well. The basic issue with all of these conditions is:

Should the jump, call, or return instruction be ignored (with program control continuing to the next sequential instruction) or not (with program control transferring to some other memory location)?

REGISTER PAIR DECODING

The six general-purpose registers are all eight bits in length. Since sixteen bits are required to address any location within the 65,536 pos-

Table 3-2. Summary of the 24 Different Conditional Instructions in the 8080 Microprocessor Instruction Set

	Jump			Call			Return	
Jump, call, or return if the result of an instruction is not zero	JNZ	302 <B2> <B3>		CNZ	304 <B2> <B3>		RNZ	300
Jump, call, or return if the result of an instruction is zero	JZ	312 <B2> <B3>		CZ	314 <B2> <B3>		RZ	310
Jump, call, or return if the result of an instruction has no carry	JNC	322 <B2> <B3>		CNC	324 <B2> <B3>		RNC	320
Jump, call, or return if the result of an instruction has a carry	JC	332 <B2> <B3>		CC	334 <B2> <B3>		RC	330
Jump, call, or return if the result of an instruction has odd parity	JPO	342 <B2> <B3>		CPO	344 <B2> <B3>		RPO	340
Jump, call, or return if the result of an instruction has even parity	JPE	352 <B2> <B3>		CPE	354 <B2> <B3>		RPE	350
Jump, call, or return if the result of an instruction is positive	JP	362 <B2> <B3>		CP	364 <B2> <B3>		RP	360
Jump, call, or return if the result of an instruction is negative	JM	372 <B2> <B3>		CM	374 <B2> <B3>		RM	370

sible locations in memory, it is convenient to have operations that employ pairs of registers rather than single registers. In this way, 16-bit words can be handled and memory locations can be addressed, if necessary, directly. Both the *stack pointer* and the *program counter* are 16-bit registers, so instructions that allow one to set the sixteen bits in these registers would be useful.

Intel Corporation has established four register pairs which correspond to the following 2-bit binary codes:

Register Pair Name	*Registers*	*2-Bit Code*
B	B and C	00
D	D and E	01
H	H and L	10
PSW	A and flags	11

Since register pairs are used to designate 16-bit memory addresses, it is important to identify a HI memory address byte and a LO memory address byte. In the above pairs, registers B, D, H, and flags are the HI bytes, i.e., the eight most significant bits in the 16-bit register pair word, and registers C, E, L, and flags are the LO bytes, i.e., the eight least significant bits in the 16-bit register pair word.

Some of the register pair instructions, such as *push* and *pop*, require a considerable amount of explanation. Since we will discuss them in a later chapter, at a time when we will have a "need to know," we won't go into any detail here. In the space below, we will briefly summarize the register pair operations and provide the byte representation for each register pair instruction. The letters rp in the byte representations refer to the 2-bit register pair code just given above.

PUSH: Push data onto stack, a single-byte instruction. The contents of the specified register pair are saved in two bytes of memory indicated by the stack pointer. (We shall discuss the stack pointer later.)

POP: Pop data off stack, a single-byte instruction. The contents of the specified register pair are restored from two bytes of memory indicated by the stack pointer. (This instruction requires more explanation, which will be given later.)

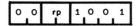

DAD: Double add, a single-byte instruction. The 16-bit number in the specified register pair is added to the 16-bit number held in the H and L registers using two's complement arithmetic. The result replaces the contents of the H and L registers. This is a useful instruction for memory indexing.

INX: Increment register pair, a single-byte instruction. The 16-bit number held in the specified register pair is incremented by one.

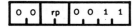

DCX: Decrement register pair, a single-byte instruction. The 16-bit number held in the specified register pair is decremented by one.

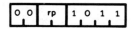

XCHG: Exchange registers, a single-byte instruction. The 16 bits of data held in the H and L registers are exchanged with the 16 bits of data held in the D and E registers.

XTHL: Exchange stack, a single-byte instruction. The 16 bits of data held in the H and L registers are exchanged with the 16 bits of data in the top two stack bytes.

SPHL: Load stack pointer from H and L, a single-byte instruction. The 16 bits of data held in the H and L registers replace the contents of the stack pointer. The contents of the H and L registers are unchanged.

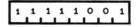

LXI: Load register pair immediate, a three-byte instruction. The third byte of the instruction (the most significant 8 bits of the 16-bit immediate data) is loaded into the first register of the specified pair, while the second byte of the instruction (the least significant 8 bits of the 16-bit immediate data) is loaded into the second register of the specified pair. *If the stack pointer is specified as the register pair, the second byte of the instruction replaces the least significant eight bits of the stack pointer, while the third byte of the instruction replaces the most significant eight bits of the stack pointer.*

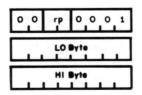

Fig. 3-11 summarizes several different register pair operations. The LXI rp command replaces the contents of one of the four register pairs by the second and third bytes in the LXI instruction. LXI SP is particularly important for locating the stack pointer immediately after you apply power to the microcomputer system. XCHG, a single-byte instruction, exchanges the contents of the D register pair with the con-

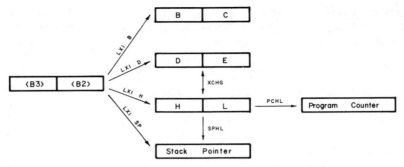

Fig. 3-11. Summary of the more important register pair operations. Both the program counter and stack pointer are 16-bit registers.

tents of the H register pair. PCHL replaces the 16-bit program counter word by the H register pair. In view of the definition for the *program counter:*

program counter—The 16-bit register in the 8080 microprocessor that contains the address of the next instruction or instruction byte that must be executed in a computer program.

it should be clear that the PCHL instruction is a jump instruction. Finally, SPHL replaces the 16-bit stack pointer value by the value of the H register pair. It is another way of relocating the stack pointer.

The *pop* and *push* instructions are defined below and summarized in Fig. 3-12.

pop—Transferring one or more bytes from a stack to some other register or group of registers. Retrieving data from a stack.

push—Replacing the contents of one or more memory locations in a stack with the contents of a register or group of registers. Putting data into a stack.

stack—The area of memory set aside by the programmer in which data or addresses are stored and retrieved.

stack pointer—The 16-bit memory address of the top of the stack.

top of stack—The memory address of the last data byte placed on a stack.

The most common information that resides in a stack is the memory address that the program will return to after execution of a subroutine. Other information, as shown in Fig. 3-12, includes the contents of the six general-purpose registers, the accumulator, and the flags.

In Fig. 3-12B, the storage location M(SP) means *the contents of that memory location whose 16-bit address is contained in the stack pointer register.* The meanings of M(SP−2), M(SP−1), and M(SP+1) should be clear. There exist four different push instructions and four different

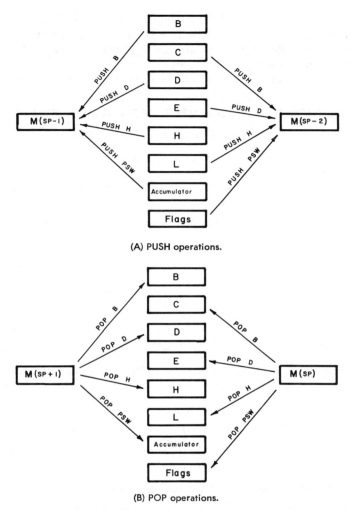

(A) PUSH operations.

(B) POP operations.

Fig. 3-12. Diagrams illustrating the PUSH and POP operations, each of which involves a
register pair and two memory locations.

pop instructions, each of which operates with a register pair and two
memory locations within the stack. For example, in the PUSH B instruction, the contents of the B register replace the contents of memory
location M(SP−1) and the contents of the C register replace the contents of memory location M(SP−2); after doing this, the stack pointer
is decremented by two to allow subsequent push instructions to put
additional data bytes on the stack. The POP B instruction reverses
this process. The contents of M(SP+1) replaces the contents of the B

register and the contents of M(SP) replaces the contents of the C register; after doing this, the stack pointer is incremented by two to make available two additional bytes at the top of the stack that can be popped into a register pair.

The push and pop operations will be discussed further in Chapter 8.

INCREMENT AND DECREMENT OPERATION DECODING

The terms *increment* and *decrement* can be defined as follows:

increment—To increase the value of a binary word. Typically, to increase the value by one.

decrement—To decrease the value of a binary word. Typically, to decrease the value by one.

The coding patterns for increment and decrement instructions are shown below.

The three-octal-digit increment instruction, in which the first octal digit is 0 and the last octal digit is 4, can be represented as follows:

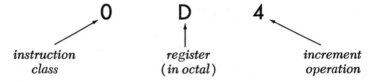

The three-octal-digit decrement instruction, in which the first octal digit is 0 and the last octal digit is 5, can be represented as follows:

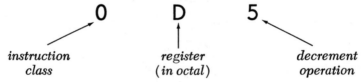

The increment and decrement instructions can be stated as follows:

increment: "Increment [register] by 1."
decrement: "Decrement [register] by 1."

The mnemonics are INR [register] and DCR [register].

We have already discussed or accounted for 218 of the 256 microprocessor instructions. It is a tedious business, and the danger is that we are considering too many different instructions without testing some of them. Our main interest has been to demonstrate how the 8080 microprocessor instructions are *decoded* by the instruction decoder. It should be apparent that there is a consistent set of coding rules behind the entire 8080 instruction set. Registers, register pairs, arithmetic operations, logical operations, conditional instructions, and the like all have specific coding patterns within the 8080 instruction set.

DATA AND MEMORY ADDRESSING MODES

Since the entire computer program and data are located in memory, it should be clear that the addressing of individual memory locations for the purpose of, for example, acquiring data bytes, is an important part of any computer program. Such addressing can be performed in a number of ways, such as:

direct addressing—An 8-bit data byte is acquired via a three-byte instruction that contains the 16-bit memory address at which the data byte is located. Byte B2 contains the LO memory address and byte B3 contains the HI memory address.

indirect addressing—An 8-bit data byte is acquired via a one-byte instruction that employs a register pair, usually H and L, to generate the 16-bit memory address. The HI memory address is stored in H and the LO memory address is stored in L. We often denote by the letter M the memory location addressed by registers H and L.

immediate addressing—An 8-bit data byte is acquired via a two-byte instruction that contains the data byte as byte B2.

stack pointer addressing—Two 8-bit data bytes are acquired via a one-byte instruction that transfers the data from a memory area called a *stack* to a register *pair* (or, if desired, to the program counter register). A *stack pointer register* provides the location of the stack, and is automatically incremented by two after each POP operation. The data in the stack has originally been entered by a PUSH operation.

In microprocessor instructions included in the "data transfer group," the memory location M refers to that location addressed by the contents of register pair H and L.

ACCUMULATOR INSTRUCTIONS

The different types of accumulator instructions described in this chapter can be classified as follows:

- Load an 8-bit data byte into the accumulator, either from memory, another register, or the second byte of an immediate instruction.
- Move an 8-bit data byte from the accumulator into either a memory location or another register.
- Load an 8-bit data byte into the accumulator from an input device.
- Move an 8-bit data byte from the accumulator into an output device.
- Rotate the contents of the accumulator.

- Complement the accumulator.
- Increment or decrement the contents of the accumulator.
- Push the contents of the accumulator on the stack, or pop the stack and replace the contents of the accumulator.
- Add, subtract, compare, AND, OR, or exclusive-OR the contents of a register, an immediate byte, or memory location with the contents of the accumulator and store the result in the accumulator.
- Clear the accumulator.

In the following subsections, we shall discuss several instructions that merit additional comment.

Rotate Contents of Accumulator

Fig. 3-13 provides schematic representations for the four different rotate instructions:

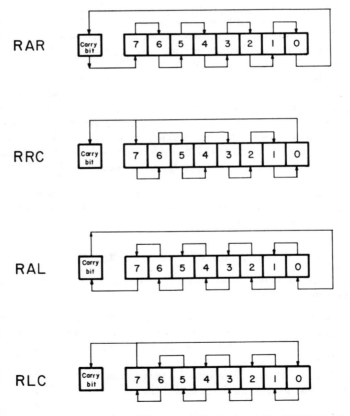

Fig. 3-13. Representations of the four different rotate instructions in the 8080 instruction set.

007 RLC Rotate contents of accumulator left one position. The least significant bit and the carry flag are both set to the value shifted out of the most significant bit position in the 8-bit accumulator byte.

017 RRC Rotate contents of accumulator right one position. The most significant bit and the carry flag are both set to the value shifted out of the least significant bit position in the 8-bit accumulator byte.

027 RAL Rotate contents of accumulator left one position through the carry flag. The least significant bit is set equal to the carry bit and the carry flag is set to the value shifted out of the most significant bit in the 8-bit accumulator byte.

037 RAR Rotate contents of accumulator right one position through the carry flag. The most significant bit is set equal to the carry bit and the carry flag is set to the value shifted out of the least significant bit in the 8-bit accumulator byte.

The carry bit and the 8-bit accumulator byte can be viewed as a 9-bit binary word, in which the ninth bit becomes logic 1 whenever the sum of two 8-bit binary words produces a carry out of the most significant bit (bit 7). The rotate instructions are useful for the following situations:

- During the multiplication of a pair of 8-bit binary data bytes. To multiply a data byte by 2, simply shift the entire data byte to the left one position.
- During the division of a pair of 8-bit binary data bytes. To divide a data byte by 2, simply shift the entire data byte to the right one position.
- During the testing of external flag bits entered into the accumulator with the aid of an IN microprocessor instruction. Each external flag can be tested in turn by rotating the accumulator through the carry bit and testing the logic state of the carry bit.

The schematic representation for the RAR instruction can be explained as follows:

The carry bit is moved to bit 7 of the accumulator byte. Simultaneous with this action, bit 7 is moved to bit 6, bit 6 is moved to bit 5, bit 5 is moved to bit 4, bit 4 is moved to bit 3, bit 3 is moved to bit 2, bit 2 is moved to bit 1, bit 1 is moved to bit 0, and bit 0 is moved to the carry bit.

The remaining rotate instructions can be explained in a similar manner. The arrows in the representations designate the destinations of each of the bits shown.

Decimal Adjust Accumulator Contents

The purpose of the DAA instruction, **047**, is to convert the result from the addition of two bcd numbers via straight binary addition into two packed binary-coded-decimal words, each of which contains four bits. This instruction can, on occasion, exhibit rather confusing behavior. To quote directly from the *Intel 8080 Assembly Language Programming Manual* (1974):

047 DAA "The eight-bit hexadecimal number in the accumulator is adjusted to form two four-bit binary-coded-decimal (bcd) digits by the following two-step process:

(1) If the least significant four bits of the accumulator represents a number greater than 9, or if the Auxiliary Carry bit is at logic 1, the accumulator is incremented by six. Otherwise, no incrementing occurs.

(2) If the most significant four bits of the accumulator now represent a number greater than 9, or if the normal bit is at logic 1, the most significant four bits of the accumulator are incremented by six. Otherwise, no incrementing occurs.

If a carry out of the least significant four bits occurs during Step (1), the Auxiliary Carry bit is set to logic 1; otherwise it is reset to logic 0. Likewise, if a carry out of the most significant four bits occurs during Step (2), the normal Carry bit is set to logic 1; otherwise, it is unaffected.

NOTE: This instruction is used when adding decimal numbers. It is the only instruction whose operation is affected by the Auxiliary Carry bit.

Condition bits affected: Zero, Sign, Parity, Carry, Auxiliary Carry."

When you use this very unusual instruction, we would encourage you to heed the following rule:

Use the decimal adjust accumulator (DAA) instruction only after an ADD, ADC, or ADI instruction.

Why? Because only after an ADD, ADC, or ADI can you be certain that the logic states of the auxiliary carry and carry bits are correct. One gimmick that you can employ is to add zero to an 8-bit byte that you wish to decimal adjust. This can be done with three consecutive instruction bytes:

306	ADI	Add following byte to contents of accumulator
000	000	Zero
047	047	Decimal adjust contents of accumulator

These three instruction bytes will allow you to decimal adjust the contents of the accumulator after the following instructions: IN <B2> and INR A. The authors have tried DCR A and SUI <B2>, but did not observe anything useful. The moral here is that you should be very careful with the DAA instruction. You might try various programs that incorporate it and demonstrate to yourself how tricky it is.

Clear Accumulator

There are two instructions that will allow you to clear the accumulator, i.e., set the contents of the accumulator register to 00000000_2:

227	SUB A	Subtract the contents of the accumulator from the contents of the accumulator
257	XRA A	Exclusive-OR the contents of the accumulator with the contents of the accumulator

Both instructions take only 2 μs execution time.

8080 INSTRUCTION GROUPS

To conclude our discussion of instruction decoding, here is a handy 8080 instruction set reference in which the 256 instructions are subdivided into the five groups suggested by Intel Corporation:

1. Data Transfer Group
2. Arithmetic Group
3. Logical Group
4. Branch Group
5. Stack, I/O, and Machine Control Group

In each group, octal instructions, mnemonics (Intel), and a description of the instruction are provided.

Data Transfer Group

100	MOV B,B	Move contents of register B to register B
101	MOV B,C	Move contents of register C to register B
102	MOV B,D	Move contents of register D to register B
103	MOV B,E	Move contents of register E to register B
104	MOV B,H	Move contents of register H to register B
105	MOV B,L	Move contents of register L to register B
106	MOV B,M	Move contents of memory location M to register B
107	MOV B,A	Move contents of accumulator to register B
110	MOV C,B	Move contents of register B to register C
111	MOV C,C	Move contents of register C to register C
112	MOV C,D	Move contents of register D to register C

113	MOV C,E	Move contents of register E to register C
114	MOV C,H	Move contents of register H to register C
115	MOV C,L	Move contents of register L to register C
116	MOV C,M	Move contents of memory location M to register C
117	MOV C,A	Move contents of accumulator to register C
120	MOV D,B	Move contents of register B to register D
121	MOV D,C	Move contents of register C to register D
122	MOV D,D	Move contents of register D to register D
123	MOV D,E	Move contents of register E to register D
124	MOV D,H	Move contents of register H to register D
125	MOV D,L	Move contents of register L to register D
126	MOV D,M	Move contents of memory location M to register D
127	MOV D,A	Move contents of accumulator to register D
130	MOV E,B	Move contents of register B to register E
131	MOV E,C	Move contents of register C to register E
132	MOV E,D	Move contents of register D to register E
133	MOV E,E	Move contents of register E to register E
134	MOV E,H	Move contents of register H to register E
135	MOV E,L	Move contents of register L to register E
136	MOV E,M	Move contents of memory location M to register E
137	MOV E,A	Move contents of accumulator to register E
140	MOV H,B	Move contents of register B to register H
141	MOV H,C	Move contents of register C to register H
142	MOV H,D,	Move contents of register D to register H
143	MOV H,E	Move contents of register E to register H
144	MOV H,H	Move contents of register H to register H
145	MOV H L	Move contents of register L to register H
146	MOV H,M	Move contents of memory location M to register H
147	MOV H,A	Move contents of accumulator to register H
150	MOV L,B	Move contents of register B to register L
151	MOV L,C	Move contents of register C to register L
152	MOV L,D	Move contents of register D to register L
153	MOV L,E	Move contents of register E to register L
154	MOV L,H	Move contents of register H to register L
155	MOV L,L	Move contents of register L to register L
156	MOV L,M	Move contents of memory location M to register L
157	MOV L,A	Move contents of accumulator to register L
160	MOV M,B	Move contents of register B to memory location M
161	MOV M,C	Move contents of register C to memory location M
162	MOV M,D	Move contents of register D to memory location M
163	MOV M,E	Move contents of register E to memory location M
164	MOV M,H	Move contents of register H to memory location M
165	MOV M,L	Move contents of register L to memory location M
166	HLT	Halt
167	MOV M,A,	Move contents of accumulator to memory location M
170	MOV A,B	Move contents of register B to accumulator
171	MOV A,C	Move contents of register C to accumulator
172	MOV A,D	Move contents of register D to accumulator
173	MOV A,E	Move contents of register E to accumulator
174	MOV A,H	Move contents of register H to accumulator
175	MOV A,L	Move contents of register L to accumulator
176	MOV A,M	Move contents of memory location M to accumulator
177	MOV A,A	Move contents of accumulator to accumulator

006	MVI B <B2>	Move immediate byte B2 into register B
016	MVI C <B2>	Move immediate byte B2 into register C
026	MVI D <B2>	Move immediate byte B2 into register D
036	MVI E <B2>	Move immediate byte B2 into register E
046	MVI H <B2>	Move immediate byte B2 into register H
056	MVI L <B2>	Move immediate byte B2 into register L
066	MVI M <B2>	Move immediate byte B2 into memory location M
076	MVI A <B2>	Move immediate byte B2 into accumulator
001	LXI B <B2> <B3>	Load immediate two bytes B2 and B3 into register pair B
021	LXI D <B2> <B3>	Load immediate two bytes B2 and B3 into register pair D
041	LXI H <B2> <B3>	Load immediate two bytes B2 and B3 into register pair H
061	LXI SP <B2> <B3>	Load immediate two bytes B2 and B3 into register pair SP
002	STAX B	Store accumulator indirect into memory location M addressed by register pair B
012	LDAX B	Load accumulator indirect from memory location M addressed by register pair B
022	STAX D	Store accumulator indirect into memory location M addressed by register pair D
032	LDAX D	Load accumulator indirect from memory location M addressed by register pair D
042	SHLD <B2> <B3>	Store L direct into memory location M addressed by two bytes B2 and B3; store H direct into the succeeding memory location
052	LHLD <B2> <B3>	Load L direct from memory location M addressed by two bytes B2 and B3; load H direct from the succeeding memory location
062	STA <B2> <B3>	Store accumulator direct into memory location M addressed by two bytes B2 and B3
072	LDA <B2> <B3>	Load accumulator direct from memory location M addressed by two bytes B2 and B3
353	XCHG	Exchange the contents of registers H and L with the contents of registers D and E, respectively
371	SPHL	Move the contents of registers H and L to stack pointer register

The above group of data transfer instructions transfer data to and from registers and memory. *Condition flags are not affected by any instructions in this group.*

Arithmetic Group

This group of instructions performs arithmetic operations on data in registers and memory. *With certain exceptions, all instructions in this group affect the zero, sign, parity, and carry flags according to the standard rules.* The only exceptions are the INR and DCR instructions (carry flag not affected), the INX and DCX instructions (no flags affected), and DAD instruction (only carry flag affected). All subtraction operations are performed via two's complement arithmetic and set the carry flag to logic 1 to indicate a borrow and clear it to indicate no borrow.

200	ADD B	Add contents of register B to contents of accumulator
201	ADD C	Add contents of register C to contents of accumulator
202	ADD D	Add contents of register D to contents of accumulator
203	ADD E	Add contents of register E to contents of accumulator
204	ADD H	Add contents o fregister H to contents of accumulator
205	ADD L	Add contents of register L to contents of accumulator
206	ADD M	Add contents of memory location M to contents of accumulator
207	ADD A	Add contents of accumulator to contents of accumulator
210	ADC B	Add carry bit and contents of register B to contents of accumulator
211	ADC C	Add carry bit and contents of register C to contents of accumulator
212	ADC D	Add carry bit and contents of register D to contents of accumulator
213	ADC E	Add carry bit and contents of register E to contents of accumulator
214	ADC H	Add carry bit and contents of register H to contents of accumulator
215	ADC L	Add carry bit and contents of register L to contents of accumulator
216	ADC M	Add carry bit and contents of memory location M to contents of accumulator
217	ADC A	Add carry bit and contents of accumulator to contents of accumulator
220	SUB B	Subtract contents of register B from contents of accumulator
221	SUB C	Subtract contents of register C from contents of accumulator
222	SUB D	Subtract contents of register D from contents of accumulator
223	SUB E	Subtract contents of register E from contents of accumulator
224	SUB H	Subtract contnets of register H from contents of accumulator
225	SUB L	Subtract contents of register L from contents of accumulator
226	SUB M	Subtract contents of memory location M from contents of accumulator
227	SUB A	Subtract contents of accumulator from contents of accumulator, *i.e., clear accumulator*
230	SBB B	Subtract carry bit and contents of register B from contents of accumulator
231	SBB C	Subtract carry bit and contents of register C from contents of accumulator
232	SBB D	Subtract carry bit and contents of register D from contents of accumulator
233	SBB E	Subtract carry bit and contents of register E from contents of accumulator
234	SBB H	Subtract carry bit and contents of register H from contents of accumulator

235	SBB L	Subtract carry bit and contents of register L from contents of accumulator
236	SBB M	Subtract carry bit and contents of memory location M from contents of accumulator
237	SBB A	Subtract carry bit and contents of accumulator from contents of accumulator
004	INR B	Increment contents of register B by one
014	INR C	Increment contents of register C by one
024	INR D	Increment contents of register D by one
034	INR E	Increment contents of register E by one
044	INR H	Increment contents of register H by one
054	INR L	Increment contents of register L by one
064	INR M	Increment contents of memory location M by one
074	INR A	Increment contents of accumulator by one
005	DCR B	Decrement contents of register B by one
015	DCR C	Decrement contents of register C by one
025	DRC D	Decrement contents of register D by one
035	DCR E	Decrement contents of register E by one
045	DCR H	Decrement contents of register H by one
055	DCR L	Decrement contents of register L by one
065	DCR M	Decrement contents of memory location M by one
075	DCR A	Decrement contents of accumulator by one
003	INX B	Increment contents of register pair B and C by one
023	INX D	Increment contents of register pair D and E by one
043	INX	Increment contents of register pair H and L by one
063	INX SP	Increment contents of stack pointer register by one
013	DCX B	Decrement contents of register pair B and C by one
033	DCX D	Decrement contents of register pair D and E by one
053	DCX H	Decrement contents of register pair H and L by one
073	DCX SP	Decrement contents of stack pointer register by one
011	DAD B	Add contents of register pair B and C to contents of register pair H and L and store in register pair H and L
031	DAD D	Add contents of register pair D and E to contents of register pair H and L and store in register pair H and L
051	DAD H	Add contents of register pair H and L to contents of register pair H and L and store in register pair H and L
071	DAD SP	Add contents of stack pointer register to contents of register pair H and L and store in register pair H and L
047	DAA	Adjust 8-bit number in the accumulator to form two 4-bit binary coded decimal digits (used after an add instruction that adds two bcd numbers)
306	ADI <B2>	Add immediate byte B2 to contents of accumulator
316	ACI <B2>	Add carry bit and immediate byte B2 to contents of accumulator
326	SUI <B2>	Subtract immediate byte B2 from contents of accumulator
336	SBI <B2>	Subtract carry bit and immediate byte B2 from contents of accumulator
270	CMP B	Compare contents of register B with contents of accumulator; the accumulator remains unchanged. The condition flags are set as a result of the subtraction of the contents of register B from the contents of the accumulator

271	CMP C	Compare contents of register C with contents of accumulator
272	CMP D	Compare contents of register D with contents of accumulator
273	CMP E	Compare contents of register E with contents of accumulator
274	CMP H	Compare contents of register H with contents of accumulator
275	CMP L	Compare contents of register L with contents of accumulator
276	CMP M	Compare contents of memory location M with contents of accumulator
277	CMP A	Compare contents of accumulator with contents of accumulator
376	CPI <B2>	Compare immediate byte B2 with contents of accumulator

Logical Group

This group of instructions performs logical operations on data in registers and memory and on condition flags. *With certain exceptions, all instructions in this group affect the zero, sign, parity, auxiliary carry, and carry flags according to the standard rules.* The only exceptions are the RLC, RRC, RAL, RAR, CMC, and STC instructions [only the carry flag is affected] and the CMA instruction [no flags affected].

240	ANA B	AND contents of register B with contents of accumulator
241	ANA C	AND contents of register C with contents of accumulator
242	ANA D	AND contents of register D with contents of accumulator
243	ANA E	AND contents of register E with contents of accumulator
244	ANA H	AND contents of register H with contents of accumulator
245	ANA L	AND contents of register L with contents of accumulator
246	ANA M	AND contents of memory location M with contents of accumulator
247	ANA A	AND contents of accumulator with contents of accumulator
250	XRA B	Exclusive-OR contents of register B with contents of accumulator
251	XRA C	Exclusive-OR contents of register C with contents of accumulator
252	XRA D	Exclusive-OR contents of register D with contents of accumulator
253	XRA E	Exclusive-OR contents of register E with contents of accumulator
254	XRA H	Exclusive-OF contents of register H with contents of accumulator
255	XRA L	Exclusive-OR contents of register L with contents of accumulator
256	XRA M	Exclusive-OR contents of memory location M with contents of accumulator
257	XRA A	Exclusive-OR contents of accumulator with contents of accumulator, *i.e., clear accumulator*
260	ORA B	OR contents of register B with contents of accumulator
261	ORA C	OR contents of register C with contents of accumulator
262	ORA D	OR contents of register D with contents of accumulator
263	ORA E	OR contents of register E with contents of accumulator
264	ORA H	OR contents of register H with contents of accumulator

265	ORA L	OR contents of register L with contents of accumulator
266	ORA M	OR contents of memory location M with contents of accumulator
267	ORA A	OR contents of accumulator with contents of accumulator
007	RLC	Rotate contents of accumulator left one position. The least significant bit and the carry flag are both set to the value shifted out of the most significant bit position
017	RRC	Rotate contents of accumulator right one position. The most significant bit and the carry flag are both set to the value shifted out of the least significant bit position
027	RAL	Rotate contents of accumulator left one position through the carry flag. The least significant bit is set equal to the carry bit and the carry flag is set to the value shifted out of the most significant bit
037	RAR	Rotate contents of accumulator right one position through the carry flag. The most significant bit is set equal to the carry bit and the carry flag is set to the value shifted out of the least significant bit
057	CMA	Complement the accumulator
067	STC	Set the carry flag, i.e., the carry bit, to logic 1
077	CMC	Complement the carry bit
346	ANI <B2>	AND immediate byte B2 with contents of accumulator
356	XRI <B2>	Exclusive-OR immediate byte B2 with contents of accumulator
366	ORI <B2>	OR immediate byte B2 with contents of accumulator

Branch Group

This group of instructions alters the normal sequential program flow. *No condition flags are affected by any instruction in this group.* The two types of branch instructions are unconditional and conditional. Unconditional transfers simply perform the specified operation on the 16-bit program counter register. Conditional transfers examine the status of one of the four processor flags (zero, sign, parity, and carry) to determine if the specified branch is to be executed. The conditions that may be specified are as follows:[7]

carry flag is at logic 1	carry flag is at logic 0
zero flag is at logic 1	zero flag is at logic 0
sign flag is at logic 1	sign flag is at logic 0
parity flag is at logic 1	parity flag is at logic 0

302	JNZ <B2> <B3>	Jump to memory location addressed by bytes B2 and B3 if zero flag is at logic 0
312	JZ <B2> <B3>	Jump to memory location addressed by bytes B2 and B3 if zero flag is at logic 1
322	JNC <B2> <B3>	Jump to memory location addressed by bytes B2 and B3 if carry flag is at logic 0
332	JC <B2> <B3>	Jump to memory location addressed by bytes B2 and B3 if carry flag is at logic 1
342	JPO <B2> <B3>	Jump to memory location addressed by bytes B2 and B3 if parity flag is at logic 0

352	JPE <B2> <B3>	Jump to memory location addressed by bytes B2 and B3 if parity flag is at logic 1
362	JP <B2> <B3>	Jump to memory location addressed by bytes B2 and B3 if sign flag is at logic 0
372	JM <B2> <B3>	Jump to memory location addressed by bytes B2 and B3 if sign flag is at logic 1
304	CNZ <B2> <B3>	Call subroutine at memory location addressed by bytes B2 and B3 if zero flag is at location 0
314	CZ <B2> <B3>	Call subroutine at memory location addressed by bytes B2 and B3 if zero flag is at logic 1
324	CNC <B2> <B3>	Call subroutine at memory location addressed by bytes B2 and B3 if carry flag is at logic 0
334	CC <B2> <B3>	Call subroutine at memory location addressed by bytes B2 and B3 if carry flag is at logic 1
344	CPO <B2> <B3>	Call subroutine at memory location addressed by bytes B2 and B3 if parity flag is at logic 0
354	CPE <B2> <B3>	Call subroutine at memory location addressed by bytes B2 and B3 if parity flag is at logic 1
364	CP <B2> <B3>	Call subroutine at memory location addressed by bytes B2 and B3 if sign flag is at logic 0
374	CM <B2> <B3>	Call subroutine at memory location addressed by bytes B2 and B3 if sign flag is at logic 1
300	RNZ	Return from subroutine if zero flag is at logic 0
310	RZ	Return from subroutine if zero flag is at logic 1
320	RNC	Return from subroutine if carry flag is at logic 0
330	RC	Return from subroutine if carry flag is at logic 1
340	RPO	Return from subroutine if parity flag is at logic 0
350	RPE	Return from subroutine if parity flag is at logic 1
360	RP	Return from subroutine if sign flag is at logic 0
370	RM	Return from subroutine if sign flag is at logic 1
303	JMP <B2> <B3>	Unconditional jump to memory location addressed by bytes B2 and B3
311	RET	Unconditional return from subroutine
315	CALL <B2> <B3>	Unconditional call of subroutine at memory location addressed by bytes B2 and B3
307	RST 0	Call subroutine at $HI = 000_8$ and $LO = 000_8$
317	RST 1	Call subroutine at $HI = 000_8$ and $LO = 010_8$
327	RST 2	Call subroutine at $HI = 000_8$ and $LO = 020_8$
337	RST 3	Call subroutine at $HI = 000_8$ and $LO = 030_8$
347	RST 4	Call subroutine at $HI = 000_8$ and $LO = 040_8$
357	RST 5	Call subroutine at $HI = 000_8$ and $LO = 050_8$
367	RST 6	Call subroutine at $HI = 000_8$ and $LO = 060_8$
377	RST 7	Call subroutine at $HI = 000_8$ and $LO = 070_8$
351	PCHL	Move contents of H and L register pair to program counter register, i.e., jump indirect to memory location M addressed by register pair H and L

Stack, I/O, and Machine Control Group

This group of instructions performs I/O, manipulates the *stack*, and alters internal control flags. *With one exception, no condition flags are affected by any instructions in this group.* The only exception is the POP PSW instruction, which affects all flags.

333	IN <B2>	Replace contents of accumulator by 8-bit data byte from input device selected by the device code given in byte B2
323	OUT <B2>	Send contents of accumulator as 8-bit data byte to output device selected by the device code given in byte B2
373	EI	Enable the interrupt system *following the execution of the next instruction*
363	DI	Disable the interrupt system *immediately following the execution of this instruction*
166	HLT	Halt the microprocessor. The registers and flags are unaffected
000	NOP	No operation. The registers and flags are unaffected
343	XTHL	Exchange the top of the stack with the contents of the H and L register pair. The contents of register L is exchanged with the contents of the memory location SP, whose address is specified by the contents of the stack pointer register. The contents of register H is exchanged with the contents of memory location SP+1
301	POP B	Pop stack and move contents to register pair B and C. Move contents of memory location SP to register C and contents of memory location SP+1 to register B. Increment contents of stack pointer register by two
321	POP D	Pop stack and move contents to register pair D and E. Move contents of memory location SP to register E and contents of memory location SP+1 to register D. Increment contents of stack pointer register by two
341	POP H	Pop stack and move contents to register pair H and L. Move contents of memory location SP to register L and contents of memory location SP+1 to register H. Increment contents of stack pointer register by two
361	POP PSW	Pop stack and move contents to the accumulator and restore the condition flags. Move contents of memory location SP to restore the condition flags and contents of memory location SP+1 to the accumulator. Increment contents of stack pointer register by two. The HI and LO bytes of the PSW register pair is given by

Accumulator Byte	S	Z	O	AC	O	P	1	C

The letters S, Z, AC, P, and C refer to the sign, zero, auxiliary carry, parity, and carry flags.

305	PUSH B	Push stack by moving contents of register pair B and C to memory locations SP−1 and SP−2, respectively. Decrement contents of stack pointer register by two
325	PUSH D	Push stack by moving contents of register pair D and E to memory locations SP−1 and SP−2, respectively. Decrement contents of stack pointer register by two
345	PUSH H	Push stack by moving contents of register pair H and L to memory locations SP−1 and SP−2, respectively. Decrement contents of stack pointer register by two

365 PUSH PSW Push stack by moving contents of accumulator and the condition flags to memory locations SP−1 and SP−2, respectively. Decrement contents of stack pointer register by two. The location of the logic states for the five flags are given for the POP PSW instruction above

8080 INSTRUCTION SUMMARY

Single-Byte Instructions

INR r	0S4	INX B	003	POP B	301	RNZ	300	XCHG	353
DCR r	0S5	INX D	023	POP D	321	RZ	310	XTHL	343
		INX H	043	POP H	341	RNC	320	SPHL	371
MOV r_1r_2	1DS	INX SP	063	POP PSW	361	RC	330	PCHL	351
ADD r	20S	DCX B	013	PUSH B	305	RPO	340	HLT	166
ADC r	21S	DCX D	033	PUSH D	325	RPE	350	NOP	000
SUB r	22S	DCX H	053	PUSH H	345	RP	360	DI	363
SBB 4	23S	DCX SP	073	PUSH PSW	365	RM	370	EI	373
ANA r	24S					RET	311	DAA	0¹7
XRA r	25S	DAD B	011	STAX B	002	RLC	007	CMA	057
ORA r	26S	DAD D	031	STAX D	022	RRC	017	STC	067
CMP r	27S	DAD H	051	LDAX B	012	RAL	027	CMC	077
		DAD SP	071	LDAX D	032	RAR	037	RST	3X7

S *and* D: B = 0, C = 1, D = 2, E = 3, H= 4, L = 5, M = 6, accumulator = 7
X: 0 through 7

Two-Byte Instructions

ADI <B2>	306	IN <B2>	333	MVI B <B2>	006
ACI <B2>	316	OUT <B2>	323	MVI C <B2>	016
SUI <B2>	326			MVI D <B2>	026
SBI <B2>	336			MVI E <B2>	036
ANI <B2>	346			MVI H <B2>	046
XRI <B2>	356			MVI L <B2>	056
ORI <B2>	366			MVI M <B2>	066
CPI <B2>	376			MVI A <B2>	076

Three-Byte Instructions

JNZ <B2> <B3>	302	CNZ <B2> <B3>	304	LXI B <B2> <B3>	001
JZ <B2> <B3>	312	CZ <B2> <B3>	314	LXI D <B2> <B3>	021
JNC <B2> <B3>	322	CNC <B2> <B3>	324	LXI H <B2> <B3>	041
JC <B2> <B3>	332	CC <B2> <B3>	334	LXI SP <B2> <B3>	061
JPO <B2> <B3>	342	CPO <B2> <B3>	344		
JPE <B2> <B3>	352	CPE <B2> <B3>	354	STA <B2> <B3>	062
JP <B2> <B3>	362	CP <B2> <B3>	364	LDA <B2> <B3>	072
JM <B2> <B3>	372	CM <B2> <B3>	374	SHLD <B2> <B3>	042
JMP <B2> <B3>	303	CALL <B2> <B3>	315	LHLD <B2> <B3>	052

ASSEMBLY LANGUAGE

Once you begin to program in binary, octal, or hexadecimal machine language, you will quickly learn that it can be rather difficult. The problem is that many machine language instructions refer to specific locations in memory. If you desire to make changes in the program, you may need to change memory locations in order to accommodate new instructions inserted at specified points in the original program. One way around this problem is to write your programs in *assembly language.*

The term *assembly* refers to the process whereby instructions written in symbolic form by the programmer are changed to machine language by a computer. Related terms include the following:

assemble—To translate from a symbolic program to a binary program by substituting binary operation codes for symbolic operation codes and replacing symbolic addresses with absolute or relocatable addresses.[4]

assembler—A program that prepares a program in machine language from a program in symbolic language by substituting absolute operation codes for symbolic operation codes and absolute or relocatable addresses for symbolic addresses.[4]

assembly language—A computer language that has one-to-one correspondence with an assembly program. The assembly program directs a computer to operate on a program in symbolic language to produce a program in machine language.[4]

assembly language programming, symbolic language programming—The writing of program instructions in a language that facilitates the translation of programs into binary code through the use of mnemonic instructions such as ADD, MPY, SUB, DIV, STO, etc.[4]

assembly program—A program that enables a computer to assemble mnemonic language into machine language. Also called assembly routine.[4]

symbolic address—Also called floating address. In digital computer programming, a label chosen in a routine to identify a particular word, function, or other information independent of the location of the information within the routine.

symbolic code—A code by which programs are expressed in source language; that is, storage locations and machine operations are referred to by symbolic names and addresses that do not depend upon their hardware-determined names and addresses. Also called pseudocode.[4]

symbolic coding—In digital computer programming, any coding system using symbolic rather than actual computer addresses.[4]

symbolic programming—A program using symbols instead of numbers for the operations and locations in a computer. Although the writing of the program is easier and faster, an assembly program must be used to decode the symbol into machine language and to assign instruction locations.[4]

It is important to understand the difference between machine and assembly languages. In machine language programming:

- Each instruction in the program is a specific binary number or group of binary numbers.
- Storage locations for data and information are given specific binary addresses in memory.
- Subroutines are located at specific binary addresses in memory.
- Each instruction in the program is located at a specific binary address in memory.
- Once written, the program is ready to run.
- As alternatives to binary memory addressing, octal or hexadecimal memory addressing can be employed.
- Changes in the program are made with difficulty. Changes in the binary addresses of instructions, data, or subroutines may be required.

In assembly language programming:

- Each instruction in the program is a single mnemonic code or group of mnemonic codes.
- Storage locations for data and information are also given symbolic (or mnemonic) names.
- Subroutines are located at addresses given by mnemonic names called *labels*.
- Each instruction in the program is located at an address characterized by a *label*.
- Once written, the program isn't ready to run. It must be passed through an assembler to convert the symbolic (or mnemonic) code into machine language.
- Binary, octal, or hexadecimal memory addressing are not usually employed, although they can be where convenient.
- Changes in the program are made with relative ease. Since none of the memory addresses for instructions, data, or subroutines have been set, new steps can be inserted anywhere in the assembly language program without causing any difficulty.

The differences between machine and assembly language instructions will be explored in the next section.

MACHINE LANGUAGE VS. ASSEMBLY LANGUAGE PROGRAMS

We will now write a simple computer program in both 8080 machine and 8080 assembly language and compare the two programs. The program is typical of that which we will use in subsequent chapters:

- Subtract the contents of the accumulator from the contents of the accumulator, i.e., clear the accumulator.
- Send a device select pulse and the contents of the accumulator to a device called "PRINTER," which has a device code of 000_8.

- Jump unconditionally to the first instruction in the program, which is at a memory location called "START," which is at the memory location $HI = 000_8$ and $LO = 000_8$.

Octal coding is used in the machine language program, which is as follows:

LO Memory Address	Octal Instruction	Comments
000_8	227	Subtract the contents of the accumulator from the contents of the accumulator, i.e., clear the accumulator
001_8	323	Send a device select pulse and the contents of the accumulator to the device given in the second byte of the instruction
002_8	000	Device code
003_8	303	Jump unconditionally to memory location given by following two bytes
004_8	000	LO memory address byte
005_8	000	HI memory address byte

And the assembly language program is:

```
          *000 000
START,    SUB A
          OUT PRINTER
          JMP START
          START
PRINTER,  000
$
```

where the *labels* are:
   START = memory address at which the program starts,
   PRINTER = name of output device.

The terms *label* and *operand* are defined as follows:

label—One or more characters that serve to define a byte of data, the location of an instruction or subroutine, or an input or output device.

operand—The quantity that is affected, manipulated, produced, or operated upon.

To emphasize a point made previously, *in assembly language programming, we desire to be able to address data locations, data bytes, devices, instructions, and subroutines by symbolic names instead of by 8-bit or 16-bit octal codes.*

Note that in the assembly language program, no octal codes are present. All instructions are written in terms of their mnemonics and the output device is given a name, PRINTER. The starting location of the program is called START rather than $HI = 000_8$ and $LO = 000_8$. The use of assembly language programming is considerably easier than machine language programming, but the latter has one important advantage: it is ready to be executed on the microcomputer, whereas the assembly language program is not. With an assembly language program, one must sort through a table and assign address values to labels and operation code values to operands. One can "hand assemble" a program by assigning address values and by looking up octal equivalents for the mnemonics. Computers are also extremely well suited to this task using "assembler" or "cross assembler" programs.

INTRODUCTION TO THE EXAMPLES

Since programming is one of the important new skills that you must master if you wish to effectively use microcomputers, here we provide a variety of programming examples that test some of the characteristics of the 8080 instruction set. Some of the more unusual instructions are emphasized, such as PUSH, POP, and DAA, along with several output programs that you can use in conjunction with an 8-bit latch/display circuit, which you will learn how to construct in Chapter 7.

EXAMPLE NO. 1

Purpose

The purpose of this example is to demonstrate how to clear the microcomputer memory.

Program

LO Memory Address	Octal Instruction	Mnemonic	Comments
000	227	SUB A	Clear the accumulator
001	041	LXI H	Load the following two data bytes into registers L and H, respectively
002	011		L data byte
003	000		H data byte
004	167	MOV M,A	Move contents of accumulator to the memory location addressed by the register pair H and L
005	043	INX H	Increment the register pair H and L by one
006	303	JMP	Unconditional jump to the memory location given in the following two bytes
007	004		LO memory address byte
010	000		HI memory address byte

Comments

This program permits you to clear read/write memory, essentially all 65,536 locations if you so desire, starting at HI = 000 and LO = 011.

As soon as it clears location HI = 377 and LO = 377, it starts to clear the program itself. It gets as far as memory location HI = 000 and LO = 004. Finally, it loops indefinitely between locations LO = 004 and LO = 010.

The NOP instruction is 000. Thus, a cleared read/write memory location, if treated as an instruction byte, will not perform any useful microcomputer operation. By clearing the read/write memory beforehand, you can prevent undesired program execution when you are testing a new program. [One problem is that you usually do not have 65K of microcomputer memory. A nonexistent memory location provides the 8080 microprocessor chip with a 377; when this is treated as an instruction byte, the 8080 calls a subroutine at locations HI = 000 and LO = 070. To minimize such a problem, you may wish to load instruction byte 166 (HLT) at HI = 000 and LO = 070.] It should be noted, however, that it is *not* necessary to clear the memory before it is used by the microcomputer.

EXAMPLE NO. 2

Purpose

The purpose of this example is to attempt to read the contents of the B and C registers, which are set to the values 010_8 and 001_8, respectively.

Program

LO Memory Address	Octal Instruction	Mnemonic	Comments
000	041	LXI H	Load the following two data bytes into registers L and H, respectively
001	200		L data byte
002	000		H data byte
003	001	LXI B	Load the following two data bytes into registers C and B, respectively
004	001		C data byte
005	010		B data byte
006	166	HLT	Halt

Comments

You should be able to successfully execute this program, but you will not know whether anything happened since all data remains within the 8080 chip. See the following example (Example No. 3) for one of the possible solutions to the problem of monitoring the contents of the internal registers.

EXAMPLE NO. 3

Purpose

The purpose of this example is to write into memory the contents of the B and C registers, which are set to the values 010_8 and 001_8, respectively.

Program

LO Memory Address	Octal Instruction	Mnemonic	Comments
000	041	LXI H	Load the following two data bytes into registers L and H, respectively
001	200		L data byte
002	000		H data byte
003	001	LXI B	Load the following two data bytes into registers C and B, respectively
004	001		C data byte
005	010		B data byte
006	160	MOV M,B	Move contents of register B to memory location addressed by the register pair H and L
007	043	INX H	Increment the register pair H and L by one
010	161	MOV M,C	Move contents of register C to memory location addressed by the register pair H and L
011	166	HLT	Halt

Comments

With Example No. 2, you learned that *it is impossible to observe directly the contents of registers, B, C, D, E, H, and L.* You can observe the contents of the accumulator more or less directly with the aid of an OUT instruction and a pair of latches (you will do this in Chapter 7). However, you must resort to some gimmicks in order to determine the contents of the six general-purpose registers. Such gimmicks include the following:

- Storing the contents of the registers in memory, then examining the contents of memory while the microcomputer is in the HOLD state.
- Pushing the contents of the registers onto the stack, then examining the contents of the memory locations in the stack while the microcomputer is in the HOLD state.
- Moving the contents of each register to the accumulator, then providing an OUT instruction and latching the contents of the accumulator. You can do this with each register in turn, and can actu-

ally follow the register contents while the microcomputer is still running.

It would be nice to have a group of seven LED registers, each register containing eight bits, that would continuously display the contents of the six general-purpose registers and the accumulator. With the 8080 microprocessor, it is not possible to do so as direct outputs from the chip.

EXAMPLE NO. 4

Purpose

The purpose of this example is to load into the stack region of memory the contents of the B and C registers, which are set to the values 010_8 and 011_8, respectively.

Program

LO Memory Address	Octal Instruction	Mnemonic	Comments
000	061	LXI SP	Load the following two data bytes into the stack pointer register
001	202		LO stack pointer byte
002	000		HI stack pointer byte
003	001	LXI B	Load the following two data bytes into registers C and B, respectively
004	001		C data byte
005	010		B data byte
006	305	PUSH B	Replace the contents of memory locations M(SP−1) and M(SP−2) by the contents of registers B and C, respectively
007	166	HLT	Halt

Comments

This program loads the contents of register B into memory location HI = 000 and LO = 201, and the contents of register C into memory location HI = 000 and LO = 200. The stack pointer is decremented by one before each register's contents is pushed on the stack. Once the program has come to a halt, you can address the stack locations and demonstrate that the register contents have been stored there.

EXAMPLE NO. 5

Purpose

The purpose of this example is to pop prestored data from the stack region in memory, increment and decrement the contents of the popped data, and then push it back on the stack. Register pair B is employed.

Program

LO Memory Address	Octal Instruction	Mnemonic	Comments
000	061	LXI SP	Load the following two data bytes into the stack pointer register
001	200		LO stack pointer byte
002	000		HI stack pointer byte
003	227	SUB A	Clear the accumulator
004	301	POP B	Replace the contents of registers B and C by the contents of stack locations M(SP+1) and M(SP), respectively
005	004	INR B	Increment contents of register B by one
006	015	DCR C	Decrement contents of register C by one
007	305	PUSH B	Replace the contents of memory locations M(SP−1) and M(SP−2) by the contents of registers B and C, respectively (Note: keep in mind that the stack pointer has been incremented by two as a result of the POP B instruction at address 004s)
010	166	HLT	Halt

Data

LO Memory Address	Memory Data
200	222
201	333

Comments

When you execute this program, you will observe octal byte 221 in memory location HI = 000 and LO = 200, and octal byte 334 in memory location HI = 000 and LO = 201. The initial contents of register B are stored at LO = 201; the initial contents of register C are stored at LO = 200. Register B is incremented, and register C is decremented. The stack pointer will first increment by two, and then decrement by two. At the end of the program, the stack pointer will be at HI = 000 and LO = 200.

EXAMPLE NO. 6

Purpose

The purpose of this example is to monitor the state of the five flags, after a simple arithmetic operation, with the aid of the PUSH PSW instruction.

Program

LO Memory Address	Octal Instruction	Mnemonic	Comments
000	061	LXI SP	Load the following two data bytes into the stack pointer register
001	202		LO stack pointer byte
002	000		HI stack pointer byte
003	227	SUB A	Subtract the contents of the accumulator from the contents of the accumulator, i.e., clear the accumulator
004	365	PUSH PSW	Replace the contents of memory locations M(SP—1) and M(SP—2) by the contents of the accumulator and the state of the five condition flags, respectively
005	166	HLT	Halt

Comments

This is a useful program that permits you to test how arithmetic and logical instructions influence the five flags: sign, zero, auxiliary carry, parity, and carry. After you perform an arithmetic operation at LO = 003, you push the contents of the flags and the accumulator onto the stack. After the microcomputer has halted, you can go directly to the stack region and determine the flag status. The 16-bit program status word appears as follows in the stack:

The accumulator byte is the HI register byte and is stored at LO = 201. The flag byte is stored at LO = 200. The letters S, Z, AC, P, and C in the above illustration refer to the sign, zero, auxiliary carry, parity, and carry flags.

When you execute this program and examine memory location LO = 200, you will observe the 8-bit byte 01010110, which signifies the following:

  $Z = 0$ Result is positive
  $S = 1$ Result is zero
  $AC = 1$ (meaningless)
  $P = 1$ Result has even parity
  $C = 0$ Result has no carry

If you modify the instruction bytes at LO = 004 through LO = 006 as shown below and then execute the program, you will observe the 8-bit byte 00000010 at LO = 200.

LO Memory Address	Octal Instruction	Mnemonic	Comments
004	074	INR A	Increment the contents of the accumulator by one
005	365	PUSH PSW	Push the contents of the accumulator and the flags onto the stack
006	166	HLT	Halt

The accumulator byte at LO = 201 will be 001. These results signify the following:

S = 0 Result is positive
Z = 0 Result is not zero
AC = 0 Result has no carry from bit D3 to bit D4 in the accumulator
P = 0 Result has odd parity
C = 0 Result has no carry

This type of program shows you the state of individual flags before you attempt to use conditional branch instructions. All logical and most arithmetic operations alter the flags. Once you know how a flag will behave, you can employ the appropriate arithmetic/logical instructions and conditional branch instructions in your main program.

EXAMPLE NO. 7

Purpose

The purpose of this example is to explore the conditional jump instructions and to determine when a jump occurs. (See Fig. 3-14.)

Program

LO Memory Address	Octal Instruction	Mnemonic	Comments
000	061	LXI SP	Load the following two data bytes into the stack pointer register
001	200		LO stack pointer byte
002	000		HI stack pointer byte
003	361	POP PSW	Pop the contents of the accumulator and the flags from the stack
004	*	*	Operation code for any of the eight conditional instructions (JNZ, JZ, JNC, JC, JPO, JPE, JP, or JM)
005	004		LO memory address byte
006	000		HI memory address byte
007	166	HLT	Halt
200	*	*	Flag data byte that will be popped off stack
201	000		Accumulator data byte that will be popped off stack

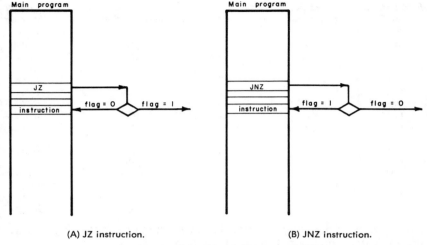

(A) JZ instruction.   (B) JNZ instruction.

Fig. 3-14. Conditional instructions JZ and JNZ.

Prior to executing this program, you first load memory with a program status word, the flag byte appearing at HI = 000 and LO = 200, and the accumulator data byte at HI = 000 and LO = 201. You also load a desired conditional jump instruction at memory address HI = 000 and LO = 004. Having done so, execution of the program permits you to test how different flag bits influence the execution of any of the eight conditional jump instructions.

To demonstrate the program, you may wish to compare the JNZ and JZ conditional jump instructions, which are represented schematically in Fig. 3-14.

With a flag byte of **002** at LO = 200 and the JNZ instruction byte, **302**, at LO = 004, you should observe that the executed program loops between LO = 004 and LO = 006. The sign flag, S, is at logic 0, which indicates to the 8080 chip that the "not zero" condition exists; a jump to HI = 000 and LO = 004 therefore occurs. If you change the flag byte from **002** to **102**, no jump will occur and the program will come to a halt.

With a flag byte of **002** and the JZ instruction byte, you should observe that the program comes to a halt. When you change the flag to **102**, the program loops between LO = 004 and LO = 006. This behavior is predictable from the nature of the JZ instruction, in which a jump occurs only if the zero flag, Z, is at logic 1.

We can summarize the program behavior for different popped flag bytes and different conditional jump instructions as shown in the following list.

Flag Byte at LO = 200	Flag Bit of Interest	Logic State of Flag Bit	Conditional Jump Instruction	Program Behavior
002	Z	0	JNZ	loops
102	Z	1	JNZ	halts
002	Z	0	JZ	halts
102	Z	1	JZ	loops
002	C	0	JNC	loops
003	C	1	JNC	halts
002	C	0	JC	halts
003	C	1	JC	loops
002	P	0	JPO	loops
006	P	1	JPO	halts
002	P	0	JPE	halts
006	P	1	JPE	loops
002	S	0	JP	loops
202	S	1	JP	halts
002	S	0	JM	halts
202	S	1	JM	loops

In each case in the above listing, we have tested one of the flag bits for the indicated conditional jump instruction.

EXAMPLE NO. 8

Purpose

The purpose of this example is to demonstrate the execution of a program that contains a *nest* of subroutines.

Program No. 1

To change the stack pointer location to HI = 003 and LO = 003, use the following program:

LO Memory Address	Octal Instruction	Mnemonic	Comments
000	061	LXP SP	Load stack pointer with address given by following two bytes
001	003		LO address byte of stack pointer
002	003		HI address byte of stack pointer
003	166	HLT	Halt

The flowchart for this program is shown in Fig. 3-15.

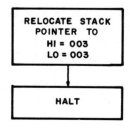

Fig. 3-15. Flowchart for Program No. 1.

Program No. 2

After executing Program No. 1, load the main program, which starts at HI = 000.

LO Memory Address	Octal Instruction	Mnemonic	Comments
000	317	RST 1	Call subroutine at HI = 000 and LO = 010
001	166	HLT	Halt
010	327	RST 2	Call subroutine at HI = 000 and LO = 020
011	311	RET	Return from subroutine
020	337	RST 3	Call subroutine at HI = 000 and LO = 030
021	311	RET	Return from subroutine
030	000	NOP	No operation
031	311	RET	Return from subroutine

The flowchart for Program No. 2 is shown in Fig. 3-16.

Comments

Since this example demonstrates how the microcomputer handles nested subroutines, the program *execution* is listed below in full detail.

Address Bytes HI	LO	Data Bus	Mnemonic	Comments
000	000	317	RST 1	Store program counter on stack, then jump to subroutine at LO = 010
003	002	000		Program counter HI address byte
003	001	001		Program counter LO address byte
000	010	327	RST 2	Store program counter on stack, then jump to subroutine at LO = 020
003	000	000		Program counter HI address byte
002	377	011		Program counter LO address byte
000	020	337	RST 3	Store program counter on stack, then jump to subroutine at LO = 030
002	376	000		Program counter HI address byte
002	375	021		Program counter LO address byte
000	030	000	NOP	No operation
000	031	311	RET	Pop program off of stack, i.e., return from Subroutine 3

Let us pause at this point in the program execution and examine what has happened so far. We have called three subroutines. Three sets of program counter bytes have been stored on the stack and the stack pointer has been shifted down. We have now executed our first RET instruction and are ready to observe the program counter bytes being popped off the stack.

| 002 | 375 | 021 | | Program counter LO address byte |
| 002 | 376 | 000 | | Program counter HI address byte |

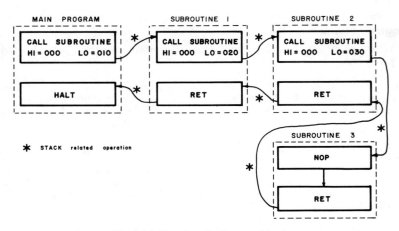

Fig. 3-16. Flowchart for Program No. 2.

000	021	311	RET	Pop program counter off of stack, i.e., return from Subroutine 2
002	377	011		Program counter LO address byte
003	000	000		Program counter HI address byte
000	011	311	RET	Pop program counter off of stack, i.e., return from Subroutine 1
003	001	001		Program counter LO address byte
003	002	000		Program counter HI address byte
000	001	000	HLT	Halt

The above program should convince you that you can nest any number of subroutines. The only requirement is that you provide sufficient read/write memory for the stack. The microcomputer will handle all of the bookkeeping chores associated with the call and return instructions. You may now wish to refer again to the flowchart for Program No. 2.

EXAMPLE NO. 9

Purpose

The purpose of this example is to demonstrate how you can determine the consequences of different accumulator instructions.

Some 8080 Accumulator Instructions

Many of the 8080 instructions involve the accumulator register, which is also known as register A. In this example, you are provided with a simple program that will allow you to test a variety of accumulator instructions, which include some of the following:

| *Octal Instruction* | *Mnemonic* | *Comments* |
| 007 | RLC | Rotate contents of accumulator left one position |

017	RRC	Rotate contents of accumulator right one position
027	RAL	Rotate contents of accumulator left one position through carry flag
037	RAR	Rotate contents of accumulator right one position through carry flag
047	DAA	Decimal adjust accumulator
057	CMA	Complement the contents of the accumulator
072 <B2> <B3>	LDA	Load the accumulator direct with the contents of the memory address given by the <B2> and <B3> address bytes
074	INR A	Increment the contents of the accumulator by one
075	DCR A	Decrement the contents of the accumulator by one
076 <B2>	MVI A	Load the accumulator with the 8-bit byte that immediately follows
170	MOV A,B	Move the contents of register B to the accumulator
171	MOV A,C	Move the contents of register C to the accumulator
172	MOV A,D	Move the contents of register D to the accumulator
173	MOV A,E	Move the contents of register E to the accumulator
174	MOV A,H	Move the contents of register H to the accumulator
175	MOV A,L	Move the contents of register L to the accumulator
176	MOV A,M	Move the contents of the memory location, whose address is given by the register pair H and L, to the accumulator
177	MOV A,A	Move the contents of the accumulator to the accumulator
200	ADD B	Add the contents of register B to the contents of the accumulator
206	ADD M	Add the contents of the memory location, whose address is given by the register pair H and L, to the contents of the accumulator
207	ADD A	Add the contents of the accumulator to the contents of the accumulator
210	ADC B	Add carry bit and contents of register B to the contents of the accumulator
217	ADC A	Add carry bit and contents of accumulator to the contents of the accumulator
220	SUB B	Subtract the contents of register B from the contents of the accumulator
227	SUB A	Clear the accumulator
230	SBB B	Subtract the carry bit and contents of register B from the contents of the accumulator
240	ANA B	AND the contents of register B with the contents of the accumulator
247	ANA A	AND the contents of the accumulator with the contents of the accumulator

Octal Instruction	Mnemonic	Comments
250	XRA B	Exclusive-OR the contents of register B with the contents of the accumulator
257	XRA A	Clear the accumulator
260	ORA B	OR the contents of register B with the contents of the accumulator
267	ORA A	OR the contents of the accumulator with the contents of the accumulator
270	CMP B	Compare the contents of register B with the contents of the accumulator
276	CMP M	Compare the contents of the memory location, whose address is given by the register pair H and L, with the contents of the accumulator
277	CMP A	Compare the contents of the accumulator with the contents of the accumulator
306 <B2>	ADI	Add the 8-bit byte that immediately follows to the contents of the accumulator
316 <B2>	ACI	Add the 8-bit byte that immediately follows and the carry bit to the contents of the accumulator
326 <B2>	SUI	Subtract the 8-bit byte that immediately follows from the contents of the accumulator
336 <B2>	SBI	Subtract the 8-bit byte that immediately follows and the carry bit from the contents of the accumulator
346 <B2>	ANI	AND the 8-bit byte that immediately follows with the contents of the accumulator
356 <B2>	XRI	Exclusive-OR the 8-bit byte that immediately follows with the contents of the accumulator
361	POP PSW	Pop the stack and store the contents in the accumulator and the flag flip-flops
366 <B2>	ORI	OR the 8-bit byte that immediately follows with the contents of the accumulator
376 <B2>	CPI	Compare the 8-bit byte that immediately follows with the contents of the accumulator

Program

LO Memory Address	Octal Instruction	Mnemonic	
000	061	LXI SP	Load the following two data bytes into the stack pointer register
001	000		LO stack pointer byte
002	001		HI stack pointer byte
003	227	SUB A	Clear the accumulator
004	016	MVI C	Move following byte into register C
005	002		Timing byte for register C
006	315	CALL	Unconditional call of subroutine located at memory address given by following two bytes

007	100		LO memory address byte
010	000		HI memory address byte
011	007	RLC	Rotate the contents of the accumulator left one position
012	074	INR A	Increment the contents of the accumulator by one
013	000	NOP	No operation
014	000	NOP	No operation
015	000	NOP	No operation
016	323	OUT	Generate device select pulse that allows an 8-bit latch to latch the contents of the accumulator
017	000	000	Device code for 8-bit latch
020	303	JMP	Unconditional jump to location given by following two address bytes
021	004		LO memory address byte
022	000		HI memory address byte

Subroutine (Generates a Time Delay)

LO Memory Address	Octal Instruction	Mnemonic	Comments
100	021	LXI D	Move following two bytes into registers E and D, respectively
101	301		Timing byte for register E
102	150		Timing byte for register D
103	035	DCR E	Decrement contents of register E by one
104	302	JNZ	If register E is 000_8, ignore this instruction; otherwise, jump to memory address given in following two bytes
105	103		LO address byte
106	000		HI address byte
107	025	DCR D	Decrement contents of register D by one
110	302	JNZ	If register D is 000_8, ignore this instruction; otherwise, jump to memory address given in following two bytes
111	103		LO address byte
112	000		HI address byte
113	015	DCR C	Decrement contents of register C by one
114	302	JNZ	If register C is 000_8, ignore this instruction; otherwise, jump to memory address given in following two bytes
115	100		LO address byte
116	000		HI address byte
117	311	RET	Unconditional return from this subroutine

Comments

This program requires an 8-bit output latch and display to permit you to observe the results of the arithmetic and logical operations that you perform on the accumulator contents. Refer to the circuits described in Chapter 7.

The subroutine starting at HI = 000 and LO = 100 generates time delays ranging from 0.200 second to 51.2 seconds through variations in the timing byte for register C at LO memory address 005.

If you execute the program as it stands, you will observe that the output display quickly fills up with logic 1's, starting from right to left. At memory addresses 011 through 015, you have five program bytes with which you can perform different types of accumulator operations. Thus, with the program segment:

011	076	MVI A	Load the following byte into the accumulator
012	360	360	Data byte corresponding to the binary word 11110000_2
013	346	ANI	AND the data that follows with the contents of the accumulator
014	252	252	Data byte corresponding to the binary word 10101010_2
015	000	NOP	No operation

you should observe that the AND operation between the byte 11110000 and the byte 10101010 produces the logical result 10100000, an operation that proceeds bit by bit. By changing the logical instruction at LO = 013, you can demonstrate the behavior of the OR and exclusive-OR instructions on the same initial data.

If you execute the following program segment contained within the main program:

011	074	INR A	Increment the contents of the accumulator by one
012	067	STC	Set the carry flag to logic one
013	077	CMC	Complement the carry flag
014	047	DAA	Decimal adjust the accumulator
015	000	NOP	No operation

you should observe a decimal output count from 0 to 99 on the output display. The **047** instruction is the decimal adjust accumulator instruction, which converts the result of adding two bcd numbers in binary back to a pair of packed bcd numbers. It is *not* a binary-to-bcd conversion instruction as such.

EXAMPLE NO. 10

Purpose

The purpose of this example is to demonstrate the BCD Input and Direct Conversion to Binary Routine, which is No. 80-147 in the Intel

Microcomputer User's Library. This program was developed by M. H. Gansler.

Program

LO Memory Address	Instruction Byte	Mnemonic	Description
000	076	MVI A	Move immediate byte to the accumulator
001	*		Two-bcd-digit data byte that is to be converted to an 8-bit binary number
002	117	MOV C,A	Move contents of accumulator to register C
003	346	ANI	AND immediate byte with contents of the accumulator
004	017	017	Mask byte that masks out the most significant bcd digit
005	137	MOV E,A	Move contents of accumulator to register E
006	171	MOV A,C	Move contents of register C to the accumulator
007	346	ANI	AND immediate byte with contents of the accumulator
010	360	360	Mask byte that masks out the least significant bcd digit
011	017	RRC	Rotate the accumulator contents one bit to the right and into the carry flag
012	017	RRC	Rotate the accumulator contents one bit to the right and into the carry flag
013	117	MOV C,A	Move contents of accumulator into register C
014	017	RRC	Rotate the accumulator contents one bit to the right and into the carry flag
015	017	RRC	Same as above
016	201	ADD C	Add contents of register C to the contents of the accumulator
017	007	RLC	Rotate the accumulator contents one bit to the left and into the carry flag
020	203	ADD E	Add contents of register E to the contents of the accumulator
021	323	OUT	Output contents of accumulator to output port given in the next instruction byte
022	000	000	Device code for output port zero
023	166	HLT	Halt

Comments

The program starts with the two-bcd-digit number in the accumulator. The result is stored in the accumulator.

To convert the program into a subroutine, substitute the RET instruction for the HLT instruction at LO = 023. The program can be located anywhere in memory.

If you attempt to execute this program, you may wish to compare your results with those shown below:

Decimal Number	Observed Binary Number
1	00000001
10	00001010
20	00010100
50	00110010
75	01001011
80	01010000
90	01011010
99	01100011

EXAMPLE NO. 11

Purpose

The purpose of this example is to demonstrate a 16-digit bcd addition subroutine, in which two bcd numbers are added together to produce a result that is less than or equal to 9,999,999,999,999,999. This program is listed and described in considerable detail in the μCOM-8 *Software Manual* and is given here courtesy of NEC Microcomputers, Inc. The program is started at memory location HI = 003 and LO = 024.

Program

LO Memory Address	Instruction Byte	Mnemonic	Description
024	021	LXI D	Load immediate two bytes into registers E and D, respectively
025	347		Registers D and E contain the 16-bit
026	003		address of the least significant digits in the augend
027	041	LXI H	Load immediate two bytes into registers L and H, respectively
030	357		Registers H and L contain the 16-bit
031	003		address of the least significant digits in the addend
ADD16: 032	365	PUSH PSW	Push the program status word onto the stack (NOTE: Make certain that you have loaded the stack pointer before you execute this program.)
033	305	PUSH B	Push the contents of register pair B,C onto the stack
034	016	MVI C	Move the immediate byte into register C
035	010		Binary number equal to one-half the number of bcd digits. Thus, for 16 bcd digits, the octal code would be 010
036	257	XRA A	Clear the accumulator and carry flag
LOOP2: 037	032	LDAX D	Load the accumulator from the memory location addressed by register pair D,E

040	216	ADC M	Add the contents of the memory location addressed by register pair H,L to the contents of the accumulator
041	047	DAA	Decimal adjust the contents of the accumulator
042	022	STAX D	Store the contents of the accumulator into the memory location addressed by register pair D,E
043	015	DCR C	Decrement contents of register C by one
044	312	JZ	Jump to the memory location DONE2 if the contents of register C are zero
045	054		LO address byte of DONE2
046	003		HI address byte of DONE2
047	053	DCX H	Decrement contents of register pair H,L by one
050	033	DCX D	Decrement contents of register pair D,E by one
051	303	JMP	Jump to the memory location LOOP2
052	037		LO address byte of LOOP2
053	003		HI address byte of LOOP2
DONE2: 054	301	POP B	Pop contents of register pair B,C off of stack
055	361	POP PSW	Pop the program status word off of stack
056	172	MOV A,D	Move contents of register D to accumulator
057	323	OUT	Output contents of accumulator
060	001	001	Device code of port one
061	173	MOV A,E	Move contents of register E to accumulator
062	323	OUT	Output contents of accumulator
063	000	000	Device code of port zero
064	166	HLT	Halt

Discussion

This program starts with a 16-digit bcd augend in LO memory addresses 340 through 347, with the least significant bcd digit in location 347 and the most significant bcd digit in location 340. The 16-digit bcd addend is initially in LO memory addresses 350 through 357, with the least significant bcd digit in location 357 and the most significant bcd digit in location 350. The terms *addend* and *augend* are defined as follows:[2]

augend—In an arithmetic addition, the number increased by having another number (called the addend) added to it.

addend—A quantity which, when added to another quantity (called the augend), produces a result called the sum.

Program execution starts at HI = 003 and LO = 024. The sum replaces the augend.

Consider an augend of 1,000,000,000,000,099 and an addend of 8,000,000,000,000,001. The memory map for these two 16-digit bcd numbers is as follows (all at HI = 003):

LO Memory Address	BCD Digits	Octal Code	Binary Code
340	1,0	020	00010000
341	0,0	000	00000000
342	0 0	000	00000000
343	0,0	000	00000000
344	0,0	000	00000000
345	0,0	000	00000000
346	0,0	000	00000000
347	9,9	231	10011001
350	8,0	200	10000000
351	0,0	000	00000000
352	0,0	000	00000000
353	0,0	000	00000000
354	0,0	000	00000000
355	0,0	000	00000000
356	0,0	000	00000000
357	0,1	001	00000001

When these two numbers are added, the sum (9,000,000,000,000,100) replaces the augend in memory locations HI = 003 and LO = 340 to HI = 003 and LO = 347.

You should observe the following sequence of bcd numbers in successive memory locations starting at LO = 340:

90
00
00
00
00
00
01
00

which correspond to the 16-digit bcd number 9,000,000,000,000,100.

You may wish to add the following bcd numbers and compare your results with the predicted sums.

Augend	Addend	Sum
3,000,000,000,000,100	1,000,000,000,000,001	4,000,000,000,000,101
0,000,000,000,123,456	0,000,000,000,240,833	0,000,000,000,364,289
0,000,000,000,927,928	0,000,000,000,844,992	0,000,000,001,772,920
9,999,999,999,999,999	0,000,000,000,000,001	0,000,000,000,000,000

EXAMPLE NO. 12

Purpose

The purpose of this example is to demonstrate the Binary to BCD Subroutine, No. 8-67 in the Intel Microcomputer User's Library. The program was developed by Niels S. Gundestrup of the Geophysical Isotope Laboratory in Denmark.

LO Memory Address	Instruction Byte	Mnemonic	Description
222	021	LXI D	Move immediate two bytes into register pair D. This is the 16-bit binary number that will be converted to a 5-bcd-digit number
223	*		Least significant 8 bits of 16-bit binary number
224	*		Most significant 8 bits of 16-bit binary number
225	041	LXI H	Move immediate two bytes into register pair D. This is the memory address of the most significant digit (MSD) of the 5-digit bcd number. The remaining four digits are stored in successive memory locations, one digit per location
226	340		L register byte
227	003		H register byte
BNBCD: 230	365	PUSH PSW	Push contents of program status word on stack
231	305	PUSH B	Push contents of register pair B on stack
232	325	PUSH D	Push contents of register pair D on stack
233	345	PUSH H	Push contents of register pair H on stack
234	353	XCHG	Exchange the contents of register pair H with the contents of register pair D
235	001	LXI B	Move immediate two bytes into register pair B (10,000)
236	360		C register byte
237	330		B register byte
240	315	CALL	Call subroutine DECNO, which performs the binary to bcd conversion (MSD)
241	276		LO address byte
242	003		HI address byte
243	001	LXI B	Move immediate two bytes into register pair B (1000)
244	030		C register byte
245	374		B register byte
246	315	CALL	Call subroutine DECNO
247	276		LO address byte
250	003		HI address byte
251	001	LXI B	Move immediate two bytes into register pair B (100)
252	234		C register byte
253	377		B register byte
254	315	CALL	Call subroutine DECNO
255	276		LO address byte

LO Memory Address	Instruction Byte	Mnemonic	Description
256	003		HI address byte
257	001	LXI B	Move immediate two bytes into register pair B (10)
260	366		C register byte
261	377		B register byte
262	315	CALL	Call subroutine DECNO
263	276		LO address byte
264	003		HI address byte
265	175	MOV A,L	Move contents of register L to the accumulator
266	306	ADI	Add immediate byte to contents of accumulator
267	000	000	[NOTE: 260 if ASCII code is desired]
270	022	STAX D	Store contents of accumulator in the memory location addressed by register pair D
271	341	POP H	Pop register pair H off stack
272	321	POP D	Pop register pair D off stack
273	301	POP B	Pop register pair B off stack
274	361	POP PSW	Pop program status word off stack
275	311	RET	Return from subroutine
DECNO: 276	076	MVI A	Move following byte to accumulator
277	000	000	[NOTE: 260 if ASCII code is desired]
300	325	PUSH D	Push register D on stack
301	135	MOV E,L	Move contents of register L to register E
302	124	MOV D,H	Move contents of register H to register D
303	074	INR A	Increment contents of accumulator by one
304	011	DAD B	Add contents of register pair B to contents of register pair H and store in register pair H
305	332	JC	Jump if carry flag is at logic 1
306	301		LO address byte
307	003		HI address byte
310	075	DCR A	Decrement contents of accumulator by one
311	153	MOV L,E	Move contents of register E to register L
312	142	MOV H,D	Move contents of register D to register H
313	321	POP D	Pop register pair D off stack
314	022	STAX D	Store contents of accumulator in the memory location addressed by register pair D
315	023	INX D	Increment contents of register pair D by one
316	311	RET	Return from subroutine DECNO

Comments

This program starts with a 16-bit binary number in register pair D,E. The number is converted into a 5-bcd-digit number that is stored starting at HI = 003 and LO = 340. The most significant bcd digit is stored at this location, and the remaining four digits in subsequent locations. The least significant bcd digit is stored at LO = 344. The program BNBCD starts at HI = 003 and LO = 230; however, the 16-bit binary number must exist in register pair D, and the location of the most significant digit in register pair H. We have used LXI instructions to set this information in the registers before BNBCD is executed.

The output can be either as decimal numerals or as 8-bit ASCII code, with the most significant bit (the parity bit) at logic 1. A slight error in the original program has been corrected to permit the LSD to be stored in ASCII code.

TEST

This test probes your understanding of the programming techniques and concepts that are described in this chapter. Please write your answers on a separate piece of paper.

3-1.   Explain the difference between the following pairs of concepts:
        instruction vs. operation
        instruction vs. program
        assembly language instruction vs. mnemonic instruction
        mnemonic instruction vs. machine language instruction
        machine code vs. mnemonic code
        register vs. register pair
        program counter vs. stack pointer
        bit vs. byte
        byte vs. word
        word vs. memory address
        HI address byte vs. LO address byte
        program vs. subroutine
        routine vs. program
        instruction register vs. instruction decoder
        jump vs. call
        zero flag vs. sign flag
        carry flag vs. auxiliary carry flag
        PUSH vs. POP
        conditional jump vs. unconditional jump
        label vs. operand
        parity flag vs. sign flag
        accumulator vs. ALU
        data byte vs. address byte
        octal code vs. hexadecimal code
        increment vs. decrement
        OR vs. exclusive OR
        subtract vs. compare
        stack vs. stack pointer
        the IN vs. OUT instructions

the B register pair vs. the H register pair
the MOV vs. MVI instructions
the ADD vs. ADC instructions
carry vs. borrow

3-2. Summarize the five basic instruction groups and provide examples of instructions within each group.

3-3. Write a simple microcomputer program in both machine code and in assembly language. With assembly language, use operands and labels.

3-4. Describe the five condition flags and the logic states that characterize specific conditions.

3-5. Explain the difference between octal code and hexadecimal code, and give several examples of 8-bit data bytes written in each type of code.

3-6. Give an example of how the PUSH instruction behaves.

3-7. Give an example of how the POP instruction behaves.

3-8. List at least nine different ways in which data can be loaded into the accumulator.

3-9. Describe the four different types of rotate instructions in the 8080 microprocessor instruction set.

3-10. What 8080 microcomputer instructions would you use to:

Clear the accumulator
Set the accumulator to 11111111_2
Output data from the accumulator to an output device
Input data into the accumulator from an input device
Move data from register E into the accumulator
Move data from the accumulator into memory location $H = 000_8$ and $L = 200_8$
Move data into the accumulator from memory location $H = 000_8$ and $L = 201_8$
Move data byte 10101110_2 into the accumulator
Check the logic state of each bit in the accumulator
Multiply the contents of the accumulator by 4
Divide the contents of the accumulator by 8
Store the contents of the accumulator in a memory location stored in register pair B and C
Load the accumulator from a memory location stored in register pair D and E
Move the contents from the accumulator to a memory location
Set the carry bit to logic 0

Use the least number of instructions that you can in each case.

Your performance on this test will be acceptable if you can answer all of the above questions correctly in a four-hour closed-book examination.

WHAT HAVE YOU ACCOMPLISHED IN THIS CHAPTER?

It was stated at the beginning of this chapter that at the end you would be able to do the following:

- Explain what the difference is between an instruction, operation, program, machine code instruction, assembly language instruction, and mnemonic instruction.

  You have learned the distinctions between the above terms in the text provided in this chapter.

- Define the terms: assemble, bit, byte, flag, mnemonic symbol, device code, HI address byte, LO address byte, increment, decrement, label, jump, call, return, label, operand, carry flag, parity flag, zero flag, sign flag, register, register pair, subroutine, two-byte instruction, three-byte instruction, unconditional operation, conditional operation, branch instruction, stack, stack pointer, program counter, accumulator, ALU, data byte, and instruction register.

  Definitions for these terms have been provided at the beginning and throughout this chapter.

- Classify the 8080 instructions into five groups.

  The five groups are: data transfer, arithmetic, logical, branch, and a final group composed of stack, I/O, and machine control instructions. An extensive list of the instruction set has been provided based on these five groups.

- Explain how an 8-bit instruction can be written in both octal code and hexadecimal code.

  This has been discussed in a section within this chapter.

- List the mnemonic codes, following the Intel Corporation recommendations, for at least ten different 8080 instructions.

  There are 78 different instructions, so this objective should be rather easy to fulfill.

- Explain the difference between machine language and assembly language.

  We have done this near the end of the chapter.

- Identify the HI address byte and the LO address byte in a 16-bit memory address word.

  You should have no difficulty with this objective.

- Explain what the differences are between a bit, a byte, a word, and an address.

  Definitions have been provided, with reference to the 8080 microprocessor.

- List at least ten different registers that can be found in the 8080 microprocessor chip.

  A list is provided in this chapter. The most important registers are the accumulator, B, C, D, E, H, L, stack pointer, and program counter registers, which total nine.

- Explain how the microprocessor decodes:
  instruction classes
  registers
  register pairs
  immediate operations
  branch operations
  condition flags
  increment operations
  decrement operations
  Much of this chapter has been devoted to this subject.

CHAPTER 4

Generating a Device Select Pulse

In this chapter, you will learn how to generate *device select pulses* from an 8080 microcomputer. These pulses will be employed in subsequent chapters in this Bugbook to latch output data and also to allow data to be input into the accumulator. The 8080 microprocessor is very powerful in that it can generate up to 256 different output device select pulses and 256 different input device select pulses. This should be more than enough for any reasonable application for the 8080 microprocessor.

OBJECTIVES

At the end of this chapter, you will be able to do the following:

- Identify the OUT and IN instructions in an 8080 microprocessor program.
- Draw a schematic diagram for a circuit that can generate up to 256 different device select pulses.
- Explain how device select pulses are generated by the 8080 microprocessor.
- Write simple microcomputer programs that employ IN or OUT instructions.
- Draw a block diagram for a 74154 four-line-to-sixteen-line decoder.

DEFINITIONS

device select pulse—A software-generated positive or negative clock pulse from a computer that is used to strobe the operation of one or more I/O devices, including individual integrated-circuit chips.

I/O—Abbreviation for input/output.[4]

I/O device—Input/output device. Any digital device, including a single integrated-circuit chip, that transmits data or strobe pulses to a computer or receives data or strobe pulses from a computer.

machine cycle—A subdivision of an instruction cycle, which is the time required to execute a complete instruction. A machine cycle is the smallest period required to perform a group of related actions during the execution of an instruction cycle.

8080 MICROPROCESSOR I/O INSTRUCTIONS

There are only two 8080 microprocessor input/output instructions:

333 <B2> IN   Generate a device select pulse to allow an 8-bit data byte to be read from the input device and *replace the contents of the accumulator.*

323 <B2> OUT   Generate a device select pulse to allow an 8-bit data byte present in the accumulator to be *sent to an output device. The contents of the accumulator remain unchanged.*

These two instructions have the following form:

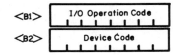

where the *device code* is an 8-bit byte that specifies one among 256 different devices. Both of the above instructions are quite similar to each other. The only difference between the two revolves around what occurs in the accumulator. With the input instruction, the accumulator contents change, whereas with the output instruction, they do not.

The term *device select pulse* can be defined in the following manner:

device select pulse—A software-generated positive or negative clock pulse from a computer that is used to strobe the operation of one or more I/O devices, including individual integrated-circuit chips.

The importance of the device select pulses resides in their use to strobe input data into the accumulator during an input instruction or to strobe the latching of output data from the accumulator during an output instruction. However, they can also be used *to strobe the operation of I/O devices under conditions where data transfer to or from the accumulator does not occur.* Thus, as pointed out in some detail in Chapter 1, device select pulses are single clock pulses that can be used in a variety of ways, for example, to simulate the behavior of a 555 astable, a pulser, or a 74121 or 555 monostable.

The mnemonics for the above two instructions are IN <B2> and OUT <B2>, and each requires ten clock cycles, or 5 μs, to execute. Neither instruction affects any of the five condition flags in the 8080 microprocessor. The symbol <B2> indicates that a second instruction byte, in this case a device address, must be present in the program immediately following the IN or OUT instruction code.

DEVICE SELECT PULSE DECODING

The generation of 256 different device codes is accomplished with the aid of the eight least-significant bits in the 16-bit memory address word, i.e., the LO memory address byte, or the eight most-significant bits in the memory address word, i.e., the HI memory address byte. *Either 8-bit byte is acceptable for the generation of the device code in the 8080 microprocessor;* we have used the LO address bus byte in our examples.

Decoders, such as the 74154 four-line-to-sixteen-line decoder, the pin configuration and block diagram of which are given in Fig. 4-1, decode the 8-bit device code into as many as 256 different device select pulses. A single decoder can provide sixteen different pulses. Four bits of the 8-bit device code are applied at the inputs A through D at pins 23 to 20. The sixteen outputs are obtained at pins 1 through 11 and 13 through 17. The two strobe inputs, G1 and G2, must both be at logic 0 to enable the chip. The unique output state is at logic 0; the remaining fifteen outputs are all at logic 1.

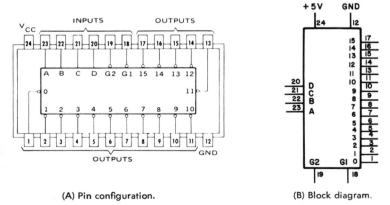

(A) Pin configuration. (B) Block diagram.

Fig. 4-1. The 74154 four-line-to-sixteen-line decoder chip.

One 74154 Decoder, Sixteen Device Select Pulses

A variety of different strategies can be employed to decode the 8-bit device code and generate individual device select pulses. The simplest decoder circuit is shown in Fig. 4-2: Sixteen different device select pulses are generated with the aid of the four least significant bits in the LO memory address word and either the $\overline{\text{IN}}$ or the $\overline{\text{OUT}}$ synchronization pulse from the 8080 microcomputer. The $\overline{\text{IN}}$ or $\overline{\text{OUT}}$ pulse strobes the decoder at G1; G2 is tied to logic 0. The device select pulse generated with this circuit is a negative clock pulse, which for some uses must be inverted with the aid of a 7404 hex inverter chip.

Most simple microcomputer interface circuits will not require more than sixteen device select pulses.

Acceptable device codes for the diagram of Fig. 4-2 include the following, where X indicates that either a logic 0 or logic 1 is acceptable in the indicated bit position:

XXXX0000	XXXX1000
XXXX0001	XXXX1001
XXXX0010	XXXX1010
XXXX0011	XXXX1011
XXXX0100	XXXX1100
XXXX0101	XXXX1101
XXXX0110	XXXX1110
XXXX0111	XXXX1111

Separate decoder chips must be used for input and output devices. Thus, a pair of 74154 decoders permits you to select up to sixteen different input devices and sixteen different output devices.

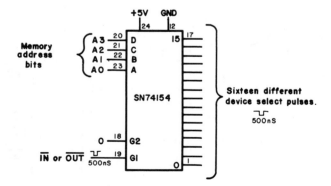

Fig. 4-2. A simple decoder circuit that can generate sixteen different device select pulses. The decoding of the address bus is not absolute.

Seventeen 74154 Decoders, 256 Device Select Pulses

A circuit that requires a single $\overline{\text{IN}}$ or $\overline{\text{OUT}}$ connection and can generate up to 256 different device select pulses is shown in Fig. 4-3. The most significant four bits in the 8-bit LO memory address word select the decoder on the right, whereas the four least significant bits select the specific output channel on the selected decoder. All device select pulses are negative clock pulses.

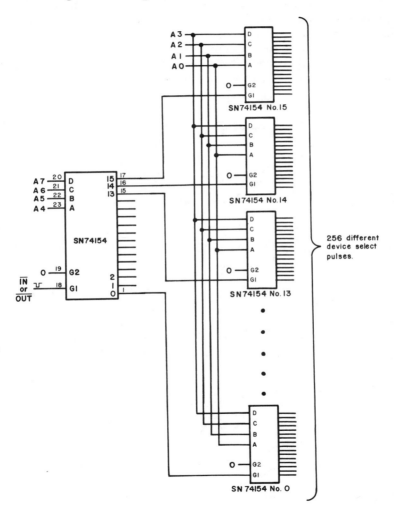

Fig. 4-3. Diagram of a circuit that can generate 256 different device select pulses.

Other Decoder Circuits

There are many other methods which may be used to generate the OUT and IN device select pulses associated with microcomputer I/O devices. While the hardware may change and may be different from application to application, the software is always the same. You always specify either an OUT (**323**) or IN (**333**) instruction and a device code.

The decoder circuit shown in Fig. 4-4 demonstrates how two 74154 decoder chips and appropriate two-input NOR gates can be used to also generate a unique one-of-256 device select pulse for each device code. While this circuit requires fewer decoders than the scheme shown in Fig. 4-3, a NOR gate is needed for each device select pulse generated. You could also use OR gates if you required negative rather

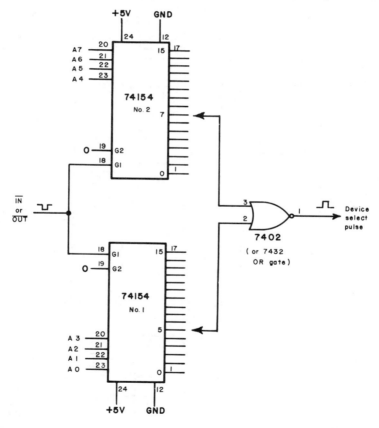

Fig. 4-4. Another circuit that can generate 256 different device select pulses. Only one of the 256 NOR gates required is shown.

than positive device select pulses. Fig. 4-5 shows how you can generate the output device select pulses 000, 001, 002, 003, and 004; the scheme decodes only output instructions. You must duplicate the Fig. 4-5 hardware for input device address decoding.

The preceding decoder schemes are used to generate input and output device select pulses for the purpose of transferring data or generating control signals only when a number of devices are located close together, usually on the same printed-circuit board. Peripheral or remote units usually have a simple decoder for the specific device. For example, if you wish to generate a unique device address, such as 371, and either an input or output device select pulse, you would employ the circuit given in Fig. 4-6.

You could use a pair of 7485 comparator chips to produce a unique device select pulse, such as the output pulse $\overline{\text{DS 306}}$, only when both sets of eight inputs exactly match (Fig. 4-7). This is a very flexible circuit that is used in systems where the device code must be changed.

If you require several device select pulses, combinations of the preceding schemes and decoders are effective. The circuit shown in Fig. 4-8 can be used to generate device addresses 070, 071, 072, and 073. The 7430 eight-input NAND gate decodes the A2 to A7 address bits. When the correct combination of address inputs appear at this gate, the 7442 decoder is enabled at input D (pin 12). The C input to the 7442 chip is used as another enable, in this case, either the $\overline{\text{IN}}$ or $\overline{\text{OUT}}$

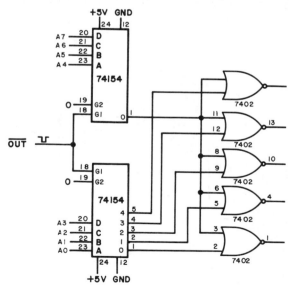

Fig. 4-5. Decoding scheme for the generation of output select pulses 000, 001, 002, 003, and 004.

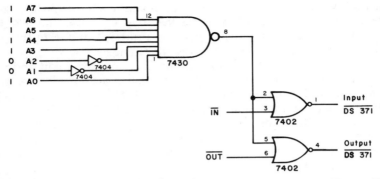

Fig. 4-6. Absolute decoder circuit based upon the use of a 7430 8-input NAND gate chip.

pulse. A pair of comparators could have been used in place of the 7430 chip and associated 7404 inverters.

While the hardware has changed in the preceding decoding circuits, the basic software necessary to generate the addresses and $\overline{IN}$ and $\overline{OUT}$ pulses remains the same.

A SAMPLE MICROCOMPUTER PROGRAM

A simple program that demonstrates the use of the OUT instruction is given on the following page.

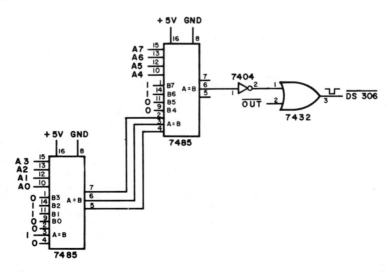

Fig. 4-7. Absolute decoder circuit based upon the use of a pair of 7485 4-bit comparator chips.

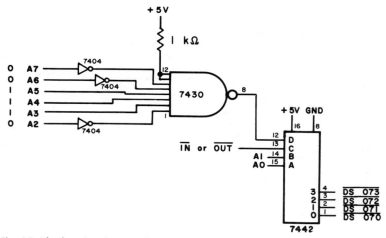

Fig. 4-8. Absolute decoder circuit based upon the use of 7430 8-input NAND gate and a 7442 decoder.

LO Memory Address	Octal Instruction	Mnemonic	Comments
000	076	MVI A	Move the following instruction byte into the accumulator
001	023	023	Data byte
002	323	OUT	Generate a device select pulse to output eight bits of accumulator data to the device with the device code given in the following byte
003	321	321	Device code for output device
004	303	JMP	Unconditional jump to the memory location given in the following two bytes
005	000		LO memory address byte
006	000		HI memory address byte

This simple program places data byte 023 into the accumulator; sends the contents of the accumulator to output device 321; and finally returns to LO memory address 000, at which point the program repeats itself. The HI memory address is 000, and all of the above numbers are in three-digit octal code.

If you were to apply an oscilloscope to an 8080 microcomputer and observe the execution of the above program, you would observe the timing diagrams shown in Fig. 4-9. The contents of the accumulator are set first and remain unchanged throughout the program; the accumulator byte has a value of 00010011, or 023 in octal code. As the OUT instruction is executed, the LO memory address lines assume the value corresponding to the device code, which is 321 in the above program. This value is held on the address lines for 1.3 μs, during which time the $\overline{OUT}$ control signal is generated, typically for 500 ns

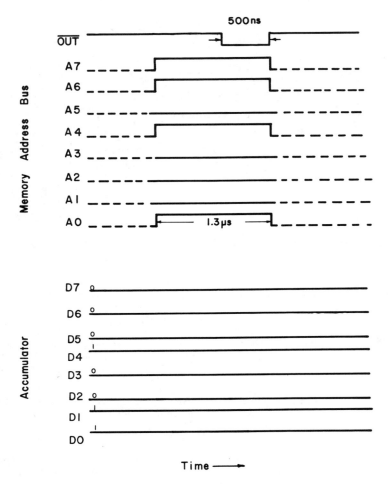

Fig. 4-9. Timing diagrams applicable for the generation of a device select pulse and the latching of accumulator output during a 5-μs OUT instruction. Information is transferred from the accumulator to an output device and a device select pulse is provided for a period of only 500 ns.

in an 8080 microcomputer that is operating at 2 MHz. The combination of the $\overline{\text{OUT}}$ control signal and the eight address lines is sufficient to generate 256 different device select pulses, as shown in Fig. 4-3. Data in the accumulator remains the same during the entire 5-μs OUT instruction. The device select pulse generated during this period can be used to latch this accumulator information, as will be discussed in Chapter 7.

DEVICE SELECT PULSES AS CONTROL PULSES

Device select pulses are not only used for strobing data transfer between the microcomputer and input/output devices. They may be used as control pulses to start or stop machines, clear devices, open valves, etc. The circuit in Fig. 4-10 shows how a device select pulse can be used to clear a 7490 decade counter integrated-circuit chip. Whenever you wish to clear the counter, insert an OUT instruction in your program with the appropriate device address. The specific device select pulse used is obtained from a decoding scheme.

A device select pulse can be used in conjunction with a latch, such as the 74175 chip shown in Fig. 4-11, to store switch data, which in this case is displayed on a seven-segment display. Data storage occurs only when the 74175 is clocked. The latch may be cleared by a different device select pulse applied at the clear input to the chip. The timing of when the latch is cleared or when switch data is stored is determined by your microcomputer program. For example, you may initially wish to clock the latch and observe the logic switch settings on the display. You do so with the aid of an output 001 device select pulse applied at pin 1 on the chip. Later in your program, you may wish to clear the latch; in this case, an output 000 device select pulse does the job. The type of program that you would use is as follows:

LO Memory Address	Octal Instruction	Mnemonic	Comments
000	323	OUT	Send out a 001 device select pulse to clear
001	001	001	the latch
.	.	.	
.	.	.	
.	.	.	
020	323	OUT	Send out a 000 device select pulse to dis-
021	000	000	play the updated logic switch data
.	.	.	
.	.	.	
.	.	.	

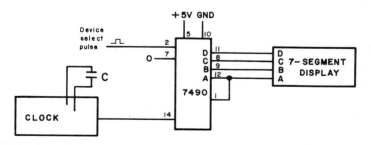

Fig. 4-10. A device select pulse can be used to clear a counter, as shown here for the 7490 chip.

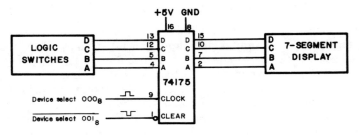

Fig. 4-11. A pair of device select pulses are used here to clock a latch and to clear it.

Notice that output instructions have been consistently used to generate the control pulses used to control the operation of the 7490 and 74175 chips. Any input device select pulse could have been used with good results, but there is an important reason why this is not done. Whenever you output data with an OUT instruction, the data in the accumulator is copied into an external output device. The microcomputer does not care whether or not a device exists to accept the data; accumulator contents are not changed. The situation is different with an IN instruction. Whenever an input device select pulse is generated, the microcomputer expects eight bits of data to be transferred to the accumulator from an input device. If no such device is present, the accumulator register is usually loaded with all logic 1's, *i.e.*, with the octal data byte 377. Therefore, you should always use OUT instructions to generate control pulses; by doing so, you continue to have control over the contents of the accumulator.

EXAMPLE

Purpose

The purpose of this example is to show how two 74154 decoders can be configured to generate sixteen contiguous device select pulses within the 256 possible device select pulses.

Program

LO Memory Address	Octal Instruction	Mnemonic	Comments
000	323	OUT	Send out a device select pulse to the device with the device code given by the following byte
001	000	000	Device code 000$_8$
002	323	OUT	Send out a device select pulse to the device with the device code given by the following byte
003	001	001	Device code 001$_8$

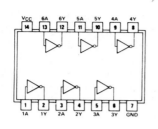

(A) 7404 chip pin configuration.

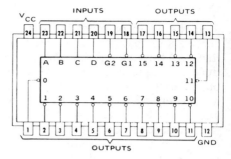

(B) 74154 chip pin configuration.

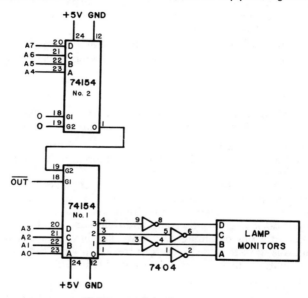

(C) Diagram of circuit.

Fig. 4-12. Circuit to generate sixteen contiguous device select pulses.

004	323	OUT	Send out a device select pulse to the device with the device code given by the following byte
005	002	002	Device code 002₈
006	323	OUT	Send out a device select pulse to the device with the device code given by the following byte
007	003	003	Device code 003₈
010	303	JMP	Unconditional jump to memory address given in following two bytes
011	000		LO memory address byte
012	000		HI memory address byte

Comments

As the microcomputer executes this program, it generates $\overline{\text{OUT}}$ synchronization pulses and provides the device code on the LO address lines, A0 through A7. This information is used by the decoders to produce a unique one-out-of-256 pulse for each device code. Although only four of the possible codes are shown in the schematic diagram and generated by the program, you can generate all sixteen pulses by adding software. The No. 1 74154 decoder already has all of the first sixteen decoded output channels available.

The No. 2 74154 decoder acts as a master decoder to enable, or turn on, the lower 74154 decoder only when the address lines A4, A5, A6, and A7 are all at logic 0. The remaining output channels on the No. 2 decoder can be used to enable more decoders to produce additional output device select pulses.

The above software contains a loop that causes the microcomputer to continuously output the four output device select pulses.

TEST

This test probes your understanding of the concepts and experiments in this chapter. Please write your answers on a separate piece of paper.

4-1. What is a device select pulse, and how is it produced with the aid of interface circuitry to the 8080 microcomputer? Use schematic diagrams in your answer to this question.
4-2. Describe ten different uses for device select pulses. You can use different integrated-circuit chips in your answer, but please do not be repetitive.
4-3. Write a simple microcomputer program that generates three different input device select pulses and two different output device select pulses.
4-4. Draw a series of timing diagrams that show how a 164_8 device select pulse is used to allow an output device to latch the contents of the accumulator, which contains data byte 11010110_2.

Your performance on this test will be acceptable if you can answer all four of these questions correctly in a 40-minute closed-book examination. You will encounter most of the answers in this book in later chapters.

WHAT HAVE YOU ACCOMPLISHED IN THIS CHAPTER?

It was stated at the beginning of this chapter that at the end you will be able to do the following:

- Identify the OUT and IN instructions in an 8080 microprocessor program.
  The operation codes for these two instructions are **323** and **333**, respectively. Whenever they appear in a microprocessor program, they are the OUT and IN instructions, without exception.

- Draw a schematic diagram for a circuit that can generate up to 256 different device select pulses.

  This circuit has been given in Fig. 4-3. It employs seventeen 74154 four-line-to-sixteen-line integrated-circuit chips.

- Explain how device select pulses are generated by the 8080 microprocessor.

  Actually, this chapter has provided only a partial explanation. Each device select pulse is produced as a consequence of an $\overline{\text{OUT}}$ or $\overline{\text{IN}}$ strobe pulse and a pulse produced by the action of decoding the 8-bit device code that appears for 1.3 μs on the memory address bus. We have not discussed how the $\overline{\text{OUT}}$ and $\overline{\text{IN}}$ pulses are produced, a topic which will be treated in Chapter 6.

- Write simple microcomputer programs that employ IN or OUT instructions.

  This has been done in several examples in this chapter. Most of the programs contain only five instruction bytes.

- Draw a block diagram for a 74154 four-line-to-sixteen-line decoder.

  We have used the 74154 chip often in this chapter, so you should be able to draw a block diagram of it and, by memory, identify some of the more important pin numbers. G1 and G2 are at pins 18 and 19, respectively. The output channels start at pin 1 and continue to pin 11. They resume at pin 13.

CHAPTER 5

Clock Cycles and Timing Loops

In this chapter, you will examine the timing of various 8080 instructions and the use of a microcomputer as a pulse or timing generator. Microcomputers are used frequently in situations where complex timing periods and sequences are required. Examples include traffic light control, oven and microwave range control, and washer and dryer control.

OBJECTIVES

At the end of this chapter, you will be able to do the following:

- Define the terms: loop, timing loop, period, clock cycle, and state.
- Program a timing loop that can generate timing delays that are multiples of 0.200 second.
- Program a timing loop that can generate timing delays that are multiples of approximately 0.5 millisecond.
- Demonstrate how a microcomputer can act as a monostable multivibrator.

DEFINITIONS

clock cycle—A single clock period.
loop—A sequence of instructions that is executed repeatedly until a terminal condition prevails.[3]

monostable multivibrator—A circuit having only one stable state, from
which it can be triggered to change the state, but only for a predetermined interval, after which it returns to the original state.

period—The time required for one complete cycle of a regular, repeating series of events.

programmable sequencer—A sequencer in which the order in which the
events or operations occur can be changed with the aid of programming.

sequencer—An electronic device that may be set to initiate a series of
events and to make the events follow in sequence, i.e., in order.[4]

state—A single clock period, or stable condition.

timing loop—A loop that requires a precise period for its execution.

MONOSTABLE MULTIVIBRATORS

A monostable multivibrator can be defined as follows:

monostable multivibrator—A circuit having only one stable state, from
which it can be triggered to change the state, but only for a predetermined interval, after which it returns to the original state.

They are used to generate individual clock pulses of precisely known
pulse width. Such clock pulses are widely used in digital electronics
to coordinate the timing in digital circuits and also to turn external
devices on and off for predetermined time intervals. The schematic
diagrams shown in Fig. 5-1 summarize the common monostable multivibrators that are in use today. The 74121, 74122, and 74123 chips
generate individual clock pulses whose pulse width varies from about
40 ns to several milliseconds. The 555 monostable can generate pulse
width that vary from several microseconds to several minutes. These
chips are discussed in greater detail in Chapter 8 in *Bugbook II*.

THE MICROCOMPUTER AS A MONOSTABLE MULTIVIBRATOR

A microcomputer, such as the 8080, can also act as a monostable
multivibrator. It is possible to write a computer program that contains
a *timing loop:*

timing loop—A loop that requires a precise period for its execution.

loop—A sequence of instructions that is executed repeatedly until a
terminal condition prevails.[3]

It should be clear that such a loop can be interposed between two
OUT instructions in a computer program. With proper external circuitry, a single clock pulse of pulse width determined by the computer
program can be produced. We might call such a pulse a software-
generated monostable pulse. The pulse width can be controlled by

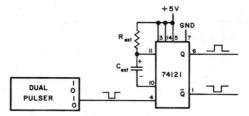

(A) The 74121 chip used as a monostable multivibrator. Monostable pulses as short as 40 ns can be generated conveniently.

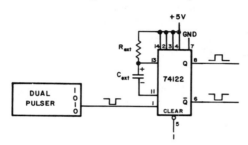

(B) The 74122 chip wired as a monostable multivibrator.

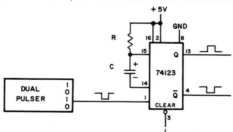

(C) The 74123 chip wired as a monostable multivibrator. Two independent monostable multivibrators are available on the 74123 chip.

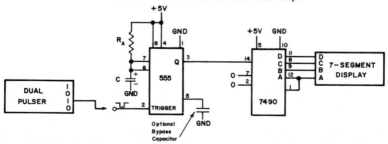

(D) The 555 timer chip used as a monostable multivibrator. Pulses shorter than several microseconds cannot be generated by this chip. The strobe pulse must be shorter than the output monostable pulse.

Fig. 5-1. Common monostable multivibrators.

making changes in the computer program rather than by changing resistors or capacitors, as would be the case for the 74121, 74122, 74123, and 555 monostable multivibrator chips.

This brings us to the question: How do we know how long it takes to execute a group of microcomputer instructions? We shall discuss this question in the following section.

HOW LONG DOES IT TAKE TO EXECUTE A MICROCOMPUTER INSTRUCTION?

A microcomputer, as any digital computer, is a clocked digital electronic device. This means that all actions occur at or during precisely defined clock intervals. For example, a typical 8080 microprocessor chip is operated at a clock rate of 2 MHz. A single clock cycle, or *state*, has a period of:

$$\text{period} = 1 \text{ cycle}/2{,}000{,}000 \text{ cycles per second (hertz)}$$
$$= 0.0000005 \text{ second}$$
$$= 0.5 \ \mu s$$
$$= 500 \text{ ns}$$

where *clock cycle*, *state*, and *period* are defined as:

period—The time required for one complete cycle of a regular, repeating series of events.
clock cycle, state—A single clock period or stable condition.

Every action within the 8080 microprocessor requires some multiple of the period of microprocessor clock. A computer instruction is a typical microprocessor "action," so it too is performed in some multiple of the period of the microprocessor clock. The fastest instruction requires only four clock periods, called states or clock cycles:

$$\text{four cycles} = 4 \times 500 \text{ ns}$$
$$= 2 \ \mu s$$

whereas the slowest instruction, XTHL, requires eighteen clock cycles:

$$\text{eighteen cycles} = 18 \times 500 \text{ ns}$$
$$= 9 \ \mu s$$

Clearly, the time required to execute a group of instructions is determined by the cumulative time to execute each of the individual instructions within the group and multiplied by the number of times such instructions are executed. If we are clever, we can arrange a group of instructions in such a manner that their execution requires a predetermined amount of time, such as 0.20 second. As long as the clock rate for the microcomputer remains at 2 MHz, it will always take 0.20 second to execute this group of instructions.

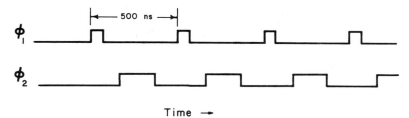

Fig. 5-2. Timing diagrams for the two-phase clock inputs to an 8080 chip.

In general, the basic "currency" of a computer is time; the faster that it can perform a series of instructions, the more powerful it is and the more useful it will be in replacing integrated-circuit chips such as those in the 7400-series of chips. At the moment, a typical operating frequency for an 8080-based microcomputer is 2 MHz; this means that a single clock period is equal to 500 ns. This is the time duration between successive pulses of one of the two clock phases, ϕ_1 and ϕ_2, as shown in Fig. 5-2.

Keep in mind, however, that the speed of 8080 chips may be increased with improvements in manufacturing techniques. It is quite possible that an improved 8080 chip may operate at a maximum speed of 4 MHz, which means that a single clock period will be only 250 ns. Naturally, the R/W, PROM, and ROM chips will also have to be faster if a useful microcomputer system is to be constructed. And the 8080 is not the last word in computer speed. Improvements in semiconductor manufacturing techniques, particularly in an area called *bipolar technology*, will lead to inexpensive and widely used microprocessor chips that are clocked at rates as high as 30 MHz, or 33.3 nanoseconds per clock period.

CLOCK CYCLE LISTING FOR THE 8080 INSTRUCTION SET

On the following page is a complete listing of the 8080 instruction set that includes the number of clock cycles required for each instruction. This page is provided by Intel Corporation. In this section, we shall summarize the conclusions that can be derived from this listing.

The shortest time during which a single instruction can be executed is four clock cycles, or 2 μs, if we assume that a single clock cycle requires 500 ns. Register arithmetic and logical operations and accumulator contents rotation can be performed in this short interval of time. Included in such a group are the ADD, ADC, SUB, SBB, ANA, XRA, ORA, CMP, RLC, RRC, RAL, and RAR instructions.

All register-to-register MOV instructions as well as increment and decrement instructions INR, DCR, INX, and DCX, are executed in five clock cycles, or 2.5 μs.

INSTRUCTION SET

Summary of Processor Instructions

Mnemonic	Description	D7	D6	D5	D4	D3	D2	D1	D0	Clock[2] Cycles
MOV r1,r2	Move register to register	0	1	D	D	D	S	S	S	5
MOV M,r	Move register to memory	0	1	1	1	0	S	S	S	7
MOV r,M	Move memory to register	0	1	D	D	D	1	1	0	7
HLT	Halt	0	1	1	1	0	1	1	0	7
MVI r	Move immediate register	0	0	D	D	D	1	1	0	7
MVI M	Move immediate memory	0	0	1	1	0	1	1	0	10
INR r	Increment register	0	0	D	D	D	1	0	0	5
DCR r	Decrement register	0	0	D	D	D	1	0	1	5
INR M	Increment memory	0	0	1	1	0	1	0	0	10
DCR M	Decrement memory	0	0	1	1	0	1	0	1	10
ADD r	Add register to A	1	0	0	0	0	S	S	S	4
ADC r	Add register to A with carry	1	0	0	0	1	S	S	S	4
SUB r	Subtract register from A	1	0	0	1	0	S	S	S	4
SBB r	Subtract register from A with borrow	1	0	0	1	1	S	S	S	4
ANA r	And register with A	1	0	1	0	0	S	S	S	4
XRA r	Exclusive Or register with A	1	0	1	0	1	S	S	S	4
ORA r	Or register with A	1	0	1	1	0	S	S	S	4
CMP r	Compare register with A	1	0	1	1	1	S	S	S	4
ADD M	Add memory to A	1	0	0	0	0	1	1	0	7
ADC M	Add memory to A with carry	1	0	0	0	1	1	1	0	7
SUB M	Subtract memory from A	1	0	0	1	0	1	1	0	7
SBB M	Subtract memory from A with borrow	1	0	0	1	1	1	1	0	7
ANA M	And memory with A	1	0	1	0	0	1	1	0	7
XRA M	Exclusive Or memory with A	1	0	1	0	1	1	1	0	7
ORA M	Or memory with A	1	0	1	1	0	1	1	0	7
CMP M	Compare memory with A	1	0	1	1	1	1	1	0	7
ADI	Add immediate to A	1	1	0	0	0	1	1	0	7
ACI	Add immediate to A with carry	1	1	0	0	1	1	1	0	7
SUI	Subtract immediate from A	1	1	0	1	0	1	1	0	7
SBI	Subtract immediate from A with borrow	1	1	0	1	1	1	1	0	7
ANI	And immediate with A	1	1	1	0	0	1	1	0	7
XRI	Exclusive Or immediate with A	1	1	1	0	1	1	1	0	7
ORI	Or immediate with A	1	1	1	1	0	1	1	0	7
CPI	Compare immediate with A	1	1	1	1	1	1	1	0	7
RLC	Rotate A left	0	0	0	0	0	1	1	1	4
RRC	Rotate A right	0	0	0	0	1	1	1	1	4
RAL	Rotate A left through carry	0	0	0	1	0	1	1	1	4
RAR	Rotate A right through carry	0	0	0	1	1	1	1	1	4
JMP	Jump unconditional	1	1	0	0	0	0	1	1	10
JC	Jump on carry	1	1	0	1	1	0	1	0	10
JNC	Jump on no carry	1	1	0	1	0	0	1	0	10
JZ	Jump on zero	1	1	0	0	1	0	1	0	10
JNZ	Jump on no zero	1	1	0	0	0	0	1	0	10
JP	Jump on positive	1	1	1	1	0	0	1	0	10
JM	Jump on minus	1	1	1	1	1	0	1	0	10
JPE	Jump on parity even	1	1	1	0	1	0	1	0	10
JPO	Jump on parity odd	1	1	1	0	0	0	1	0	10
CALL	Call unconditional	1	1	0	0	1	1	0	1	17
CC	Call on carry	1	1	0	1	1	1	0	0	11/17
CNC	Call on no carry	1	1	0	1	0	1	0	0	11/17
CZ	Call on zero	1	1	0	0	1	1	0	0	11/17
CNZ	Call on no zero	1	1	0	0	0	1	0	0	11/17
CP	Call on positive	1	1	1	1	0	1	0	0	11/17
CM	Call on minus	1	1	1	1	1	1	0	0	11/17
CPE	Call on parity even	1	1	1	0	1	1	0	0	11/17
CPO	Call on parity odd	1	1	1	0	0	1	0	0	11/17
RET	Return	1	1	0	0	1	0	0	1	10
RC	Return on carry	1	1	0	1	1	0	0	0	5/11
RNC	Return on no carry	1	1	0	1	0	0	0	0	5/11

Mnemonic	Description	D7	D6	D5	D4	D3	D2	D1	D0	Clock[2] Cycles
RZ	Return on zero	1	1	0	0	1	0	0	0	5/11
RNZ	Return on no zero	1	1	0	0	0	0	0	0	5/11
RP	Return on positive	1	1	1	1	0	0	0	0	5/11
RM	Return on minus	1	1	1	1	1	0	0	0	5/11
RPE	Return on parity even	1	1	1	0	1	0	0	0	5/11
RPO	Return on parity odd	1	1	1	0	0	0	0	0	5/11
RST	Restart	1	1	A	A	A	1	1	1	11
IN	Input	1	1	0	1	1	0	1	1	10
OUT	Output	1	1	0	1	0	0	1	1	10
LXI B	Load immediate register Pair B & C	0	0	0	0	0	0	0	1	10
LXI D	Load immediate register Pair D & E	0	0	0	1	0	0	0	1	10
LXI H	Load immediate register Pair H & L	0	0	1	0	0	0	0	1	10
LXI SP	Load immediate stack pointer	0	0	1	1	0	0	0	1	10
PUSH B	Push register Pair B & C on stack	1	1	0	0	0	1	0	1	11
PUSH D	Push register Pair D & E on stack	1	1	0	1	0	1	0	1	11
PUSH H	Push register Pair H & L on stack	1	1	1	0	0	1	0	1	11
PUSH PSW	Push A and Flags on stack	1	1	1	1	0	1	0	1	11
POP B	Pop register pair B & C off stack	1	1	0	0	0	0	0	1	10
POP D	Pop register pair D & E off stack	1	1	0	1	0	0	0	1	10
POP H	Pop register pair H & L off stack	1	1	1	0	0	0	0	1	10
POP PSW	Pop A and Flags off stack	1	1	1	1	0	0	0	1	10
STA	Store A direct	0	0	1	1	0	0	1	0	13
LDA	Load A direct	0	0	1	1	1	0	1	0	13
XCHG	Exchange D & E, H & L Registers	1	1	1	0	1	0	1	1	4
XTHL	Exchange top of stack, H & L	1	1	1	0	0	0	1	1	18
SPHL	H & L to stack pointer	1	1	1	1	1	0	0	1	5
PCHL	H & L to program counter	1	1	1	0	1	0	0	1	5
DAD B	Add B & C to H & L	0	0	0	0	1	0	0	1	10
DAD D	Add D & E to H & L	0	0	0	1	1	0	0	1	10
DAD H	Add H & L to H & L	0	0	1	0	1	0	0	1	10
DAD SP	Add stack pointer to H & L	0	0	1	1	1	0	0	1	10
STAX B	Store A indirect	0	0	0	0	0	0	1	0	7
STAX D	Store A indirect	0	0	0	1	0	0	1	0	7
LDAX B	Load A indirect	0	0	0	0	1	0	1	0	7
LDAX D	Load A indirect	0	0	0	1	1	0	1	0	7
INX B	Increment B & C registers	0	0	0	0	0	0	1	1	5
INX D	Increment D & E registers	0	0	0	1	0	0	1	1	5
INX H	Increment H & L registers	0	0	1	0	0	0	1	1	5
INX SP	Increment stack pointer	0	0	1	1	0	0	1	1	5
DCX B	Decrement B & C	0	0	0	0	1	0	1	1	5
DCX D	Decrement D & E	0	0	0	1	1	0	1	1	5
DCX H	Decrement H & L	0	0	1	0	1	0	1	1	5
DCX SP	Decrement stack pointer	0	0	1	1	1	0	1	1	5
CMA	Complement A	0	0	1	0	1	1	1	1	4
STC	Set carry	0	0	1	1	0	1	1	1	4
CMC	Complement carry	0	0	1	1	1	1	1	1	4
DAA	Decimal adjust A	0	0	1	0	0	1	1	1	4
SHLD	Store H & L direct	0	0	1	0	0	0	1	0	16
LHLD	Load H & L direct	0	0	1	0	1	0	1	0	16
EI	Enable Interrupts	1	1	1	1	1	0	1	1	4
DI	Disable interrupt	1	1	1	1	0	0	1	1	4
NOP	No operation	0	0	0	0	0	0	0	0	4

NOTES: 1. DDD or SSS – 000 B – 001 C – 010 D – 011 E – 100 H – 101 L – 110 Memory – 111 A.
2. Two possible cycle times, (5/11) indicate instruction cycles dependent on condition flags.

Most of the instructions in which transfers of information to or from memory occur require at least seven clock cycles, or 3.5 μs. Included in this group are the register-to-memory or memory-to-register MOV instructions; the ADD M, ADC M, SUB M, SBB M, ANA M, XRA M, ORA M, CMP M, MVI, ADI, ACI, SUI, SBI, ANI, XRI, ORI, and CPI instructions; and the STAX and LDAX instructions.

The conditional and unconditional jump instructions, MVI M, INR M, DCR M, RET, IN, OUT, LXI, DAD, and POP instructions all require ten clock cycles, or 5 μs, for execution.

The conditional call instructions require either eleven or seventeen clock cycles, depending upon whether or not the subroutine is called. If it is called, then seventeen clock cycles, or 8.5 μs, are required. If not, only eleven clock cycles, or 5.5 μs, are required to perform this type of instruction.

Similar considerations apply to the conditional return instructions. If the flag is at such a logic state that a return occurs, then eleven clock cycles, or 5.5 μs, are required. If no return occurs, then only five clock cycles, or 2.5 μs, are required for the conditional return instruction.

If you are planning a timing loop of precise time duration, you will require this listing. You may desire to make a copy of it for your use while you are programming. Such a listing is also included in the *Intel 8080 Microcomputer System Manual*.

COUNTING CLOCK CYCLES: SOME SIMPLE MICROCOMPUTER PROGRAMS

In this section, we shall consider a number of simple computer programs and learn how to count clock cycles.

Program No. 1

LO Memory Address	Octal Instruction Byte	Mnemonic	Comments
000	303	JMP	Unconditional jump to memory address given in following two bytes
001	000		LO address byte
002	000		HI address byte

If you look at the Intel instruction set listing, you will observe that a JMP instruction requires ten clock cycles for execution. Since this program does not contain any IN or OUT instructions, you will have a somewhat difficult time in measuring, or employing this program to generate, 5-μs monostable pulses. This program can be discarded for such a purpose. It is important to note that all three bytes of the JMP instruction are "used" in ten clock cycles. This overall time applies to all bytes in a multibyte instruction.

Program No. 2

LO Memory Address	Octal Instruction Byte	Mnemonic	Clock Cycles	Comments
000	323	OUT	10	Generate device select pulse for device with following device code
001	000	000		Device code
002	323	OUT	10	Generate second device select pulse for same device
003	000	000		Device code
004	166	HLT	7	Halt

This program is executed in 27 clock cycles, or 13.5 μs. What is interesting about the program, however, is that two device select pulses are generated and sent to the same device. One pulse is used to turn the device on, and the other to turn it off. What device can be turned on and off from a single input? As one example, consider the toggled J-K flip-flop circuit shown in Fig. 5-3.

The preset, clear, J, and K inputs are all left unconnected, which means they are all at a logic 1 state. Therefore, each clock pulse applied to the clock input at pin 1 of the 7476 chip will cause the flip-flop to *toggle*, i.e., to change state. Let us assume that the flip-flop output, Q, is initially at logic 0. The first OUT instruction in Program No. 2 generates a single device select pulse which toggles the flip-flop to logic 1. This output is used as a gating signal to the two-input 7408 AND gate, and permits signals from the ϕ_2 clock to pass through the gate to the five-decade counter, where they are counted. The second OUT instruction in Program No. 2 generates a device select pulse that causes the Q output at pin 15 to return to logic 0; this action disables the 7408 gate and stops the counting by the five-decade counter.

How long will the counter count? This question can best be answered with the aid of information supplied in Chapter 6. We can anticipate such information by pointing out that the device select pulse is not sent to the 7476 flip-flop until the last 500 ns in the 5-μs OUT instruction. It can be shown that the flip-flop is at a logic 1 state for

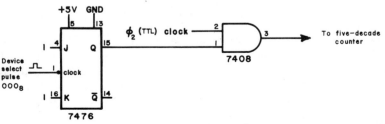

Fig. 5-3. A 7476 flip-flop toggled at the clock input can be used to gate clock pulses from the master clock in an 8080-based microcomputer.

only ten clock cycles, or 5 μs: 500 ns during the first OUT instruction and 4.500 μs during the second OUT instruction. The 5-μs time interval is quite exact: It is not 4.93 μs or 5.05 μs, but precisely 5.0000 μs for a crystal-controlled 2-MHz 8080 clock input.

Program No. 3

LO Memory Address	Octal Instruction Byte	Mnemonic	Clock Cycles	Comments
000	323	OUT	10	Generate device select pulse
001	000	000		Device code
002	*	*	*	Arithmetic, logical, or other single-byte instruction
003	323	OUT	10	Generate device select pulse
004	000	000		Device code
005	166	HLT	7	Halt

Program No. 3 is similar to Program No. 2, except that we have inserted an instruction between the two OUT instructions. All single-byte instructions with the exception of the return instructions can be tested. For example, if the RLC instruction, which requires four clock cycles, were inserted at memory address 002_8, the total counting time, as measured by the five-decade counter and the 7476 circuit shown on the preceding page, would be:

$$\begin{aligned} \text{counting time} &= (4 + 10) \times 500 \text{ ns} \\ &= 7000 \text{ ns} \\ &= 7.0 \ \mu\text{s} \end{aligned}$$

If you would subtract 5 μs, the time required for Program No. 2, from this value, you would measure a time of 2.0 μs for the RLC instruction, a time that corresponds to four clock cycles, as indicated in the 8080 timing chart.

Program No. 4

LO Memory Address	Octal Instruction Byte	Mnemonic	Clock Cycles	Comments
000	323	OUT	10	Generate device select pulse that sets the 7476 flip-flop
001	000	000		Device code
002	323	OUT	10	Generate device select pulse that clears the 7476 flip-flop
003	001	001		Different device code
004	166	HLT	7	Halt

Rather than toggle the 7476 flip-flop, you can connect two different device select signal lines to the preset and clear inputs of the flip-flop. The circuit is shown in Fig. 5-4. It should be apparent that this is an equally, or perhaps more, effective way to change the output states on a flip-flop. In this case, though the 7476 flip-flop is a single "device,"

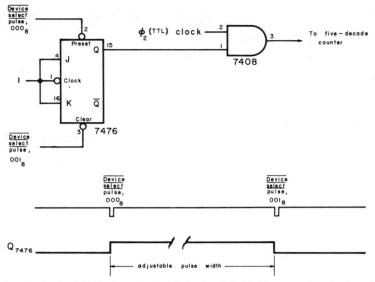

Fig. 5-4. A simple 7476 flip-flop circuit and associated timing diagrams. This circuit can be used to count clock cycles in an 8080 microcomputer.

two "device select pulses" are required to control it. There need not be any correlation between the number of devices present and the number of device select pulses required to service such devices.

Program No. 5

LO Memory Address	Octal Instruction Byte	Mnemonic	Clock Cycles	Comments
000	006	MVI B	7	Move following data byte into B register
001	*			Data byte
002	323	OUT	10	Generate device select pulse that sets the 7476 flip-flop
003	000	000		Device code
004	005	DCR B	5	Decrement contents of register B by one
005	302	JNZ	10	Conditional jump. If contents of B register are 000, ignore this instruction and go to memory address 010. Otherwise, jump to memory address given in following two bytes
006	004			LO address byte
007	000			HI address byte
010	323	OUT	10	Generate device select pulse that clears the 7476 flip-flop
011	001	001		Different device code
012	166	HLT	7	Halt

This interesting program contains:

- A conditional jump instruction [at memory address 005]
- A timing loop [at memory addresses 004 through 007]
- A data byte that determines the time duration of the timing loop [at memory address 001]
- Two OUT instructions that generate two different device select pulses

The circuit that accompanies this program, along with a pair of timing diagrams, is shown in Fig. 5-4. The first OUT instruction sends a device select pulse to the preset input to the 7476 flip-flop at pin 2. The flip-flop output, Q, is thus set to logic 1, which opens the 7408 gate. The OUT instruction appearing at memory address 010_8 in the program clears the flip-flop and closes the gate.

The conditional jump instruction, JNZ, at memory address 005 permits a jump only when the zero *flag* is at logic 0. The decrement instruction at memory address 004 will decrease the contents of the B register by one on each pass through the loop. Eventually, the B register becomes equal to 000, at which time program control moves to the instruction at memory address 010 owing to the JNZ instruction. The magnitude of the data byte at memory address 001 determines the number of loops that occur during the execution of the program. If this data byte is **001**, the program will make only a single pass through the instructions at memory addresses 004 through 007. On the other hand, if the data byte is initially **000**, the program will loop 256 times. This is because the data byte is decremented before being tested.

Each time the program loops through addresses 004 through 007, there is a delay of fifteen clock cycles, or 7.5 μs. This time is multiplied by the number of loop passes that occur. Added to this figure is 5 μs, the time associated with clearing the flip-flop via the OUT instruction at memory address 010.

The asterisk (*) at memory address 001 indicates that this data byte can vary from **000** to **377**, in octal code. Some calculations will demonstrate how you can vary the time that Program No. 5 is executed. The objective here is to demonstrate, via calculations, *how the microcomputer can be used to generate time delays in external digital circuitry. It generates these delays through the use of device select pulses and timing loops.*

Assume that the data byte at memory address 001 is equal to **001**. This is the content of the B register at the end of the instruction byte at memory address 003_8. At memory address 004, the contents of the B register are decremented by 1, and become equal to 000. With the aid of the conditional jump instruction that follows, program control is transferred to memory address 010, at which point a device select pulse is generated to clear the flip-flop. The total number of clock cycles between the first and second OUT instructions is:

$$\text{number of clock cycles} = [\text{DCR}] + [\text{JNZ}] + [\text{OUT}]$$
$$= \quad 5 \quad + \quad 10 \quad + \quad 10$$
$$= 25$$

At 500 ns per clock cycle, the total elapsed time is:

$$\text{elapsed time} = 25 \times 500 \text{ ns}$$
$$= 12.5 \ \mu\text{s}$$

The five-decade counter in the circuit indicated in Fig. 5-4 counts clock pulses for this period.

Now assume that the data byte at memory address 001 is **002**. The total number of clock cycles between the first and second OUT instructions is now:

$$\text{number of clock cycles} = 2 \, [\text{DCR}] + 2 \, [\text{JNZ}] + [\text{OUT}]$$
$$= \quad 10 \quad + \quad 20 \quad + \quad 10$$
$$= 40$$

which is equivalent to a total elapsed time of:

$$\text{elapsed time} = 40 \times 500 \text{ ns}$$
$$= 20.0 \ \mu\text{s}$$

If the data byte at memory address 011 is **000**, there are 256 passes through the timing loop. The number of clock cycles and total elapsed time between OUT instructions is:

$$\text{number of clock cycles} = 256 \, [\text{DCR}] + 256 \, [\text{JNZ}] + [\text{OUT}]$$
$$= \quad 1280 \quad + \quad 2560 \quad + \quad 10$$
$$= 3850$$

$$\text{elapsed time} = 3850 \times 500 \text{ ns}$$
$$= 1925 \ \mu\text{s}$$
$$= 1.925 \text{ ms}$$

This elapsed time of 1.925 milliseconds refers to the time that the 7476 flip-flop output is at a logic 1 state, not to the total elapsed time of the program.

It should be clear that the pulse width shown in Fig. 5-4 is adjustable. The exact width is determined by the location of the first and second OUT instructions (the ones that generate device select pulses 000 and 001) in the microcomputer program. For example, the pulse width would have the following values as the magnitude of the data byte present at memory address 001 varies from 000 to 377:

Data Byte at LO Memory Address 001	Number of Clock Cycles	Pulse Width (ms)
000	3850	1.925
001	25	0.0125
002	40	0.02
003	55	0.0275
004	70	0.035
005	85	0.0425
010	130	0.065
020	250	0.125
050	610	0.305
100	970	0.485
200	1930	0.965
300	2890	1.445
350	3490	1.745
377	3835	1.9175

You should carefully study the discussion of Program No. 5. It provides the simplest example of a timing loop that can be written.

TIMING LOOPS

The definition of a *timing loop* has been given previously in this chapter. Timing loops are widely employed in microprocessor programs in systems that control or sequence instruments and machines. Some characteristics of such loops include the following:

- Timing loops of different time durations are required: microseconds, milliseconds, and seconds.
- The timing loops are used frequently.
- Since they are used frequently, they usually appear in the microcomputer program as subroutines.

We will now consider such a subroutine, one which we have loaded into PROM starting at memory location H = 060 and L = 000. This subroutine will generate a timing delay that is precisely equal to 0.2000 second.

Subroutine No. 1

Memory Address H	L	Octal Instruction Byte	Mnemonic	Clock Cycles	Comments
060	000	021	LXI D	10	Move following two bytes into registers E and D, respectively
060	001	301	301		Timing byte for register E
060	002	150	150		Timing byte for register D
060	003	035	DCR E	5	Decrement register E by one
060	004	302	JNZ	10	If register E is 000_8, ignore this instruction; otherwise, jump to memory address given in the following two bytes

Memory Address H	L	Octal Instruction Byte	Mnemonic	Clock Cycles	Comments
060	005	003			LO address byte
060	006	060			HI address byte
060	007	025	DCR D	5	Decrement register D by one
060	010	302	JNZ	10	If register D is 000_8, ignore this instruction; otherwise, jump to memory address given in the following two bytes
060	011	003			LO address byte
060	012	060			HI address byte
060	013	015	DCR C	5	Decrement register C by one
060	014	302	JNZ	10	If register C is 000_8, ignore this instruction; otherwise, jump to memory address given in the following two bytes
060	015	000			LO address byte
060	016	060			HI address byte
060	017	311	RET	10	Unconditional return from this subroutine

A flowchart for this 0.200-second subroutine is shown in Fig. 5-5. Note that the subroutine is entered with a timing byte already present in register C. As can be seen from the flowchart, there is an E register loop within a D register loop, which is within a C register loop. A program that employs this subroutine is given below.

Program No. 6

LO Memory Address	Octal Instruction Byte	Mnemonic	Clock Cycles	Comments
100	061	LXI D	10	Move following two bytes into the stack pointer
101	200	200		LO address byte
102	000	000		HI address byte
103	016	MVI C	7	Move following byte into register C
104	°	°		Timing byte for register C
105	323	OUT	10	Generate device select pulse that sets the 7476 flip-flop
106	000	000		Device code
107	315	CALL	17	Unconditional call of subroutine located at memory address given by following two bytes
110	000			LO address byte
111	060			HI address byte
112	323	OUT	10	Generate device select pulse that clears the 7476 flip-flop
113	001	001		Different device code
114	166	HLT	7	Halt

Let us assume that the timing byte for register C at memory address $H = 000_8$ and $L = 001_8$ is **001**. The steps that occur in both Program No. 6 and Subroutine No. 1 can be summarized as follows:

a. The stack pointer within the 8080 is set to $HI = 000$ and $LO = 200$. A timing byte is moved into register C. This takes a total of seventeen clock cycles. However, the five-decade counter connected to the 7476 flip-flop does not measure this time.

b. A device select pulse is generated via an OUT instruction. This sets the 7476 flip-flop to logic 1 and starts the counter.

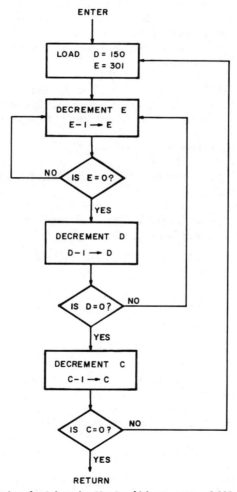

Fig. 5-5. Flowchart for Subroutine No. 1, which generates a 0.200-second delay.

c. A subroutine at memory address H = 060 and L = 000 is called unconditionally. This takes seventeen clock cycles, or 8.5 μs, a time that is measured by the counter.

d. In the subroutine, timing bytes are moved into registers D and E. This takes ten clock cycles.

e. A timing loop is established with register E. The contents of this register are decremented 193 times. A total of $193 \times 15 = 2895$ clock cycles are required.

f. The contents of the D register are decremented by one. This takes fifteen clock cycles.

g. A second timing loop is established with register E, only this time the contents of this register are decremented 256 times. This takes 3840 clock cycles.

h. The contents of the D register are decremented by one. This takes fifteen clock cycles.

i. Steps g and h are repeated 103 times. The total clock cycles required are 3840×103 plus 15×103 clock cycles.

j. The contents of the C register are decremented by one. This takes five clock cycles. Since the C register is now 000_8, the zero flag is set to logic 1.

k. Ten cycles are consumed with the JNZ instruction at memory location H = 060 and L = 014.

l. There is an unconditional return from the subroutine. This takes ten clock cycles.

m. Finally, a device select pulse is generated via an OUT instruction. This takes ten clock cycles. The 7476 flip-flop is cleared to logic 0 and the counting stops.

How many clock cycles are there in all? We calculate the following:

a.		i.	397,065	
b.		j.	5	
c.	17	k.	10	
d.	10	l.	10	
e.	2,895	m.	10	
f.	15			

The total number of clock cycles is 400,037. At 500 ns per clock cycle, this translates into a timing delay of 0.2000185 second. The timing subroutine is programmed in such a manner that, if the timing byte for register C were **002**, the total number of clock cycles would be 800,037, or 0.4000185 second. Each time register C is set at one bit larger than the previous time, an additional 0.2000000 second is added to the timing delay.

You will find that a subroutine that generates a 0.200-second timing delay is quite handy. The maximum time delay that you can generate is 51.2000185 seconds using only the C, D, and E registers. A sampling of typical time delays is given below.

Timing Byte for Register C	Time delay (seconds)
001	0.2000185
002	0.4000185
005	1.0000180
012	2.0000185
031	5.0000185
062	10.0000185
144	20.0000185
372	50.0000185

While the maximum time delay is somewhat over 50 seconds, longer delays may be necessary. These longer times may be obtained by *nesting* subroutines so that a 30-second time delay subroutine is used 120 times to provide an overall time delay of one hour. Program No. 7 shows how this is done.

Program No. 7

LO Memory Address	Octal Instruction Byte	Mnemonic	Clock Cycles	Comments
000	061	LXI SP	10	Move following two bytes into the stack pointer
001	200	200		LO address byte
002	000	000		HI address byte
003	001	LXI B	10	Move following two bytes into registers C and B, respectively
004	226	226		C register byte
005	170	170		B register byte
006	315	CALL	17	Unconditional call of subroutine located at memory address given by the following two bytes
007	000			LO address byte
010	060			HI address byte
011	005	DCR B	5	Decrement register B by one
012	302	JNZ	10	If register B is 000_8, ignore this instruction; otherwise, jump to the memory address given in the following two bytes
013	006			LO address byte
014	000			HI address byte
015	166	HLT	7	Halt

Here we are using Subroutine No. 1 to generate a 30.000-second time delay. The timing byte C has a value of 226_8, which corresponds to decimal 150. This 30-second time delay is called 120 times, or 170_8 in octal code, to produce a total time delay of one hour. This is done with only 30 instruction bytes located in memory. We use the principle of loop *nesting* to accomplish our desired result:

nesting—In a computer, the inclusion of a loop or routine within a larger loop or routine.

SEQUENCING WITH A MICROCOMPUTER

In Chapter 4 and in this chapter, you have learned how to:

- Generate individual device select pulses, up to a total of 512 different pulses.
- Write time delay routines that create time delays ranging from 5 μs to minutes or even hours.
- Toggle an external J-K flip-flop to turn on and off a digital device such as a counter.
- Write program loops that will repeat a sequence of operations after a predetermined time interval.

Thus, you already have the ability to create a variety of programmable sequencers, in which you sequence a series of operations at preset time intervals that are determined by the programmed time delays. Some definitions are in order:

sequential operation—The carrying out of operations one after the other.[4]

sequencer—An electronic device that may be set to initiate a series of events and to make the events follow in sequence, i.e., in order.[4]

programmable sequencer—A sequencer in which the order in which the events or operations occur can be changed with the aid of programming.

These concepts are discussed in some detail in Chapter 5 in *Bugbook I*.

An example of how device select pulses and time delay routines can be used to perform sequential operations is shown in Fig. 5-6. In this example, two liquid streams are added to a large tank, the resulting solution is heated and stirred to allow a reaction to occur, and finally the tank contents are drained. Eight different devices are present; a power switch, three valves, three motors, and a heater. Two device select pulses are employed per device: one to turn it on and the other to turn it off. A variety of time delays are required, varying from 0.01 hour, or 36 seconds, to 65.4 minutes, and all can be readily programmed in the microcomputer. The 36-second time delay is used at least seven times. The important point about this system is that *the sequence of operations, and the time intervals between them, can be readily changed simply by altering the microcomputer program.* Again, this is an example of software replacing hardware. No counters or special logic circuits

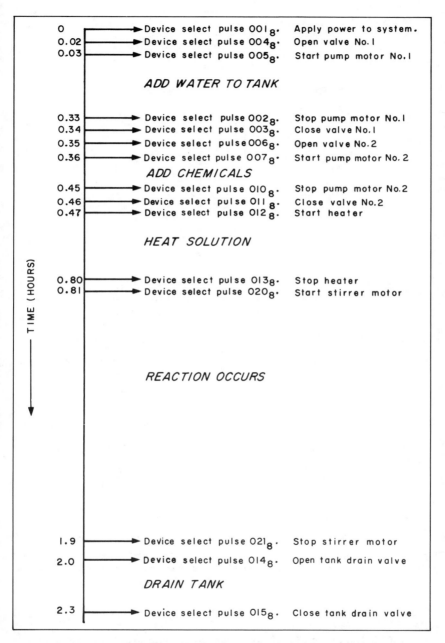

Fig. 5-6. A sequence of operations associated with a batch reactor, a piece of equipment used by chemical engineers to perform chemical reactions.

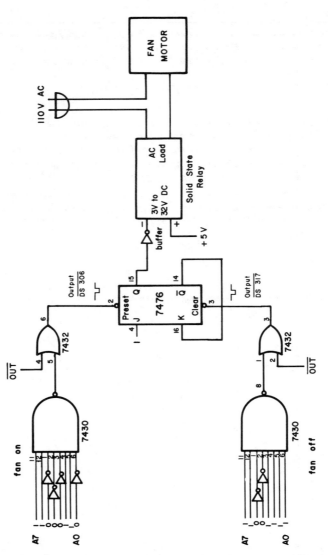

Fig. 5-7. This circuit demonstrates (a) the use of 8-input 7430 NAND gates to decode the 8-bit device code from the microcomputer, and (b) the use of an optically isolated solid-state relay to drive a fan motor from a TTL input signal.

are required to sequence the operations. The microcomputer can do the whole thing with the aid of device select pulses, eight flip-flops, eight TTL buffers, and eight optoelectronic relays that control ac power with logic 0 and logic 1 signals from a TTL circuit. The extension of

Fig. 5-8. Typical optically isolated solid-state relays that are available for a price of $10 to $20 in quantities of one. Such relays can control up to 10 A of 115 V ac power from a single TTL output. The relay at the lower right (AC IN) converts ac power to a dc signal, thus permitting you to detect when a fan motor or other power-consuming device is in the "on" state. The small chip is not a semiconductor device, but rather a reed relay that can operate from +5 volts TTL. The Aristan time capsule is a solid-state time delay device.

these ideas to traffic lights, building protection, machine operation, and a variety of other situations that require sequential operations should be clear.

CONTROLLING POWER WITH A MICROCOMPUTER

Fig. 5-7 shows a circuit in which a 7476 flip-flop controls ac power to a fan motor. This is done with the aid of an optically isolated solid-state relay (Fig. 5-8), a type of relay that has become very popular within the last several years. A simple TTL input to this relay can easily control 10 amperes at 115 volts ac. Although we shall not discuss such relays in this book, it should be clear that a microcomputer can readily control the fan. The LO memory address is connected to each of the two 7430 eight-input NAND gates, which decode the 8-bit device code produced by the OUT instruction. The unique logic 0 state produced by the 7430 gate is then ORed with the $\overline{\text{OUT}}$ pulse.

TEST

This test probes your understanding of the concepts and experiments in this chapter. Please write your answers on a separate piece of paper.

5-1. Define the following terms: loop, timing loop, period, clock cycle, and state.

5-2. Draw a simple digital circuit that can count clock cycles.

5-3. Write a microcomputer program that will generate timing delays that are multiples of approximately 100 microseconds.

Your performance on this test will be acceptable if you can answer all of the above questions correctly in a one-hour closed-book examination. You will frequently encounter timing loops in microcomputer programs.

WHAT HAVE YOU ACCOMPLISHED IN THIS CHAPTER?

It was stated at the beginning of this chapter that at the end you would be able to do the following:

- Define the terms: loop, timing loop, period, clock cycle, and state.
  This was done at various places in the chapter.

- Program a timing loop that can generate timing delays that are multiples of 0.200 second.
  You did this in Subroutine No. 1.

- Program a timing loop that can generate timing delays that are multiples of approximately 0.5 millisecond.
  You did this in Program No. 6.

- Demonstrate how a microcomputer can act as a monostable multivibrator.
  You actually generated single timing pulses with the aid of the microcomputer program and the 7476 flip-flop.

CHAPTER 6

Generating Status Information

It becomes ever more clear that one of the important functions of the 8080 microprocessor chip is to control the transfer of eight bits of digital information, called a *byte*, between the internal data bus, located within the 8080 chip itself, and the external data bus, located external to the chip. Internally, information can be stored in registers such as the accumulator, the general-purpose registers, the program counter, stack pointer, and instruction register. Externally, information is stored in memory, the status latch, and input/output devices. In this chapter, you will learn quite a bit more concerning how all this is done. You will gain a general understanding of how the microprocessor operates and interacts with the "outside world" external to the chip.

This is a somewhat advanced chapter, one that you can skip for the moment if your time is limited. If you wish, you may read Chapters 7 and 8 first, for they will round out your interfacing skills. Then return to this chapter; you will not miss needed information by skipping it.

OBJECTIVES

At the end of this chapter, you will be able to do the following:

- Explain the differences between the internal and external busses in an 8080-based microcomputer system.
- List the sources and destinations of information that appears on the external data bus.
- Explain the differences between a state, clock cycle, instruction cycle, and machine cycle.

- Explain what a status bit and a status byte are.
- Describe the nine different types of machine cycles.
- Describe the function of each of the eight different status bits.
- Explain how the control outputs on the 8080 chip can be combined logically with one or more of the status bits, and provide at least one example of such a logical combination.
- Draw timing diagrams that depict the behavior of typical microcomputer instructions. Such diagrams should clearly demonstrate the logic states of the more important control inputs, control outputs, and status bits.
- Explain the different types of data that can appear on the external data bus.
- Explain state timing for typical machine cycles.
- Explain how single stepping of an 8080 microcomputer occurs, complete with timing diagrams and circuit diagrams.
- Discuss the characteristics of the 8212 eight-bit input/output port integrated-circuit chip.

DEFINITIONS

bus—A path over which digital information is transferred, from any of several sources to any of several destinations. Only one transfer of information can take place at any one time. While such transfer is taking place, all other sources that are tied to the bus must be disabled.

to bus—To interconnect several digital devices that either receive or transmit digital signals by a common set of conducting paths, called a bus, over which all information between such devices is transferred.

control input—An input pin on the 8080 chip that controls the behavior of the microprocessor.

control output—An output pin on the 8080 chip that controls the behavior of external chips and devices connected to the 8080 chip.

data bus buffer/latch—An 8-bit latch with three-state buffer outputs that controls the transfer of information between the internal data bus within the 8080 microprocessor chip and the external data bus.

execution—One of the two functional parts of an instruction cycle.

external bus—The 8-bit bidirectional data bus located external to the 8080 microprocessor chip and to which is connected memory, output latches and output devices, and input buffers from input devices.

fetch—One of the two functional parts of an instruction cycle. The collective actions of acquiring a memory address and then an instruction or data byte from memory.

instruction cycle—A successive group of machine cycles, as few as one or as many as five, which together perform a single microprocessor instruction within the microprocessor chip.

internal bus—A bidirectional data bus located within the 8080 microprocessor chip and to which is connected the accumulator, instruction register, general-purpose register, a temporary register, and the arithmetic/logic unit.

machine cycle—A subdivision of an instruction cycle during which time a related group of actions occur within the microprocessor chip. In the 8080 microprocessor, there exist nine different machine cycles. All instructions are combinations of one or more of these machine cycles.

nonoverlapping two-phase clock—A two-phase clock in which the clock pulses of the individual phases do not overlap.

state—A constant interval equal in length to the period of the clock oscillator that drives the central processing unit.

status bit—A single bit of output information that is placed on the external data bus early during the execution of a machine cycle and is latched by an integrated-circuit chip called a status latch. Since this bit is acquired early by the latch, it can be used to control external events that occur later in the machine cycle.

status byte—An 8-bit byte, i.e., a unit of 8 bits, that contains eight different status bits.

status latch—An integrated-circuit chip, such as, for example, the Intel 8212, that latches the eight status bits when they appear on the external data bus.

three-state device—A semiconductor logic device in which there exist three possible output states: (1) a "logic 0" state, (2) a "logic 1" state, or (3) a state in which the output is, in effect, disconnected from the rest of the circuit and has no influence upon it.

two-phase clock—A two-output timing device that provides two continuous series of timing pulses that are synchronized together, with a single clock pulse from the second series always following a single clock pulse from the first series. Depending on the type of two-phase clock, the pulses in the first and second series may or may not overlap each other.

THE BIDIRECTIONAL DATA BUS

The *8-bit bidirectional data bus* is the main data communications link between the accumulator in the 8080 microprocessor chip and memory, input devices, output devices, and the *status latch*. By *bidirectional* it is meant that data can flow in both directions on the bus, from the chip to a device, and from a device into the chip. The bus is *three-state*. A schematic diagram of data flow on the bus is shown in Fig. 6-1.

In the discussion of *bus* in Chapter 7 of *Bugbook II*, the following definitions were provided:

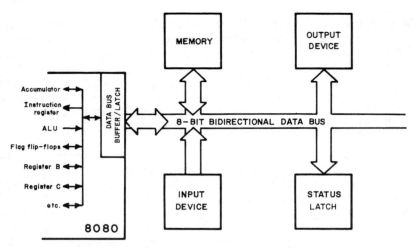

Fig. 6-1. The data bus buffer/latch within the 8080 chip serves as an internal interface between the internal data bus and the external bidirectional data bus.

bus—A path over which digital information is transferred, from any of several sources to any of several destinations. Only one transfer of information can take place at any one time. While such transfer is taking place, all other sources that are tied to the bus must be disabled.

to bus—To interconnect several digital devices which either receive or transmit digital signals by a common set of conducting paths, called a bus, over which all information between such devices is transferred.

three-state device—A semiconductor logic device in which there are three possible output states: (1) a "logic 0" state, (2) a "logic 1" state, or (3) a state in which the output is, in effect, disconnected from the rest of the circuit and has no influence upon it.

In the preceding definition for a bus, the important point is that *only one transfer of information can take place at any one time.* Since a bus is a shared group of conducting paths, chaos would result if all the transmitters on the bus attempted to send information simultaneously. The basic purpose of a bus is to minimize the number of interconnections required to transfer information between digital devices. The fewer the interconnections, the easier it is to lay out printed-circuit boards. Even within the integrated-circuit chip itself, *internal busses* are employed to facilitate chip fabrication. The 8080 microprocessor chip has an internal bus and communicates with external devices over an *external bus* present on printed-circuit boards.

In Fig. 6-1 is given a functional block diagram of the external 8-bit bidirectional data bus. On the following page is provided a functional block diagram of the 8080 chip itself. Note the *data bus buffer/latch* at the top middle part of the diagram. This portion of the 8080 chip is the buffer between the internal and external data busses. When the latch is enabled, data can pass in either direction between the two data busses.

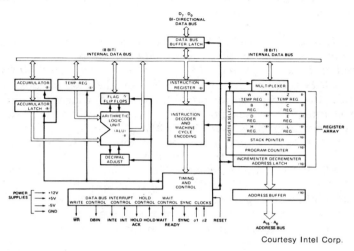

Courtesy Intel Corp.

On the 8-bit bidirectional data bus (the external bus), there are three transmitters:

- memory,
- any input device, and
- the data bus buffer/latch within the 8080 chip;

and four receivers:

- memory,
- any output device,
- the status latch, and
- the data bus buffer/latch within the 8080 chip.

Information that appears on the external bus can be one of the following:

- A data byte that is being transferred from memory, through the data bus buffer/latch, into the accumulator (or one of the six general-purpose registers);
- An instruction byte that is being transferred from memory, through the data bus buffer/latch, into the instruction register;
- A data byte from an input device that is being transferred through the data bus buffer/latch into the accumulator;
- A data byte from the accumulator that is being transferred through the data bus buffer/latch to an output device;

- A *status byte* that is being transferred through the data bus buffer/latch to the status latch; and
- An instruction byte from an input device that is being transferred, during an interrupt condition, through the data bus buffer/latch into the instruction register;

and perhaps others as well. Clearly, the microprocessor has a considerable timing problem: *It must coordinate the transfer of information between all transmitters and all receivers on the external 8-bit bidirectional data bus.* It has the same problem on the internal bus as well. How does the microprocessor do all this? This is what we shall discuss in this chapter. This discussion will give you a "feeling" for what happens within a microprocessor chip without bogging you down in the many subtle details of microprocessor operation. For further details, see the Intel Corporation literature, specifically their *8080 Microcomputer System Manual* and the *Intellec 8/Mod 80 Microcomputer Development System Reference Manual,* both of which provide useful information and timing diagrams on what occurs during the different microcomputer machine cycles.[8,9] Some of the material provided below is from these two manuals, courtesy of the Intel Corporation.

INSTRUCTION CYCLES

To quote the *Intellec 8/Mod 80 Microcomputer Development System Reference Manual:*

"The 8080 is driven by a two-phase clock oscillator, at a maximum frequency of 2.08 MHz. All processing activities are referred to the period of this clock. The two nonoverlapping clock phases, labeled ϕ_1 and ϕ_2, are furnished by external circuitry. The ϕ_1 clock divides the processing cycle into *states.* A state is the smallest unit of processing activity (480 ns when the processor is operating at maximum speed) and is defined as the interval between two successive positive-going transitions of the ϕ_1 clock. Timing logic within the 8080 uses the clock inputs to produce a SYNC pulse, which identifies the first state of every machine cycle. . .

". . . As shown in Fig. 6-2, the SYNC signal is related to the leading edge of the ϕ_2 clock. There is a delay between the low-to-high transition of ϕ_2 and the positive-going edge of the SYNC pulse. There also is a corresponding delay between the next ϕ_2 pulse and the falling edge of the SYNC signal. Status information is displayed on D0 through D7 during this same interval. Switching of the status signals (occurs only when ϕ_2 is at logic 1) . . ."

"An *instruction cycle* consists of two functional parts, the *fetch* and the *execution.* Each of these functional parts, in turn, consists of a number of *machine cycles.* During the fetch, a selected instruction

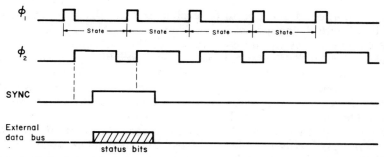

Fig. 6-2. Clocks ϕ_1 and ϕ_2 and SYNC timing. SYNC does not occur in the second and third machine cycles of a DAD instruction.

(one, two, or three bytes) is extracted from memory and deposited in the CPU's instruction register. During the execution part, the instruction is decoded and translated into specific processing activities. The fetch routine requires one machine cycle for each byte to be fetched. The duration of the execution portion of the instruction cycle *depends upon the kind of instruction that has been fetched.* Some instructions do not require any machine cycles other than those necessary to fetch the instruction; other instructions, however, require additional machine cycles to write or read data to/from memory or I/O devices. The DAD instruction is an exception in that it requires two additional machine cycles to complete an internal register-pair add.

"Every instruction cycle contains one, two, three, four, or five machine cycles. Each machine cycle, in turn, consists of three, four, or five states. A state is defined as a constant interval, equal in length to the period of the clock oscillator which drives the CPU (a phase). That is, a state is so defined in all but three cases. Exceptions to the rule are the WAIT state, the hold (HLDA) state, and the halt (HLTA) state, . . . A moment's consideration will show that this is reasonable, since the WAIT, the HLDA, and the HLTA states depend on external events and are, by their nature, of indeterminate length. Observe, however, that even these exceptional states must be synchronized with the pulses of the driving clock. Thus the durations of all states, including these, are integral multiples of the clock phase.

"To summarize then, each clock *phase* marks a *state;* three to five states constitute a *machine cycle;* and one to five machine cycles comprise an *instruction cycle.* A full instruction cycle requires anywhere from four to eighteen phases for its completion (2.0 microseconds to 9.0 microseconds), depending on the kind of instruction involved."

The preceding paragraphs are well written and need little elaboration. The important point is that a microprocessor is a clocked digital electronic device. Clock pulses are required to synchronize and cause specific operations to occur. A sufficient number of operations within the microprocessor must occur for each instruction that it is not possible to do all with a single clock train. Thus, a two-phase clock with non-overlapping pulses ϕ_1 and ϕ_2 is required. For the simplest instruction cycles, *eight individual clock pulses are available to coordinate the actions within the microprocessor.* For simple instructions, this is all that is required. However, for more complicated instructions, *additional clock pulses are required to coordinate the microprocessor actions.* The most complicated instruction in the 8080 instruction set is the XTHL instruction, which requires eighteen states, or *36 individual clock pulses,* for its completion. Treat the 8080 microprocessor as *a digital circuit that you could, if you so desired, wire on breadboarding sockets.* It wouldn't be practical for you to do so, because of the many wire connections which might be required. Nevertheless, you shouldn't view the internal workings of the 8080 chip as a mystery. What is inside is simply a clocked digital circuit that is run via a pair of synchronized clock trains called a two-phase clock. Much of the internal circuitry within the 8080 chip is bus oriented, so fewer wire connections are required than you would ordinarily expect.

Fig. 6-3 is a schematic diagram of a group of three microcomputer instructions, SUB A, OUT <B2>, and CALL <B2> <B3>, which respectively require four, ten, and 17 states (or clock cycles). This diagram will be discussed in greater detail in the following section.

MACHINE CYCLES

In Fig. 6-3 is a group of three microcomputer instructions each of which requires its own instruction cycle. The SUB A instruction has one machine cycle and a total of four states. The two-byte OUT <B2> instruction requires three machine cycles and a total of ten states. Finally, the three-byte CALL <B2> <B3> instruction requires five machine cycles and a total of seventeen states. The different machine cycles within each instruction are labeled M_1, M_2, . . . , and M_5. Five machine cycles is the maximum number required for any of the three

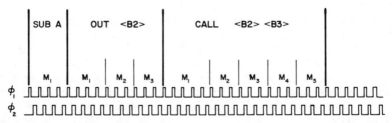

Fig. 6-3. State, machine cycle, and instruction cycle timing. There are three microcomputer instructions shown: **SUB A, OUT <B2>,** and **CALL <B2> <B3>,** which are, respectively, single-byte, two-byte, and three-byte instructions requiring four, ten, and seventeen clock cycles.

instructions shown in the figure. In this section, we shall discuss the individual machine cycles within the overall instruction cycle.

There are nine types of machine cycles that *may occur* within an instruction cycle, although not more than five machine cycles will appear in any given instruction cycle. These types of machine cycles include the following:

- *Fetch*—This machine cycle consists of either four or five states, with the exception of the WAIT, HLDA, and HLTA states, which contain any integral number of states greater than three. During this cycle, the memory address is acquired, status bits are made available on the 8-bit external data bus, register transfers occur within the 8080 chip, and simple arithmetic or logical operations are performed. With some microcomputer instructions, this is the only machine cycle required. Any microcomputer instruction that requires only four or five states requires only the fetch machine cycle. This machine cycle acquires its name from the fact that, during the cycle, the operation code for the instruction is "fetched" from the memory location present in the program counter. This operation code is transferred to the instruction register within the 8080 chip, where it is subsequently decoded by the instruction decoder into a series of actions that the microprocessor performs. During this cycle, the program counter is incremented by one, thus giving the location of the next instruction byte.
- *Memory read*—This machine cycle consists of three states. During this cycle, a byte present in the memory location indicated by the program counter is transferred from memory to one of the registers within the 8080 chip. Such registers include the accumulator, B, C, D, E, H, and L.
- *Memory write*—This machine cycle consists of either three or four states, during which the contents of a register are transferred to the memory location pointed to by the H and L registers. The H and L pointer registers may also be incremented or decremented during this machine cycle.
- *Output*—This machine cycle consists of three states, during which the output device code is made available on the 16-bit memory address bus and the contents of the accumulator are made available on the 8-bit external bidirectional data bus.
- *Input*—This machine cycle also consists of three states, during which the input device code is made available on the 16-bit memory address bus and the data bus buffer/latch within the 8080 microprocessor is enabled to allow input data appearing on the external bus to be transferred to the accumulator.
- *Stack write*—During this three-state machine cycle, an 8-bit data byte is placed upon the external data bus and transferred to the

memory location given by either $M(SP-1)$ or $M(SP-2)$, where SP is the stack pointer register within the 8080 microprocessor.

- *Stack read*—During this three-state machine cycle, an 8-bit data byte is transferred from the memory location given by either $M(SP)$ or $M(SP+1)$ via the external data bus to the microprocessor registers, such as H, L, B, C, D, E, or the program counter.
- *Halt*—This machine cycle can contain any integral number of states greater than three. The microprocessor remains in a WAIT state for as long as the READY input to the 8080 chip is at logic 0. The WAIT output from the 8080 chip is at logic 1 to acknowledge that the CPU is in a WAIT state.
- *Interrupt*—This five-state machine cycle resembles the fetch machine cycle, except that the program counter, which has already been incremented in the fetch cycle, is not incremented. This allows the pre-interrupt status of the counter to be saved in the stack and permits an orderly return to the interrupted program after the interrupt request has been processed.

The following machine cycles occur for the instructions present in Fig. 6-3.

Fetch: M_1 in SUB A, OUT <B2>, and CALL <B2> <B3>
Memory read: M_2 in OUT <B2> and both M_2 and M_3 in CALL
             <B2> <B3>
Output: M_3 in OUT <B2>
Stack Write: Both M_4 and M_5 in CALL <B2> <B3>

You might wonder why two similar machine cycles are required during the same instruction cycle, as occurs in the CALL instruction. The answer is that information is being transferred to or from different registers within the 8080 chip during the memory read and stack write machine cycles; consequently, two different cycles are required in each case. It is not hard to imagine that the microprocessors of the future, which will all be much faster than the 8080, will require more machine cycles than five to perform still more complicated instructions such as multiply or divide.

Additional information on machine cycles can be found in References 8 and 9. Both sources were used in writing this section.

MACHINE CYCLE IDENTIFICATION

A question that bothers many people when they first learn about the 8080 microprocessor is: How can one determine which machine cycles comprise a microcomputer instruction? The Intel literature describes typical machine cycles for instructions such as INP, OUT, ADD, CALL, HALT, and others, but such descriptions are far from being a complete inventory of the entire 78-instruction set. We may believe that we can decipher most of the instructions given sufficient time and patience, but is there any way to do this while the microcomputer is in operation?

The answer to the preceding question is that it is indeed possible to determine which machine cycles comprise a microcomputer instruction; it can be done while the microcomputer is in operation. The details will be provided in the subsections that follow. Much of the information is contained in References 8 and 9.

Latching the Status Bits

How does the microcomputer identify the machine cycle in progress? *It does so by transmitting an 8-bit status signal during the first state, T_1, of every machine cycle.* These status signals appear on the external 8-bit bidirectional data bus, and are latched by the 8212 *status latch circuit* shown in Fig. 6-4. There are eight status bits, and we shall discuss them shortly. The important point is that *the status bits are the first information applied to the external data bus during a new instruction cycle.* Thus, the status bits precede an instruction or data byte from memory or an input or output data byte on the external data bus. Such information comes after the status bits, not before it.

How are the status bits latched? This is shown in both Fig. 6-4 and 6-5. Observe in Fig. 6-4 that the SYNC output from the 8080 chip is connected to the DS_2 input on the 8212 chip. When DS_2 is at logic 1

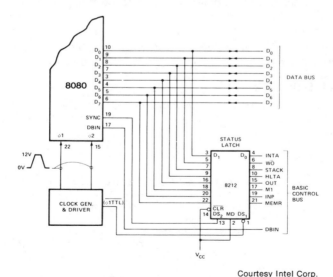

Courtesy Intel Corp.

Fig. 6-4. Diagram of circuit for latching the eight status bits that appear on the external data bus during the T_1 and T_2 states.

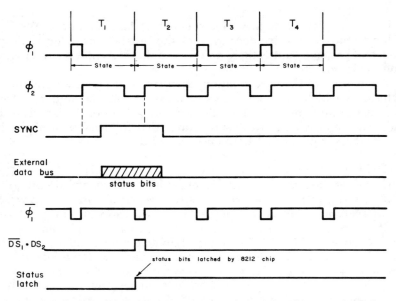

Fig. 6-5. Timing diagram that illustrates how the status bits on the 8-bit external data bus are latched by the 8212 chip.

and $\overline{DS}_1$ is at logic 0, the status information available on the external data bus is latched and appears at the 8212 output pins 4, 6, 8, 10, 15, 17, 19, and 21. The input to pin 1 on the 8212 chip is ϕ_1; when this input goes to logic 0 with SYNC at logic 1, the latching action occurs (Fig. 6-5). The $\overline{DS}_1 \cdot DS_2$ pulse has a pulse width of 500 ns. A typical 8080 microcomputer has such a latch, as shown in Fig. 6-6.

The Eight Status Bits

The eight status bits that appear on the external data bus during the T_1 and T_2 states of a machine cycle have the following symbols and definitions:

Symbol	Data Bus Bit	Description
INTA	D0	Acknowledge signal for INTERRUPT request, at which time it is a logic 1. This signal should be used to gate a restart instruction, RST, onto the data bus when DBIN (pin 17 on the 8080 chip) is at logic 1.
$\overline{WO}$	D1	If the operation in the current machine cycle is a WRITE memory or OUTPUT function, this status bit will be at logic 0. If the operation is a READ memory or INPUT, this status bit will be at logic 1.
STACK	D2	A logic 1 indicates that the 16-bit memory address bus holds the stack address from the stack pointer, SP.

HLTA	D3	Acknowledge signal for a HALT instruction. When the machine cycle is a HALT instruction, this status bit will be at logic 1.
OUT	D4	A logic 1 for this status bit indicates that the 16-bit memory address bus contains the 8-bit device code of the output device and that the external data bus will contain the output data when $\overline{WR}$ (pin 18 on the 8080 chip) is at logic 0.
M_1	D5	This status bit provides a logic 1 signal to indicate that the CPU is in the fetch cycle for the first byte of an instruction.
INP	D6	A logic 1 for this status bit indicates that the 16-bit memory address bus contains the 8-bit device code of the input device and that the input data should be placed on the external data bus when DBIN (pin 17 on the 8080 chip) is at logic 1.
MEMR	D7	A logic 1 indicates that the external data bus will have data coming from memory during this machine cycle.

To quote from Reference 8:

"The machine cycles that actually do occur in a particular instruction cycle depend upon the kind of instruction, with the overriding stipulation that the first machine cycle in any instruction cycle is always a FETCH.

"The processor identifies the machine cycle in progress by transmitting an 8-bit status signal during the first state of every machine cycle. Updated status information appears on the 8080's data lines (D0 through D7) during the SYNC interval. This data may be saved in latches, decoded, and used to develop control signals for external circuitry. Table 6-1 shows how the status information is distributed on the microprocessor's data bus.

Status latch

Fig. 6-6. The location of the 8-bit status latch on the CPIC-80/B printed-circuit board. This board is part of an 8080 microcomputer system manufactured by E&L Instruments, Inc.

"Status signals are provided principally for the control of external circuitry. Simplicity of interface, rather than machine identification, dictates the logical definition of individual status bits. You will therefore observe that certain processor machine cycles are uniquely identified by a single status bit, but that others are not. The M_1 status bit, D5, for example, unambiguously identifies a FETCH machine cycle. A STACK READ, on the other hand, is indicated by the coincidence of STACK and MEMR signals. Machine cycle identification data can also be valuable in the test and debugging phases of system development."

As indicated in the preceding quote, to identify a specific machine cycle, we employ the truth table shown as Table 6-1.

8080 Control Inputs and Outputs

In Chapter 1 we discussed the control inputs and outputs to and from the 8080 microprocessor chip. The control inputs include (Fig. 6-7):

RESET (pin 12)
INT (pin 14)
READY (pin 23)
HOLD (pin 13)

and the control outputs are:

WAIT (pin 24)
$\overline{WR}$ (pin 18)
HLDA (pin 21)
INTE (pin 16)
SYNC (pin 19)
DBIN (pin 17)

The above control inputs and outputs can be combined logically with the eight status outputs:

INTA
$\overline{WO}$
STACK
HLTA
OUT
M_1
INP
MEMR

latched by the 8212 buffer/latch chip to coordinate and control data transfer into and out of the microprocessor. This is a very important point. *You are not limited to the four control input pins and six control output pins on the 8080 chip (Fig. 6-7); the latched status bits can be used as well.* The $\overline{IN}$ and $\overline{OUT}$ strobe outputs are not located on the

Table 6-1. Truth Table Relating Type of Machine Cycle to
Individual Status Bits in 8-Bit Status Word Appearing
on the External Data Bus During State T_1

Type of Machine Cycle	Data Bus Bit and Status Information							
	MEMR D7	INP D6	M_1 D5	OUT D4	HLTA D3	STACK D2	$\overline{WO}$ D1	INTA DO
Instruction Fetch	1	0	1	0	0	0	1	0
Memory Read	1	0	0	0	0	0	1	0
Memory Write	0	0	0	0	0	0	0	0
Stack Read	1	0	0	0	0	1	1	0
Stack Write	0	0	0	0	0	1	0	0
Input	0	1	0	0	0	0	1	0
Output	0	0	0	1	0	0	0	0
Interrupt	0	0	1	0	0	0	1	1
Halt	1	0	0	0	1	0	1	0
Interrupt While Halt	0	0	1	0	1	0	1	1

8080 chip; you derive them from the status bits after they are latched. The latching of status bits is a very clever piece of digital electronic design, one that maximizes the use of the data bus and eliminates the need for extra output pins on the microprocessor chip. Although it may appear that the price you pay for this capability is one state per machine cycle to latch the status bits, keep in mind that during the same

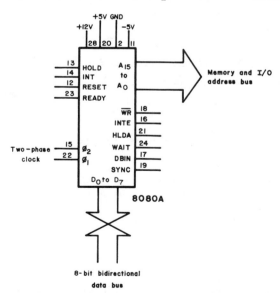

Fig. 6-7. Block diagram of the 8080 microprocessor chip showing the control inputs and outputs as well as the memory address bus and the 8-bit bidirectional data bus (the external data bus).

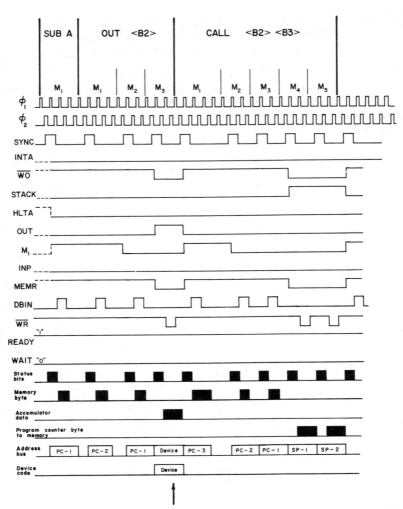

Fig. 6-8. Timing diagrams for signals present on the data bus, address bus, and control bus. Note changes in the status bit outputs.

state the 16-bit memory address is being loaded into the program counter.

Timing Diagrams for Typical 8080 Instructions

We shall now discuss the preceding points with the aid of Fig. 6-8, which shows timing diagrams for the following digital signals:

- the 8080 two-phase clock and several control inputs and outputs (Fig. 6-9),

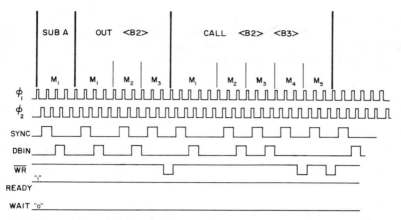

Fig. 6-9. The two-phase clock inputs and several control input and output signals found on the 8080 microprocessor chip.

- the latched status bits (Fig. 6-10),
- the different types of data that appear on the external data bus (Fig. 6-11),
- the memory address and I/O device code information that appears on the memory address bus (Fig. 6-12).

The letters PC and SP stand for program counter and stack pointer, respectively, which are 16-bit registers within the 8080 microprocessor chip. By "PC − 1" is meant that the information on the 16-bit external address bus is one less than the contents of the program counter. *The program counter contains the address of the next instruction to be executed, not the address of the current instruction being executed.*

The three instructions that will be discussed include: SUB A, a single-byte instruction that clears the accumulator; OUT <B2>, a two-byte instruction that provides an $\overline{\text{OUT}}$ strobe pulse that allows an external device to latch the contents of the accumulator, which appears

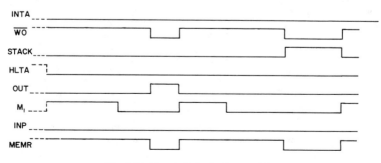

Fig. 6-10. The eight latched status bits.

for a fleeting instant on the external data bus; and CALL <B2> <B3>, a three-byte instruction that unconditionally calls a subroutine at the memory address given by bytes B2 and B3. A simple program that incorporates these instructions in sequence is as follows:

LO Memory Address	Octal Instruction	Comments
000	227	Subtract contents of accumulator from accumulator, i.e., clear the accumulator
001	323	Generate a device select pulse to output eight bits of accumulator data to the device with the device code given in the following byte
002	000	Device code for output device
003	315	Unconditional call of subroutine located at memory location given in the following two bytes
004	040	LO memory address byte
005	000	HI memory address byte
006	166	Halt
040	311	Unconditional return to main program from this subroutine

We should note that the stack pointer, SP, has been previously located at $LO = 200_8$ and $HI = 000_8$ and that the preceding program can be run repeatedly simply by resetting the program counter to $HI = 000_8$ and $LO = 000_8$ with the aid of the manual RESET control switch on the front panel of an 8080 microcomputer. The execution of this program can be summarized as follows:

LO Memory Address Bus	Bidirectional Data Bus		MEMR	INP	M_1	OUT	HLTA	STACK	$\overline{WO}$	INTA
								Status Bits		
377	377	Mnemonic	1	0	0	0	1	0	1	0

NOTE: At the moment, the microcomputer is in the HALT state. The eight status bits are latched in the states shown. To start the computer program, we use the RESET control switch to reset the program counter to $HI = 000_8$ and $LO = 000_8$. The reason that we have supplied the above information will become apparent below.

000	227	SUB A	1	0	1	0	0	0	1	0
001	323	OUT	1	0	1	0	0	0	1	0
002	000	<B2>	1	0	1	0	0	0	1	0
000*	000	Data output on bus	0	0	0	1	0	0	0	0
003	315	CALL	1	0	1	0	0	0	1	0
004	200	<B2>	1	0	1	0	0	0	1	0
005	000	<B3>	1	0	1	0	0	0	1	0
177	000	Stack write	0	0	0	0	0	1	0	0
176	006	Stack write	0	0	0	0	0	1	0	0
040	311	RET	1	0	1	0	0	0	1	0
177	006	Stack read	1	0	0	0	0	1	1	0
176	000	Stack read	1	0	0	0	0	1	1	0
006	166	HLT	1	0	1	0	0	0	1	0
377	377	---	1	0	0	0	1	0	1	0

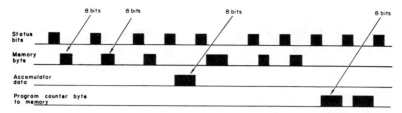

Fig. 6-11. Representation of the types of data that appear on the external bidirectional data bus. Observe that no two different types of data are present on the data bus simultaneously.

After execution of the above program, the microcomputer is in the HALT state. The asterisked (*) instruction shows the data output machine cycle. The device code for the output device selected at LO = 002_8 is 000_8.

Fig. 6-8 provides the timing diagrams for the first nine machine cycles in the above program listing. The entire program requires thirteen machine cycles; no further execution occurs in the HALT state at the end of the program. If you study the figure well, you will develop a good understanding of most of the important concepts of microprocessor operation. Focus upon the following:

- The time before the first machine cycle, M_1, in the SUB A instruction.

  Here we assume that the microcomputer is in the HALT state, in which the eight status bits are latched in the 8212 chip in the following states: INTA = STACK = OUT = M_1 = INP = logic 0 and $\overline{WO}$ = HLTA = MEMR = logic 1.

- The unique time when the OUT status bit is latched by the 8212 chip to a logic 1 state.

  Note that at no other time is the OUT status bit at a logic 1. This condition allows you to uniquely determine two important conditions that occur simultaneously: (1) the I/O device code is present as two identical 8-bit bytes on the 16-bit memory address bus, and (2) the contents of the accumulator are present on the 8-bit external bidirectional data bus. These conditions occur *only when the OUT status bit is latched at logic 1.* Clearly, the OUT status bit can be used to generate

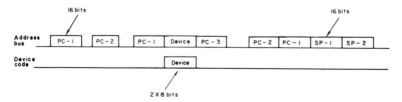

Fig. 6-12. Representation of the types of data that appear on the 16-bit address bus.

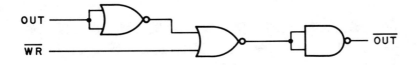

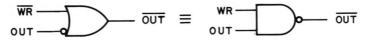

Fig. 6-13. Logic circuitry for the generation of the $\overline{\text{OUT}}$ control signal.

device select pulses that can strobe data from the accumulator to a specified output device. In Fig. 6-8 a vertical arrow is drawn near the bottom of the figure to denote the time at which output data from the accumulator can be latched by an external device.

An 8080 microcomputer will generate a 500-ns $\overline{\text{OUT}}$ pulse during the time that the OUT status bit is at logic 1. The logic circuitry employed to do this is shown in Fig. 6-13, i.e., a simple two-input NAND gate that is enabled only when WR and OUT are both at logic 1. The 500-ns pulse width is a consequence of the $\overline{\text{WR}}$ input, which remains at logic 0 for only 500 ns, as can be seen in Fig. 6-7.

Although the input instruction is not shown, it functions in a manner similar to the output instruction. The INP status bit is latched by the 8212, and a device select pulse is generated while it is latched with the aid of the logic circuit shown in Fig. 6-14. The negative clock pulse, $\overline{\text{IN}}$, is generated for 500 ns when both DBIN and INP are at logic 1.

- The status bit M_1 is at a logic 1 state only during the first machine cycle of an instruction.
- The status bit $\overline{\text{WO}}$ is at logic 0 when data is being written into memory or an output device. This status bit is at logic 1 while an instruction byte is being read from memory. During a multibyte

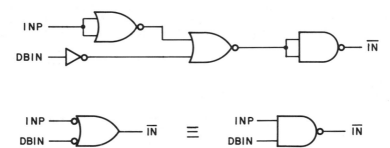

Fig. 6-14. Logic circuitry for the generation of the $\overline{\text{IN}}$ control signal.

instruction, $\overline{\text{WO}}$ remains latched at logic 1 until the full multibyte instruction has been read from memory.

- The SYNC output at pin 19 of the 8080 chip is at logic 1 at the same time that the eight status bits are present on the external data bus.
- The HLTA status bit is latched at logic 1 only when the microcomputer is in the halt state.
- The $\overline{\text{WR}}$ output at pin 18 of the 8080 chip is at logic 0 only when data is being written into memory or an output device. When $\overline{\text{WR}}$ is at logic 0, the status bit MEMR must be at a logic 0 state (since no data is being read from memory).
- A logic 1 at the MEMR status bit indicates that the external data bus will have data coming from memory during this machine cycle.
- The DBIN output at pin 17 on the 8080 chip is at logic 1 only when data from memory or an input device is present on the external data bus. This is the signal that indicates that data is coming from memory into the 8080 chip.
- The STACK status bit is usually latched at logic 0. It is latched at logic 1 only when the 16-bit address bus contains the address of a memory location on the stack.
- At least four types of 8-bit bytes can appear on the external data bus: the eight status bits, an 8-bit data or instruction byte from memory, eight bits of data from the accumulator, or an 8-bit address byte that is being transferred from memory to the program counter. *Only one 8-bit byte appears on the external data bus at a time.* There are no circumstances under which two different 8-bit bytes are simultaneously present on the external data bus.
- The program counter always contains the 16-bit memory address of the next instruction byte to be executed. The memory address of the existing instruction byte is therefore always one less than the current value of the program counter.
- The device code appears on the memory address bus as two identical 8-bit bytes, one occupying the LO address byte and the other occupying the HI address byte.
- The number of executed instructions in a program can be counted simply by applying the DBIN output at pin 17 on the 8080 chip and the latched M_1 status bit to a two-input 7408 AND gate. Each pulse from the gate output corresponds to a single instruction.

A schematic diagram that shows a status latch connected to an 8080 microprocessor chip is shown in Fig. 6-15. Some status signals are not often used. Among the most important signals derived from the status latch and the 8080 control signals are $\overline{\text{MEMR}}$, $\overline{\text{MEMW}}$, $\overline{\text{INTA}}$, $\overline{\text{I/O R}}$, and $\overline{\text{I/O W}}$. In this book, we have used the letters $\overline{\text{IN}}$ for $\overline{\text{I/O R}}$ and $\overline{\text{OUT}}$ for $\overline{\text{I/O W}}$. The $\overline{\text{MEMR}}$ and $\overline{\text{MEMW}}$ control signals indicate a

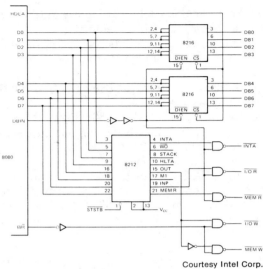

Fig. 6-15. Diagram of a typical 8080 control circuit that employs an 8212 chip. I/O R in the diagram is equivalent to $\overline{\text{IN}}$, and I/O W is equivalent to $\overline{\text{OUT}}$.

memory read or memory write operation. The $\overline{\text{IN}}$, $\overline{\text{OUT}}$, and $\overline{\text{INTA}}$ control signals have been mentioned previously.

The 8216 and 8212 chips in Fig. 6-15 have been eliminated through the introduction by Intel Corporation of the 8228 system controller and bus driver chip, which contains a status latch and the necessary gating inside the chip to generate the control signals $\overline{\text{INTA}}$, $\overline{\text{MEMR}}$, $\overline{\text{MEMW}}$, $\overline{\text{I/O R}}$, and $\overline{\text{I/O W}}$, as shown in Fig. 6-16. The 8228 chip also acts as a bidirectional bus driver, which allows the bidirectional data bus to be connected to more TTL loads than is possible with a bare 8080 chip. While the 8228 chip replaces several TTL chips, it is still relatively expensive. This discussion is only to call your attention to this chip and other new chips that help to simplify your microcomputer design task. Most individuals will be microcomputer users rather than microcomputer designers, and will not be involved with designs that start with the CPU chip and work up. This chapter gives you some idea of the design considerations required to convert an 8080 microprocessor chip into a full microcomputer. If you are interested in designing microcomputers using microprocessor chips, take a careful look at manufacturers' literature and periodicals. Others may have already encountered and solved your problems.

State Timing

Each different machine cycle is subdivided into from three to five 500-ns *states* labeled T_1, T_2, T_3, T_4, and T_5. Three additional states—

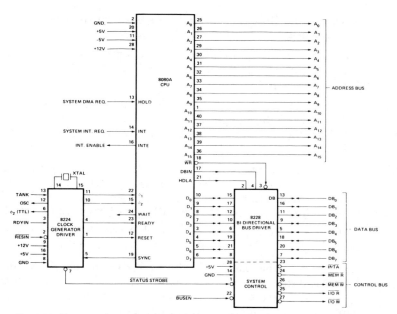

Fig. 6-16. Diagram of a typical 8080 control circuit that is based on the 8228 chip.

WAIT, HOLD, and HALT—last from three to an indefinite number of 500-ns clock periods, as controlled by external signals that determine the termination time of such states. The total number of states per instruction is determined by the number of machine cycles and by the number of states in each machine cycle. The simplest 8080 instructions have four states; the most complicated one has eighteen. The 8080 chip does not indicate its internal state directly, by broadcasting a "state control" output during each state; instead, the 8080 supplies direct control outputs (INTE, HLDA, DBIN, $\overline{WR}$, and WAIT) for use by external circuitry.[8]

The 8080 passes through at least three states in every machine cycle, with each state defined by successive positive leading edge transitions of the ϕ_1 clock. Each state contains two clock pulses: a ϕ_1 pulse and a ϕ_2 pulse. Events that occur in each state are referred to transitions in the ϕ_1 and ϕ_2 clock pulses; such events usually occur at the leading edge or within 50 ns of the leading edge.

The activities, or actions, that occur during each state, as explained in References 8 and 9, can be summarized in the following manner:

State	Associated Activities
T_1	The memory address from the program counter, the H and L register pair, or the stack pointer, *or* an I/O device number, is

255

placed on the 16-bit memory address bus near the positive leading edge of the ϕ_2 clock pulse.

The SYNC output pin on the 8080 microprocessor chip goes to logic 1 slightly after the positive leading edge of the ϕ_2 clock pulse.

The eight status bits (INTA, $\overline{\text{WO}}$, STACK, HLTA, OUT, M, INP, and MEMR) are placed on the external 8-bit bidirectional data bus slightly after the positive leading edge of the ϕ_2 clock pulse.

T_2 The logic states of the HOLD and READY input pins to the 8080 chip and the presence of a HALT instruction are tested. If the READY input is at logic 1, state T_3 can be entered; if the READY input is at logic 0, the CPU goes into a wait state, T_w.

The SYNC output pin on the 8080 chip goes to logic 0 slightly after the positive leading edge of the ϕ_2 clock pulse.

Slightly after the positive leading edge of the ϕ_2 clock pulse, the 8-bit status word on the external data bus is replaced either by an 8-bit instruction or data byte from memory, *or* by a data byte from the accumulator or an input device.

The contents of the 16-bit memory address bus do not change during this state. DBIN on the 8080 chip goes to logic 1 at ϕ_2 leading edge.

T_w An optional wait state. The CPU enters this state if the READY input to the 8080 chip is at logic 0 or if a HALT instruction has been executed. If a HALT instruction is encountered, the CPU will remain in this state until an interrupt is received or the program counter is reset. The CPU acknowledges the wait state by placing the WAIT output pin on the 8080 chip at a logic 1 state at the positive leading edge of the ϕ_1 clock pulse.

The HOLD state is a bit more complex and will not be discussed here.

A wait period may be of indefinite duration. The processor remains in the waiting condition until its READY input line again goes to logic 1. The instruction cycle may then proceed, beginning with the positive leading edge of the next ϕ_1 clock pulse. A WAIT interval will therefore consist of an integral number of T_w states and will always be a multiple of the clock period.[8]

The contents of the 16-bit memory address bus do not change during this state unless the CPU is in the HOLD state.

T_3 Data coming from memory and present on the 8-bit external data bus can be transferred to the instruction register, the accumulator, or to one of the general-purpose registers.

Data coming from an input device and present on the external data bus can be transferred to the accumulator.

Data coming from the accumulator and present on the external data bus can be transferred to memory or to an output device.

Data coming from one of the general-purpose registers and present on the external data bus can be transferred to memory.

The DBIN output pin on the 8080 chip returns to logic 0 at the positive leading edge of the ϕ_2 clock pulse.

The $\overline{WR}$ output pin on the 8080 chip goes to logic 0 at the positive leading edge of the first ϕ_1 clock pulse following state T_2. Note that this could occur either in state T_w or state T_3, usually the latter.

A variety of activities can occur during state T_3, depending upon the type of machine cycle. To summarize, an instruction byte (fetch machine cycle), data byte (memory read, stack read, or input machine cycle), or interrupt instruction (interrupt cycle) is input to the CPU from the 8-bit external data bus; *or* a data byte (memory write, stack write, or output machine cycle) is output onto the external data bus.[8]

T_4, T_5 Two optional states available for the execution of a particular instruction if required. If not, the CPU may skip one or both of them. These states are only used for internal processor operations.[8] The contents of the memory address bus change slightly after the positive leading edge of the ϕ_2 clock pulse in these states.

T_1 The $\overline{WR}$ output pin on the 8080 chip returns to a logic 1 at the positive leading edge of the ϕ_1 clock pulse during this state. This is the first state of a new instruction cycle.

The above descriptions are summarized in Figs. 6-17 and 6-18. Fig. 6-17 is a five-state machine cycle, the fetch cycle, in which a memory byte is transferred to the instruction register. As long as the READY output pin is at logic 1 during state T_2, state T_3 can be entered. We have not specified what occurs during states T_4 and T_5. Fig. 6-18 is a three-state machine cycle in which a data byte is written into memory or an output device. Note that the $\overline{WR}$ output pin on the 8080 chip is at logic 0 during state T_3. DBIN remains at logic 0 during a write or output machine cycle.

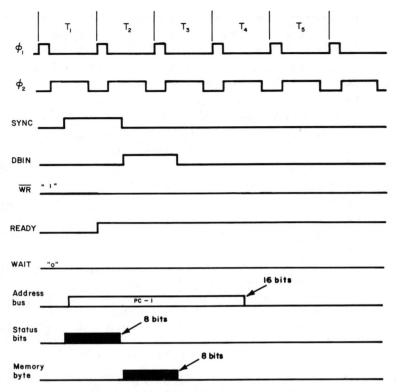

Fig. 6-17. A five-state machine cycle, the fetch cycle, in which a memory byte is transferred to the instruction register.

This concludes our discussion of "state timing" in the 8080 micro-processor chip. It would be worth your time to study Figs. 6-11 and 6-12 and also to obtain copies of References 8 and 9, which go into state timing in considerably greater detail.

SINGLE STEPPING AN 8080 MICROCOMPUTER

Fig. 6-19 shows a circuit used with an 8080 microcomputer to single step through the execution of a computer program. It is described here because it will give a bit more insight into the WAIT state of the 8080 microprocessor.

The basic function of the circuit in Fig. 6-19 is to generate, via a debounced pulser on the front panel of the microcomputer, a 550-ns monostable pulse at the D input to the 7474 positive-edge-triggered flip-flop. As shown in Fig. 6-20, the ϕ_1 TTL clock input to the 7474 flip-flop allows a logic 1 state to exist at pin 23, the READY input, of

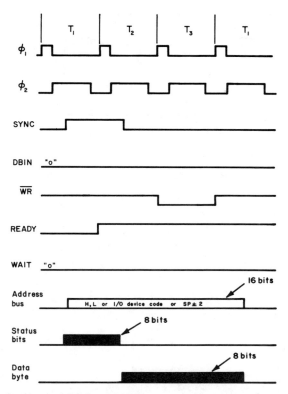

Fig. 6-18. A three-state machine cycle in which a data byte is written into memory or an output device. Note that $\overline{WR}$ is at logic 0 during state T_3.

the 8080 microprocessor chip. A logic 1 exists for only 500 ns, but this period is sufficient to allow the machine cycle to continue into state T_3 from the series of wait states T_w. Beyond state T_3 are either states T_4 and perhaps T_5, or else a new machine cycle, which starts with state T_1. In other words, the single-step pulser on the front panel allows the machine cycle to enter state T_3 from a wait state. Note that the WAIT output on the 8080 chip goes to logic 0 at the beginning of state T_3.

The debounced logic switch allows you to disable the single-step pulser circuit. In its quiescent state, the debounced logic switch applies a logic 0 at pin 2 of the 7400 NAND gate. This forces the output from the gate to be at logic 1, a logic state that is clocked through the 7474 flip-flop to pin 23 of the 8080 chip. As long as the READY input of the 8080 chip is at logic 1, it is not possible to single step through the program.

Note that the single-step pulser has a quiescent state of logic 1. This allows you to employ an external clock to clock the 74123 monostable

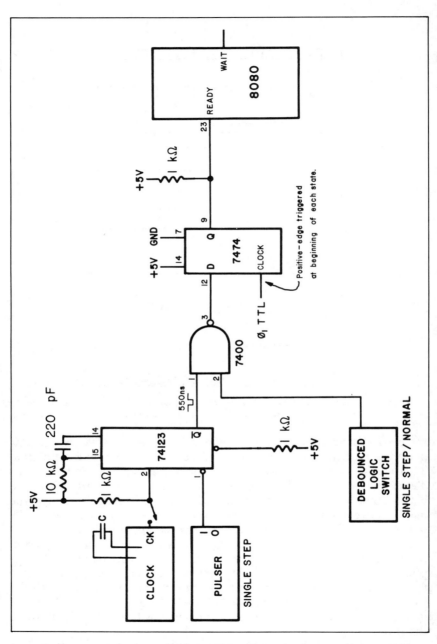

Fig. 6-19. The circuit employed in an 8080-based microcomputer to permit single-step execution of a computer program. The clock frequency is 2 MHz.

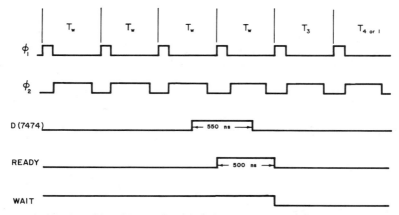

Fig. 6-20. Timing diagrams for the single-step circuit shown in Fig. 6-19.

at pin 2. The authors have found an external clock, consisting of a 555 timer chip with a clock frequency of about 1 Hz, to be quite useful.

There is one final question about the single-step circuit: How fast does the 8080 microcomputer execute a single instruction when in the single-step mode? The answer is: At the full internal clock frequency of 2 MHz. With the single-step capability, you simply force the microcomputer to remain in a wait state. When you bring the READY input to logic 1 for 500 ns, you allow the microcomputer to execute states T_3, T_4, and T_1 and T_2 of the next machine cycle at a clock rate of 500 ns per state. *You are not able to control the speed with which a single state is executed. As long as the internal clock frequency is 2 MHz, such a speed will always be 500 ns per state.*

A second and superior single-step circuit, one based on the use of a 7474 flip-flop in 8080 systems that contain an 8224 clock generator/ driver chip, is shown in Fig. 6-21. The behavior of this circuit can be

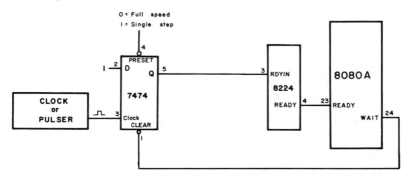

Fig. 6-21. A simple single-step circuit for an 8080-based microcomputer that employs an 8224 chip. This circuit can operate at any system clock frequency.

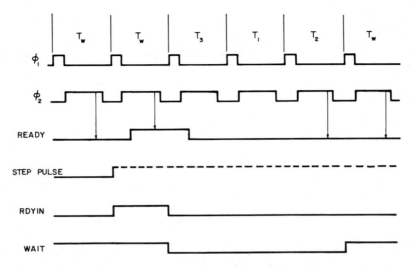

Fig. 6-22. Timing diagrams for the circuit given in Fig. 6-21. The step pulse is the pulse applied at pin 3 on the 7474 chip; it may be generated by a manual pulser.

understood with the aid of the timing diagrams shown in Fig. 6-22. The key to the operation of the circuit is, as it was in the preceding circuit, the fact that a logic 0 at the READY input to the 8080 chip will force the chip into a wait state. As can be seen from the block diagram for the 8224 chip, the ϕ_2 clock signal clocks a D-type latch within the 8224 that latches the RDYIN input and outputs it to the READY input of the 8080. The sequence of actions that occurs in the single-step circuit is as follows:

- A clock pulse, "step pulse," applied at pin 3 of the 7474 flip-flop, produces a logic 1 at the output Q, which is connected to the RDYIN input of the 8224 chip.
- At the positive edge of ϕ_2, the READY output from the 8224 chip goes to logic 1.
- The 8080 chip samples the READY input line during ϕ_2; with the READY input now at logic 1, the 8080 finishes the execution of the current machine cycle.
- At the end of the second wait state in the timing diagram, the WAIT output line of the 8080 chip returns to logic 0, which clears the 7474 flip-flop.
- RDYIN returns to logic 0, which is clocked within the 8224 chip to the READY output at pin 4.
- After state T_2 of the next machine cycle, the 8080 microprocessor again enters a wait state since the READY input is again at logic 0.

If RDYIN is maintained at logic 1, which it can be if the preset input to the 7474 flip-flop is maintained at logic 0, READY will always be at logic 1 and the 8080 chip will be prevented from entering a wait state.

The author is indebted to Mr. William Dalton, a computer science student at VPI&SU, for pointing out the utility of this circuit, including the fact that it does not require an RC timing circuit and thus can operate any system clock frequency.

The specifications for the 8224 clock generator and driver chip are provided on the following two pages.

THE 8212 EIGHT-BIT INPUT/OUTPUT PORT CHIP

The 8212 eight-bit input/output port integrated-circuit chip is destined to be a very popular buffer/latch, so it is worthwhile to understand how it operates. Basically, the chip is a group of eight 7475-type latches each of which has a three-state output buffer (Fig. 6-23).

You may recall that the output from the latch in Fig. 6-23 follows the data input as long as the clock input is at logic 1. A logic 0 at the $\overline{\text{CLR}}$ input clears the latch. The enable input, EN, to the three-state buffer must be at logic 1 for data to appear at the output of the buffer.

An important section of the 8212 is devoted to control logic. The logic diagram shown in Fig. 6-24 will make the circuitry easier to understand. The five control inputs can be summarized as follows:

$\overline{\text{DS1}}$, DS2 Device select. These two inputs are used for device selection. When $\overline{\text{DS1}}$ is at logic 0 and DS2 is at logic 1, the device is selected. In the selected state, the output buffer is enabled and the service request flip-flop (SR) is set to logic 1. When the MD input is at logic 1, the source of clock pulses to the eight latches is from the device select inputs. When the MD input is at logic 0, the output buffer state is determined by the device select inputs.

MD Mode. This input is used to control the state of the output buffer and to determine the source of clock input to the eight latches. When MD is at logic 1, the output buffers are enabled and the source of clock pulses is from the device select inputs. When MD is at logic 0, the output buffer state is determined by the device select inputs and the source of clock pulses to the eight latches is from the STB input.

STB Strobe. This input clocks the eight latches when the MD input is at logic 0. This input also synchronously clears the service request flip-flop to Q = 0.

intel®

Schottky Bipolar 8224

CLOCK GENERATOR AND DRIVER
FOR 8080A CPU

- Single Chip Clock Generator/Driver for 8080A CPU
- Power-Up Reset for CPU
- Ready Synchronizing Flip-Flop
- Advanced Status Strobe

- Oscillator Output for External System Timing
- Crystal Controlled for Stable System Operation
- Reduces System Package Count

The 8224 is a single chip clock generator/driver for the 8080A CPU. It is controlled by a crystal, selected by the designer, to meet a variety of system speed requirements.

Also included are circuits to provide power-up reset, advance status strobe and synchronization of ready.

The 8224 provides the designer with a significant reduction of packages used to generate clocks and timing for 8080A.

PIN CONFIGURATION

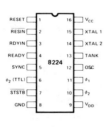

BLOCK DIAGRAM

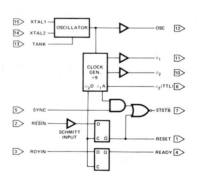

PIN NAMES

RESIN	RESET INPUT		XTAL 1	CONNECTIONS
RESET	RESET OUTPUT		XTAL 2	FOR CRYSTAL
RDYIN	READY INPUT		TANK	USED WITH OVERTONE XTAL
READY	READY OUTPUT		OSC	OSCILLATOR OUTPUT
SYNC	SYNC INPUT		ϕ_2 (TTL)	ϕ_2 CLK (TTL LEVEL)
STSTB	STATUS STB (ACTIVE LOW)		V_{CC}	+5V
ϕ_1	8080		V_{DD}	+12V
ϕ_2	CLOCKS		GND	0V

SCHOTTKY BIPOLAR 8224

FUNCTIONAL DESCRIPTION

General

The 8224 is a single chip Clock Generator/Driver for the 8080A CPU. It contains a crystal-controlled oscillator, a "divide by nine" counter, two high-level drivers and several auxiliary logic functions.

Oscillator

The oscillator circuit derives its basic operating frequency from an external, series resonant, fundamental mode crystal. Two inputs are provided for the crystal connections (XTAL1, XTAL2).

The selection of the external crystal frequency depends mainly on the speed at which the 8080A is to be run at. Basically, the oscillator operates at 9 times the desired processor speed.

A simple formula to guide the crystal selection is:

$$\text{Crystal Frequency} = \frac{1}{t_{CY}} \text{ times 9}$$

Example 1: (500ns t_{CY})
2mHz times 9 = 18mHz*

Example 2: (800ns t_{CY})
1.25mHz times 9 = 11.25mHz

Another input to the oscillator is TANK. This input allows the use overtone mode crystals. This type of crystal generally has much lower "gain" than the fundamental type so an external LC network is necessary to provide the additional "gain" for proper oscillator operation. The external LC network is connected to the TANK input and is AC coupled to ground. See Figure 4.

The formula for the LC network is:

$$F = \frac{1}{2\pi \sqrt{LC}}$$

The output of the oscillator is buffered and brought out on OSC (pin 12) so that other system timing signals can be derived from this stable, crystal-controlled source.

*When using crystals above 10mHz a small amount of frequency "trimming" may be necessary. The addition of a small capacitance (3pF - 10pF) in series with the crystal will accomplish this function.

Clock Generator

The Clock Generator consists of a synchronous "divide by nine" counter and the associated decode gating to create the waveforms of the two 8080A clocks and auxiliary timing signals.

The waveforms generated by the decode gating follow a simple 2-5-2 digital pattern. See Figure 2. The clocks generated; phase 1 and phase 2, can best be thought of as consisting of "units" based on the oscillator frequency. Assume that one "unit" equals the period of the oscillator frequency. By multiplying the number of "units" that are contained in a pulse width or delay, times the period of the oscillator frequency, the approximate time in nanoseconds can be derived.

The outputs of the clock generator are connected to two high level drivers for direct interface to the 8080A CPU. A TTL level phase 2 is also brought out ϕ_2 (TTL) for external timing purposes. It is especially useful in DMA dependant activities. This signal is used to gate the requesting device onto the bus once the 8080A CPU issues the Hold Acknowledgement (HLDA).

Several other signals are also generated internally so that optimum timing of the auxiliary flip-flops and status strobe ($\overline{STSTB}$) is achieved.

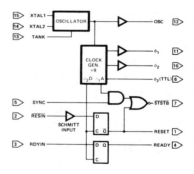

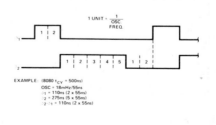

EXAMPLE: (8080 t_{CY} = 500ns)
OSC = 18mHz/55ns
ϕ_1 = 110ns (2 x 55ns)
ϕ_2 = 275ns (5 x 55ns)
ϕ_2-ϕ_1 = 110ns (2 x 55ns)

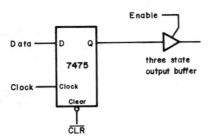

Fig. 6-23. A typical latch/buffer cell in the 8212 integrated-circuit chip. There are eight of these cells on the chip.

CLR   Clear. A logic 0 at this input asynchronously clears the eight latches and asynchronously sets the service request flip-flop to $Q = 1$. When the service request flip-flop is set, it is in the noninterrupting state.

The three outputs resulting from the above five control inputs can be described as follows:

INT   A logic 0 at this output may be used to interrupt the microcomputer. The output must be inverted and then connected to pin 14 of the 8080 chip. *Appears as an external output pin.*

Clock   A logic 1 enables the eight D-type latches, which follow the data input. Latching occurs when this output returns to a logic 0 state. *Occurs internally within the chip.*

Enable   A logic 1 enables the eight three-state output buffers, one on each latch. A logic 0 forces the buffers into their high-impedance state. *Occurs internally within the chip.*

Table 6-2 summarizes the behavior of the circuitry in Figs. 6-23 and 6-24.

Table 6-2. Inputs and Outputs of the 8212 Chip.

Control Inputs								
CLR	DS2	DS1	MD	STB	Enable	Clock	Q(SR)	INT
1	1	⎍	1	1	1	⎍	1	⎍
1	⎍	0	1	1	1	⎍	1	⎍
1	1	⎍	0	1	⎍	1	0	⎍
1	⎍	0	0	1	⎍	1	0	⎍
1	1	0	0	⎍	1	⎍	0	0

The Intel Corporation literature on the 8212 eight-bit input/output port provides a variety of application notes for the use of this chip as a gated buffer, bidirectional bus driver, interrupting input port, interrupt instruction port, output port, and 8080 status latch. Four pages from

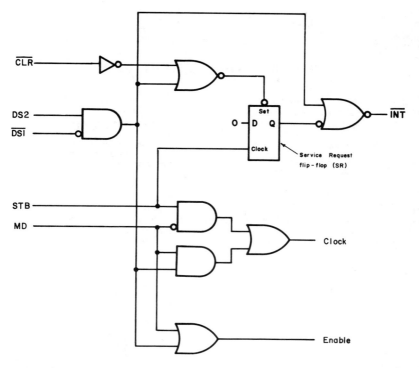

Fig. 6-24. Details of the control and device select logic for the 8212 integrated-circuit chip. The clock and enable outputs are connected directly to the 7475-type D latches within the chip itself, as shown in Fig. 6-23. They do not exist as outputs from the 8212 chip.

the Intel literature are provided on the following pages. The chip is fast, with most actions occurring in no more than 40 ns.

TEST

This test probes your understanding of the advanced concepts discussed in this chapter. Please write your answers on a separate piece of paper.

6-1. What is the difference between a clock cycle, machine cycle, and instruction cycle?

6-2. What types of 8-bit information can appear on the external data bus? Give as much detail as you can.

6-3. Which of the data storage elements listed below are connected to the external data bus, and which are connected to the internal data bus?
accumulator
B register

Schottky Bipolar 8212
EIGHT-BIT INPUT/OUTPUT PORT

- **Fully Parallel 8-Bit Data Register and Buffer**
- **Service Request Flip-Flop for Interrupt Generation**
- **Low Input Load Current — .25 mA Max.**
- **Three State Outputs**
- **Outputs Sink 15 mA**

- **3.65V Output High Voltage for Direct Interface to 8080 CPU or 8008 CPU**
- **Asynchronous Register Clear**
- **Replaces Buffers, Latches and Multiplexers in Microcomputer Systems**
- **Reduces System Package Count**

The 8212 input/output port consists of an 8-bit latch with 3-state output buffers along with control and device selection logic. Also included is a service request flip-flop for the generation and control of interrupts to the microprocessor.

The device is multimode in nature. It can be used to implement latches, gated buffers or multiplexers. Thus, all of the principal peripheral and input/output functions of a microcomputer system can be implemented with this device.

PIN CONFIGURATION

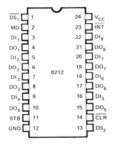

PIN NAMES

DI_1-DI_8	DATA IN
DO_1-DO_8	DATA OUT
$\overline{DS_1}$, DS_2	DEVICE SELECT
MD	MODE
STB	STROBE
$\overline{INT}$	INTERRUPT (ACTIVE LOW)
$\overline{CLR}$	CLEAR (ACTIVE LOW)

LOGIC DIAGRAM

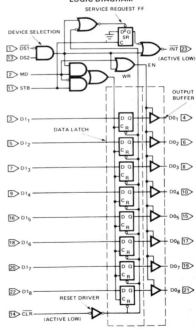

Applications Of The 8212 -- For Microcomputer Systems

I	Basic Schematic Symbol	VII	8080 Status Latch
II	Gated Buffer	VIII	8008 System
III	Bi-Directional Bus Driver	IX	8080 System:
IV	Interrupting Input Port		8 Input Ports
V	Interrupt Instruction Port		8 Output Ports
VI	Output Port		8 Level Priority Interrupt

I. Basic Schematic Symbols

Two examples of ways to draw the 8212 on system schematics—(1) the top being the detailed view showing pin numbers, and (2) the bottom being the symbolic view showing the system input or output as a system bus (bus containing 8 parallel lines). The output to the data bus is symbolic in referencing 8 parallel lines.

BASIC SCHEMATIC SYMBOLS

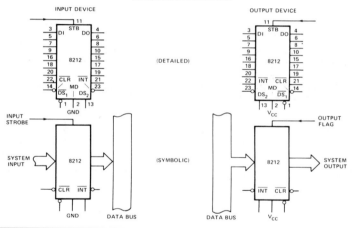

II. Gated Buffer (3 - STATE)

The simplest use of the 8212 is that of a gated buffer. By tying the mode signal low and the strobe input high, the data latch is acting as a straight through gate. The output buffers are then enabled from the device selection logic $\overline{DS1}$ and DS2.

When the device selection logic is false, the outputs are 3-state.

When the device selection logic is true, the input data from the system is directly transferred to the output. The input data load is 250 micro amps. The output data can sink 15 milli amps. The minimum high output is 3.65 volts.

GATED BUFFER
3-STATE

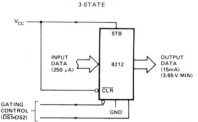

III. Bi-Directional Bus Driver

A pair of 8212's wired (back-to-back) can be used as a symmetrical drive, bi-directional bus driver. The devices are controlled by the data bus input control which is connected to $\overline{DS1}$ on the first 8212 and to DS2 on the second. One device is active, and acting as a straight through buffer the other is in 3-state mode. This is a very useful circuit in small system design.

BI-DIRECTIONAL BUS DRIVER

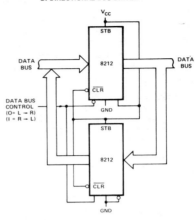

IV. Interrupting Input Port

This use of an 8212 is that of a system input port that accepts a strobe from the system input source, which in turn clears the service request flip-flop and interrupts the processor. The processor then goes through a service routine, identifies the port, and causes the device selection logic to go true — enabling the system input data onto the data bus.

INTERRUPTING INPUT PORT

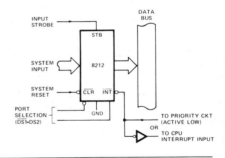

V. Interrupt Instruction Port

The 8212 can be used to gate the interrupt instruction, normally RESTART instructions, onto the data bus. The device is enabled from the interrupt acknowledge signal from the microprocessor and from a port selection signal. This signal is normally tied to ground. ($\overline{DS1}$ could be used to multiplex a variety of interrupt instruction ports onto a common bus).

INTERRUPT INSTRUCTION PORT

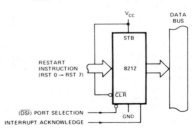

270

SCHOTTKY BIPOLAR 8212

VI. Output Port (With Hand-Shaking)

The 8212 can be used to transmit data from the data bus to a system output. The output strobe could be a hand-shaking signal such as "reception of data" from the device that the system is outputting to. It in turn, can interrupt the system signifying the reception of data. The selection of the port comes from the device selection logic. ($\overline{DS1} \cdot DS2$)

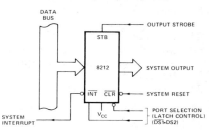

OUTPUT PORT (WITH HAND-SHAKING)

VII. 8080 Status Latch

Here the 8212 is used as the status latch for an 8080 microcomputer system. The input to the 8212 latch is directly from the 8080 data bus. Timing shows that when the SYNC signal is true, which is connected to the DS2 input and the phase 1 signal is true, which is a TTL level coming from the clock generator; then, the status data will be latched into the 8212.

Note: The mode signal is tied high so that the output on the latch is active and enabled all the time.

It is shown that the two areas of concern are the bidirectional data bus of the microprocessor and the control bus.

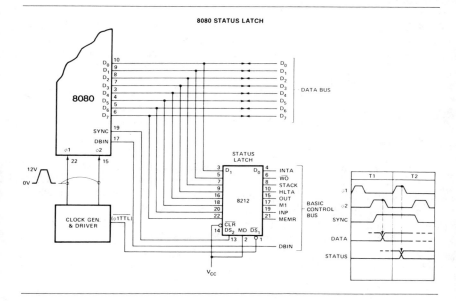

8080 STATUS LATCH

a R/W memory byte
an input device
an output device
instruction register
flags
PROM memory byte

6-4. Describe five of the eight status bits and explain what type of information they provide.

6-5. Describe five of the nine machine cycles.

6-6. Both the status bits and output pins from the 8080 microprocessor chip can be used to provide output signals to interface circuits. Explain how this is done.

6-7. Describe the different types of states that can comprise a machine cycle.

Your performance on this test will be acceptable if you can answer all of the above questions correctly in a 90-minute closed-book examination. The above concepts are advanced concepts that you may not immediately need to know. With time, however, you will find them to be quite important as you develop more complex interface circuits.

WHAT HAVE YOU ACCOMPLISHED IN THIS CHAPTER?

It was stated at the beginning of this chapter that at the end you will be able to do the following:

- Explain the differences between the internal and external busses in an 8080-based microcomputer system.
  This was done in the section on the bidirectional data bus. The single 8080 microprocessor sheet from the Intel literature gives an excellent view of the internal data bus.

- List the sources and destinations of information that appears on the external data bus.
  This was also done in the section on the bidirectional data bus.

- Explain the differences between a state, clock cycle, instruction cycle, and machine cycle.
  A state and a clock cycle are the same. A machine cycle consists of three or more states. An instruction cycle consists of one to five machine cycles. All of these concepts have been discussed in some detail.

- Explain what a status bit and a status byte are.
  A status byte consists of eight different status bits, which are discussed in the section on machine cycle identification.

- Describe the nine different types of machine cycles.
  They are fetch, memory read, memory write, output, input, stack write, stack read, halt, and interrupt. These nine types of cycles are discussed in considerable detail in the section on machine cycles.

- Describe the function of each of the eight different status bits.
  The eight status bits are given in the section on machine cycle identi-

Fig. 6-21 provides the circuit that may be used with an 8080-based microcomputer.

- Discuss the characteristics of the 8212 eight-bit input/output port integrated-circuit chip.

  We did this at the end of the chapter. Manufacturer's literature was provided.

  fication. They are used to identify the type of machine cycle that is being executed.

- Explain how the control outputs on the 8080 chip can be combined logically with one or more of the status bits, and provide at least one example of such a logical combination.

  In the text we have logically combined the following signals:

  > OUT and $\overline{\text{WR}}$
  > INP and DBIN
  > M_1 and DBIN

  The first pair generated a 500-ns $\overline{\text{OUT}}$ pulse, the second pair generated a 500-ns $\overline{\text{IN}}$ pulse, and the third pair generated a single clock pulse at the beginning of each instruction cycle.

- Draw timing diagrams that depict the behavior of typical microcomputer instructions. Such diagrams should clearly demonstrate the logic states of the more important control inputs, control outputs, and status bits.

  This was done in considerable detail in this chapter. See Fig. 6-7.

- Explain the different types of data that can appear on the external data bus.

  Data are emphasized here, not instruction bytes. Data can come from the accumulator, from memory, from an input device, from the second and third bytes of an instruction, and from a register.

- Explain state timing for typical machine cycles.

  This has been done in the subsection on state timing. Six different states were discussed. Figs. 6-17 and 6-18 provide examples.

- Explain how single stepping of an 8080 microcomputer occurs, complete with timing diagrams and circuit diagrams.

  Fig. 6-21 provides the circuit that may be used with an 8080-based microcomputer.

- Discuss the characteristics of the 8212 eight-bit input/output port integrated-circuit chip.

  We did this at the end of the chapter. Manufacturer's literature was provided.

CHAPTER 7

Microcomputer Input/Output

In this chapter, you will learn how to use device select pulses to latch output data from the accumulator and to input data into the accumulator. Circuits will be provided for six different latch chips and two different input buffer chips. You will also learn how to test a variety of accumulator instructions, including the decimal adjust accumulator instruction, which allows you to perform binary-coded-decimal operations.

OBJECTIVES

At the end of this chapter, you will be able to do the following:

- Latch the output from the accumulator of an 8080-based microcomputer with the aid of any one of six different integrated-circuit chips: 7475, 74100, 74175, 75193, 74198, and 8212.
- Input TTL data into the accumulator with the aid of either the 8095 or 8212 buffer chips.
- Explain what a data logger is.
- Calculate the timing delays required to data-log digital information appearing at different rates.

DEFINITIONS

accumulator—The register and associated digital electronic circuitry in the arithmetic unit of a computer in which arithmetic and logical operations are performed.

autoranging instrument—A digital instrument that changes scales auto-matically.

buffer—A digital device that isolates one digital circuit from another. (Note: There exist a variety of other meanings for the term *buffer*).

bus monitor—A device for checking digital signals that appear on a bus.

data point—All of the bits required to characterize the sign and magni-tude of a measured digital quantity. A data point typically consists of many bits.

decimal adjust accumulator—An 8080 microprocessor instruction that permits binary-coded-decimal operations.

data logger—An instrument that automatically scans data produced by another instrument or process and records readings of the data for future use.

input/output—General term for the equipment used to communicate with a computer and the data involved in the communication.[4]

I/O—Abbreviation for input/output.[4]

latch—A simple logic storage element.

log—To automatically scan data produced by an instrument or process and record readings of the data for future use.

monitor—A device used for checking signals.[4]

rotate—A computer instruction that causes the contents of the accumu-lator to move, bit by bit, to the left or right by one position.

INPUT/OUTPUT

When the term, *input/output*, or *I/O*, is employed, what is usually meant is that one or more data bytes are transferred between an input/output device and the microcomputer. A pair of schematic dia-grams that depict how this is done are shown in Figs. 7-1 and 7-2. The important points provided by these two figures can be summarized as follows:

- Input-output of a data byte occurs between an external I/O device and the *accumulator* within the 8080 chip.
- The function pulses, $\overline{\text{IN}}$ and $\overline{\text{OUT}}$, are produced by the 8080 microprocessor (along with additional circuitry, as described in Chapter 6) to allow an I/O device to know whether it is trans-ferring a data byte to the microcomputer or receiving a data byte from it.
- An 8-bit device code available at the time that an $\overline{\text{IN}}$ or $\overline{\text{OUT}}$ pulse is generated permits the generation of 256 different input device select pulses and 256 different output device select pulses.

In other words, quite a bit of digital information is transferred from one point to another within an interfaced microcomputer system dur-ing either an IN or OUT microcomputer instruction cycle.

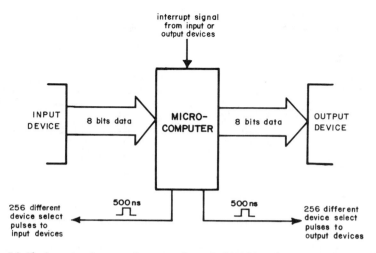

MICROCOMPUTER OUTPUT CIRCUITS

The basic "gimmick" that you employ to acquire data output from the accumulator is quite simple: *You use a single output device select pulse to enable a latch that "latches" a data byte from the bidirectional data bus.* The data goes in and out over the same signal lines on the 8080 chip: D0 through D7. Depending upon the type of latch chip,

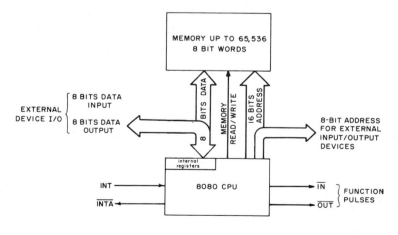

MICROCOMPUTER

Fig. 7-2. Typical inputs and outputs from an 8080 microprocessor chip. The $\overline{\text{IN}}$ and $\overline{\text{OUT}}$ function pulses are generated with the aid of additional circuitry, i.e., an 8212 status latch.

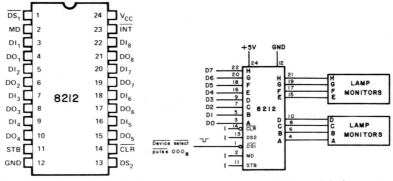

(A) Pin configuration of the 8212 chip.

(B) A circuit in which an 8212 chip serves as an output latch.

Fig. 7-3. Microcomputer output circuit based on an 8212 chip.

either a positive or a negative device select pulse is used to strobe, pulse, or latch data. Device select pulses are produced with the aid of a decoder chip, such as the 7442 or 74154, in which the address bus and $\overline{\text{IN}}$ or $\overline{\text{OUT}}$ control signals are gated together. Based upon the information provided in Chapter 4, you should be able to sketch various decoder and gating schemes to derive input and output device select pulses.

Typical microcomputer output circuits include those based upon the 8212 chip (Figs. 7-3A and 7-3B), the 74100 eight-bit D-type latch (Figs. 7-4A and 7-4B), a pair of 7475 D-type latches (Figs. 7-5A and 7-5B), the 74198 eight-bit shift register chip and a pair of 74175 positive-edge triggered latches (Figs. 7-6A, 7-6B, and 7-6C), and even a pair of 74193 up/down counters (Figs. 7-7A and 7-7B).

When using the 8212 chip as an output latch, you should make certain that the clear input, $\overline{\text{CLR}}$, at pin 14 is tied to logic 1. This input should normally "float" to logic 1 when unconnected, but experience has shown that this is not always the case.

MICROCOMPUTER INPUT CIRCUITS

The basic "gimmick" that you employ to input data into the accumulator from an input device is equally simple: *You use a single input device select pulse to enable a three-state buffer chip, which transfers a data byte to the bidirectional data bus.* You can employ a three-state buffer/latch chip such as the 8212 (Fig. 7-8), or a pair of 8095 (74365) three-state buffer chips, which are relatively inexpensive (Figs. 7-9A and 7-9B).

In this case, the enabled buffers permit data to be transferred to the bidirectional data bus, D0 through D7, *i.e.* pins 3 through 10 on the

8080 chip. The accumulator acquires the data during the 500-ns input device select pulse. In the preceding illustrations, the device select pulse is a negative clock pulse, as indicated by the bars over the words "Device select pulse."

The inputs of the 8095 three-state buffers are connected to logic switches, but they can be connected to any source of eight bits of TTL binary or encoded data. This data is transferred through the 8095 buffers, placed on the data bus, and copied into the accumulator during an IN microcomputer instruction. Data is input each time that the IN instruction is executed.

INPUT/OUTPUT INSTRUCTIONS

We will repeat the two 8080 microprocessor input/output instructions given in Chapter 4:

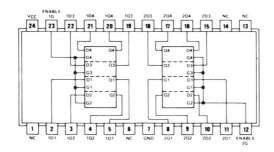

(A) Pin configuration of the 74100 eight-bit latch chip.

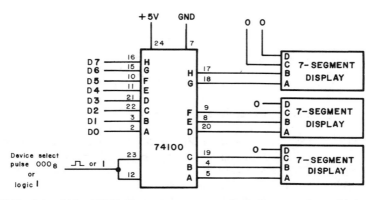

(B) Circuit in which a 74100 chip serves as an output latch. The output is provided as a three-digit octal word.

Fig. 7-4. Microcomputer output circuit based on the 74100 latch.

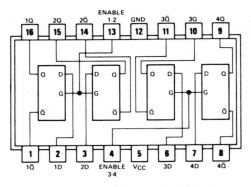

(A) Pin configuration of the 7475 four-bit latch chip.

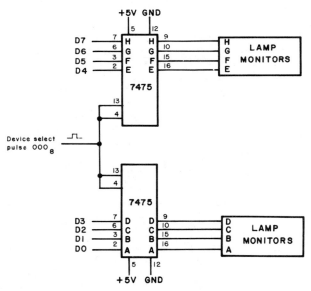

(B) Circuit in which a pair of 7475 D-type latches serve as an output port for
the microcomputer.

Fig. 7-5. Microcomputer output circuit based on a 7475 latch.

| 333 | <B2> | IN | Generate an input device select pulse to allow an 8-bit data byte to be read from an input device and replace the contents of the accumulator. |
| 323 | <B2> | OUT | Generate an output device select pulse to allow an 8-bit data byte present in the accumulator to be sent to an output device. The contents of the accumulator remain unchanged. |

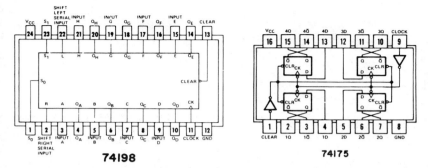

74198

74175

(A) Pin configurations of the 74198 eight-bit shift register and the 74175 four-bit latch chips. Both chips contain positive-edge–triggered flip-flops of the 7474 type.

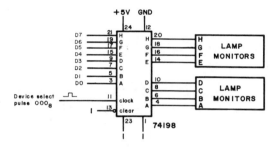

(B) Circuit in which a 74198 shift register chip latches the accumulator data.

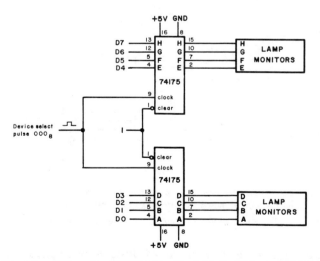

(C) Circuit in which a pair of 74175 latch chips latch the 8-bit accumulator data.

Fig. 7-6. Microcomputer output circuits based on the 74198 and 74175 chips.

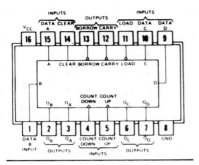

(A) The 74192 or 74193 up/down counter chip. This chip contains a built-in four-bit latch of the 7475 type.

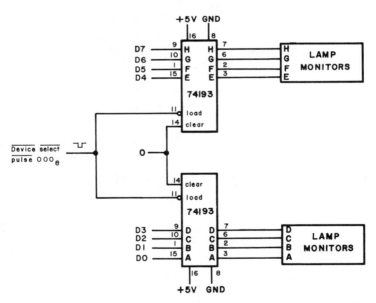

(B) Output latch circuit that employs a pair of 74193 up/down counter chips. The microcomputer is used to preset a count in these counters.

Fig. 7-7. Microcomputer output circuit based on a 74193 chip.

The second byte in each of the above instructions, <B2>, is an 8-bit device code that permits you to select any of 256 different input devices or 256 different output devices.

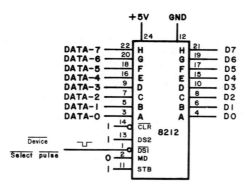

Fig. 7-8. Circuit in which an 8212 chip is used as an input buffer to an 8080-based microcomputer.

INPUT/OUTPUT PROGRAMS

A simple program to input the logic switch data in Fig. 7-9B into the accumulator and then immediately output it to one of the microcomputer output circuits shown previously is as follows:

LO Memory Address	Octal Instruction	Mnemonic	Comments
000	333	IN	Input data from input device 004
001	004	004	Device code 004
002	323	OUT	Output data to output device 000
003	000	000	Device code 000
004	166	HLT	Halt

This program will input the logic switch data, output it to an output latch, and then halt. To input and output the data continuously, you would change the above program to the following:

LO Memory Address	Octal Instruction	Mnemonic	Comments
000	333	IN	Input data from input device 004
001	004	004	Device code 004
002	323	OUT	Output data to output device 000
003	000	000	Device code 000
004	303	JMP	Unconditional jump to the memory location given by the following two bytes
005	000		LO address byte
006	000		HI address byte

To store the input data into a memory location and update the memory contents each time new data is input, you would use the following program:

LO Memory Address	Octal Instruction	Mnemonic	Comments
000	333	IN	Input data from input device 004
001	004	004	Device code 004
002	323	OUT	Output data to output device 000
003	000	000	Device code 000
004	062	STA	Store the accumulator contents in the memory location given by the following two bytes
005	200		LO address byte
006	003		HI address byte
007	303	JMP	Unconditional jump to the memory location given by the following two bytes
010	000		LO address byte
011	000		HI address byte

The program is similar to that shown previously in this section, but this time a STA <B2> <B3> instruction has been added to permit you to store the accumulator contents into a specific memory location, the contents of which are updated during each program loop. You may ask: "How can data be stored when it has previously been sent out to display, which in the above program example is output device 000? Is not the data 'used up' when it is output to a device?" The answer is no. When a data byte is transferred from one location to another, it *copied* to the new location. It is not used up; the original data is still present in its initial location, be it the accumulator, a register, or a memory location. Data present in a given location, such as the accumulator, can be copied indefinitely.

While the concept of using input device select pulses to input eight bits of logic switch data is straightforward, once you have input the data you can perform interesting programming tricks to take advantage of the power of the 8080 chip. For example, assume that the eight bits of data from the logic switches are really the 8-bit ASCII code from a standard ASCII keyboard that has TTL output. Each time eight new bits of data are input, they are tested to determine whether or not they are the ASCII equivalent to the letter E, which has an ASCII code of 305. If so, the input data will be output and also stored in memory. If not, the program will immediately loop back to the IN instruction and input new data. The applicable flowchart for this program is provided in Fig. 7-10 and the program is:

LO Memory Address	Octal Instruction	Mnemonic	Comments
000	333	IN	Input data from input device 004
001	004	004	Device code 004
002	376	CPI	Compare the accumulator contents with the following data byte. If they are identical, set the zero flag
003	305	305	Data byte that is the ASCII code for the letter E

004	302	JNZ	Jump to the memory location given by the following two bytes if the zero flag is reset, *i.e.*, at logic 0
005	000		LO address byte
006	000		HI address byte
007	323	OUT	Output data to output device 000
010	000	000	Device code 000
011	062	STA	Store the accumulator contents in the memory location given by the following two bytes
012	200		LO address byte
013	003		HI address byte
014	166	HLT	Halt

The compare immediate instruction at LO memory addresses 002 and 003 permits you to compare the ASCII byte 305 with the contents of the accumulator *without altering the contents of the accumulator.* Only the flag contents are changed. If the ASCII byte for the letter E and the accumulator contents are identical, the zero flag is set to logic 1; otherwise, it is reset to logic 0. The flag state is then used in the following conditional jump instruction, JNZ, to decide whether to continue looping or to continue to the OUT instruction at LO memory address 007.

MICROCOMPUTER OUTPUT TO A MULTIPLEXED DISPLAY

One important characteristic of microcomputers is their ability to replace hardware, i.e., integrated-circuit chips, wires, capacitors, etc., with software. The preceding example, in which a microcomputer program tested the input for the ASCII code equivalent of the letter E, is a good illustration. Simple modifications of earlier input/output programs changed the entire nature of what the microcomputer system did. These same changes would take much more time to develop and test if they were performed with hardware only.

A multiplexed display is a good example of a hardware-software tradeoff. Assume that you wish to display up to five decimal digits on an indicator display. The classical hardware approach would be to use a latch, a decoder-driver, and a seven-segment display for each numeral. This can be an expensive approach that also consumes a great deal of power.

An alternative approach, one that requires both hardware and software, is shown in Fig. 7-11. You use the microcomputer to *multiplex,* or scan, the digits very quickly. By doing so at a sufficiently fast rate, it appears to the human eye that each digit is on continuously, as would be expected for a normal display. The main features of the circuit are a 74175 latch to temporarily store the data to be displayed, a 7448 decoder/driver to decode this data into an output for each of the seven light-emitting diode (LED) segments in the display, and a

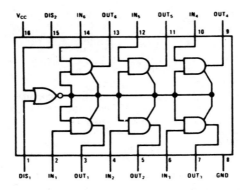

(A) The 8095 three-state buffer chip. All six three-state buffers are gated simultaneously, and there is a two-input NOR gate at the enable inputs.

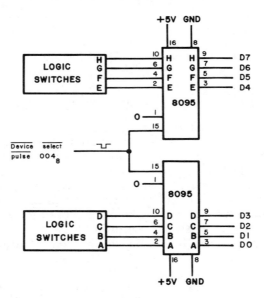

(B) Input circuit that employs two 8095 three-state buffer chips. The logic switches can be replaced by any 8-bit source of TTL data.

Fig. 7-9. Microcomputer input circuit based on 8095 chips.

74154 decoder to select the individual digits in the five-digit display. The 7448 encodes the proper segments to be displayed at the same time that the 74154 decoder chooses a single digit. In practice, a high-current decoder such as the 74145 would be used in place of the 74154.

The program for the multiplexed display is straightforward. No decision-making is necessary, so there are no conditional jumps.

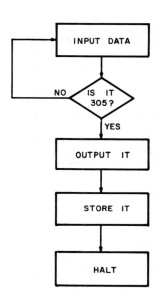

Fig. 7-10. Program flowchart that tests an input character to determine whether or not it is the ASCII character E. When an E is finally detected, the program outputs it, stores it, and then comes to a halt.

LO Memory Address	Octal Instruction	Comments
000	227	Clear the accumulator
001	323	Generate a device select pulse that can be used for some other operation, such as clearing the 74175 latch (wiring not shown in the schematic diagram)
002	005	Device code for other operation
003	041	Load the following two bytes into the L and H registers, respectively
004	200	L register byte
005	001	H register byte
006	176	Move the contents of memory location addressed by the register pair H and L to the accumulator
007	323	Generate device select pulse that applies a logic 0 to pin 7 of the Hewlett-Packard five-digit display.
010	000	Device code for pin 7 of the display
011	043	Increment the contents of the register pair H and L by one
012	176	Move contents of memory location addressed by register pair H and L to accumulator (NOTE: The register pair has been incremented by 1 from its value at memory address 006)
013	323	Generate device select pulse that applies a logic 0 to pin 4 of the Hewlett-Packard five-digit display
014	002	Device code for pin 4 of the display
015	043	Increment the contents of the register pair H and L by one
016	176	Move contents of memory location addressed by register pair H and L to accumulator
017	323	Generate device select pulse that applies a logic 0 to pin 13 of the Hewlett-Packard five-digit display

LO Memory Address	Octal Instruction	Comments
020	003	Device code for pin 13 of the display
021	043	Increment the contents of the register pair H and L by one
022	176	Move contents of memory location addressed by register pair H and L to accumulator
023	323	Generate device select pulse that applies a logic 0 to pin 1 of the Hewlett-Packard five-digit display
024	044	Device code for pin 1 of the display
025	076	Move the following byte to the accumulator
026	017	This byte, which is input to the 7448 chip, blanks the seven segments of the display at pin 9 and allows only the decimal point to appear
027	323	Generate device select pulse that applies a logic 0 at pin 9 and a logic 1 at pin 5 of the Hewlett-Packard five-digit display
030	001	Device code for pin 9 and pin 5 of the display
031	303	Unconditional jump to memory location given by following two bytes
032	000	LO address byte
033	000	HI address byte

The numbers to be displayed must be present within the microcomputer memory before this program is executed. For example, the digits 7, 3, 0, and 5 are stored in memory locations HI = 001 and LO = 200 to 203. The decimal-point position is hardwired; the blank position is generated in software. The numbers are output from right to left in the circuit, so the data is stored in memory as follows:

LO Memory Address	Data Byte
200	007
201	003
202	000
203	005

A previously executed program or program segment could have placed such data in the indicated memory locations. Such data could be input data from some other device, or it could be the result of arithmetic operations. Today, multiplexed displays are the rule rather than the exception. Almost every hand calculator display is multiplexed.

The flowchart for the preceding program is shown in Figure 7-12. Note that there is a single loop, one that is executed at the full microcomputer speed.

DATA LOGGING WITH AN 8080 MICROCOMPUTER

A *data logger* can be defined as follows.

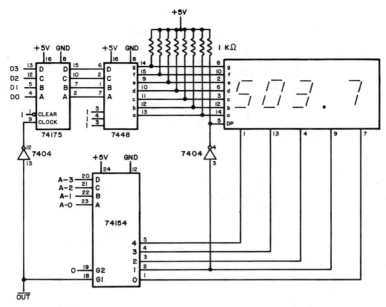

Fig. 7-11. A multiplexed Hewlett-Packard five-digit seven-segment LED display.

data logger—An instrument that automatically scans data produced by another instrument or process and records readings of the data for future use.

It should be clear that a microcomputer can be a data logger. Data from an instrument can be put into the accumulator and then stored in memory. At a later time, this stored information can be read out in any one of a variety of ways. Data logging will become a common application for microcomputers in the future.

Perhaps the most important questions to consider when you plan to log data from an instrument are the following: (1) How many data points do you wish to log? (2) How much time will it take to log all of these points? (3) How much digital information is contained in a single data point? (4) What do you wish to do with the logged data once it has been acquired? (5) Do you need short-term or long-term data storage? We shall now discuss each of these questions.

How Many Data Points?

The number of data points that you wish to log and the time that you will need to store them will dictate the type of storage device required. If you need to log 1,000,000 four-digit binary-coded-decimal words, you will require a memory capacity of sixteen million bits. You will therefore require some form of magnetic tape or magnetic disk.

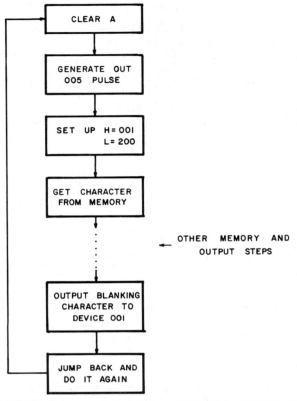

Fig. 7-12. Flowchart for the operation of the multiplexed Hewlett-Packard five-digit seven-segment display shown in Fig. 7-11.

On the other hand, if you need to log 100 points, each containing four bcd digits, and store the data only for several hours, only 1600 bits of memory are required. A simple R/W memory would do quite nicely for such an application.

Short-Term or Long-Term Storage?

Read/write memory is not, in general, suitable for long-term storage of data. For one reason, such memory is volatile; if a power failure occurs, all of the data will be lost. Core memory is not volatile, but on the other hand it is quite expensive and generally not suited for long-term storage of data unless the amount of data stored is limited in amount. The best data storage devices at present appear to be magnetic tape, such as a cassette, and magnetic disk, such as the increasingly popular "floppy disks." A high-quality tape cassette can store as many as 500,000 bits of information on a single cassette that costs no more than $10. If you are willing to gamble, you can put your own clock track on a high-quality audio cassette and reduce tape costs to about $4 per cassette. The authors have done so with considerable success.

An inexpensive and long-term storage technique is the use of perforated paper tape. However, it should be pointed out that it takes considerable time to punch such tape as well as to read it back into a computer.

How Much Information in a Single Data Point?

A typical data point is usually a several-digit binary-coded-decimal or binary number that contains both a decimal point or range as well as a sign. Usually, the decimal point or range is fixed and the sign is positive, but this is not always the case. New digital devices are increasingly incorporating an *autoranging* capability, which simply means that the device decides where to place the decimal point. In general, you can plan on a data point containing at least sixteen bits of digital information. With 100 data points, you must multiply 100 by the number of bits per data point, 16, to obtain the total memory capacity required, i.e., 1600 bits. Frequency meters typically have many more bits per data point. A seven-digital frequency meter has at least 28 bits per data point.

What Will You Do With the Logged Data?

Some logged data can be considered only to be "raw" data that must be manipulated and interpreted to produce a useful final result. For example, it might be necessary to convert a digital voltage into a force. With such cases, the logged data will require mathematical computations that are best performed soon after the data is acquired. Clearly, with data that requires additional treatment, it is best to keep the data in digital electronic form until it can be treated. Read/write memory and magnetic tape are both quite suitable for such a purpose. Once the data is in a final form, it can be printed out. Keep in mind that the printing of data is a type of long-term data storage. It is certainly the least expensive type of long-term storage around, but you pay a penalty in that you must consume time to convert it back to an electronic or magnetic type of storage if you wish to perform additional mathematical manipulations on the data.

How Many Data Points per Second?

This is a question that is of fundamental importance in all data logging operations. The data can, for example:

- appear quite slowly and take considerable periods, such as a day, for its acquisition, or

- appear extremely rapidly, and take only milliseconds for the acquisition of hundreds of data points.

Both extremes in data acquisition rates point to the need for automated data acquisition techniques, such as the use of a microcomputer-based data logger. There is no question that data in the laboratory, as well as elsewhere, will increasingly be logged automatically by built-in microcomputers. Chart recorders may still be used, but they will no longer need to be of the quality required in previous years. In the future, a major use for chart recorders may simply be to allow the eye to visually "integrate" a block of data to detect curvature, linearity, etc.

As a demonstration of data logging, we would like to provide a computer program that enables us to log 256 eight-bit data points as fast as the microcomputer can input and store them. For example, let us assume that we are logging data from a pair of 7490 decade counters, as shown in Fig. 7-13. The question that we seek to answer is: What is the minimum amount of time required to log 256 data points from the two counters, where each data point contains two bcd digits?

LO Memory Address	Octal Instruction	Clock Cycles	Comments
000	061	10	Load the following two bytes into the stack pointer register
001	100		LO stack pointer byte
002	003		HI stack pointer byte
003	006	7	Load the following data byte into the B register
004	000		Number of points that will be logged by the microcomputer
005	041	10	Load the following two bytes in the register pair L and H
006	000		L register byte
007	001		H register byte
010	323	10	Generate device select pulse to set the 7476 flip-flop
011	000		Device code for preset input
012	333	10	Generate device select pulse that allows eight bits of data from a pair of 7490 counters to be input into the accumulator
013	000		Device code for input buffer chips
014	167	7	Move the contents of the accumulator to the memory location given by the register pair H and L
015	043	5	Increment the register pair H and L by one
016	005	5	Decrement the contents of register B by one
017	302	10	If register B is 000₈, ignore this instruction. Otherwise, jump to the memory address given by the following two bytes
020	012		LO address byte

021	000		HI address byte
022	323	10	Generate device select pulse that clears the 7476 flip-flop
023	001		Device code for clear input
024	166		Halt

In the program, we have provided a pair of OUT instructions to allow us to employ the techniques described in Chapter 5 to count clock pulses, such as the 7476 flip-flop circuit shown in Fig. 7-14. Device select pulse 000 sets the flip-flop, and device select pulse 001 clears it. While it is set, the five-decade counter counts clock cycles from the microcomputer clock.

Thirty-seven clock cycles are required for each 8-bit data point acquired by the microcomputer program. For 256 data points and a microcomputer operating at 2 MHz, a total of $256 \times 37 = 9472$ clock cycles, or 4.741 ms, are required in all. At 18.5 μs per 8-bit data point, approximately 54,000 data points per second can be logged by the microcomputer. And this is not even the limit.

If you desire to log data at a slower rate, you will need to insert a time delay subroutine in the above program. The 0.2-second subroutine described in Chapter 5 should be quite convenient for slow data rates. The modifications necessary to the above program are rather simple:

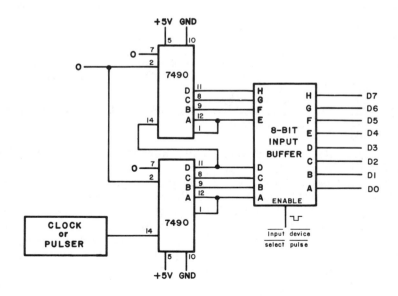

Fig. 7-13. Simple data logging circuit that employs a pair of cascoded 7490 counters.

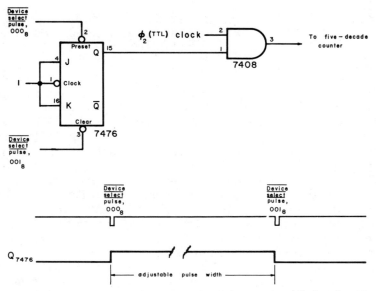

Fig. 7-14. The 7476 latch circuit permits you to determine experimentally how long it takes to log and store 256 data points. The behavior of the circuit is shown in the timing diagram.

016	016	7	Load the following byte into the C register
017	*		Timing byte for time delay subroutine
020	315	17	Call subroutine at memory address given by following two bytes
021	000		LO address byte
022	060		HI address byte
023	005	5	Decrement contents of register B by one
024	302	10	If register B is 000₈, ignore this instruction. Otherwise, jump to the memory address given by the following two bytes
025	012		LO address byte
026	000		HI address byte
027	323	10	Generate device select pulse that clear the 7476 flip-flop
030	003		Device code
031	166		Halt

If the data byte at memory address 017 is set at 001, corresponding to a 0.20-second time delay per data point, it will now require about 51.3 seconds to log all 256 points. Simply by changing the data byte at memory address 017, you can change the time per data point from 0.20 second per point to 51.2 seconds per point. This capability points up the advantages of microcomputers as data loggers.

To output the file of 256 data points, you employ a circuit which resembles that shown in Fig. 7-15. The program that you use to sequentially output the stored data points is similar to the program that you initially used to log them. Thus, in the preceding program in this section, make the following program changes:

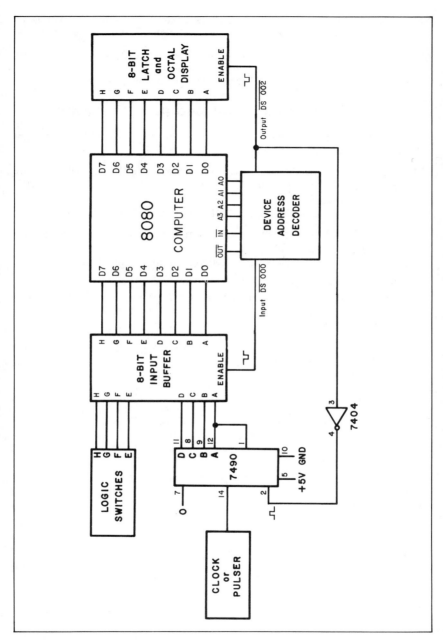

Fig. 7-15. Data logging circuit that outputs ASCII coded numeric data. Logic switches HGFE should be set at 1011, respectively.

012	176	MOV, M,A	7	Move the contents of the memory location given by the register pair H and L to the accumulator
013	323	OUT	10	Output the accumulator data to the 8-bit latch and octal display
014	002	002		Device code for the latch/display

WHAT HAVE YOU ACCOMPLISHED IN THIS CHAPTER?

It was stated at the beginning of this chapter that at the end you will be able to do the following:

- Latch the output from the accumulator with the aid of any one of six different integrated-circuit chips: 7475, 74100, 74175, 74193, 74198, and 8212.

  This was done in the section "Microcomputer Output Circuits."

- Input TTL data into the accumulator with the aid of either the 8095 or 8212 buffer chips.

  This was done in the section "Microcomputer Input Circuits."

- Explain what a data logger is.

  A discussion concerning data loggers was provided in the text. A circuit and a program were provided to create a simple microcomputer based data logger.

- Calculate the timing delays required to data log digital information appearing at different rates.

  This was discussed in the text.

CHAPTER 8

Subroutines, Interrupts, External Flags, and Stacks

In this chapter you will focus your attention primarily upon the fourth and final fundamental task of computer interfacing: *the servicing of interrupts*. We have already discussed some of the details of interrupt servicing in Chapter 1. Here, you will learn how to construct an external flag and how to interface such a flag to the microcomputer. Microcomputers are typically operated in the interrupt mode, so the concepts described in this chapter are quite important. Study them carefully and review the examples.

OBJECTIVES

At the end of this chapter, you will be able to do the following:

- Define the terms: subroutine, SSI, MSI, LSI, allocate, stack, interrupt, polling, software driver, vectored interrupt, disabled interrupt, external flag, deferred interrupt, and sense register.
- Explain how you would mask an 8-bit word to obtain the logic state of bit 5, or the logic state of any of the other seven bits.
- Explain how digital information is loaded and removed from the 8080 microcomputer stack.
- Perform an approximate calculation that will tell you when to use a subroutine.
- Describe how you would interface an ASCII keyboard.

DEFINITIONS

allocate—In a computer, to assign storage locations to main routines and subroutines, thus fixing the absolute values of symbolic addresses.[4]

breakpoint—A place in a routine specified by an instruction, instruction digit, or other condition, where the routine may be interrupted by external intervention or by a monitor routine.[4]

breakpoint instruction—In the programming of a digital computer, an instruction, which, together with a manual control, causes the computer to stop.[4]

breakpoint switch—A manually operated switch that controls conditional operation at breakpoints; it is used primarily in debugging.[4]

deferred interrupt—A computer interrupt that occurs at some time after an external flag is set.

disable interrupt—To disable the interrupt flag within a microprocessor chip.

enable interrupt—To enable the interrupt flag within a microprocessor chip.

external flag—A digital circuit, usually containing a single flip-flop, which indicates a condition that exists with an input/output device.

flag—In a computer, an indication that a particular operation has been completed.[4] Also, a flag is a flip-flop that can be either set or cleared in response to operations that are occurring within a microcomputer.

immediate interrupt—A computer interrupt that occurs as soon as an external flag is set.

internal flag—A digital circuit, usually containing a single flip-flop, which indicates a condition that exists internally within the microprocessor chip.

interrupt—In a computer, a break in the normal flow of a system or routine such that the flow can be resumed from that point at a later time. The source of the interrupt may be internal or external.[4]

interrupt flag—A flip-flop within the microprocessor chip that can be enabled or disabled by microprocessor software and which can detect an interrupt pulse and remember the fact that an interrupt occurred.

large-scale integration—Monolithic digital integrated-circuit chips with a typical complexity of 100 or more gates or gate-equivalent circuits. The number of gates per chip used to define LSI depends upon the manufacturer. Abbreviated LSI.[4]

large-scale programs—Programs that contain from 1000 to 10,000 instruction bytes. Abbreviated LSP.

mask—A logical technique in which certain bits of a word are blanked out or inhibited.[4]

medium-scale integration—Integrated-circuit chips that function as simple, self-contained logic systems, such as decade counters, small read/write memories, decoders, multiplexers, and shift registers. Such chips usually contain from 20 to 100 gates. Medium-scale integration is abbreviated MSI.

medium-scale programs—Programs that contain from 100 to 1000 instruction bytes. Abbreviated MSP.

multilevel interrupt—An interrupt system in which there exist many interrupt lines to the microcomputer, each line being tied to a separate I/O device. The microcomputer does not need to scan the devices to determine which one caused the interrupt.

nesting—In a computer, the inclusion of a routine or block of data within a larger routine or block of data.

polling—Periodic interrogation of each of the devices that share a communication line to determine whether it requires servicing. The multiplexer or control station sends a poll that has the effect of asking the selected device, "Do you have anything to transmit?"[4]

priority—The condition in which input/output devices are ordered in importance so that some devices take precedence over others.

response time—The time between the interrupt request by a device and the first instruction byte of the software driver that services it.

sense—To examine or determine the status of some system component.[4]

service routine—In digital computer programming, a routine designed to assist in the actual operation of the computer.[4] This term may also mean a subroutine that services an interrupt signal from an external device.

single-line interrupt—An interrupt system in which there is a single interrupt line. Multiple devices must be ORed to this line. Each input to the OR gate is from an I/O device. Once it receives an interrupt, the microcomputer must scan all of the devices to determine which one generated the interrupt.

small-scale integration—Integrated circuits that provide only simple gates, buffers, or flip-flops. Such chips usually contain no more than ten to twenty gates. Abbreviated SSI.

small-scale programs—Programs that contain up to 100 instruction bytes. Abbreviated SSP.

stack—A region of memory that stores temporary information, typically the contents of the internal registers within a microprocessor chip.

software driver—A subroutine or part of a computer program that transfers information between the computer and a specified input/output device.

status—The contents of the internal registers, including the flag bits, in a microprocessor during program execution, at a given instant.

subroutine—A small subprogram not stored in the main path of the routine. Such a subroutine is entered by a jump operation known as a call; provision is made to return control to the main program at the end of the subroutine.

vectored interrupt—An interrupt system in which the interrupt causes a direct branch to that part of the program that services the interrupt. This is the fastest mode of interrupt operation.

vector bits—The individual bits that designate the branch location in a vector interrupt instruction.

very large-scale integration—Monolithic digital integrated-circuit chips with a typical complexity of 2000 or more gates or gate-equivalent circuits. Abbreviated VLSI.

very large-scale programs—Programs that contain more than 10,000 instruction bytes. Abbreviated VLSP.

WHAT IS A SUBROUTINE?

A *subroutine* can be defined as follows:

subroutine—A small subprogram not stored in the main path of the routine. Such a subroutine is entered by a jump operation known as a call; provision is made to return control to the main program at the end of a subroutine.

The call instruction causes the microcomputer to transfer program control to the selected subroutine. Subroutines are generally dedicated to specific repeated tasks, so when a task is finished we would like the microcomputer to return to the main program that issued the call and resume operation there. Whenever a call instruction is used, whether it is conditional or unconditional, the microcomputer stores a return address on its *stack* so that we have a way of knowing at which point to return when the subroutine execution is finished. A *stack* is a region of read/write memory that you allocate for the storage of temporary information, such as return addresses from subroutines and the contents of the internal registers within a microprocessor chip.

What return address is stored on a stack? Is it always the same 16-bit address? Fig. 8-1 provides answers to these two questions:

Once we execute a three-byte call instruction and the associated subroutine, *we would like to return to the instruction byte that immediately follows the three-byte call instruction.* Thus, the 16-bit address of instruction byte A, shown in Fig. 8-1, is the one that is stored on the stack. If "x" is the 16-bit address of the call instruction, then "$x+3$" is the 16-bit address that is stored on the stack. Since only eight bits at a time can be stored in the read/write memory of an 8080 microcomputer, two consecutive memory locations in the stack are required to store the full 16-bit return address. *The 8080 microprocessor chip automatically stores these two return address bytes on the stack whenever*

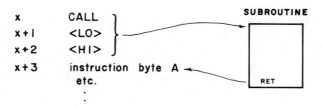

Fig. 8-1. The return address that is stored on the stack is x + 3, the address of the instruction byte that immediately follows the three-byte call instruction.

we execute a call instruction. The process is called *pushing* an address on the stack.

All subroutines must end, in one way or another, with a return instruction. The return instruction may be conditional or unconditional. In either case, a return causes the 8080 microprocessor chip to retrieve the 16-bit return address from the stack. This address is placed in the chip's program counter, and program execution resumes again at the correct point, such as "x+3" in our example.

We do not have to be concerned with the methods that the 8080 chip uses to store or retrieve information from the stack. However, we must be certain that we do have a stack area available in read/write memory before we attempt to call any subroutine. We can locate the stack anywhere within the available 65,536 bytes of memory by using the LXI SP instruction, a three-byte instruction in which the second and third bytes contain the 16-bit stack address, which is stored in a 16-bit register within the 8080 chip that is called a *stack pointer register*. If you wish, for example, to set the starting address of the stack at HI = 003 and LO = 300, you would use the instruction byte sequence:

LO Memory Address Byte	Octal Instruction Byte	Mnemonic	Comments
000	061	LXI SP	Load the stack pointer register with the following two address bytes
001	300	300	LO address byte
002	003	003	HI address byte

Upon execution of this instruction, the stack pointer will contain the 16-bit address given by HI = 003 and LO = 300. The setting of the stack pointer is one of the most important initialization conditions that you must execute at the very beginning of an 8080 microcomputer program.

In the preceding program, we have assumed that we have only 1K of read/write memory. We have located the stack near the "top" of this memory, *i.e.*, near the highest (or largest) memory locations. The reason for doing so is that the stack, as information is added to it, grows down toward lower memory addresses. In fact, the address HI = 003 and LO = 300 is only a temporary address for the stack. If we were to call a subroutine, we would observe that the return address (also called the *linking address*) is stored as an 8-bit HI address byte at HI = 003 and LO = 277, and an 8-bit LO address byte at HI = 003 and LO = 276. The stack pointer would then be decremented by two. Most 8080 users are not concerned about the order with which the address is pushed on the stack. For your information, the HI address (or data) byte is always pushed first on the stack and the LO address (or data) byte second. *The first byte to be removed, or popped from a stack is always the LO address (or data) byte.* This is entirely consistent with the way that the 8080 chip handles three-byte instructions: The LO address (or data) byte is always loaded first into the LO byte of a 16-bit register, such as the program counter, stack pointer, or the register pairs DE, BC, or HL.

The stack pointer is always decremented (to a lower address) *before data or address information is pushed onto the stack.* The stack pointer is always incremented (to a higher address) *after data or address information is popped from the stack.* If we would examine the stack area in memory after a number of subroutines had used it, we would find that some information was still there. Is this important? Not really, since the appropriate information has long ago been copied back into the 8080 microprocessor chip where it was needed. The old information is meaningless to the microcomputer; the information will be written over whenever the stack is used again.

USE OF THE STACK FOR DATA AND STATUS STORAGE

Most subroutines employ the general-purpose registers or the internal flags within an 8080 chip. Problems occur when we have data in registers that the subroutine will also use. Imagine that the microcomputer is in the middle of a lengthy numerical calculation when a subroutine call is caused by an interrupt. What happens to the temporary data in the registers? Are they destroyed? Must the calculation be repeated? Can we overcome this serious limitation?

Clearly, we must have the ability to store the program *status,* which can be defined as the contents of the internal registers, including the flag bits, that exist inside a microprocessor chip during the execution of a program at a given instant. For an 8080 chip, the status is contained within the following registers:

program counter
accumulator
register B
register C

register D
register E
register H
register L
five flag bits

If we know this information, program execution can be interrupted.

We store the program status in the stack using a group of four instructions, called *push* instructions and a single call subroutine instruction. At the end of a subroutine, we retrieve the program status using four *pop* instructions and a subroutine return instruction. The eight push and pop instructions can be listed as follows:

305	PUSH B	Store contents of register pair B,C on the stack
325	PUSH D	Store contents of register pair D,E on the stack
345	PUSH H	Store contents of register pair H,L on the stack
365	PUSH PSW	Store program status word (PSW), i.e., the contents of the accumulator and the five flags, on the stack
301	POP B	Return the top two stack bytes to the register pair B,C
321	POP D	Return the top two stack bytes to the register pair D,E
341	POP H	Return the top two stack bytes to the register pair H,L
361	POP PSW	Return the top two stack bytes to the accumulator and flag flip-flops

All stack push and pop operations involve either the program counter or a register pair; they are 16-bit operations that are performed upon two 8-bit bytes, a LO address or data byte and a HI address or data byte. The program status word (PSW) is the accumulator register, A, and the five 8080 chip flags—carry, zero, parity, sign, and auxiliary carry—along with three dummy bits. Fig. 8-2 illustrates the push and pop instructions. SP is the 16-bit address contained in the stack pointer register within the 8080 chip.

The stack is a last-in first-out (LIFO) stack. The last data that is pushed onto the stack must be the first data to be popped from the stack. This is easy to see with the aid of Fig. 8-3. Note that the push and pop orders are the reverse of each other. In this example, the subroutine did not affect registers D or E, so there was no need to place them on the stack.

The push and pop instructions permit great programming flexibility, since we can store our temporary data before a subroutine is executed and retrieve it after we have finished the subroutine. This brings up one interesting question: Would the push and pop instructions be lo-

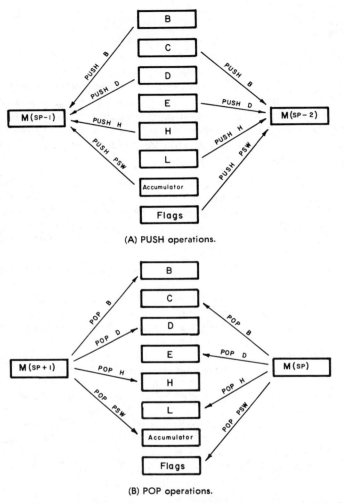

(A) PUSH operations.

(B) POP operations.

Fig. 8-2. The PUSH and POP operations, each of which involves a register pair and two memory locations.

cated before and after the call instruction, or would they be included in the subroutine? Fig. 8-4 presents the two alternatives.

The answer to this question is that you would include them in the subroutine. It makes more sense to place them in the subroutine rather than repeat them every time there is a call instruction. The stack thus stores both the return address (the *linking address*) as well as the original data in all register pairs affected in the subroutine itself. When we assign a location for the stack in read/write memory, we must make

```
PUSH   H
PUSH   PSW
PUSH   B

┌──────────────┐
│              │
│  Subroutine  │
│              │
└──────────────┘

POP    B
POP    PSW
POP    H
```

Fig. 8-3. Proper procedure for pushing and popping information on the stack.

certain that there exists sufficient memory for the status information associated with several nested subroutine calls. Since the stack grows down toward lower memory addresses, we usually place the initial stack location at the highest available read/write memory address. Finally, subroutines must contain the same number of push and pop instructions, in reverse order, as well as a conditional or unconditional return instruction. If these conditions are not met, your stack could "run away" in read/write memory and destroy any program or data that exists in read/write memory. For an 8080 microcomputer oper-

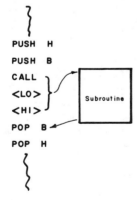

(A) In this program the PUSH and POP instructions are provided in the main program as needed.

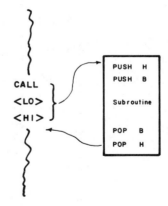

(B) In this program the PUSH and POP instructions are incorporated only in the subroutine.

Fig. 8-4. Two alternatives for locating the PUSH and POP instructions associated with a subroutine call.

ated at 2 MHz, it takes only several seconds to wipe out 65,536 memory bytes.

Let us finish our discussion with the aid of Fig. 8-5, which shows the contents of the stack after a call and four successive push instructions. Please note the following:

- Before we called the subroutine, the original location of the *stack pointer* was HI = 003_8 and LO = 303_8.
- After we pushed PSW on the stack, the new location of the stack pointer was HI = 003_8 and LO = 271_8. *We can therefore conclude*

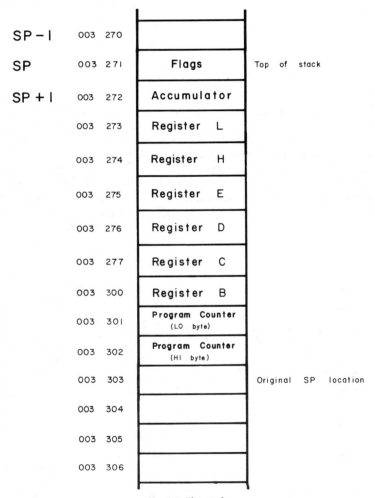

Fig. 8-5. The stack.

that the stack pointer "points" to the top filled memory location in the stack, not the first empty stack location.

- The stack is a *first-in, last-out stack.* The first bytes in were the program counter bytes from the call instruction. They are the last to be popped from the stack. The last bytes in were the flags and accumulator contents; they are the first to be popped out.
- The HI byte of the program counter or HI byte of a register pair is the first to be placed on the stack and the last of the two bytes to be removed. When a register pair is popped, the LO byte of the pair always is popped first.
- In a push instruction, the HI byte or register is stored in stack location $SP - 1$ and the LO byte or register is stored in stack location $SP - 2$. The stack pointer, SP, is decremented by two to produce a new value of the stack pointer.
- In a pop instruction, the LO byte or register is popped from stack location SP and the HI byte or register is popped from stack location $SP + 1$. The stack pointer, SP, is incremented by two to produce a new value of the stack pointer.

WHEN IS A SUBROUTINE USED?

When do you use a subroutine? This depends upon two factors: the number of steps in the subroutine, and the number of times you call the subroutine from the main program. Some general rules are as follows:

- If the proposed subroutine will contain only three or four instruction bytes, there is little incentive for you to write the subroutine no matter how many times you call it in the main program.
- If the proposed subroutine will be used only once in a program or group of programs, you might as well incorporate it into the main program and not use it as a subroutine.
- If the proposed subroutine will be used by other people as a component of their programs, then you should definitely write it as a subroutine and pay particular attention to where it is located in memory.
- If you wish to minimize the time it takes to perform a group of instructions, you should minimize the number of subroutines present.
- You should minimize the length of your main program and maximize the length of your subroutines.

Basically, your long-term goal should be to acquire a repertoire of subroutines that make microcomputer programming easy.

Your decision on when to use a subroutine can perhaps be facilitated by the use of Fig. 8-6, in which we plot C, the number of times a sub-

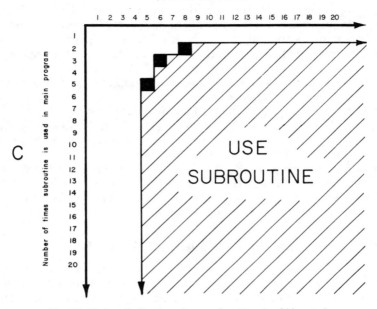

Fig. 8-6. Diagram indicating when a subroutine should be used.

routine is used in a main program, versus X, the number of instruction bytes (less call and return instructions) used in the subroutine. We have used the equation

$$F = \frac{CX}{X + 4C}$$

to determine when a subroutine should be employed. When $F > 1$, a subroutine should be used; when $F < 1$, a subroutine is not needed. A toss-up situation occurs when $F = 1$ (black squares). In the equation, the quantity CX is the total number of instruction bytes used in the entire main program (less the call and return instructions). The quantity $X + 4C$ is related to the number of instruction bytes in the entire main program required to repeatedly call and return from the subroutine. The ratio of these two terms, F, is a measure of their relative importance. You should use your own judgment concerning when to use a subroutine.

The authors believe that subroutines will become increasingly important as microcomputers proliferate. In the following sections, a point of view is presented concerning subroutines.

HARDWARE INTEGRATION: SSI, MSI, LSI, AND VLSI

Let us briefly summarize the incredible progress that has occurred in digital electronics within the last ten to fifteen years. This progress is basically reflected in the acronyms SSI, MSI, LSI, and VSLI, which we shall now define:

small-scale integration (SSI)—Integrated-circuit chips that provide only simple gates or flip-flops. Such chips usually contain no more than ten to twenty gates. Abbreviated SSI.

medium-scale integration (MSI)—Integrated-circuit chips that function as simple, self-contained logic systems, such as decade counters, small read/write memories, decoders, multiplexers, and shift registers. Such chips usually contain from 20 to 100 gates. Abbreviated MSI.

large-scale integration (LSI) — Monolithic digital integrated-circuit chips with a typical complexity of 100 to 5000 gates or gate-equivalent circuits. The number of gates per chip used to define LSI depends on the manufacturer. Abbreviated LSI.

very large-scale integration (VLSI)—Monolithic digital integrated-circuit chips with a typical complexity of 5000 or more gates or gate-equivalent circuits. Abbreviated VLSI.

The scale subdivisions are a bit arbitrary. Nevertheless, progress in the area of digital electronics is closely reflected in the scale of integration that has been achieved at any given time. In the mid-1960's, small-scale integration emerged as an important force in electronics. The chips were expensive, and many of them were required to build a useful instrument or computer. By the late 1960's, medium-scale integration began to cut the cost of digital instruments by reducing the chip count and labor required. The early 1970's saw large-scale integration emerge: large memories and UART integrated-circuit chips. The electronics industry barely caught its breath when very-large-scale integration appeared and gave a hint as to the incredible impact that electronics will have still in the future. The 16K static random access memories such as the Intel 8185, 32K EPROMs such as the Intel 2732, 8-bit microprocessors such as the 8085, and various peripheral interface chips provide individuals with an opportunity to construct powerful computers for only several hundred dollars. Sixteen-bit microcomputers—the 8086, Z8000, and 68000—are in wide use, specially in industry, and 32-bit microcomputers—for example, the Intel iAPX32—have already been introduced. We are now in the age of VLSI. However, if you are a novice, the 8-bit microcomputers still provide your best pathway to learning about microcomputer programming and interfacing.

SOFTWARE INTEGRATION: SSP, MSP, LSP, AND VLSP

You can also observe progress in the area of digital electronics by watching what happens to memory chips. The trends are:

- New memory chips will contain more memory per chip.

  The 4K dynamic RAMs and 16K EPROMs were available in 1976. By 1981, the 64K dynamic RAMS and 64K EPROMs were commercially available. Yet to come are the 256K and 1M RAMs, ROMs, EPROMs, and EAROMs. You should note that it takes only an 18-bit memory address word to address any location among 262,144 different locations.

- The fast memory chips will become faster.

  A tradeoff exists between the size of memory and the basic speed of a memory cell, but improvements in technology are paving the way to large memories that are faster than today's chips.

Memory speed and memory size are the important variables for the future. The speed of memory basically determines the execution time of an instruction in a computer. The faster the memory, the more instructions that can be executed in a given period, and the more powerful programs that can be used. A good measure of the progress yet to be made by microcomputers is the length of microcomputer programs employed. Parallel to the abbreviations, SSI, MSI, LSI, and VLSI, they would like to suggest the following indicators of program complexity:

small-scale programs (*SSP*)—Programs that contain up to 100 instruction bytes. Abbreviated SSP.

medium-scale programs (*MSP*)—Programs that contain from 100 to 1000 instruction bytes. Abbreviated MSP.

large-scale programs (*LSP*)—Programs that contain from 1K to 16K instruction bytes. Abbreviated LSP.

very-large-scale programs (*VLSP*)—Programs that contain more than 16K instruction bytes. Abbreviated VLSP.

In order to execute a 16K byte programs, your computer must have both a large memory and also a very fast one. With an 8-bit computer, 16K instruction bytes corresponds to 128,000 memory bit. Personal computers, however, commonly have 48K to 64K of memory in 1981.

Have you tried to write a 1000-instruction-byte program? It takes quite a bit of time, especially if the program is carefully written and performs some interesting function.

What this discussion is leading up to is the importance of subroutines. A subroutine can be of any length. If a variety of subroutines are readily available, they will save you time since you do not have to rewrite them. Thus, a 1000-instruction-byte program might be very easy to write, provided that it consists of 200 bytes of main program and 800 bytes of subroutines that others have worked out for you.

You ought to think about subroutines with every MSP program that you write. What program functions are required? Time delays? Multi-bit addition, subtraction, multiplication, or division? Put them in subroutines. Do you need to log data from a four-bcd-digit instrument? Write a data logging subroutine in which you can set in the main program the number of points desired and the time between individual points. Do you need to output information to a teletype via a UART chip and 20-mA current loop? Write a *software driver,* a computer subroutine that handles the data transfer requirements.

THE 8080 SUBROUTINE INSTRUCTIONS

We consider there to be 26 subroutine instructions in the 8080 microprocessor instruction set:

- A three-byte unconditional call instruction, CALL

  315 CALL <B2> <B3>   Unconditional call of subroutines at memory location addressed by bytes B2 and B3

- A one-byte unconditional return instruction, RET
  311 RET   Unconditional return from subroutine

- Eight different one-byte restart instructions, RST
  307 RST 0   Call subroutine at $HI = 000_8$ and $LO = 000_8$
  317 RST 1   Call subroutine at $HI = 000_8$ and $LO = 010_8$
  327 RST 2   Call subroutine at $HI = 000_8$ and $LO = 020_8$
  337 RST 3   Call subroutine at $HI = 000_8$ and $LO = 030_8$
  347 RST 4   Call subroutine at $HI = 000_8$ and $LO = 040_8$
  357 RST 5   Call subroutine at $HI = 000_8$ and $LO = 050_8$
  367 RST 6   Call subroutine at $HI = 000_8$ and $LO = 060_8$
  377 RST 7   Call subroutine at $HI = 000_8$ and $LO = 070_8$

- Eight different one-byte conditional return instructions
  300 RNZ   Return from subroutine if zero flag is at logic 0
  310 RZ   Return from subroutine if zero flag is at logic 1
  320 RNC   Return from subroutine if carry flag is at logic 0
  330 RC   Return from subroutine if carry flag is at logic 1
  340 RPO   Return from subroutine if parity flag is at logic 0

350	RPE		Return from subroutine if parity flag is at logic 1
360	RP		Return from subroutine if sign flag is at logic 0
370	RM		Return from subroutine if sign flag is at logic 1

- Eight different three-byte conditional call instructions

304	CNZ	\<B2> \<B3>	Call subroutine at memory location addressed by bytes B2 and B3 if zero flag is at logic 0
314	CZ	\<B2> \<B3>	Call subroutine at memory location addressed by bytes B2 and B3 if zero flag is at logic 1
324	CNC	\<B2> \<B3>	Call subroutine at memory location addressed by bytes B2 and B3 if carry flag is at logic 0
334	CC	\<B2> \<B3>	Call subroutine at memory location addressed by bytes B2 and B3 if carry flag is at logic 1
344	CPO	\<B2> \<B3>	Call subroutine at memory location addressed by bytes B2 and B3 if parity flag is at logic 0
354	CPE	\<B2> \<B3>	Call subroutine at memory location addressed by bytes B2 and B3 if parity flag is at logic 1
364	CP	\<B2> \<B3>	Call subroutine at memory location addressed by bytes B2 and B3 if sign flag is at logic 0
374	CM	\<B2> \<B3>	Call subroutine at memory location addressed by bytes B2 and B3 if sign flag is at logic 1

You may refer to Chapter 3 or the appendix for a more detailed discussion of the above instructions. We need not repeat it here.

THE 8080 STACK INSTRUCTIONS

There exist fourteen stack operations in addition to the subroutine instructions given in the above section. We consider a stack instruction to be one in which the location of the stack pointer or the contents of the stack, or both, are altered. Rather than discuss the stack operations in detail, we shall simply list them here and you may refer to Chapter 3 or the appendix for a more extensive discussion.

- A three-byte load immediate instruction, LXI SP
  061 LXI <B2> <B3>   Load immediate two bytes B2 and B3 into the stack pointer register

- A data transfer instruction, SPHL
  371 SPHL   Move the contents of registers H and L to the stack pointer register

- Two increment and decrement instructions, INX SP and DCX SP
  063 INX SP   Increment contents of stack pointer register by one
  073 DCX SP   Decrement contents of stack pointer register by one

- An arithmetic instruction, DAD SP
  071 DAD SP   Add contents of stack pointer register to contents of register pair H and L and store in register pair H and L

- A stack contents exchange instruction, XTHL
  343 XTHL   Exchange the top of the stack with the contents of the H and L register pair

- Four single-byte stack pop instructions, POP
  301 POP B   Pop stack and move contents to register pair B and C. Increment stack pointer register by two
  321 POP D   Pop stack and move contents to register pair D and E. Increment stack pointer register by two
  341 POP H   Pop stack and move contents to register pair H and L. Increment stack pointer register by two
  361 POP PSW   Pop stack and move contents to accumulator and restore the condition flags. Increment stack pointer register by two

- Four single-byte stack push instructions, PUSH
  305 PUSH B   Push contents of register pair B and C on stack. Decrement stack pointer register by two
  325 PUSH D   Push contents of register pair D and E on stack. Decrement stack pointer register by two
  345 PUSH H   Push contents of register pair H and L on stack. Decrement stack pointer register by two

365 PUSH PSW   Push contents of accumulator and the condition flags on stack. Decrement stack pointer register by two

MEMORY ALLOCATION

We are about ready to discuss the question "What is a stack?" in greater detail. Before we do so, however, we should briefly consider the *allocation* of memory in a microcomputer. The term *allocate* means:

allocate—In a computer, to assign storage locations to main routines and subroutines, thus fixing the absolute values of symbolic addresses.

Basically, allocation means how we subdivide a memory section or block into smaller groups of locations, each of which contains one of the following:

- A *main program*, at which the microcomputer starts execution. The main program need not be long. In fact, it can mainly consist of calls of subroutines and wait loops.
- One or more *subroutines*, where most of the computing work is performed. The subroutines can be time delays, arithmetic calculation routines, software drivers, and service routines, to mention a few types.
- Up to eight small *interrupt service routines*, which respond to different interrupt conditions and restart instructions, RST, jammed into the microcomputer.
- A single *stack*, where temporary information is stored while subroutines are being executed. You can consider the stack to be the computer's bookkeeper. It keeps track of all the subroutines that have been called.

Several hypothetical locations for the above groups are illustrated in Fig. 8-7, which fits all of them into the first 1K memory section of the microcomputer. Note that it is not necessary to crowd the different types of memory regions together. The stack, if at all possible, should be separated from the other program regions. This is because it grows from the end of memory toward the beginning.

MODES OF MICROCOMPUTER OPERATION

In this book, we have written only simple microcomputer programs and have constructed quite simple microcomputer interfaces that employ only a few 7400-series integrated-circuit chips (plus the 8212 buffer/latch and the 8095 buffer chips). Although you will continue in the same vein in this chapter as well, the real world of microcom-

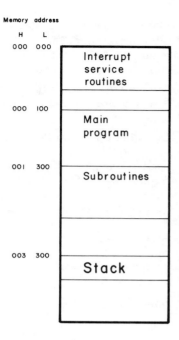

Memory address

H	L	
000	000	Interrupt service routines
000	100	Main program
001	300	Subroutines
003	300	Stack

Fig. 8-7. A hypothetical memory allocation scheme for the first 1K memory section. Here the stack is located at the top of the memory section, somewhat removed from all other memory regions.

puter interfacing will demand from you at least an order-of-magnitude increase in programming and interfacing sophistication. In the real world, you will be required to interface instruments and machines and to communicate between the microcomputer and a teletype, cathode-ray tube (crt) display, another microcomputer, a minicomputer, a cassette tape unit, a magnetic disk, and the like. In short, a single 8080 microcomputer may be required to communicate with a number of input/output devices, all of which seek the attention of the microcomputer.

How does a single microcomputer handle many I/O devices? *It handles only one device at a time!* However, the way it handles "only one device" can be quite clever and interesting. There are two main modes of microcomputer operation: *polled* and *interrupt*. These modes will now be discussed in turn.

Polled Operation

Graf has defined *polling* as:

polling—Periodic interrogation of each of the devices that share a communications line to determine whether it requires servicing. The multiplexer or control station sends a poll that has the effect of asking the selected device: "Do you have anything to transmit?"[4]

When a microcomputer *services* a device, it simply exchanges digital information with the device in a manner that is prescribed by some segment of the microcomputer program. The particular program segment is frequently called a *software driver,* which can be defined as:

software driver—A subroutine or part of a computer program that transfers information between the computer and a specified input/output device.

In polled operation, the microcomputer simply sequences through devices tied to the microcomputer looking for individual devices that need servicing. When it finds a device that needs servicing, it stops sequencing, calls up a software driver, and services the device. Once it has finished, it continues sequencing through the devices.

Polled operation is most useful with relatively slow devices that do not require frequent servicing, or at least can wait to be serviced. Advantage is taken of the differences in speed between the microcomputer and the polled devices, each of which might be serviced in only a fraction of a second. In 100 ms, the 8080 microcomputer can execute approximately 20,000 instructions.

Interrupt Operation

Graf has defined an *interrupt* as:

interrupt—In a computer, a break in the normal flow of a system or routine such that the flow can be resumed from that point at a later time. The source of the interrupt may be internal or external.[4]

Interrupt operation is a much more sophisticated mode of microcomputer operation, one that can circumvent most of the inherent disadvantages of polled operation. Thus, in polled operation:

- The microcomputer spends much of its time sequencing through the devices tied to it.
- Once a device is serviced, it must wait its turn until all other devices are sequenced and, if necessary, also serviced. In other words, there is no *priority* in polled operation. All devices are treated equally.
- The *response time* between when a device wants servicing and when it is serviced can be substantial, at least by microcomputer standards.

In contrast, in interrupt operation:

- The microcomputer may spend much of its time in a wait loop, waiting for a device to ask for servicing.
- There can exist *priority* in interrupt operation. The most important devices can be serviced more often than the less important devices.

- The *response time* between when an important device wants servicing and when it is serviced can be very short, even by microcomputer standards. With the 8080 microcomputer, this time is usually no more than 10 μs.
- Software becomes much more complex.

The terms *priority* and *response time* are defined in the following ways:

priority—The condition in which input/output devices are ordered in importance so that some devices take precedence over others.
response time—The time between the interrupt request by a device and the first instruction byte of the software driver that services it.

Interrupt operation is depicted schematically in Fig. 8-8. In 8080 microcomputers, an I/O device that interrupts the microcomputer sends both an interrupt clock pulse—a single pulse—as well as an 8-bit instruction byte that tells the microcomputer what to do after it has been interrupted. With the 8080 microcomputer this 8-bit instruction is one of the eight different restart instructions (RST), which are single-byte instructions that call a subroutine at one of eight different locations: $HI = 000_8$ and $LO = 000, 010, 020, 030, 040, 050, 060,$ or 070_8. The 8080A microprocessor chip permits multibyte interrupt instructions. We will not discuss this possibility in this book, but be aware that it exists.

Clearly, in interrupt operation, the 8080 microcomputer services its devices on demand, perhaps with the aid of priority considerations. If no device needs servicing, the microcomputer simply idles in a wait

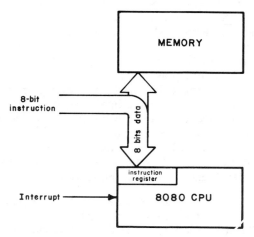

Fig. 8-8. During an interrupt an 8-bit instruction is "jammed" into the instruction register within the 8080 chip.

loop or performs other software tasks. It must be clear that *interrupts are complex, require additional software, and are difficult to debug.* Many individuals keep their interrupt use to a minimum.

BASIC TYPES OF INTERRUPTS

There exist three types of interrupts: *single-line, multilevel,* and *vectored.* They can be defined as follows:

single-line interrupt—An interrupt system in which there is a single interrupt line. Multiple devices must be ored to this line. Each input to the or gate is from an I/O device. Once it receives an interrupt, the microcomputer must scan all of the devices to determine which one generated the interrupt.

multilevel interrupt—An interrupt system in which there exist many interrupt lines to the microcomputer, each line being tied to a separate I/O device. The microcomputer does not need to scan the devices to determine which one caused the interrupt.

vectored interrupt—An interrupt system in which the interrupt causes a direct branch to that part of the program that services the interrupt. This is the fastest mode of interrupt operation.

These three types of interrupts are shown schematically in Fig. 8-9.

The single-line interrupt is a popular type of interrupt with microcomputers and one that is easy to implement. There exists no limit to the number of devices that can be ored together to a single interrupt line. Three devices are shown in Fig. 8-9A. However, the more devices, the longer the time required to scan them. Priority is determined by the order in which the devices are scanned under software control.

The multilevel interrupt, shown in Fig. 8-9B, is an effective technique if a sufficient number of interrupt pins exist on the microprocessor chip. This is rarely the case. Existing microprocessor chips have no more than four interrupt pins.

The vectored interrupt technique (Fig. 8-9C) permits direct branching to the part of a program, most likely a subroutine called a *service subroutine,* that immediately services the interrupt. The interrupt pulse is first sent to the microprocessor chip, followed by an 8-bit single-byte instruction that is *jammed* into the microprocessor immediately after the interrupt pulse. The Intel 8080 provides eight different restart instructions, as mentioned in a previous section:

307	RST 0	Call subroutine at $HI = 000_8$ and $LO = 000_8$
317	RST 1	Call subroutine at $HI = 000_8$ and $LO = 010_8$
327	RST 2	Call subroutine at $HI = 000_8$ and $LO = 020_8$
337	RST 3	Call subroutine at $HI = 000_8$ and $LO = 030_8$
347	RST 4	Call subroutine at $HI = 000_8$ and $LO = 040_8$

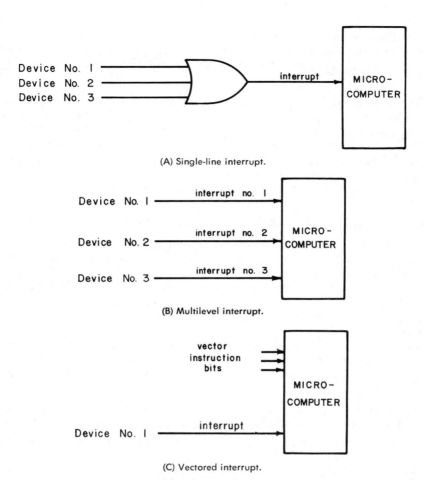

(A) Single-line interrupt.

(B) Multilevel interrupt.

(C) Vectored interrupt.

Fig. 8-9. Three different types of interrupt techniques.

357	RST 5	Call subroutine at HI $= 000_8$ and LO $= 050_8$
367	RST 6	Call subroutine at HI $= 000_8$ and LO $= 060_8$
377	RST 7	Call subroutine at HI $= 000_8$ and LO $= 070_8$

You should observe that only three of the eight bits are changed in the above restart (RST) instructions. Intel Corporation has taken advantage of this fact and has provided a special chip, called the 8214 priority interrupt control unit, that contains all the logic needed to:

- Cause an interrupt to the 8080 microprocessor chip.
- Jam three vector bits, in combination with five other vector bits, into the 8080 microprocessor chip immediately after the interrupt.

- Provide eight levels of priority, e.g., the eight RST instructions.
- Provide open-collector outputs for both the interrupt and vector outputs, thus permitting interrupt capability by more than eight devices.

The manufacturer's specifications for the chip are shown in Chapter 1.

One would expect the interrupt hardware within microprocessor chips to improve with time. The 8080A and 8228 chips permit multibyte instructions to be entered immediately after an interrupt. However, special digital circuitry external to the chip is required to take advantage of this feature. A new interface chip, the Intel 8259 programmable interrupt controller, performs some of these functions.

ENABLE AND DISABLE INTERRUPT INSTRUCTIONS

It is not uncommon for a computer to have a variety of I/O devices connected to it, each demanding attention constantly. The use of priority levels helps with the problem of servicing such devices, but occasionally the computer may want to know that an interrupt has arrived without the necessity of servicing the interrupt. This is particularly true during a complex or time-dependent piece of software. For this purpose, there is a piece of internal circuitry within the microprocessor and software to allow it to turn a "deaf ear" to all interrupts. The circuitry is an *interrupt flip-flop* or *flag* (the terms mean the same thing) that can be enabled or disabled by single-byte microcomputer instructions. Some definitions are in order:

interrupt flag, interrupt flip-flop—A flip-flop within the microprocessor chip that can be enabled or disabled by microprocessor software and can detect an interrupt pulse and remember the fact that an interrupt occurred.

disable interrupt—To disable the interrupt flag within a microprocessor chip.

enable interrupt—To enable the interrupt flag within a microprocessor chip.

The enable interrupt and disable interrupt instructions in the 8080 microprocessor instruction set are:

373 EI Enable the interrupt system within the microprocessor chip *following the execution of the next instruction.*

363 DI Disable the interrupt system within the microprocessor chip *immediately following the execution of this instruction.*

If the interrupt flag is enabled, then an interrupt will be serviced immediately. However, even if the interrupt flag is disabled, the computer can still detect whether or not an interrupt has occurred. If an interrupt did occur while the interrupt flag was disabled, then an interrupt would occur as soon as the flag is enabled. Only one interrupt event is remembered.

EXTERNAL FLAGS

The term *flag* has been defined in Chapter 1 as:

flag—In a computer, an indication that a particular operation has been completed.[4] Also, a flip-flop that can be either set or cleared in response to operations occurring in the microcomputer.

Such a flag can more correctly be called an *internal flag*, since it is located within the circuitry internal to the 8080 microprocessor chip. An extremely important, but quite simple, interface circuit is an *external flag*, which can be defined as follows:

external flag—A digital circuit, usually containing a single flip-flop, which indicates a condition that exists with an input/output device.

"Internal flag" can be defined in a similar manner. Thus:

internal flag—A digital circuit, usually containing a single flip-flop, which indicates a condition that exists internally within the microprocessor chip.

The really important word in the preceding definitions is *condition*. A flag is able to detect a change in condition almost instantaneously; it is then able to remember this condition until it is cleared by a clock pulse from the microprocessor or, if the flag is internal, until the executed program changes the logic state of the flag. It might be more appropriate to call an external flag an *external condition flag*. This term is redundant, however.

External flags indicate the conditions that exist with an input/output device; thus, they are able to synchronize the operation of the device with that of the microcomputer. They are no less important in a properly functioning interfaced microcomputer system than the device select pulses that we discussed previously. The different types of conditions that the flag can indicate include, but are not limited to, the following:

- Data is available to be input into the microcomputer from the device.
- The device is ready to accept output data from the microcomputer.
- The device has finished one operation, and is ready to start a new operation.

- The device is busy and does not wish to be disturbed.
- A power failure has occurred; the microcomputer must react immediately to save valuable data and programs.
- The device is not in operation at the moment.
- A controlled quantity has exceeded the danger zone.
- The value of a controlled quantity is too high.
- The value of a controlled quantity is too low.

A schematic diagram of a typical external flag circuit is shown in Fig. 8-10. The authors prefer this circuit to one that can be constructed from a 7476 J-K flip-flop. The 7474 flip-flop is positive-edge–triggered, whereas the 7476 flip-flop is level-triggered, but both flip-flops are effective.

A positive edge clocks the Q output of the flip-flop to logic 1. This logic state is input into a 7400 two-input NAND gate, which inverts the signal and applies logic 0 to the interrupt terminal of the 8080. *While the 8080 chip itself requires a logic 1 to generate an interrupt at pin 14 on the chip, the figure shows a logic 0 generating the interrupt. This means that the interrupt input is inverted before it enters the 8080. The active low (logic 0) condition is the authors' design condition in the 8080-based microcomputer that they used.*

The second input on the 7400 NAND gate can be used to gate the interrupt into the microcomputer. If the arm flag within the microprocessor has been previously enabled by an EI instruction, the microcomputer is interrupted and the program branches to a subroutine indicated by an 8-bit instruction that is "jammed" into the computer via external circuitry. The "jammed" instruction is usually a restart instruction, RST n, *but may be any other single-byte instruction.* You should be aware of the fact that the new 8080A microprocessor chip, available from Intel and others, permits the jamming of a multibyte

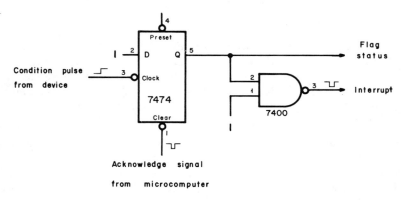

Fig. 8-10. An external flag circuit.

instruction, such as a subroutine call, during an interrupt. Extra hardware, including the 8228 chip, is required to do so, however.

It is poor design procedure to drive long lines, wires, etc., directly from flip-flop or latch outputs. The 7400 two-input NAND gate has been added to provide the drive capability and to buffer the flip-flop output.

A more useful representation of the external flag circuit is shown in Fig. 8-11. This circuit is called "external flag 0," and the following inputs and outputs of the flag are identified:

- The condition pulse, which is usually from some instrument or device.
- The clear input, $\overline{\text{CLR-0}}$. A negative clock pulse will clear the flag.
- The preset input, $\overline{\text{PR-0}}$. A negative clock pulse will set the flag.
- The flag output, STAT-0. This output is typically sent as input into the microcomputer through a three-state input port.
- The interrupt output from the flag, $\overline{\text{INT-0}}$. A negative clock pulse from this output will interrupt the microcomputer.

"External flag 1" would have input $\overline{\text{CLR-1}}$ and $\overline{\text{PR-1}}$ and outputs STAT-1 and $\overline{\text{INT-1}}$. Similar considerations apply for other flags.

Clearing an External Flag

The obvious way to clear an interrupt flag is through the use of the INTA status bit, which goes to logic 1 early in a machine cycle when there is an interrupt condition. This logic 1 state can be inverted and applied to the $\overline{\text{CLR-0}}$ input of external flag 0 or any other flag, as shown schematically in Fig. 8-12.

The clearing operation can sometimes occur very quickly, in as little as 2 μs. A more typical value is 7 μs. We will not consider all of the subtleties associated with this type of clearing operation, but

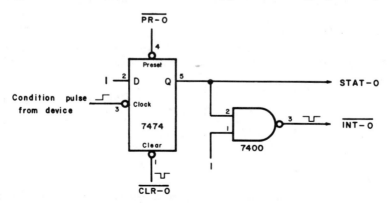

Fig. 8-11. Circuit for external flag 0.

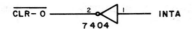

Fig. 8-12. External flags, such as flag 0, can be cleared via the use of the INTA status signal.

$\overline{\text{CLR-0}}$ ——— 2 ◁ 1 ——— INTA

7404

the key variables are the instruction being executed and the machine cycle within the instruction cycle at the time that the interrupt occurs.

It is usually quite desirable to provide a manual clear capability from the front panel of an interfaced instrument. One example of how this can be done is shown in Fig. 8-13. Note that either the INTA signal or the pulser can apply a clear pulse to the flag. Naturally, a 7408 AND gate can be substituted for the combination of a NAND gate and 7404 inverter.

An equally interesting type of flag clearing circuit is one in which the clear pulse is generated by software, i.e., via an output device select pulse from the microcomputer. A negative device select pulse is required, and this is noted by the symbol $\overline{\text{DS}}$, where there is a bar indicating inversion over the letters DS. Circuits employing such a clear signal are shown in Fig. 8-14.

Deferred and Immediate Interrupts

The terms *deferred interrupt* and *immediate interrupt* can be defined as follows:

deferred interrupt—A computer interrupt that occurs at some time after an external flag goes to logic 1.

immediate interrupt—A computer interrupt that occurs as soon as an external flag goes to logic 1.

An example of an immediate interrupt is where the interrupting signal is applied directly to the 8080's interrupt input (pin 14).

For external flag 0, as soon as STAT-0 goes to logic 1, $\overline{\text{INT-0}}$ goes to logic 0 and the microcomputer is interrupted. A simple deferred interrupt circuit is shown in Fig. 8-15. The reason why the circuit is deferred is that you can control when $\overline{\text{INT}}$ goes to logic 0 by the gating signal DS 002_8. Naturally, this signal is generated by the microcomputer software, so a considerable period can elapse between the time that Q goes to logic 1 and the time that the output from the 7400

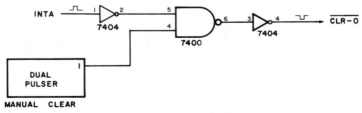

Fig. 8-13. A circuit that permits both a manual and an interrupt acknowledge input to the clear input of external flag 0.

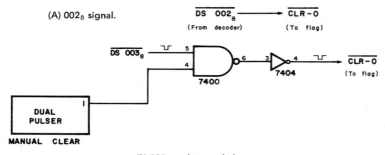

(A) 002_8 signal.

DS 002_8 ⟶ $\overline{CLR-0}$

(From decoder)   (To flag)

DS 003_8

7400   7404

$\overline{CLR-0}$
(To flag)

DUAL
PULSER

MANUAL CLEAR

(B) 003_8 and manual clear.

Fig. 8-14. Use of device select pulses to clear external flag 0.

NAND gate goes to logic 0. You will see this in another example in this chapter. This circuit is an example of how software can replace hardware. With the DS 002_8 device select pulse, you can control the time delay. This circuit is especially useful in polled interrupt systems; the device select pulse serves as the polling signal.

External Flag Output

Not too many tricks are performed with output STAT-0 from an external flag such as external flag 0. Usually, you input this bit into the microcomputer. Thus, for the STAT-4 output from external flag 4, you can use either of the three-state circuits shown in Fig. 8-16. These circuits employ three-state buffers such as the 74125 or 74126. You may recall that we talked about these buffers in Chapter 7 in *Bugbook II*. A device select pulse, generated by an IN instruction, is used to input data into the accumulator. The pin configurations for the two chips are provided in Fig. 8-17.

If you wish to input the STAT outputs from several external flags, the authors would recommend the use of an 8212 three-state buffer/latch chip (Fig. 8-18). Such a circuit is very useful in polled interrupt operation. Once you have input the logic states of the external flags

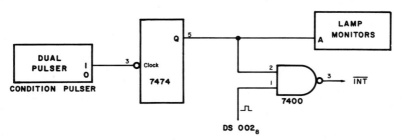

DUAL
PULSER

CONDITION PULSER

Clock

7474

LAMP
MONITORS

7400 $\overline{INT}$

DS 002_8

Fig. 8-15. A deferred interrupt circuit. $\overline{INT}$ does not become logic 0 until both Q is logic 1 and a device select pulse is applied to the 7400 NAND gate.

Fig. 8-16. The use of three-state buffers to input status bits into the 8080.

into the microcomputer, you can perform logical manipulations and rotations to determine which flags are at a logic 1 state, which are at logic 0, which have changed from logic 0 to logic 1, and which have changed from logic 1 to logic 0. You can use any of these conditions or logic state changes to call subroutines that service the devices tied to the external flags.

As a final point, the sequence of events that occurs in conjunction with an interrupt can be listed as follows:

- The external flag output, STAT, goes to logic 1.
- Essentially immediately (if an immediate interrupt) or after some time delay (if a deferred interrupt), a logic 0 is applied to the interrupt terminal, $\overline{\text{INT}}$.
- A pulse is generated by the microprocessor chip to acknowledge the interrupt ($\overline{\text{INTA}}$). This pulse can be used to "jam" a single-byte instruction into the microprocessor chip and, if desired, to also clear the flag.
- The external flag is cleared as soon as it receives the clear pulse. STAT returns to logic 0 and $\overline{\text{INT}}$ returns to logic 1.

The vector restart instruction, RST n, is applied to the data bus only during the interrupt acknowledge ($\overline{\text{INTA}}$) time. *Unlike all other input bytes, the 8-bit restart instruction byte goes directly to the instruction register within the 8080 microprocessor chip, where it is executed.* We shall discuss vector restart instructions in a later example.

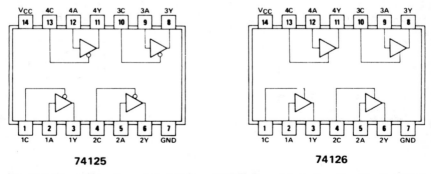

Fig. 8-17. Pin configurations of the 74125 and 74126 three-state buffer chips. For the 74125 chip a logic 0 enables the buffer; in the 74126 a logic 1 enable signal is required.

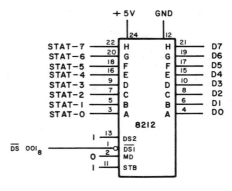

Fig. 8-18. An 8212 chip used as an input buffer for the status outputs from eight different external flags. This type of circuit is called a status register.

Single-Line Interrupt (Polled Interrupt)

If you have only a single interrupt terminal and are not able to employ the vector interrupt feature of the 8080 microcomputer, you can still wire the circuit shown in Fig. 8-19. You can poll the four external flags with the aid of four different device select pulses, each gated with an external flag in the manner shown in Fig. 8-20.

INTERRUPT MASK

In polled interrupt operation, you typically sense the logic states of the external flags with the aid of a status register (Fig. 8-18), which inputs the bits into the accumulator of the microcomputer. Once the bits are in the accumulator, the question arises: What do you do next? You have several possibilities:

- Rotate each bit, in turn, into the carry flag and employ a conditional call instruction that is dependent upon whether the carry flag is at logic 0 or logic 1. In this way, you poll the status of each external flag and are able to call the subroutine required if a given flag is set.
- *Mask* each 8-bit sense word with a *mask word* that basically makes it easy to determine whether a given external flag is set or cleared. Once the mask operation has been completed, different arithmetic or logical operations can be employed to immediately determine whether the external flag is set or cleared. Once this is done, a conditional call instruction can be employed. Typically an AND operation does the masking.

The term *mask* can be defined in the following manner:

mask—A logical technique in which certain bits of a word are blanked out or inhibited.[4]

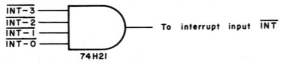

Fig. 8-19. If any of the interrupt inputs, $\overline{\text{INT-n}}$, to the 72H21 AND gate become logic 0, an interrupt signal is output from the gate.

It is useful to give an example of a *mask operation*. Assume that there exist eight different external flags that are attached to the following devices:

Flag Number	Device
0	Teletype
1	Paper tape reader
2	Cathode-ray–tube display
3	Minicomputer
4	Temperature recorder
5	Digital voltmeter
6	Pressure indicator
7	Unassigned

Each device has its own external flag, and all eight flags are connected to a 8212 status register.

If we wish to determine whether or not the microcomputer flag is set, *i.e.*, at logic 1, we can employ the following program:

LO Memory Address	Octal Instruction	Mnemonic	Comments
.	.		.
.	.		.
.	.		.
150	333	IN	Generate input device select pulse that inputs the flag bits at the status register into the accumulator
151	001	001	Device code for status register
152	346	ANI	AND the contents of the accumulator with the following mask word
153	010	010	Mask word that masks all flag bits except flag bit 3
154	302	JNZ	If the contents of the accumulator are not zero, jump to the memory location given by the following address bytes. Otherwise, ignore this instruction

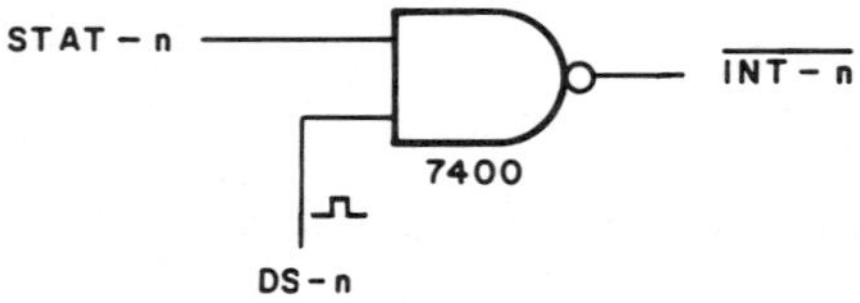

Fig. 8-20. The $\overline{\text{INT-n}}$ is not generated until both STAT-n and DS-n are at logic 1. This permits you to "poll" each external flag using software.

155	000	LO address byte
156	002	HI address byte
.	.	.
.	.	.
.	.	.

Presumably a service routine is present at memory location $H = 002$ and $L = 000$ to handle the situation when the external flag for the mini-computer is set.

INTERFACING A KEYBOARD

In this section we shall discuss how to interface an ASCII keyboard. Some of the schematics shown will be simplified for clarity.

Recall the keyboard example in Chapter 7 where you input a keyboard code and compared it with the ASCII code for the letter E. The flowchart was as shown in Fig. 8-21. The program remains in a very tight input loop, even when no key is pressed and no ASCII code is present at input port 004. Such a program is inefficient in that it wastes the valuable time of the microcomputer, which could be performing more meaningful tasks.

Flag Bit Testing

Most ASCII keyboards generate a short output pulse, which is called READY or VALID, each time a key is pressed on the keyboard. In the case of one keyboard, this pulse has a duration of 1 μs, a pulse width that is much too short to be entered directly into the microcomputer.

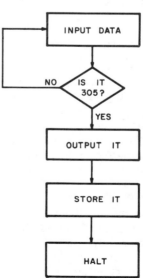

Fig. 8-21. Flowchart that tests an input character to determine whether or not it is ASCII character E. When an E is finally detected, the program outputs it, stores it, and then comes to a halt.

The reason is that most timing loops that test for a single input bit consume at least 12 μs for a 2-MHz microcomputer. For a 1-μs input pulse, the odds are that 92 percent of the time it will not be detected.

The solution to this problem is to connect the VALID output signal from the keyboard to an external flag, the output of which is input and tested by the microcomputer. A simplified circuit is shown in Fig. 8-22.

The 7474 flip-flop is the flag, which is clocked to a logic 1 output state by the 1-μs signal pulse from the keyboard. The microcomputer program tests for the logic state of the flag output, clears the flag with device select pulse $\overline{\text{OUT 065}}$, and inputs the keyboard data into the accumulator. The actual program is as follows:

LO Memory Address	Octal Instruction	Mnemonic	Comments
000	333	IN	Input flag data from 8212 status register
001	017	017	Device code for 8212 status register
002	346	ANI	Mask the accumulator contents with the following data byte
003	010	010	Mask data byte for input bit D3
004	312	JZ	If the result of the masking operation is zero, jump to HI = 000 and LO = 000 and test flag again
005	000		LO address byte
006	000		HI address byte
007	323	OUT	Clear the flag by sending a device select pulse to the CLR input
010	065	065	Device code for CLR input of flag
011	333	IN	Input keyboard data into the accumulator
012	005	005	Device code for 8212 input port
013	.	.	.
014	.	.	.

The flowchart for this program is provided in Fig. 8-23.

Flag bit D3 can be tested in other ways, such as by rotating it into the carry bit and testing the carry bit with a JC or JNC instruction. There are many different ways to test status or flag bits.

When the keyboard/microcomputer system is first turned on, it is important to *initialize* the system by clearing all flags. Traditionally, this has been done through the use of one or more manual RESET switches, which are gated with device select pulses such as $\overline{\text{OUT 065}}$. An alternative to the use of manual switches is a short initialization program that generates all necessary clear flag pulses, including $\overline{\text{OUT 065}}$.

Vectored Interrupts

Even though the VALID flag testing program is more efficient than the program in Chapter 7 that simply input keyboard data, most microcomputers have more important things to do than monitor a single flag bit. In some cases, hundreds of flags need to be tested. In other cases, the microcomputer is performing a complex mathematical calculation

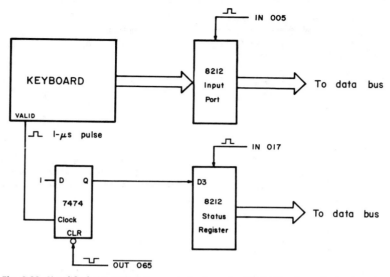

Fig. 8-22. Simplified circuit that demonstrates how the VALID flag from the keyboard is tested by the 8080 microcomputer.

that requires considerable computation time. The point is that most microcomputers should be interfaced in such a way that they respond only when a key is pressed on the keyboard; at all other times, the keyboard is ignored. A good typist will type five to ten characters per second, or 100 to 200 ms per ASCII character. This is very slow by microcomputer standards, and the microcomputer can be doing many other things between keystrokes. However, once a key is pressed, it would be useful for the microcomputer to respond immediately. With an 8080-based microcomputer, "immediate" response can be accomplished through the use of *vectored interrupts.*

A vectored interrupt has been previously defined in this chapter as an interrupt system in which the interrupt causes a direct branch to that part of the program that services the interrupt. The necessary circuitry for our keyboard example is shown in Fig. 8-24. Observe that the 8212 input port remains the same, but that the VALID pulse is now input to the INTERRUPT input of our 8080-based microcomputer. In this case, the interrupt input requires a negative interrupt pulse; if you input directly into the 8080 microprocessor chip, you will require a positive interrupt pulse, INT.

Once the 8080 chip receives an interrupt pulse, and if the interrupt flag within the chip has been previously enabled by an enable interrupt instruction, EI, *the 8080 finishes the execution of its current instruction and then sends out an interrupt acknowledge signal, $\overline{INTA}$, that is used to gate a single-byte restart instruction, RST n, directly into the instruc-*

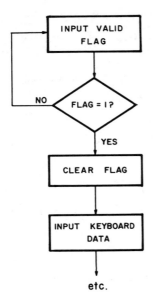

Fig. 8-23. Flowchart for the program that tests for the VALID flag. When VALID = 1, a single character is entered from the keyboard.

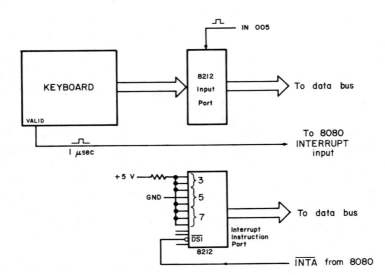

Fig. 8-24. Simplified vector interrupt for the ASCII character keyboard. If there are other interrupting devices in the system, a NAND gate must be used prior to the INTERRUPT input on the 8080 chip.

tion register within the 8080 chip. This is the only time in which you can, using an external three-state buffer chip, input directly into the *instruction register* rather than the accumulator or other general-purpose register. In effect, you "jam" an instruction byte into the instruction register. The hardware used to jam an instruction byte is shown in Fig. 8-24. It consists of an 8-bit gated driver chip that is called the *interrupt instruction port.* In Fig. 8-24 the jammed instruction is a RST 5, or **357**, instruction, which causes the microcomputer to immediately go to the subroutine located at HI = 000 and LO = 050.

Let us examine the software required for a vectored interrupt system. Since the RST n is a call subroutine instruction, you must first set up a stack pointer within read/write memory. You then write an enable interrupt instruction, EI, to permit the 8080 microprocessor chip to be interrupted by an external signal applied at the INT input pin. Next, you jump to an area of memory that we shall call MAIN TASK. This is the main program, most likely located in ROM or EPROM, that will be periodically interrupted. MAIN TASK can be located anywhere in memory, but the authors recommend that it be located away from the interrupt service routines area of memory, which starts at HI = 000 and LO = 000 and continues to approximately HI = 000 and LO = 077. Note, however, that the final interrupt subroutine location, at LO = 070, can accommodate a subroutine of any length.

We can summarize the preceding comments by listing the program that we have developed so far. Thus:

LO Memory Address	Octal Instruction	Mnemonic	Comments
000	061	LXI SP	Locate the stack within read/write memory by inputing the following two address bytes into the stack pointer within the 8080 chip
001	300	300	LO address byte
002	003	003	HI address byte
003	373	EI	Enable the interrupt flag within the 8080 chip
004	303	JMP	Jump to MAIN TASK
005	*		LO address byte of MAIN TASK
006	*		HI address byte of MAIN TASK
.			
.			
050	333	IN	Input keyboard data into the accumulator
051	005	005	Device code for 8212 input port
.			
.		This section of memory contains other software associated with the keyboard service routine. Most likely, there is a jump instruction to some other memory address away from the interrupt service subroutine area.	
.			
.			
057	311	RET	Return from subroutine, the last instruction in the keyboard service routine

It should be clear that an interrupt from the keyboard will force the microcomputer to jam a RST 5 instruction into the instruction register. Upon execution, this instruction byte will call the keyboard service routine that starts at HI = 000 and LO = 050. This subroutine ends with a RET statement, which permits the microcomputer to return to MAIN TASK, which could be a simple control loop or a complicated mathematical program. They keyboard service routine will usually be short and not consume much time.

The preceding program will work, but if you try to execute it, you will observe a number of operating difficulties. First, you will not be able to execute the keyboard service routine more than once. Why not? You have failed to re-enable the interrupt flag within the 8080 chip. Remember the following rule:

> *During an interrupt machine cycle, the internal interrupt flag within the 8080 chip is first disabled, then an interrupt acknowledge signal, $\overline{INTA}$, is generated to permit a RST n instruction to be jammed into the instruction register.*

The key point here is that the interrupt flag is disabled to prevent further interrupts while the microcomputer is servicing the current interrupt. *If you wish to re-enable the interrupt flag, you must do so by providing an EI instruction in the interrupt service routine.* The interrupt flag is not automatically enabled.

It is common practice to provide an enable interrupt instruction, EI, immediately before the RET instruction of the interrupt service subroutine. Since the *interrupt flag does not become active until after the next instruction has been executed,* you can return to MAIN TASK before another interrupt is accepted by the 8080 chip. If this capability were not provided, there would be the danger that you would fill much of read/write memory with linking return addresses waiting to be used, because interrupt service routines were interrupted again, before they had a chance to return.

In all other respects, you treat your vector subroutines as normal subroutines. If the contents of the registers are important, you use the PUSH and POP instructions to save and restore registers. A typical interrupt subroutine would appear as shown in Fig. 8-25.

Since there exist only seven memory locations between our vector address at LO = 050 and the next vector address at LO = 060, you will not be able to fit in four PUSH instructions, four POP instructions, one EI instruction, one RET instruction, and the keyboard service instructions without encroaching on the next one or two vector subroutine locations. Instead, you place a jump instruction at LO = 050, 051, and 052 that transfers control to an area of memory where you will have more room for software. At the end of the service routine, the RET instruction will still return program control to the point where the MAIN

Fig. 8-25. A typical interrupt subroutine. The first instructions, the PUSH instructions, save the microcomputer status. Near the end of the subroutine, the microcomputer status is popped back into the internal registers.

TASK was interrupted. The relationship between the MAIN TASK, vector jump instruction at $HI = 000$ and $LO = 050$, and keyboard service software is shown in Fig. 8-26. The interfacing of the keyboard could have been made more complex. For example, deferred interrupts or priority interrupts could have been used. In the preceding example, there was little incentive to do so.

PRIORITY INTERRUPTS

Priority interrupts are interrupts that are ordered in importance so that some interrupting devices take precedence over others. They are

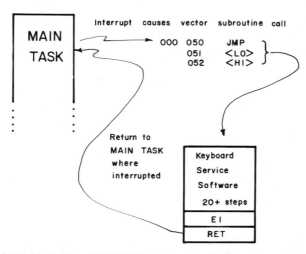

Fig. 8-26. Relationship between MAIN TASK, the vector subroutine jump, and the keyboard service software, which is located elsewhere in memory.

used whenever a number of interrupts can occur at the same time, or whenever there is a need to determine which interrupting devices are the most important.

Of various ways to establish priority, the easiest way is to set priority in software and then to poll the interrupting devices and determine which devices should be serviced in which order. For example, consider the interface circuit in Fig. 8-27. Three interrupts are shown, but many more could be included in a practical system. An interrupt occurs whenever one of the flag flip-flops becomes set by a pulse at its clock input. We show this as a positive interrupt pulse, which is what is required for most 8080-based microcomputers. If the interrupt pulse is applied directly to the 8080 chip, a 7410 chip should be used, as shown in Fig. 8-27. When the 8080 accepts the interrupt, it generates an $\overline{\text{INTA}}$ pulse that gates the RST instruction code **357**, which is pre-

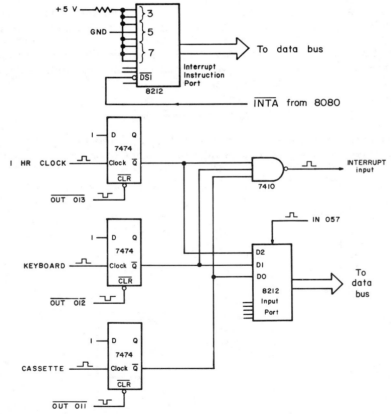

Fig. 8-27. Polled interrupt circuit that consists of three interrupting devices. The positive interrupt pulse is connected directly to the INT input pin on the 8080 microprocessor chip.

wired at the interrupt instruction port, directly into the instruction register. Upon execution of the RST 5 instruction, a subroutine at HI = 000 and LO = 050 is called. The RST 5 instruction causes a *vector*, or branch, to the indicated subroutine, where the software polling of the interrupting devices takes place.

Each flag bit for the one-hour clock, keyboard, and cassette shown in Fig. 8-27 is input at logic 1 to the 7410 three-input NAND gate if service is not needed, and as logic 0 if service is needed. The normal logic state of the output from the 7410 gate is logic 0; a positive clock pulse at this output is required to interrupt most 8080-based microcomputers. In the program, which is given below, the priority is set so that the tape cassette has the highest priority (high-speed device), the keyboard is next in priority (low-speed device), and the one-hour clock is last in priority (unbelievably slow device). The software is as follows:

LO Memory Address	Octal Instruction	Mnemonic	Comments
050	333	IN	Input status bits of three flags
051	057	057	Device code for 8212 input port
052	057	CMA	Complement the status bits $(1 \rightarrow 0$ and $0 \rightarrow 1)$
053	346	ANI	Mask out all bits except bits D0, D1, and D2
054	007	007	Mask byte
055	037	RAR	Rotate accumulator contents right through carry (bit D0 is rotated into the carry bit)
056	332	JC	If carry bit is logic 1, jump to the cassette service routine located at HI = 003 and LO = 100
057	100		LO address byte of cassette service routine
060	003		HI address byte of cassette service routine
061	037	RAR	Rotate accumulator contents right once again (bit D1 is now rotated into the carry bit)
062	332	JC	If carry bit is logic 1, jump to the keyboard service routine located at HI = 003 and LO = 200
063	200		LO address byte of keyboard service routine
064	003		HI address byte of keyboard service routine
065	037	RAR	Rotate accumulator contents right (bit D2 is now rotated into the carry bit)
066	332	JC	If carry bit is logic 1, jump to the one-hour clock service routine located at HI = 003 and LO = 300
067	300		LO address byte of one-hour clock service routine
070	003		HI address byte of one-hour clock service routine
071	166	HLT	If you got to this point, something is wrong. The microcomputer is halted; find out what the problem is.

Note the use of the CMA instruction at LO = 052. Normally, the flag would be at logic 1 if service is needed and logic 0 if service is not needed. In the example in Fig. 8-26 the situation is just the opposite. The use of the CMA instruction illustrates how easy it is to invert eight bits of accumulator data.

The ANI instruction at LO = 053 masks out bits D3 through D7 as an illustration of how a masking operation can be used. However, since RAR instructions are used, and since we keep track of how many times we rotate the accumulator contents, the ANI instruction is not really needed here. Other bit-testing methods could be implemented in software. These service routines are very similar to those used with regular vector service routines, as shown in Fig. 8-25. Such routines generally end with an enable interrupt instruction, EI, and a return instruction, RET. Even when polling is used, we still must return to the main program that was interrupted.

The above polling routine runs through vector addresses LO = 060 and LO = 070. This is not an error; there exist no other interrupts which use these vector addresses.

Other variations in the polling program are possible. Since the interrupt flags are input into the accumulator, we may wish to save the contents of the accumulator and flags at the time that MAIN TASK was interrupted. To do so, we would provide a PUSH PSW instruction at LO = 050. Each service subroutine would require a POP PSW instruction immediately before the EI instruction. Other PUSH and POP instructions would be required to save the register contents. Finally, it is quite likely that the first instruction in each service routine would clear the flag associated with the subroutine. Thus, as shown in Fig. 8-27, an $\overline{\text{OUT 011}}$ pulse would clear the cassette flag, an $\overline{\text{OUT 012}}$ would clear the keyboard flag, and an $\overline{\text{OUT 013}}$ would clear the one-hour clock flag.

The authors have found the above polling program to be very useful in their own work. Other polling software schemes will work equally well, but the one given above is simple and effective.

The one-hour clock raises an important question: Why would you build an external one-hour hardware clock when you already have software to do the same thing in under 50 instruction bytes? The answer to this question depends on how you use your computer. If your computer can sit and do the one-hour software and nothing else, or if you are using interrupts and can tolerate a small amount of error in the hour time-delay subroutine (owing to the time that the microcomputer spends with the interrupts), then use software. If you need to know the exact time, use hardware. Remember, when you use interrupts and interrupt service routines, you are essentially interjecting additional software into the MAIN TASK program flow. This additional software takes time. You must not only check the interrupting device, but you must also service it. If you interrupt a one-hour software time delay routine four times with a two-minute device service routine, the execution of the time delay routine will take one hour and eight minutes rather than one hour. The one-hour software routine operations are suspended when there is an interrupt that requires some other task to be performed. The one-hour external clock can be called a *real-time clock*, since it keeps real time, as opposed to microcomputer software time.

HARDWARE PRIORITY INTERRUPTS

Interrupt priorities may also be generated using hardware. Hardware priority interrupts are very important when a number of interrupting devices are connected to a microcomputer and all require relatively fast service. The "gimmick" employed is simple: *Each interrupting device generates its own restart instruction, RST n, which, when input into the 8080 microcomputer, causes an immediate vector to location HI = 000 and LO = 0N0, where N can be 0, 1, 2, 3, 4, 5, 6, or 7.* In addition, priority is automatically assigned by the hardware, so that device 7 has higher priority than device 6, which has higher priority than device 5, etc. In other words, if $>$ represents priority, then:

$$7 > 6 > 5 > 4 > 3 > 2 > 1 > 0$$

The circuit that you would use is shown in Fig. 8-28.

The 74148 eight-line-to-three-line priority-encoder integrated-circuit chip is a sixteen-pin chip that has the pin configuration and truth table shown in Fig. 8-29. Note that the data inputs and outputs are active at the low logic level. The 74148 chip will accept up to eight logic 0 inputs from flags, such as those shown in Fig. 8-28 and will output *the binary code for the highest numbered input that is at logic 0.* For

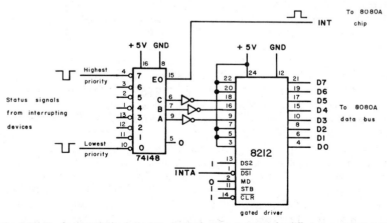

Fig. 8-28. Hardware priority interrupt circuit that generates eight different vector restart instructions, RST n, that have priority 7 $>$ 6 $>$ 5 $>$ 4 $>$ 3 $>$ 2 $>$ 1 $>$ 0.

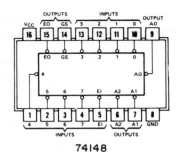

SN54148, SN74148
FUNCTION TABLE

INPUTS									OUTPUTS				
EI	0	1	2	3	4	5	6	7	A2	A1	A0	GS	EO
H	X	X	X	X	X	X	X	X	H	H	H	H	H
L	H	H	H	H	H	H	H	H	H	H	H	H	L
L	X	X	X	X	X	X	X	L	L	L	L	L	H
L	X	X	X	X	X	X	L	H	L	L	H	L	H
L	X	X	X	X	X	L	H	H	L	H	L	L	H
L	X	X	X	X	L	H	H	H	L	H	H	L	H
L	X	X	X	L	H	H	H	H	H	L	L	L	H
L	X	X	L	H	H	H	H	H	H	L	H	L	H
L	X	L	H	H	H	H	H	H	H	H	L	L	H
L	L	H	H	H	H	H	H	H	H	H	H	L	H

74148

Fig. 8-29. Pin configuration and truth table for the 74148 eight-line-to-one-line priority encoder chip.

example, if you have simultaneous interrupt requests from both device 5 and device 7, device 7 has the higher priority and the 74148 chip and inverters will supply an octal 7 for the middle octal digit in the restart instruction, 3N7. This vectors the program to location HI = 000 and LO = 070. The RST 0 instruction is not often used since its only effect is to reset the microcomputer and start the MAIN TASK program again.

Fig. 8-28 has been simplified for clarity. The necessary flags and flag clearing lines are not shown. Additional hardware refinements could be added to the circuit to make it more efficient. These would include an additional 7442 decoder to generate the flag clearing pulses without using OUT instructions, and a mask register so that various devices could be masked on or off via external hardware. The modified circuit is shown in Fig. 8-30. It is a very sophisticated priority interrupt scheme that provides great flexibility in the use of vectored interrupts in conjunction with an 8080-based microcomputer.

You must first decide which devices will be allowed to interrupt the microcomputer and which will not. You develop an 8-bit mask pattern in which interrupting devices are assigned a logic 1 and noninterrupting devices are assigned a logic 0. These eight bits are output from the accumulator to the two 7475 latches shown at the left in Fig. 8-30. An OUT 030 instruction is used for this purpose. Bit position D7 corresponds to interrupting device 7, which has the highest priority and can generate a vector to the address HI = 000 and LO = 070. Those devices that are masked will probably use a status register input to request service, as shown previously in this chapter.

Interrupt requests from flags are gated with the OR gates (one is shown at the left of Fig. 8-30) tied to the 7475 mask register and nonmasked interrupt requests are passed to the 74100 8-bit latch. Whenever the interrupt flag within the 8080 chip is enabled, INTE is high and enables the 74100 chip. The actions of the 74148 priority encoder and interrupt instruction port have been described previously. When

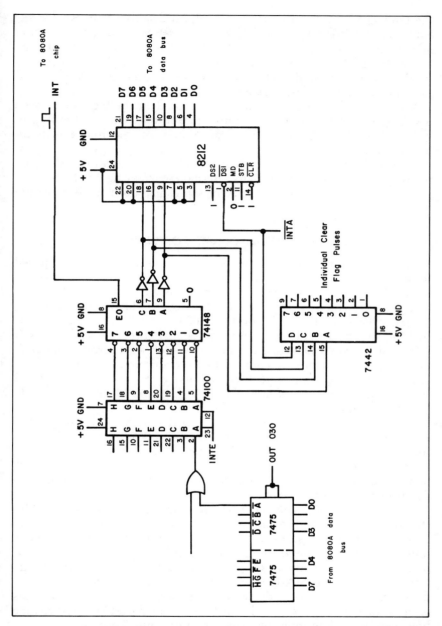

Fig. 8-30. Example of a sophisticated priority interrupt circuit that generates individual flag clear pulses and has a mask register so that devices can be masked on or off via external hardware.

the interrupt is received by the 8080 chip, it disables its internal interrupt enable flip-flop and the INTE output returns to logic 0, latching any interrupts present at the 74100 chip. The $\overline{\text{INTA}}$ signal not only inputs the RST n instruction byte; it also pulses the 7442 decoder to produce a clear pulse that clears the flip-flop associated with the vector interrupt currently being serviced.

Many other interrupt schemes can be used, including those based upon the Intel 8214 priority interrupt control unit. The Intel 8259 programmable interrupt controller can generate eight vectored priority interrupts for an 8080 microprocessor chip and is cascadable for up to 64 vectored priority interrupts without additional circuitry. Although interrupts permit fast response to external events or demands for service, their use requires some degree of sophistication in both hardware and software.

PRIORITY INTERRUPT SOFTWARE

As the final topic in this chapter, let us consider the software required for a priority interrupt system. Assume that we have only two interrupting devices: high-priority device 7 and low-priority device 2. Each device generates its own restart instruction byte, which causes a vector to either location LO = 070 or LO = 020, respectively. Also assume that the high-priority device interrupts the main program, called MAIN TASK, on a regular basis and is quickly serviced via software. Device 2, the low-priority device, is assumed to interrupt on an irregular schedule. It requires considerable time to service. For example, device 2 could be another microcomputer that is dumping blocks of data into our microcomputer.

The most important software is the MAIN TASK software that is executed whenever the external devices are not being serviced. If the software were not important, it would not be the "main task" performed by our microcomputer. Early in MAIN TASK, we locate the stack pointer with an LXI SP intruction and also enable the interrupt flip-flop using an EI instruction.

Since the interrupts can occur at any time, both PUSH and POP instructions are required in the interrupt service routines. Such instructions will save and restore any registers that are altered in the service routines. The execution of the software can be graphically represented by a *time line*, as shown in Fig. 8-31. Notice that the high-priority device has interrupted MAIN TASK four times, whereas the low-priority device has only interrupted once. The high-priority device interrupts on a regular basis, as shown by its spacing on the MAIN TASK time line. The heavy line indicates when the interrupt is enabled.

Fig. 8-32 shows a more realistic time line. The time line in Fig. 8-31 is somewhat deceptive since only the time spent in MAIN TASK is

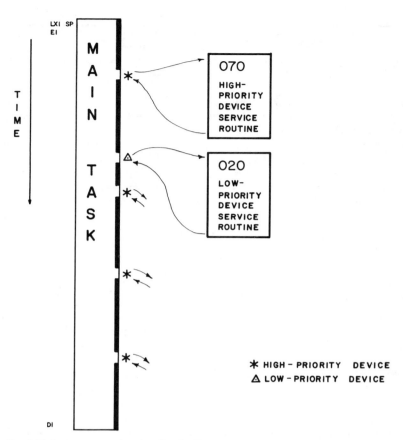

Fig. 8-31. Program execution time line for MAIN TASK. Interrupts by the high- and low-priority devices are denoted by the symbols * and △, respectively.

shown. It is more correct to show the real time spent in both MAIN TASK and in the subroutines. In Fig. 8-32 the MAIN TASK starts operating and is interrupted by the high-priority device. After executing the high-priority device service subroutine, control is returned to MAIN TASK, which is interrupted by the low-priority device later on the time line. Control is eventually returned to MAIN TASK, which is then interrupted at repeated intervals by the high-priority device. Clearly, it takes considerably longer to reach the end of MAIN TASK when it is repeatedly interrupted by other devices, each requiring service. During a critical timing period, such interruptions would be disastrous if we are relying on programmed time-delay loops to generate the time delay.

We have assumed that the high-priority device interrupts on a regular basis. It probably tried to interrupt the execution of the low-priority

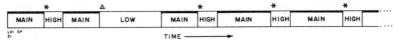

Fig. 8-32. Program execution time line for MAIN TASK and both the low- and high-priority device service subroutines.

service subroutine shown in Fig. 8-32. If high had a higher priority than low, why didn't an interrupt occur? The answer is that the interrupt flag within the 8080 chip *was not enabled during the execution of the low-priority device service subroutine.* In our first attempt at writing the interrupt service software, we forgot to take this possibility into account. As a result, data or signals from the high-priority device were lost during the low-priority device service software. We can correct our software easily by placing the enable interrupt instruction, EI, at the beginning of the low-priority device service subroutine. We can also design hardware to store data or signals that occur during a missed interrupt.

By moving the enable interrupt instruction, EI, to the beginning of the low-priority device service subroutine, we may encounter a new problem: a chopped-up low-priority device software flow, as shown in Fig. 8-33. To emphasize the point, we have assumed that the high-priority device interrupts the low-priority device service software twice, chopping the low-priority software into three pieces. With the low-priority device software so split up, we must inquire whether we are able to complete the low-priority software *before the low-priority device generates a new interrupt.* It is entirely possible for the low-priority device to interrupt the microcomputer while it is still trying to service the last interrupt request from the low-priority device. While the interrupt response is fast, the actual execution time may be much slower than the time required for a single pass through the interrupt service software. This is a consequence of the fact that we can interrupt our interrupts. Such considerations should give you a good idea of the care needed when using priority interrupts. It is very easy for a microcomputer to become *interrupt bound,* i.e., it spends all of its time checking and servicing interrupts and has no time left for its MAIN TASK software.

In our MAIN TASK software, we may wish to prevent interrupts from occurring during sensitive time-delay software or complex time-dependent tasks or calculations. The disable interrupt instruction, DI, allows the microcomputer to be immune to external interrupts. Such a

Fig. 8-33. Program execution time line that demonstrates the interrupting of an interrupt service routine. The "low" interrupt software is interrupted twice by the "high" priority device.

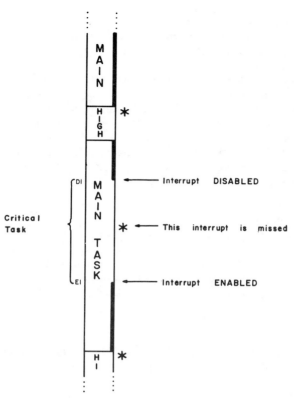

Fig. 8-34. Program execution time line that demonstrates the use of DI and EI instructions to permit a critical task to be performed in MAIN TASK. In this case, however, an interrupt is missed or delayed while the critical task is being executed.

situation is shown in Fig. 8-34. The interrupt flip-flop is disabled to permit a critical task to be performed, and then re-enabled. Unfortunately, the time line for the execution of MAIN TASK shows that an interrupt from the high-priority device was missed. Without additional, and usually complex, hardware as a back up, it is very easy to loose signals or data from interrupting devices while the interrupt flag is disabled. The important point here is that *we do not know when an external device will interrupt MAIN TASK, and we cannot be sure that it will not do so during the period that the interrupt flip-flop is disabled.* How do we circumvent this problem? It isn't easy, and this is why we must use a great deal of caution when using interrupts.

Another type of interrupt which may be of interest is a *time-oriented interrupt.* Only one interrupt is used: a clock. The clock interrupts every 10 milliseconds, or other reasonable period. When interrupted, the microcomputer uses a look-up table to determine which devices to check to see if they need service. Some devices are always checked, while other slower devices might be checked once every one thousand times. This is a useful technique, but it requires considerable amounts of software to work well.

The newer 8080-type microprocessor chips permit multibyte instructions to be input during an interrupt, so that a complete three-instruction-byte call or jump could be inserted. The ability to "jam" a three-byte instruction eliminates the need to use the restart instructions and associated vector locations, and provide you with much greater flexibility in the use of hardware and software. It appears that the Intel 8259 programmable interrupt controller will allow you to perform direct calls to interrupt service subroutines, but it is a complex device, not for the beginner.

We shall finish this chapter with some final notes of caution. Interrupts are difficult to debug. Since interrupts can occur at almost any time, typical software debugging programs are difficult to apply; most are ineffective. Special diagnostic software is required to test interrupts in specific applications. *If you can avoid the use of interrupts, do so.* Spend your valuable time on other noninterrupt approaches, if possible. Your efforts will usually be well rewarded.

TEST

This test probes your understanding of the interrupt techniques discussed in this chapter. Please write your answers on a separate piece of paper.

8-1. Describe how the following sequence of stack instructions are loaded on the stack: PUSH D, PUSH B, PUSH PSW, PUSH H.

8-2. Draw a simple circuit for an external flag and explain all of the inputs and outputs.

8-3. A small routine requires four instruction bytes and is used ten times in an 8080 microcomputer program. Explain how you would decide whether or not the routine should be made into a subroutine, complete with a return instruction.

8-4. Describe the different types of subroutine instructions in the 8080 microprocessor instruction set.

8-5. Describe the different types of stack instructions in the 8080 microprocessor instruction set.

8-6. Explain the differences between the following types of interrupts:
   deferred
   vectored
   single-line
   immediate
   multilevel
   polled

Your performance on this test will be acceptable if you can answer all of the above questions correctly in a 90-minute closed-book examination.

WHAT HAVE YOU ACCOMPLISHED IN THIS CHAPTER?

It was stated at the beginning of this chapter that at the end you would be able to do the following:

- Define the terms: subroutine, SSI, MSI, LSI, allocate, stack, interrupt, polling, software driver, vectored interrupt, disabled interrupt, external flag, deferred interrupt, and sense register.
  Definitions for these terms have been provided in the chapter in several locations.

- Explain how you would mask an 8-bit word to obtain the logic state of bit 5.
  As an example, we provided a simple program in which bit 3 in an 8-bit word was masked. You should be able to apply similar techniques to bit 5.

- Explain how digital information is loaded and removed from the 8080 microcomputer stack.
  We did this in conjunction with Fig. 8-3, which is a very interesting diagram of a typical stack.

- Perform an approximate calculation that will tell you when to use a subroutine.
  See Fig. 8-6 and the associated discussion.

- Describe how you would interface an ASCII keyboard.
  This subject is discussed in considerable detail near the end of the chapter.

CHAPTER 9

Advanced Input/Output Techniques

As the complexity of microcomputer systems increases, so must the sophistication of the input/output (I/O) techniques used. In Chapter 7, you learned how to perform simple input/output (called unconditional I/O), and in Chapter 8, you learned how to use flags and interrupts to synchronize input/output processes. In this chapter, you will learn some of the finer distinctions between different input/output techniques, such as conditional and unconditional input/output, unidirectional and bidirectional input/output, double-buffered input/output, and the 2-wire and 3-wire handshake protocols (the 3-wire handshake protocol is used in the IEEE 488 hardware bus). You will also learn the difference between a flag and a semaphore, why a semaphore is superior to a flag, and under what conditions it can be replaced by a flag. In preparation for the discussions of different I/O techniques, you will review several important techniques used in computer engineering, including block diagrams, flowcharts, timing diagrams, and structure charts.

OBJECTIVES

At the end of this chapter, you will be able to do the following:

- List the elementary mechanisms of structured programming.
- Explain the difference between a flowchart and a structure chart.
- List some techniques used in computer engineering and computer science.
- Provide a set of diagrams that demonstrate currently used timing diagram conventions.

- Define block diagram and discuss an example.
- Explain the difference between a flag and a semaphore.
- Explain the difference between conditional and unconditional I/O.
- Provide two different ways to achieve double-buffered I/O.
- Provide a series of timing diagrams that demonstrate how the NDAC, NRFD, and DAV signal lines function in the IEEE 488 3-wire handshake protocol.
- Explain how the 74LS373 chip can be used to achieve double-buffered I/O between a pair of 8080A-based microcomputers.
- Explain how the 8255 chip can be used to achieve a variety of different interfaces between a pair of 8080A microcomputers.
- Explain the characteristics of the 8255 semaphores.
- Compare the timing diagrams with the flowcharts for the IEEE 488 hardware bus.
- Compare the timing diagrams for unconditional input, conditional input using a flag (with and without a buffer), and conditional input using a semaphore.
- Compare the timing diagrams for unconditional output, conditional output using a flag (with and without a buffer), and conditional output using a semaphore.
- Explain when master/slave is a more acceptable pair of terms than source/acceptor.
- Compare the rates of performing a memory-to-memory transfer of 64 data bytes using various input/output techniques and a pair of 8080A microcomputers.

DEFINITIONS

acceptor—A device that accepts information.

bidirectional I/O—A computer input/output technique in which data can be either input or output, but not both simultaneously, over the same group of signal lines.

block diagram—A diagram of a device, system, instrument, computer or program in which selected portions are represented by annotated boxes and interconnecting lines that indicate, for example, the flow of information, energy, or mass. A block diagram shows both the basic functions as well as the functional relationships between the parts.

bused flag—A flag whose output is connected to the outputs of other flags, typically via open collector busing.

buffer—A device used to compensate for a difference in rate of flow of information or time of occurrence of events when transmitting information from one device to another[16].

CASE mechanism—One of the elementary mechanisms of structured programming.

conditional input—A computer input/output technique in which there is synchronization between the input device and the computer. The synchronization typically is accomplished using one or more flags or semaphores.

conditional output—A computer input/output technique in which there is synchronization between the output device and the computer. The synchronization typically is accomplished using one or more flags or semaphores.

double-buffered conditional I/O—A computer conditional input/output technique in which there are two buffers in the data transfer path between the computer and the I/O device. Typically, one of the buffers is a latch and the other is a 3-state buffer.

DO-WHILE mechanism—One of the elementary mechanisms of structured programming.

DO-UNTIL mechanism—One of the elementary mechanisms of structured programming. Also known as the REPEAT-UNTIL mechanism.

flag—In a computer, an indication that a particular operation has been completed, a condition exists, or an event has occurred. Typically, a flip-flop that can be either set or cleared in response to operations occurring in the computer. The status of the flag is tested by a single communicating device or program and synchronizes its behavior.

flowchart—A graphic representation of a program or a routine[16]. A programmer's tool for determining a sequence of operations as charted using sets of symbols, direction marks, and other representations to indicate stepped procedures of computer operation[14].

handshake cycle—The process whereby digital signals effect the transfer of each data byte across the interface by means of an interlocked sequence of status and control signals. Interlocked denotes a fixed sequence of events in which one event in the sequence must occur before the next event may occur[30].

hold time—The time subsequent to a designated time during which data is stable. Typically, the designated time is the positive or negative edge of a pulse.

IF-THEN-ELSE mechanism—One of the elementary mechanisms of structured programming.

input/output—General term for the equipment used to communicate with a computer and the data involved in the communication[4].

I/O—Abbreviation for input/output.

listener—A device that accepts information.

LOOP-FOREVER mechanism—One of the elementary mechanisms of structured programming, more commonly called the REPEAT mechanism.

master—The primary digital device, typically a computer, among a group of two or more communicating devices.

protocol—A set of conventions between communicating processes on the format and content of messages to be exchanged[14].

REPEAT mechanism—One of the elementary mechanisms of structured programming. Also known as the LOOP-FOREVER mechanism.

REPEAT-UNTIL mechanism—One of the elementary mechanisms of structured programming, more commonly called the DO-UNTIL mechanism.

semaphore—In a computer, an indication that a particular operation has been completed, a condition exists, or an event has occurred. Typically, a flip-flop that can be either set or cleared in response to operations occurring in the computer. The status of the semaphore is tested by two communicating devices or programs and synchronizes their behavior.

SEQUENCE mechanism—In structured programming, a single instruction or computational statement, or any sequence of computational statements, with only one entry and one exit.

setup time—The time prior to a designated time during which data is stable. Typically, the designated time is the positive or negative edge of a pulse.

slave—A secondary digital device among a group of two or more communicating devices.

source—A device that supplies information.

strobed input—A conditional input technique in which input data is latched by a buffer prior to being transferred to the accumulator or internal register of a computer. The use of a buffer permits the acquisition of input data that is available only for a short period of time.

structure chart—Another form of graphic representation of a program or a routine that accomplishes the same objective as a flowchart.

structured programming—A set of conventions and rules that yield programs that are easy to write, test, modify and read.

talker—A device that supplies information.

time line—A technique in which intervals required by individual steps or tasks in a sequential process are plotted on a linear axis.

timing diagram—A graphical representation of a single digital signal that shows the variations in logic state as a function of time.

top-down structured programming—A method for solving a given problem or implementing a given definition in which the problem or definition is more specifically refined at each step of the procedure until a final step of refinement results in executable code.

transparent latch—A latch in which the output follows the input when the latch is enabled, and in which the input data is latched at the trailing edge of the enable pulse.

unconditional input—A computer input technique in which there is no synchronization between the input device and the computer.

unconditional output—A computer output technique in which there is no synchronization between the output device and the computer.

unidirectional I/O—A computer input/output technique in which data is transferred over a group of signal lines only in a single direction between the computer and the I/O device.

SOME TECHNIQUES IN COMPUTER ENGINEERING AND COMPUTER SCIENCE

When you enter the world of computers, you are confronted with a wide variety of devices and machines—*hardware*—some examples of which are integrated circuits, printed-circuit boards, microcomputers, minicomputers, printers, crt terminals, keyboards, keypads, lamp monitors, etc. You are also confronted with a wide variety of programs and programming languages—*software*—including machine code, assembly language, subroutines, BASIC, PASCAL, FORTRAN, FORTH, CO-BOL, compilers, interpreters, debuggers, operating systems, editors, assemblers, peripheral interchange programs, linker/loaders, etc. When these programs are placed into hardware, via integrated circuit memories such as ROMs, PROMs, and EPROMs, the term used to describe such devices is *firmware*. Hardware, software, and firmware: these terms seem to describe the world of computers.

There is another segment of the field of computers that has no specific name associated with it but could be considered to be as important as hardware, software, and firmware. These are the "techniques" of computer engineering and computer science by which professionals communicate approaches, ideas, and concepts to each other, and by which tomorrow's generation of professionals is taught. Some examples of these "techniques" are:

binary code
machine code
assembly language
program
high-level language
structured programming
timing diagram
flowchart
structure chart
block diagram
schematic diagram
pin configuration
truth table
Warnier-Orr diagram

Karnaugh map
Vetch diagram
Backus-Nur representation
. . . and others

These "techniques" and methods of representation of devices, information flow, and information structure are to the broad field that the Europeans call *informatica* (*information science*) as the chemical symbols, formulas, and equations are to chemistry, mathematical symbols and equations are to physics, and alphabets are to written languages. Without the "techniques" of information science, it would be impossible to record and convey ideas.

In this chapter, we wish to discuss some different approaches to microcomputer input/output. We will use some special terms to distinguish between the approaches, including *unconditional* vs *conditional*, *buffered* vs *unbuffered*, *unidirectional* vs *bidirectional*, and *2-wire handshake* vs *3-wire handshake*. Before we discuss these approaches, it is appropriate to comment on the "techniques" that we shall use: timing diagrams, flowcharts, and block diagrams.

WHAT IS A TIMING DIAGRAM?

A *timing diagram* can be defined as a graphical representation of a single digital signal that shows the variations in logic state as a function of time. As an example, the rather complex timing diagrams that characterize the behavior of the pins on the 8080A microprocessor chip are shown—for the instructions SUB A, OUT <B2>, and CALL <B2> <B3>—in Figs. 6-8 through 6-12. Timing diagrams are extremely popular with electrical engineers. They are used not only to represent logic states and transitions between states, but also timing relationships between individual signals. Instruments have been developed that plot a series of eight or more timing diagrams on an oscilloscope screen. It has been said that "one picture is worth a thousand words." Timing diagrams are pictures of logic relationships, and confirm this popular statement.

TIMING DIAGRAM CONVENTIONS

You should be aware of timing diagram conventions that are likely to be encountered in the study of signal timing in microcomputer systems. This section draws together the different conventions and illustrations (adapted from References 13 and 15) to provide you with a convenient overview of current practice.

Conventions used in the representation of a single signal are given in Fig. 9-1. A low level, for transistor-transistor (TTL) logic inputs

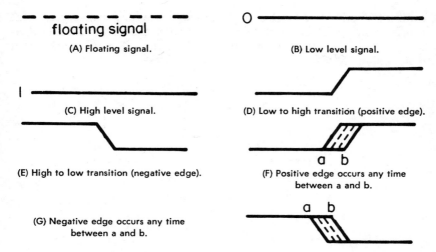

Fig. 9-1. Timing diagram conventions for a single signal. Horizontal lines combine with diagonal lines, which indicate transitions in logic levels.

and outputs, typically is a voltage that is near ground potential. A high level, for TTL inputs and outputs, typically is a potential that ranges from 3.5 V to 5.0 V. A floating signal occurs when the output from a 3-state device (see Chapter 7) is in its high-impedance state; the representation is a dashed line that is halfway between the low and high logic levels. Positive-edge and negative-edge transitions are shown as diagonal rather than vertical lines to account for the fact that the transitions are not instantaneous, as well as to permit the choice of a specific voltage when delay times are provided on the timing diagram. If the time when the transition occurs can vary, then a series of parallel diagonal lines are used to represent this fact, as shown in Figs. 9-1F and 9-1G.

Several timing diagram conventions apply when one signal influences another signal (Fig. 9-2). Signal A is the input signal, and signal B is the resulting output signal. As a function of time, signal A exhibits both steady logic levels (logic 0 and logic 1) and also transitions between these two levels (the 0-to-1 transition, known as a positive edge, and the 1-to-0 transition, known as a negative edge).

Depending upon the type of digital function—gate, edge-triggered latch, transparent latch, 3-state buffer, etc.—that is employed, signal B can respond to signal A in four ways. As depicted in Fig. 9-2, a transition in signal A can cause either a transition in signal B, as would occur in a simple gate or gating circuit, or else a steady logic level, as would occur with an edge-triggered flip-flop such as the 7474 chip. When signal A reaches and remains at a specific logic level, then signal B can exhibit a steady logic level, as would be the case for a transparent latch (such as the 7475) or a 3-state buffer (such as the 8095/74365); otherwise, signal B can undergo a transition in logic levels—a situation that is not common.

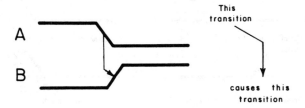

(A) Transition in signal A causes transition in signal B.

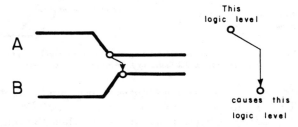

(B) Specific logic level in signal A causes specific logic level in signal B.

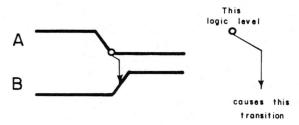

(C) Transition in signal A causes specific logic level in signal B.

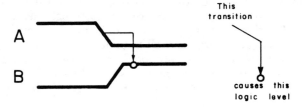

(D) Specific logic level in signal A causes transition in signal B.

Fig. 9-2. Timing diagram conventions for a pair of signals illustrate four ways in which one signal can gate or strobe (trigger) another signal.

Fig. 9-3 presents some conventions that represent parallel buses containing two or more signals, examples of which are the data bus or address bus of a microprocessor. The "signals change" notation in Fig. 9-3A and Fig. 9-3E indicates that one or more of the parallel signals change level, but that exact details of the changes in logic states need not be specified. A floating bus is represented by a dashed line that is halfway between the two logic levels (Fig. 9-3B). In Fig. 9-3C, the

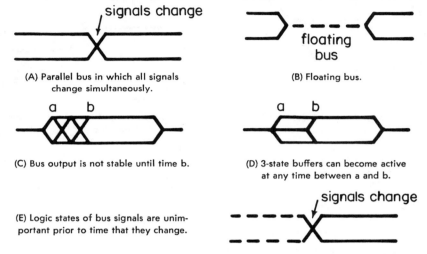

(A) Parallel bus in which all signals change simultaneously.

(B) Floating bus.

(C) Bus output is not stable until time b.

(D) 3-state buffers can become active at any time between a and b.

(E) Logic states of bus signals are unimportant prior to time that they change.

Fig. 9-3. Timing diagram conventions for a bus consisting of two or more signals.

3-state buffers become active at time a, but the output is not guaranteed to be stable until time b. In the Fig. 9-3D, the 3-state buffers can become active at any time between a and b.

Several applications of the conventions given in Figs. 9-1 through 9-3 are identified in Fig. 9-4, which has been adapted from Reference 13. In Fig. 9-4A, a low level from signal A triggers a bus change of state. In Fig. 9-4B, a low level from signal A and a transition in signal B trigger a third event. In Fig. 9-4C, a positive edge from signal A triggers changes in both signals B and C. Finally, two signals at different logic levels can result in a third signal's transition, while one signal can produce transitions in two other signals.

There are several ways to represent delay times that occur when one signal influences another signal. Four possibilities are shown in Fig. 9-5. The small circle represents the time when a specific logic level is reached; the cross represents that specific amplitude—a voltage—on a logic level transition from which the time is measured.

We shall use these conventions later in this chapter to describe the sequence of events that occur in specific I/O techniques.

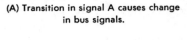

(A) Transition in signal A causes change in bus signals.

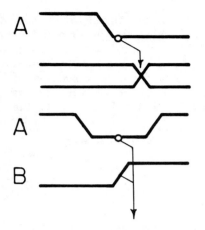

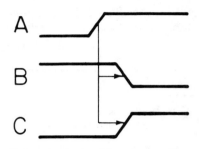

(B) Transition in signal B and logic 0 state in signal A causes third event to occur.

(C) Transition in signal A causes transitions in signals B and C.

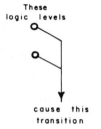

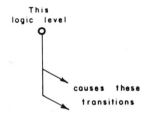

(D) Two signals at specific logic levels cause transition in third signal.

(E) Specific logic level in signal causes transitions in two other signals.

Fig. 9-4. Applications of timing diagram conventions to combinations of signal transitions and logic states that cause changes in other signals.

WHAT IS A FLOWCHART?

A *flow diagram,* also called a *flowchart,* is a graphic representation of a program or a routine[16]. A more extensive definition is given by Sippl[14]: "A flowchart is a programmer's tool for determining a sequence of operations as charted using sets of symbols, directional marks, and other representations to indicate stepped procedures of computer operation. Flowcharts also enable the designer to conceptualize the procedure necessary and to visualize each step and item on a program. A completed flowchart is often a necessity to the achievement of accurate final code."

The three basic flowchart symbols are shown in Fig. 9-6[17]: the action or process symbol—a box; the decision symbol—a diamond—which asks

358

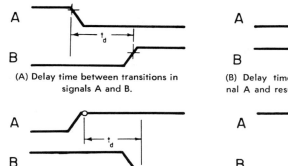

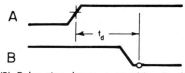

(A) Delay time between transitions in signals A and B.

(B) Delay time between transition in signal A and resulting logic level of signal B.

(C) Delay time between resulting logic level of signal A and resulting logic level of signal B.

(D) Delay time between resulting logic level of signal A and transition in signal B.

Fig. 9-5. Timing diagram conventions for a pair of signals illustrates the representation of delay times.

a question and is answered by yes or no (logic 0 or logic 1); and the terminal symbol—an ellipse—which is used to denote an initial or final state.

Another definition for a flowchart is[14]: "A graphical representation for the definition, analysis, or solution of a problem, in which symbols are used to represent operations, data, flow, equipment, etc." In the sense of this definition, IBM has produced a flowcharting template that provides symbols for: process, input/output, document, manual operation, preparation, merge, communications link, decision, magnetic tape, display, auxiliary operation, keying, extract, collate, terminal interrupt, punched card, punched tape, online storage, preparation, transmittal tape, and offpage connector. We shall restrict our flowcharts to the symbols shown in Fig. 9-6.

WHAT IS A STRUCTURE CHART?

Like a flowchart, a *structure chart* is a graphic representation of a program or a routine. The more extensive definition for flowchart given by Sippl, and quoted in the preceding section, also applies. The structure chart is not popular in the United States, but is quite popular in Europe. The large German electronics firm, Siemens, has provided texts and courses on microcomputer programming in which they use the structure chart notation throughout. Rather than provide basic structure chart forms, it is more appropriate to describe structure charts in the context of the elementary mechanisms found in structured programming. This will be done in the next section, where the flowchart and structure chart notations will be compared.

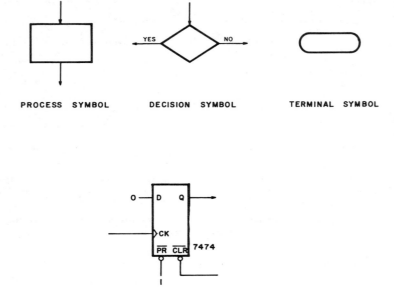

Fig. 9-6. Standard flowcharting symbols.

WHAT IS STRUCTURED PROGRAMMING?

Structured programming is a set of conventions and rules that yield programs that are easy to write, test, modify, and read[18]. Turner defines top-down structured programming as a method for solving a given problem or implementing a given definition in which the problem or definition is more specifically refined at each step of the procedure until a final step of refinement results in executable code. The same limited set of syntactic structures is used at every stage of the problem's refinement[19]. References [18] through [20] discuss structured programming in the context of microcomputers. The basic approach was first proposed by Dijkstra[21, 22]; another useful reference is the book by Yourdon[23].

This widespread technique, discussed and employed in most recent computer science texts, is still not commonly taught to engineers and scientists, who usually learn either FORTRAN or BASIC. Due to space limitations, only the common "structures"—the basic building blocks of structured programming—will be discussed. These "structures" or *elementary mechanisms* include the following:

SEQUENCE
DO-WHILE
DO-UNTIL (also known as REPEAT-UNTIL)
IF-THEN-ELSE
CASE
REPEAT (also known as LOOP-FOREVER)

In the following section, three types of representations will be given for each of these structures: (1) flowchart, (2) structure chart, and (3) written statement. You will encounter these representations frequently.

BASIC MECHANISMS OF STRUCTURED PROGRAMMING

The first structure or mechanism, the *SEQUENCE* block, is a single instruction or computational statement, or any sequence of computa-

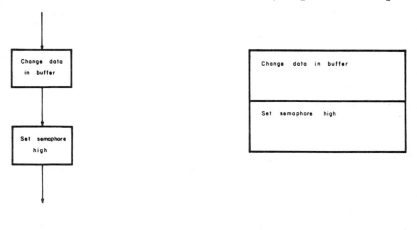

Fig. 9-7. Pair of SEQUENCE mechanisms. Flowchart, structure chart, and written statements for two sequential operations are depicted.

tional statements, with only one entry and one exit. Fig. 9-7 depicts a pair of SEQUENCE blocks. The first computational statement in this pair is "change data in buffer," and the second statement is "set semaphore high." These two statements can be combined into a single SEQUENCE block. In Fig. 9-7, the pair of SEQUENCE blocks is represented in flowchart notation, structure chart notation, and in written statement form. Figs. 9-8 through 9-12 are set up following the same format. Computer scientists find the written statement form convenient when developing programs on cathode-ray tube (crt) terminals.

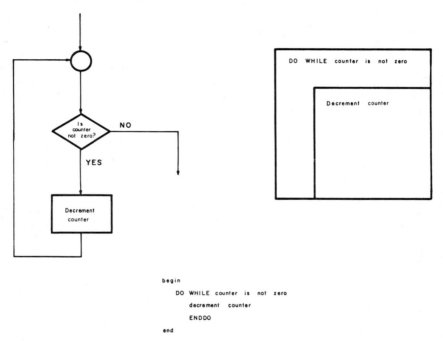

Fig. 9-8. DO-WHILE mechanism. Generalized loop-and-test structure shows microcomputer timing loop.

The second structure is a generalized loop-and-test structure, usually called the *DO-WHILE* block or mechanism. Again, observe that there is only one entry and one exit (Fig. 9-8), a fundamental characteristic of all basic structures (mechanisms) in structured programming. In Fig. 9-8, the loop-and-test structure is a microcomputer timing loop, in which a counter is successively decremented until it reaches zero, at which time the loop is exited. A related loop-and-test structure is the *DO-UNTIL* block or mechanism, also known as the *REPEAT-UNTIL* block. Fig. 9-9 provides the form of the timing loop that is typically employed with microcomputers (see Chapter 5); in other words, the counter usually is first decremented, then the zero flag is tested, and finally a branch occurs depending upon the logic state of the flag.

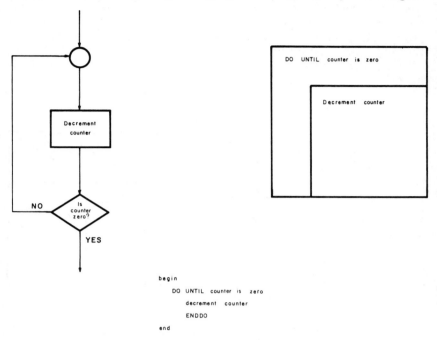

```
begin
    DO UNTIL counter is zero
        decrement counter
    ENDDO
end
```

Fig. 9-9. DO-UNTIL (REPEAT UNTIL) mechanism. This form of timing loop is typical of that used in microcomputers.

A selection-based-on-a-test structure is the third basic form, universally called the *IF-THEN-ELSE* block or mechanism. With still only one entry and one exit, the example in Fig. 9-10 is a simple binary test—yes or no. If the answer is yes, the THEN alternative is executed; if the answer is no, the ELSE alternative is executed.

The SEQUENCE, DO-WHILE, and IF-THEN-ELSE mechanisms comprise the three basic structures of structured programming. Two other structures commonly found in microcomputer programs are the CASE and REPEAT mechanisms. The *CASE* block or mechanism in Fig. 9-11 is also a selection-based-on-a-test structure, but with more than two alternatives to select from. This type of structure can be implemented with microcomputers in several ways, such as by a sequence of IF-THEN-ELSE statements or by a command decoder. Single entry to and single exit from the structure are basic characteristics shared in Figs. 9-7 through 9-11.

Fig. 9-12 depicts the *REPEAT* mechanism, also known as the *LOOP-FOREVER* mechanism, which is not one of the basic structures in structured programming since there is a single entry to but no exit from the structure. Nevertheless, it is occasionally used in microcomputer programs, such as those that employ interrupt-driven input/output. In such situations, the microcomputer program loops (perhaps forever) until an interrupt occurs.

The above approach is patterned after the Swiss article by Baumann[24].

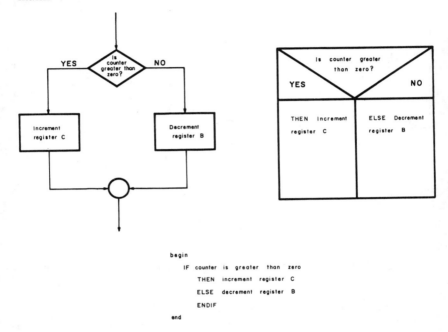

```
begin
    IF counter is greater than zero
        THEN increment register C
        ELSE decrement register B
    ENDIF
end
```

Fig. 9-10. IF-THEN-ELSE mechanism. A simple binary test executes THEN for a yes answer and ELSE for a no answer.

WHAT IS A BLOCK DIAGRAM?

A *block diagram* is a diagram of a device, system, instrument, computer, or program in which selected portions are represented by annotated boxes and interconnecting lines that indicate, for example, the flow of information, energy, or mass. A block diagram shows both the basic functions as well as the functional relationships between the parts. In the field of control systems, special rules—for example, a block can have only a single entry and a single exit—govern the construction of block diagrams. With computers, integrated circuits, and related

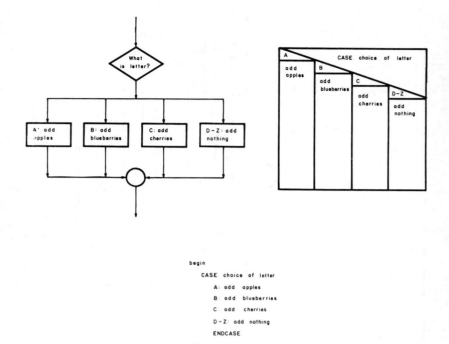

```
begin
    CASE choice of letter
        A: add  apples
        B: add  blueberries
        C: add  cherries
        D-Z: add nothing
        ENDCASE
end
```

Fig. 9-11. CASE mechanism. Also based on a test, this mechanism can select from more than two alternatives.

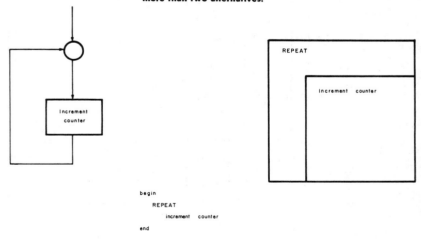

```
begin
    REPEAT
        increment  counter
end
```

Fig. 9-12. REPEAT (LOOP-FOREVER) mechanism.

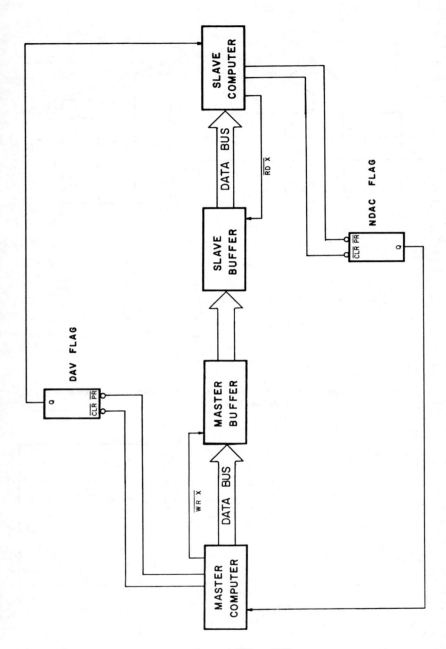

Fig. 9-13. Example of a block diagram. $\overline{PR}$ and $\overline{CLR}$ are flag inputs, and Q is a flag output.

devices, there can be many input and output digital signals. Usually these signals are grouped together in terms of function, for example, data bus, address bus, select lines, etc. In the discussion of I/O techniques that follows, each technique will be represented by (a) a block diagram, (b) a set of timing diagrams, and (c) a pair of flowcharts.

Fig. 9-13, which will be shown again later, is an example of a block diagram that depicts the information flow in a two-computer two-buffer two-flag system. Observe that there are six devices, but that information does not flow bidirectionally between all of the devices. The wide arrows represent eight bits of data. Data flows in one direction from the master microcomputer to the master buffer, slave buffer, and, finally, the slave microcomputer. The master microcomputer sends a pair of signals to the DAV flag to set or reset it; the slave microcomputer performs a similar function with the NDAC flag. The DAV flag output is input to and tested by the slave microcomputer; the NDAC flag output is input to and tested by the master microcomputer. Finally, the $\overline{\text{WR X}}$ signal permits the master buffer to latch output data from the master microcomputer; the $\overline{\text{RD X}}$ signal enables the 3-state output lines in the slave buffer, thus permitting the transfer of data to the slave microcomputer.

SOURCE/ACCEPTOR, MASTER/SLAVE, TALKER/LISTENER, AND TRANSMITTER/RECEIVER

When you perform an input/output (I/O) operation, there is a transfer of information between a pair of devices. One device sends information and the other device receives it. All I/O operations should be viewed in this way, that is, in terms of a pair of devices between which information is transferred.

In discussions of I/O situations, various terms have been used to characterize the pair of devices:

    source and acceptor
    master and slave
    transmitter and receiver
    talker and listener
    computer and input device
    computer and output device
    local and remote
    host and remote

We will use several of these pairs of terms in our discussions of I/O techniques. The pair of terms, *talker/listener,* are commonly used in discussions of the *2-wire* and *3-wire handshake protocols,* and we will follow this custom. In general, we prefer to use *source/acceptor* and *master/slave,* and will do so with many of the flowcharts shown in subsequent sections.

FLAG VS SEMAPHORE

A *flag* has already been defined in Chapters 1 and 8 as:

flag—In a computer, an indication that a particular operation has been completed[4]. Also, a flip-flop that can be either set or cleared in response to operations occurring in the computer.

A distinction was also made between an external flag—a digital circuit, usually containing a single flip-flop, which indicates a condition that exists with an I/O device—and an internal flag—a digital circuit, usually containing a single flip-flop, which indicates a condition that exists internally within the microprocessor chip.

In software, a related concept, that of a semaphore, is very popular. What is a *semaphore?* It can be set and cleared, and acts like a flag. It is widely used when two programs compete for a common "resource," for example, a memory region, a subroutine, or some physical device. Is there a fundamental difference between a flag and a semaphore? Can the concept be applied to hardware? The answer to these last two questions is yes.

Both the flag and the semaphore are single flip-flops that indicate when a condition exists or an event has occurred. However, as shown in Fig. 9-14, a flag outputs its state to a single device—either a source or acceptor—whereas a semaphore outputs its state to two devices, both the source and the acceptor. Clearly, a semaphore is more useful since

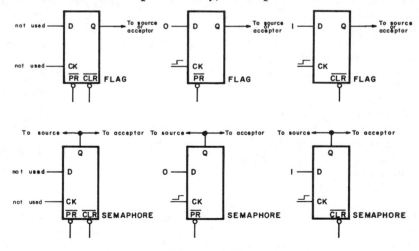

Fig. 9-14. Some different types of flags and semaphores.

the two communicating devices can individually determine the status of the condition or event. You will not find semaphore mentioned in the popular dictionaries of electronics and computers[4, 14, 16].

Refined definitions for the concepts of flag and semaphore are:

flag.—In a computer, an indication that a particular operation has been completed, a condition exists, or an event has occurred. Typically, a flip-flop that can be either set or cleared in response to operations occurring in the computer. The status of the flag is tested by a single communicating device or program and synchronizes its behavior.

semaphore—In a computer, an indication that a particular operation has been completed, a condition exists, or an event has occurred. Typically, a flip-flop that can be either set or cleared in response to operations occurring in the computer. The status of the semaphore is tested by two communicating devices or programs and synchronizes their behavior.

You will see how useful a semaphore is in a subsequent section.

CONDITIONS AND EVENTS ASSOCIATED WITH FLAGS AND SEMAPHORES

Both a semaphore and a flag indicate that a condition exists or an event has occurred. The following are typical conditions and events that are encountered in input/output operations:

$\overline{\text{busy}}$/done
$\overline{\text{data not available}}$/data accepted
$\overline{\text{data not accepted}}$/data accepted
$\overline{\text{data not valid}}$/data valid
$\overline{\text{data available}}$/data accepted
$\overline{\text{not ready for data}}$/ready for data
$\overline{\text{data accepted}}$/data available
$\overline{\text{busy}}$/ready

The bar represents the logic 0 condition of the flag or semaphore. Often you will see these conditions abbreviated and used to represent the status of the flag or semaphore. For example, you will encounter the abbreviations NDAC (not data accepted), DAV (data available), and NRFD (not ready for data) in all discussions of the IEEE 488 hardware bus.

UNCONDITIONAL INPUT

The simplest input/output technique can be called unconditional I/O, a form of data transfer in which it is assumed that the external

I/O device is always available and ready for communication with the microcomputer[25]. Figs. 9-15 through 9-17 provide block diagrams, flowcharts, and timing diagrams, respectively, for *unconditional input*. $\overline{RD}$ X is a device select pulse that simultaneously selects the input device and initiates the data transfer. X is a device code or device address, typically an 8- to 16-bit signal. When 8080A, 8085, or Z80 microcomputers are employed in this and other books by the author, this pulse is labeled $\overline{IN}$ X and data transfer occurs between the input device and the accumulator. The data bus in Fig. 9-15 is bidirectional.

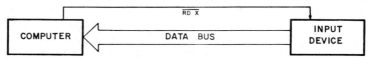

Fig. 9-15. Unconditional input: block diagram.

In Fig. 9-16, observe that there are no dotted lines between the source and acceptor flowcharts. There is no communication or synchronization between the input device (source) and the microcomputer (acceptor). The input device is assumed always to be available. The microcomputer, through the use of a software loop or a realtime clock, determines how often the data transfer occurs. In Fig. 9-17, the data to be input may need to be stable for a significant period of time, such as milliseconds or seconds. The rate at which it can change is determined by the nature of the input device, the repetition rate associated

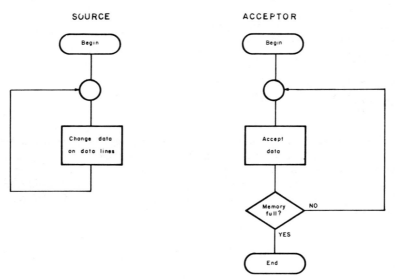

Fig. 9-16. Unconditional input: flowcharts for source and acceptor.

with the input and processing of new data by the microcomputer, and whether every new data point needs to be input and processed.

In unconditional input, the input device can be said to be "dumb" in that it does not influence the timing of the data transfer in any way. The microcomputer neither needs nor requests confirmation that the device is operating. When the device operates continuously, unconditional input techniques are acceptable; when it operates at sporadic

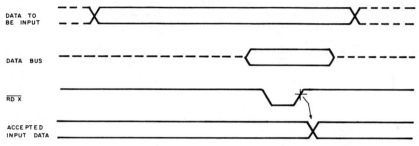

Fig. 9-17. Unconditional input: timing diagrams.

time intervals, the use of a flag is more appropriate since the flag is set only when the device is ready to send data. Thus, the use of a flag frees the microcomputer to direct its attention to other tasks. Examples of unconditional input are given in Chapter 7.

UNCONDITIONAL OUTPUT

Figs. 9-18 through 9-20 provide a block diagram, flowcharts, and timing diagrams, respectively, for *unconditional output*. Note their resemblance to the corresponding figures—Figs. 9-15 through 9-17—for unconditional input. In Fig. 9-18, $\overline{\text{WR X}}$ is a device select pulse that

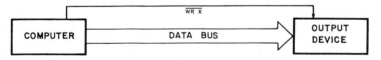

Fig. 9-18. Unconditional output: block diagram.

simultaneously selects the output device and initiates the output data transfer. X is an 8-bit device code or 16-bit address. In Chapter 7 of this book, we have used $\overline{\text{OUT X}}$ as the label for the pulse rather than $\overline{\text{WR X}}$, and data transfer occurs between the accumulator and the output device.

Note again that there are no dotted lines present between the flowcharts in Fig. 9-19. Their absence indicates that there is no communication or synchronization between the microcomputer (source) and the

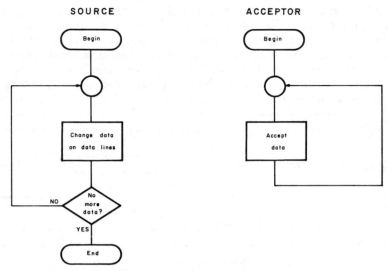

Fig. 9-19. Unconditional output: flowcharts for source and acceptor.

output device (acceptor). The output device is assumed always to be available, just as was the case with the input device in Fig. 9-15. The microcomputer determines how often the data transfer occurs.

In unconditional output, the output device also can be said to be "dumb" in that it does not influence the timing of the data transfer in any way. As was the case with unconditional input, the microcomputer

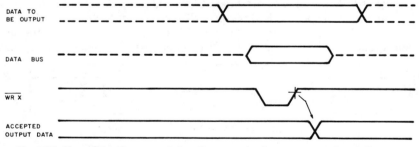

Fig. 9-20. Unconditional output: timing diagrams. A microcomputer software loop or realtime clock frequently determines when data transfer occurs between the source and acceptor.

neither needs nor requests confirmation that the output device is operating. When the device cannot accept data too quickly, the use of a flag is more appropriate since the flag is set only when new data can be output. Thus, the use of a flag frees the microcomputer to execute other tasks. Examples of unconditional output are given in Chapter 7.

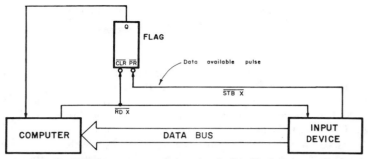

Fig. 9-21. Conditional input using a flag and no buffer: block diagram. The flag outputs information on status of input device to the microcomputer.

CONDITIONAL INPUT USING A FLAG

Conditional input techniques that employ flags can be distinguished by whether or not they have a buffer between the input device and the microcomputer. Consider Figs. 9-21 and 9-22. In each case, a single flag serves to communicate the status of the input device to the microcomputer. For microcomputer input, a strobe signal ($\overline{\text{STB X}}$) from the input device sets the flag to a logic 1, thus indicating to the microcomputer that data is available. Upon detecting this logic 1 state, the microcomputer proceeds to input the data and at the same time clears the

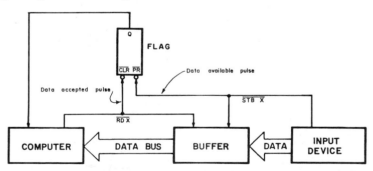

Fig. 9-22. Conditional input using a flag and a buffer: block diagram. The input device strobes data into a buffer rather than the microcomputer.

flag, with both operations being accomplished by the $\overline{\text{RD X}}$ pulse. The difference between Figs. 9-21 and 9-22 is mainly associated with the operations performed by the $\overline{\text{STB X}}$ pulse. In Fig. 9-21, the $\overline{\text{STB X}}$ pulse only sets the flag. In Fig. 9-22, *buffered conditional input,* the $\overline{\text{STB X}}$ pulse both transfers data to the buffer and sets the flag. The buffer can hold only a single data word, typically eight or sixteen bits. The behavior of the buffer can be summarized as:

Q (flag)	Buffer condition
0	empty
1	full

A simplified flowchart in Fig. 9-23 depicts the data transfer between an input device (source) and a microcomputer (acceptor) in the presence of a single flag. A high (logic 1) condition for the flag indicates to the microcomputer that new data is available, while a low (logic 0) condition indicates that new data is not available. When a flag is used, only the microcomputer tests its logic state, as can be seen by the direction of the dotted line and the decision symbol, "Is the

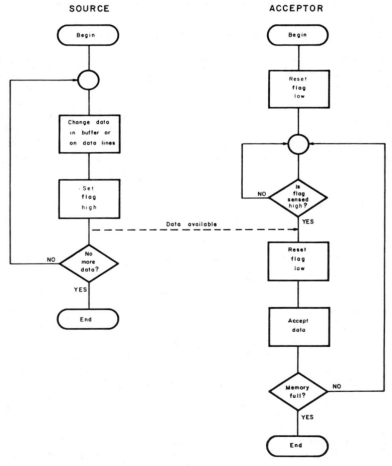

Fig. 9-23. Conditional input using a flag: flowcharts for source and acceptor.

flag sensed high?" that appears only in the acceptor flowchart. The input device does not know when data has been accepted. Therefore, the microcomputer alone has the responsibility for synchronizing data transfer.

Figs. 9-24 and 9-25 provide timing diagrams for conditional input using a flag in the presence and absence, respectively, of a buffer. Three questions associated with data input to the microcomputer should be kept in mind:

1. What is the repetition rate of the data, in units of data points/sec?
2. For what duration of time is each data point stable?
3. Is it necessary to input each new data point?

When input data is stable for only a very short time, an input buffer must be used in addition to the flag. This situation is illustrated by the timing diagrams in Fig. 9-24. The flag is set by the positive-edge transition of the $\overline{\text{STB X}}$ pulse, which is generated by the input device, and reset by the logic 0 condition of the $\overline{\text{RD X}}$ pulse, which is generated by the microcomputer. Data to be input must be stable for a period of time that is typically in the order of 150 to 200 ns; this time is the sum of the *setup time*—the time prior to the positive edge of the $\overline{\text{STB X}}$ pulse, during which the input data is stable—and the *hold time*—the time subsequent to the positive edge of the $\overline{\text{STB X}}$ pulse, during which the input data must also be stable. An estimate of the maximum repetition rate for data input can be obtained from a full flag period, from positive edge to next successive positive edge. Depending upon the method by which the flag is tested (polled loop, polled interrupt, vectored interrupt, etc.) and the importance of input device X relative to other microcomputer tasks, the calculated repetition rate may be low or high. Careful programming may be required to make certain that input data is not lost. On the other hand, it may not be necessary to input every new data point. Only periodic data input, where the period is determined by software or by a realtime clock, may be required.

The timing diagrams in Fig. 9-25 portray the situation when a flag, but not an input buffer, is present. Data to be input must be stable for a substantially longer time than that shown in Fig. 9-24. The sequence of events in Fig. 9-25 can be summarized as follows: the input device supplies new input data, the $\overline{\text{STB X}}$ pulse sets the flag and, after a period of time, the microcomputer detects the availability of new data, enables the data bus, and finally generates an $\overline{\text{RD X}}$ pulse that resets the flag and inputs the new data to the microcomputer. This technique is widely used with "slow" input devices (500 bytes/sec or less) that have latched data (which means that they have an internal buffer) and in which data input timing is not critical. Counter/timers are examples of such devices. The use of the flag permits the microcomputer (acceptor) to ignore the input device (source) for as long as the flag is low (logic 0). Such a characteristic frees the microcomputer to perform other processing tasks while it awaits new input data.

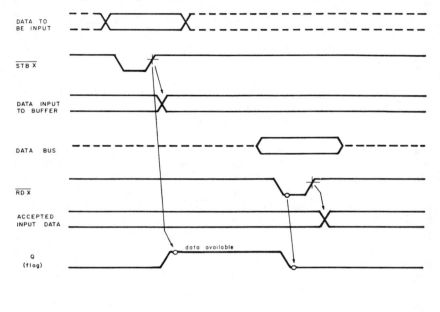

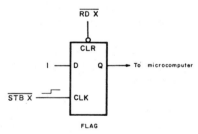

Fig. 9-24. Conditional input using a flag and a buffer: timing diagrams.

CONDITIONAL OUTPUT USING A FLAG

As was the case for conditional input using a flag, *conditional output* techniques that employ flags can be distinguished by whether or not there is a buffer between the microcomputer and the output device. The block diagrams shown in Figs. 9-26 and 9-27 portray these two situations. In Fig. 9-26, the $\overline{\text{WR X}}$ pulse simultaneously writes data into the output device and also sets the flag. The output device acknowledges the receipt of this data by sending an $\overline{\text{ACK X}}$ pulse to clear the

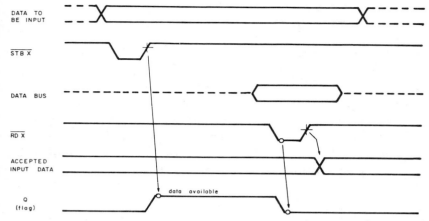

Fig. 9-25. Conditional input using a flag and no buffer: timing diagrams. The flag shown in Fig. 9-24 applies to this set of timing diagrams as well.

flag. In Fig. 9-27, the $\overline{\text{WR X}}$ pulse writes data into the buffer and sets the flag, and the $\overline{\text{ACK X}}$ pulse simultaneously transfers data from the buffer to the output device and clears the flag. Note that the output from the flag goes only to the microcomputer.

Fig. 9-28, which can be compared to Fig. 9-23, depicts the data transfer between a microcomputer (source) and an output device (acceptor) in the presence of a single flag. A low (logic 0) condition for the

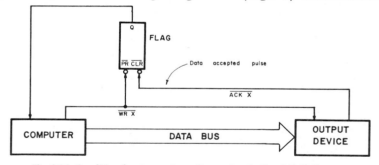

Fig. 9-26. Conditional output using a flag and no buffer: block diagram.

flag indicates to the microcomputer that previous output data has been accepted. A high (logic 1) condition indicates that the previous data has not been accepted. When a flag is used, only the microcomputer tests its logic state, as can be seen by the direction of the dotted line and the decision symbol, "Flag sensed low?" that only appears in the source flowchart. The output device does not know when new data is available. Thus, as was the case with conditional input using a flag, the

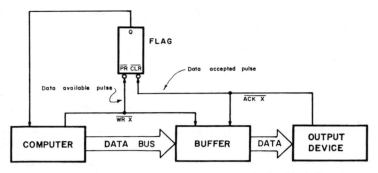

Fig. 9-27. Conditional output using a flag and a buffer: block diagram.

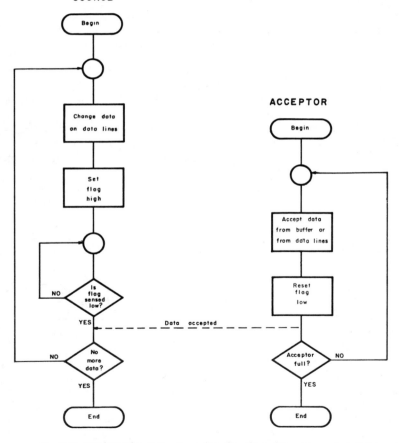

Fig. 9-28. Conditional output using a flag: flowcharts for source and acceptor.

microcomputer alone has responsibility for synchronization of data transfer.

The flag is used to synchronize data transfer between the microcomputer and the output device. To see how such a transfer occurs, consider Fig. 9-29, which gives the timing diagrams when a single flag, but no output buffer, is present. The flag is reset by the positive edge transition of the $\overline{\text{ACK X}}$ pulse, which is generated by the output device, and set by the logic 0 condition of the $\overline{\text{WR X}}$ pulse, which is generated by the microcomputer. As a result, the output device sends an $\overline{\text{ACK X}}$ signal that clears the flag and indicates to the microcomputer that the previous data has been received and processed. Then, after a period

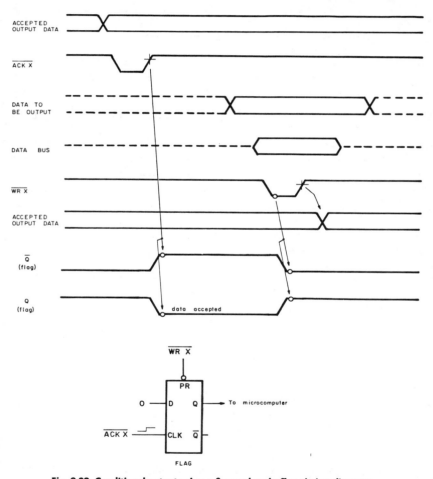

Fig. 9-29. Conditional output using a flag and no buffer: timing diagrams.

of time, the microcomputer places new output data in the accumulator, enables the data bus, and generates a $\overline{\text{WR X}}$ pulse that sets the flag and causes the output device to latch the data from the data bus. At this point, the output device has the data, but it must do something with it, such as convert it to analog voltages, print it, store it on disk or tape, or display it. In other words, the output device must process the data before it sends another $\overline{\text{ACK X}}$ pulse, which indicates its readiness to receive additional data. The repetition rate at which the output device can receive data can be estimated from a full flag period, from positive edge to next successive positive edge.

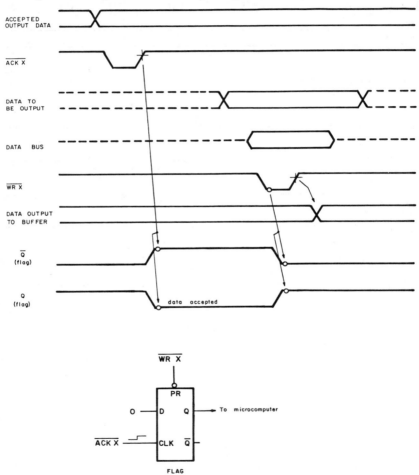

Fig. 9-30. Conditional output using a flag and a buffer: timing diagrams. The flag shown in Fig. 9-29 applies to this set of timing diagrams as well.

Output devices that can generate an acknowledge signal, $\overline{\text{ACK X}}$, typically also have an output buffer, so the situation depicted in Figs. 9-26 and 9-29 is the exception rather than the rule. The more commonly encountered situation is given in Fig. 9-27 and also in Fig. 9-30, which shows the timing diagrams for an output device that has both a flag and an output buffer. As indicated in Fig. 9-30, the acceptance and processing of previous data is acknowledged by the $\overline{\text{ACK X}}$ signal, which resets the flag. After a period of time, new data to be output appears in the accumulator and then on the data bus. Finally, the new data is latched by the buffer with the aid of the microcomputer-generated $\overline{\text{WR X}}$ pulse, which also sets the flag. The next $\overline{\text{ACK X}}$ pulse appears only when the output device is ready to receive additional data.

Use of the flag permits the microcomputer (source) to ignore the output device (acceptor) for as long as the flag is high (logic 1). Such a characteristic frees the microcomputer to perform other processing tasks while it waits for an acknowledge signal, and is very useful with "slow" output devices (500 bytes/sec or less).

CONDITIONAL I/O USING A SEMAPHORE

Figs. 9-31 and 9-32 demonstrate the use of a *semaphore*, the basic principle behind the conditional I/O technique known as "strobed" I/O. A single flip-flop is used, as in Figs. 9-21, 9-22, 9-26, and 9-27, but in this instance the output from flip-flop—the semaphore—is sent both to the microcomputer and to the I/O device.

With an input device, as shown in Fig. 9-31, the buffer stores a single input data word. When the buffer is full, the semaphore is at logic 1, when empty, the semaphore is at logic 0. An input device first tests the semaphore to determine that the buffer is empty, and, if so, simultaneously inputs a new data byte and sets the semaphore to logic 1 using the $\overline{\text{STB X}}$ pulse. The microcomputer tests the semaphore to determine

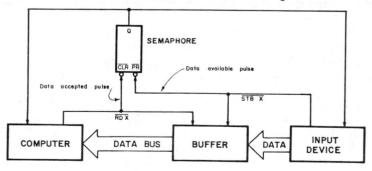

Fig. 9-31. Conditional input using a semaphore: block diagram.

when it becomes logic 1; at that time, the microcomputer simultaneously inputs the data from the buffer and uses the $\overline{\text{RD X}}$ pulse to clear the semaphore to logic 0. The distinction between a semaphore and a flag is thus clear: a semaphore is tested by both the microcomputer and the input device, whereas a flag is tested by only one of the two devices, usually the microcomputer.

In the case of the output device in Fig. 9-32, the microcomputer first tests the semaphore to determine that it is logic 0, which means that the buffer is empty. When this condition is satisfied, the microcomputer simultaneously outputs a data byte to the buffer and sets the semaphore using the $\overline{\text{WR X}}$ pulse. The output device tests the semaphore to determine when the buffer is full; when such a condition is detected, an $\overline{\text{ACK X}}$ pulse simultaneously transfers data from the buffer to the output device and clears the semaphore.

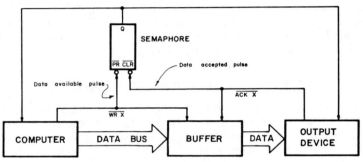

Fig. 9-32. Conditional output using a semaphore: block diagram.

The simplified flowchart in Fig. 9-33 depicts the transfer between a source of data and an acceptor of data in the presence of a semaphore. As discussed in the preceding paragraphs, there are two semaphore states. A high (logic 1) condition indicates that data is available to the acceptor from the buffer; a low (logic 0) condition indicates that data has been received by the acceptor from the buffer and that the buffer is now empty and can accept new data from the source. The dotted lines, which represent the semaphore output, indicate how the source and acceptor influence each other's sequence of events. For example, as long as the semaphore is sensed high by the source, no new data can be provided to the buffer; while the semaphore is sensed low by the acceptor, the acceptor cannot acquire new data from the buffer.

The timing diagrams depicted in Fig. 9-34 and the flowcharts in Fig. 9-33 are based upon the *strobed input* mode for the Intel 8155/8156 and 8255 integrated circuits, as provided on pp. 9-75 and 11-62, respectively, of the 1979 Intel Component Data Catalog. Assume that the source is an 8-bit analog-to-digital converter, and the acceptor is a microcomputer. $\overline{\text{STB X}}$ is a timing signal that inputs data to the buffer from the input device, as discussed previously. X represents a device code that is associated with input device X, distinguishing it from other input devices that are also present in the system. Typically, $\overline{\text{STB X}}$ is generated by the input device X. $\overline{\text{RD X}}$ is a timing signal generated by the microcomputer to input data from the buffer. A logic 0 condition for $\overline{\text{STB X}}$ sets the semaphore, and a positive-edge transition in $\overline{\text{RD X}}$ clears the semaphore. The sequence of events in Fig. 9-34 can be summarized as follows:

1. The input device detects that the semaphore is reset (low, or logic 0), and therefore that new data can be input to the buffer.

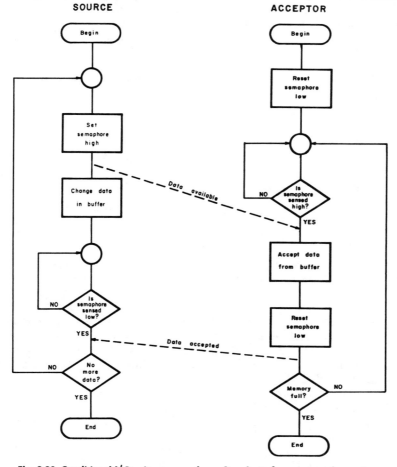

Fig. 9-33. Conditional I/O using a semaphore: flowcharts for source and acceptor.

383

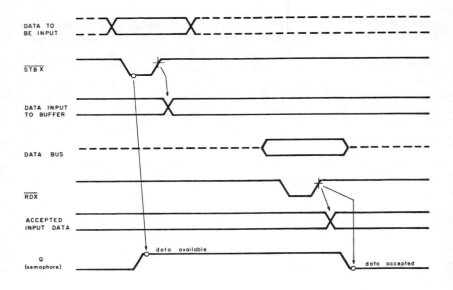

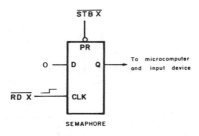

Fig. 9-34. Conditional input using a semaphore: timing diagrams. Note that the positive edge of the $\overline{\text{RD X}}$ signal clears the semaphore.

2. The input device uses the logic 0 condition of the $\overline{\text{STB X}}$ pulse to set (high, or logic 1) the semaphore, thus indicating that new data is available and the buffer is full. (See additional comments on the order of steps (2) and (3) at the end of this section.)
3. The input device transfers data to the buffer with the aid of the positive edge of the $\overline{\text{STB X}}$ pulse.
4. The microcomputer detects that the semaphore is set, and therefore that data is available in the buffer.
5. After a period of time, the microcomputer enables the data bus to permit the input of data.
6. The microcomputer inputs data to the accumulator (or other internal register).

7. The microcomputer resets the semaphore to indicate to the input device that data has been input and that the buffer is empty.
8. This set of operations is repeated at step 1.

The term "empty buffer" must be used with caution. All that happens is that a copy of the buffer data is transferred to the microcomputer. The original data still remains in the buffer. However, with a copy stored safely in the microcomputer, the original has little value and can be replaced by new data. Perhaps we should use the term "useless buffer data" to characterize the situation immediately after the $\overline{RD\ X}$ pulse.

A final situation, shown in Figs. 9-32 and 9-35, uses an output device, such as a display terminal, as the acceptor and a microcomputer as the source. The sequence of events shown in Fig. 9-35 is based upon the strobed output mode for the Intel 8155/8156 and 8255 integrated circuits. For the DATA ACCEPTED state, the semaphore output from the 8155/8156 is a logic 1, whereas from the 8255 it is a logic 0. The two pin functions are listed as BF and $\overline{OBF}$, respectively, and this explains the presence of the complementary output in Fig. 9-35.

In Fig. 9-35, $\overline{ACK\ X}$ is a timing signal from the output device that acknowledges the acceptance of data. The microcomputer generates timing signal $\overline{WR\ X}$ to output data to the buffer. A logic 0 condition for $\overline{ACK\ X}$ clears the semaphore, while a positive-edge transition in $\overline{WR\ X}$ sets the semaphore. The sequence of events in Fig. 9-35 can be summarized as follows:

1. The output device detects that the semaphore is set (high, or logic 1), and accepts the data from the buffer.
2. The output device uses the logic 0 condition of the $\overline{ACK\ X}$ pulse to reset (low, or logic 0) the semaphore, thus indicating that data has been accepted and that the buffer is empty.
3. The microcomputer detects that the semaphore is reset, and therefore that output data has been accepted.
4. After a period of time, the microcomputer selects new data to be output and enables the data bus to permit the output of data.
5. The microcomputer sets the semaphore to indicate to the output device that the buffer is full. (See additional comments on the order of steps 5 and 6 at the end of this section.)
6. The microcomputer outputs new data to the buffer from the accumulator (or other internal register).
7. This process is repeated starting at step 1.

Clearly, a semaphore synchronizes data transfer between a microcomputer and an I/O device; each knows when the other has acted. In Fig. 9-34, the input device (source) does not input new data to the buffer until the semaphore is reset. The microcomputer (acceptor) does not accept data from the buffer until the semaphore becomes set. In Fig. 9-35, the microcomputer (source) does not output new data to the buffer until the semaphore is reset. The output device (acceptor)

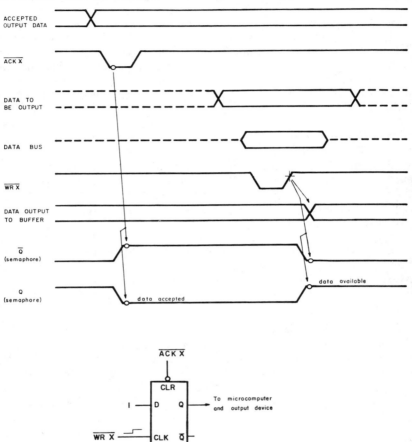

Fig. 9-35. Conditional output using a semaphore: timing diagram. Note that the positive edge of the $\overline{WR\ X}$ signal sets the semaphore.

does not accept data until the semaphore is set. In these two figures, only the source can set the semaphore and only the acceptor can reset it, but both can test it.

Integrated circuits that exhibit conditional I/O typically present the semaphore output bit both as an internal status register bit, to be input and tested by the microprocessor, and as an external output pin,

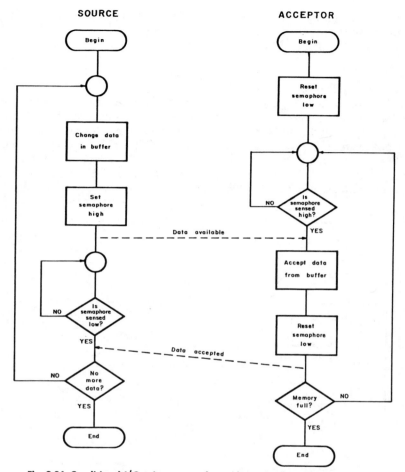

Fig. 9-36. Conditional I/O using a semaphore: alternative flowchart for source.

to be connected to the I/O device. The Intel 8255 programmable peripheral interface chip is an excellent chip with which to test the above concepts.

The flowchart and timing diagrams for individual integrated circuits may differ somewhat from those shown in Figs. 9-33 through 9-35. An alternative flowchart is shown in Fig. 9-36. Observe that now the data in the buffer is changed BEFORE the semaphore is set. This sequence is the more prudent course to follow, both with hardware and with software. However, with hardware (such as the 8155, 8156, and 8255 chips), the interval between changing the data in the buffer and setting the semaphore high may be so short that either step could be first. For

Fig. 9-36 to apply, steps (2) and (3) in the discussion of conditional input would have to be interchanged, as would steps (5) and (6) in the discussion of conditional output.

TIME LINES

Time lines, which depict the intervals required by individual steps or tasks in a sequential process, can be used to demonstrate how source and acceptor perform their data processing tasks in a conditional input/output system. Fig. 9-37 provides a general flowchart for conditional I/O using a semaphore (compare it to Fig. 9-33). Processing tasks can include arithmetic, memory storage and retrieval, and command word test operations. For the specific situation in which acceptor processing

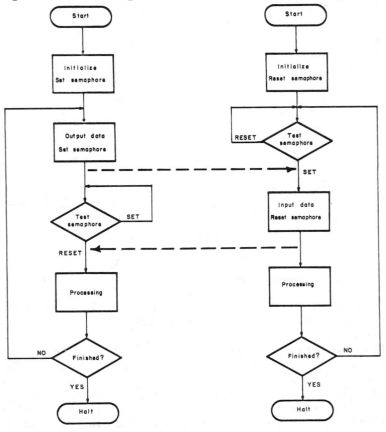

Fig. 9-37. Conditional I/O using a semaphore: generalized flowchart. The source is on the left and acceptor on the right.

time is much greater than source processing time, there is a corresponding set of time lines (Fig. 9-38). From these illustrations, it can be seen that the source outputs data to the acceptor, sets the semaphore, and

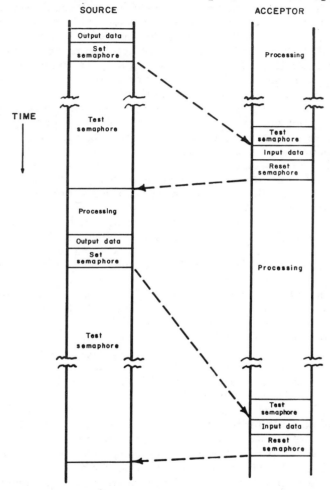

Fig. 9-38. Conditional I/O using a semaphore: time lines for source and acceptor.

then repeatedly tests the semaphore for the reset condition. The acceptor repeatedly tests the semaphore for the set condition; when such a condition is met, the acceptor inputs the data, resets the semaphore, and proceeds to the processing of the input data.

After the source detects the reset condition of the semaphore, it proceeds to its own processing tasks, which can be as simple as retrieving new data from memory and incrementing the memory pointer. Dotted arrows in Figs. 9-37 and 9-38 represent the communication of the one bit of semaphore information between source and acceptor.

A time line representation can be a valuable pedagogical tool in answering questions associated with the choice of I/O technique. Typical questions such as the following must be answered. Is a flag or semaphore needed? If a flag is needed, should the source or acceptor test the flag output? Does the source or acceptor spend too much time in a test loop? Can the use of interrupts improve performance by releasing the source or acceptor to perform other tasks?

For example, in Fig. 9-38, the source sets the semaphore considerably before—not during—the acceptor test loop. Consequently, only a single pass is made through the acceptor test loop, and it can be eliminated. Removal of this loop converts the semaphore into a flag that is tested only by the source, as shown in Fig. 9-39. Comparison of Figs. 9-38 and 9-39 demonstrates that when the processing time of the acceptor is much greater than that of the source, the acceptor test loop can be eliminated and a flag substituted for the semaphore.

Furthermore, the source wastes time testing for the reset condition of the flag (see Fig. 9-39). An alternative choice of I/O technique would employ an *interrupt* (Chapter 8). By using an interrupt, the source test loop would be eliminated, the source would be diverted to processing tasks associated with other acceptors, and the flag would generate the interrupt signal whenever the acceptor required service. For 8080A-based microcomputers operating at 2 MHz, interrupt overhead—the time associated with stack operations that do not contribute to data processing tasks—falls within the range of 25 to 50 microseconds, whereas a single pass through a test flag loop consumes about 14 microseconds. Therefore, use of an interrupt, including the additional hardware required, may not be justified if the source makes only a few passes through the test loop shown in Fig. 9-37.

A semaphore, like a flag, is used to synchronize the asynchronous source and acceptor for the transfer of data from one to the other. Use of a semaphore becomes justified when processing times of source and acceptor are comparable, or are both comparable and variable, as shown in Fig. 9-40; either can be greater than the other. It can be seen from Figs. 9-37 and 9-40 that the basic software principle behind the synchronization is the test-semaphore loop.

For example, time lines in Fig. 9-40 depict source and acceptor initially to be performing their respective processing tasks. Then the source outputs data, sets the semaphore, and proceeds to test the semaphore for the reset condition. At about the same time, the acceptor tests the semaphore for the set condition, detects the condition, inputs data, resets the semaphore, and proceeds to process the input data. The subsequent acceptor processing time is shown to be short, so the acceptor

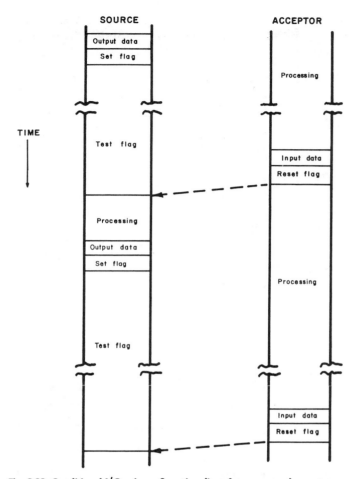

Fig. 9-39. Conditional I/O using a flag: time lines for source and acceptor.

spends considerable time in its test loop awaiting the source to output new data and set the semaphore once again. The acceptor test loop can be viewed as the means whereby the acceptor resynchronizes itself to the source and, in a similar fashion, the source test loop can be viewed as the means whereby the source resynchronizes itself to the acceptor.

Use of semaphores currently appears to be more common in software than in hardware. In fact, semaphore as a term is rarely mentioned in hardware textbooks or specifications sheets. An excellent example of the use of a pair of semaphores is the Mode 2, 8080-to-8080 interface circuit described in the Intel Peripheral Design Handbook[26]. The

$\overline{\text{OBF}}$ and IBF semaphores associated with the 8255 programmable interface chip synchronize bidirectional transfer of data between the two microcomputers. This example will be discussed in greater detail in a subsequent section.

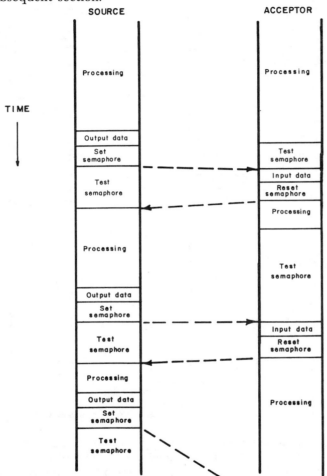

Fig. 9-40. Conditional I/O using a semaphore: specific case of time lines for source and acceptor.

The trend in hardware continues to move towards the distribution of process tasks—to peripheral chips such as I/O, math, fast Fourier transform (FFT), firmware data processors, and stepper motor controllers. Given the increase in sophistication of microprocessors, it appears that hardware semaphore use will become more prevalent.

EXAMPLE 1: UNIDIRECTIONAL CONDITIONAL I/O USING A SEMAPHORE

In this example, a source 8080A microcomputer transmits data to an acceptor 8080A microcomputer via a 74LS373 buffer/latch integrated circuit (Fig. 9-41). The heart of the circuit is the 74LS373 buffer/latch, which contains eight transparent D-type latches with 3-state outputs. The 74LS373 is equivalent to two 7475s connected to two 74365s (8095s) in a single 20-pin DIP package. The term, *transparent latch,* means that while the enable is high, the output of the latches follows the data input. When the enable goes low, the outputs become latched at the level of the data that was set up. All eight latches are enabled simultaneously at pin 11, the latch enable (LE) input, and all eight 3-state buffers are also enabled simultaneously at pin 1, the output enable ($\overline{\text{OE}}$) input.

The device select pulses (see Chapter 4) shown in Fig. 9-41 are summarized in Table 9-1. The source $\overline{\text{OUT 05H}}$ pulse (05H represents 00000101) sets the semaphore, and the acceptor $\overline{\text{OUT 06H}}$ pulse resets the semaphore, which is a 7474 D-type edge-triggered flip-flop with preset and clear. Two $\overline{\text{IN 04H}}$ pulses input the semaphore output, Q,

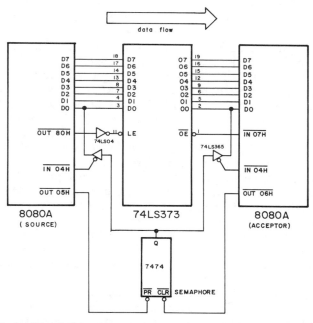

Fig. 9-41. Conditional I/O using two microcomputers and a semaphore: circuit diagram. Data flow is from left to right, from source microcomputer, through the 74LS373 buffer/latch, to the acceptor microcomputer.

Table 9-1. Input and Output Device Select Pulses

SOURCE 8080A MICROCOMPUTER	
$\overline{\text{IN 04H}}$	Inputs semaphore (flag) bit into the source microcomputer
$\overline{\text{OUT 05H}}$	Sets semaphore (flag)
$\overline{\text{OUT 80H}}$	Outputs data from source microcomputer to 74LS373 buffer
ACCEPTOR 8080A MICROCOMPUTER	
$\overline{\text{IN 04H}}$	Inputs semaphore (flag) bit into the acceptor microcomputer
$\overline{\text{OUT 06H}}$	Resets semaphore (flag)
$\overline{\text{IN 07H}}$	Inputs data from the 74LS373 buffer to the acceptor microcomputer

to the D0 position in the accumulator of the source and acceptor microcomputers, respectively. Once input to the accumulator, the D0 bit is rotated into the carry position and the logic state of the carry tested either with a JC or a JNC instruction. Output from the source microcomputer is latched into the 74LS373 with the aid of the $\overline{\text{OUT 80H}}$ pulse, and data in the 74LS373 is input to the acceptor microcomputer with the aid of the $\overline{\text{IN 07H}}$ pulse.

It is possible, in principle, to eliminate the source $\overline{\text{OUT 05H}}$ and acceptor $\overline{\text{OUT 06H}}$ device select pulses and to replace them with $\overline{\text{OUT 80H}}$ and $\overline{\text{IN 07H}}$, respectively. Since the circuit in Fig. 9-41 is designed for educational purposes, it is more useful to provide independent data I/O and semaphore set/reset capabilities.

Fig. 9-42 provides flowcharts and 8080A assembly language listings for conditional I/O using a semaphore. Programs for source and acceptor microcomputers both were started at memory location 0300H. The objective of the programs was to transfer 64 successive bytes from memory locations 0380H through 03BFH in the source microcomputer to memory locations 0380H through 03BFH in the acceptor microcomputer. Data stored in these locations was 00H, 01H, 02H, 03H, . . . 3FH, which permitted ease of observation of the process of data transfer. Data transfer from source to acceptor was monitored using a hexadecimal latch/display output port on each microcomputer. A successful transfer of 64 bytes was concluded by the appearance of the number 3FH on the hexadecimal latch/display output port on each microcomputer, and with one or both microcomputers in the halt state.

The data processing routine for the source microcomputer consisted of retrieving a single byte of data from a memory location, executing a time-delay routine, incrementing the memory pointer, and testing the memory pointer to see if any more data needed to be output. The data processing routine for the acceptor microcomputer consisted of storing input data into a memory location, executing a time-delay routine, incrementing the memory pointer, and testing the memory pointer to determine if memory was full. The source and acceptor microcomputers were identical, but the source had a clock frequency of approximately 0.75 MHz, while the acceptor microcomputer had a clock frequency of 1.17 MHz.

In the absence of a time-delay routine in either the source or acceptor programs, it was possible to transfer data from source memory to acceptor memory at a rate of 134 μs/byte. If both microcomputers were

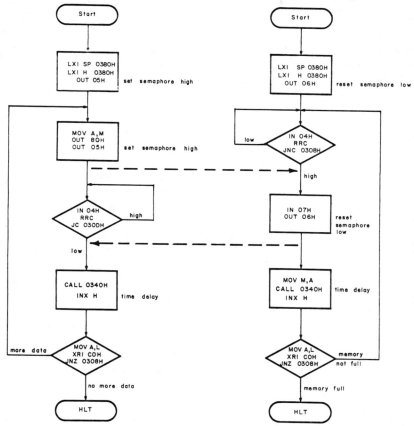

Fig. 9-42. Conditional I/O using two microcomputers and a semaphore: flowcharts and assembly language programs for source and acceptor. The source program is on the left, and the acceptor program on the right.

operated at 2 MHz, the data transfer rate would be approximately 50 μs/byte. When a 6.131-ms delay was added to the acceptor program, with the source program running as fast as possible, the data transfer rate slowed to 6.235 ms/byte. Conversely, when a 9.506-ms delay was added to the source program, with the acceptor program running as fast as possible, the data transfer rate became 9.695 ms/byte. These results confirm the expectation that the longest time delay, whether in the source or acceptor programs, governs the data transfer rate.

The semaphore in Fig. 9-41 can be converted to a flag simply by deleting the flag-testing loop in either the source or acceptor program. Details are provided in Table 9-2. For conditional output with flag, a 6.131-ms delay in the acceptor program, with the source program running as fast as possible, produced a data transfer rate of 6.189 ms/byte. For conditional input with flag, a 9.530-ms delay in the source program, with the acceptor program running as fast as possible, provided a data transfer rate of 9.642 ms/byte.

Using a pair of microcomputers to demonstrate characteristics of conditional I/O techniques has advantages. Influences of time delays in source or acceptor can be explored simply by making software changes. The longest time delay governs the data transfer rate. Software changes also can be made to determine the type of I/O operation performed, and whether a flag or semaphore is used.

Table 9-2. Modifications of the Assembly Language Programs in Fig. 9-42

Type of I/O Operation	Modifications Required
Conditional I/O with semaphore	Use source and acceptor programs as given.
Conditional output with flag	Use source program as given. Eliminate first OUT 06H and IN 04H, RRC, and JC 0308H from acceptor program.
Conditional input with flag	Use acceptor program as given. Eliminate first OUT 05H and IN 04H, RRC, and JC 030DH from source program.
Unconditional I/O	Difficult to synchronize the data transfer of 64 bytes from source memory to acceptor memory.

EXAMPLE 2: BIDIRECTIONAL CONDITIONAL I/O USING TWO SEMAPHORES

The Intel 8255 programmable peripheral interface chip contains a bidirectional conditional I/O port that is particularly useful for interfacing a pair of microcomputers in a master/slave relationship. *Bidirectional conditional I/O* can be represented schematically as shown in Fig. 9-43. In this case, the master microcomputer is on the left and the slave microcomputer is on the right. The terms, source and acceptor, no longer apply since either computer could be a source or acceptor. The buffer is a programmable peripheral interface chip that communicates directly with the master using accumulator I/O or memory read/write instructions. Strobe signals utilized by the master are the $\overline{RD}$ X and $\overline{WR}$ X device select pulses (also known as $\overline{IN\ X}$ and $\overline{OUT\ X}$, respectively, for 8080A microcomputers), which input and output data and also clear the input and output semaphores. Compare Fig. 9-43 to

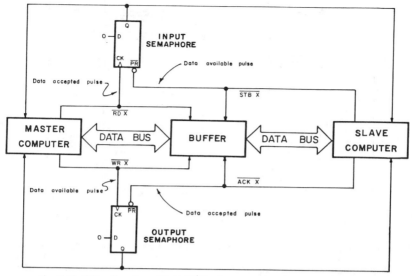

Fig. 9-43. Bidirectional conditional I/O using two semaphores: block diagram.

Figs. 9-31 and 9-32. The buffer can store only a single byte of data. Thus, it can be viewed as a half-duplex parallel data transmission device: data can be transmitted from master to slave, or slave to master, but not in both directions simultaneously.

The slave microcomputer communicates with the buffer via the $\overline{\text{STB X}}$ and $\overline{\text{ACK X}}$ pulses. The $\overline{\text{STB X}}$ pulse loads slave data into the buffer and simultaneously sets the input semaphore; the $\overline{\text{ACK X}}$ pulse acknowledges the receipt of buffer data by the slave and simultaneously sets the output semaphore. In transferring a block of data from master to slave, only the output semaphore is tested by each microcomputer. After processing in the slave, the data may be sent as a block back to the master, in which case only the input semaphore is tested. Both semaphores are tested by the two microcomputers if data bytes or words are continuously sent to the slave, processed in the slave, and immediately returned to the master.

The 8255 chip is interfaced directly to the address, data, and control buses of the master 8080A microcomputer (Fig. 9-44). This interface is simple: only two 74LS04 inverters and 16 wire interconnections are required. The slave 8080A microcomputer is interfaced to the bidirectional buffer (port A) and also to the preset and semaphore output signals of the IBFA and $\overline{\text{OBFA}}$ semaphores. Three 74LS32 OR gates generate the device select pulses, and two 74LS125 (8095) 3-state buffers input the semaphore signals IBFA and $\overline{\text{OBFA}}$ into bit positions D5 and D7, respectively, of the slave accumulator, where they are tested.

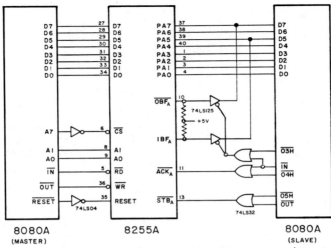

Fig. 9-44. Bidirectional conditional I/O using two semaphores: master/slave interface circuit diagram. The 8255 chip is operated in the mode 2 configuration. One kilohm pull-up resistors are used with OBFA and IBFA. The notations 03H, 04H, and 05H represent decoded 8-bit address pulses.

Both microcomputers employ the accumulator I/O instructions summarized in Table 9-3. Use of these instructions can best be seen by observing which pulses are needed to transfer a data byte from the master to the slave and back to the master. The master first tests the $\overline{\text{OBFA}}$ semaphore to determine whether or not port A is full. If it is not full, an OUT 80H instruction is executed, and data is transferred from the accumulator in the master to the 8255 buffer. Concurrently, $\overline{\text{OBFA}}$ is set. The slave uses the IN 03H instruction to input the semaphore bits into the accumulator, where they are tested for an output semaphore that is set. If $\overline{\text{OBFA}}$ is set, the slave executes the IN 04H instruction and inputs data to its accumulator.

Table 9-3. Input and Output Instructions for Master and Slave Microcomputers

MASTER 8080A MICROCOMPUTER	
IN 80H	Inputs data from the 8255A Port A and resets input semaphore IBF$_A$
IN 82H	Inputs semaphore bits $\overline{\text{OBF}}_A$ and IBF$_A$
OUT 80H	Outputs data to the 8255A Port A and resets output semaphore $\overline{\text{OBF}}_A$
OUT 83H	Outputs control word to the 8255A control register.

SLAVE 8080A MICROCOMPUTER	
IN 03H	Inputs semaphore bits $\overline{\text{OBF}}_A$ and IBF$_A$
IN 04H	Inputs data from the 8255A Port A and sets output semaphore $\overline{\text{OBF}}_A$
OUT 05H	Outputs data to the 8255A Port A and sets input semaphore IBF$_A$

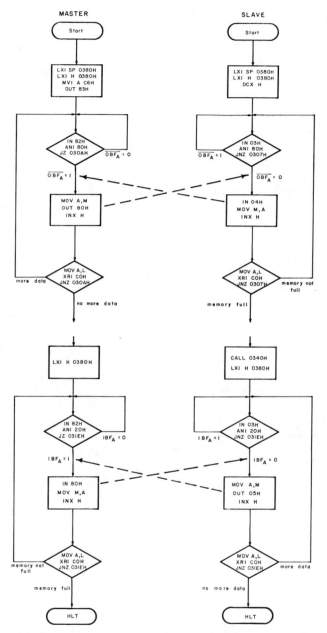

Fig. 9-45. Bidirectional conditional I/O using two semaphores: flowcharts and assembly language programs for master and slave.

After processing the data byte, the slave tests the IBFA semaphore to determine that the input buffer is empty. If it is empty, the slave executes an OUT 05H instruction that strobes the data byte into port A and also sets the IBFA semaphore. Next, the master tests the IBFA semaphore. If it is set, the master executes an IN 80H instruction to input the data byte into the accumulator. Concurrently, IBFA is cleared.

A pair of master and slave microcomputer programs that transfer a block of 64 successive data bytes from master to slave, process it in the slave, and then transfer the processed bytes back to the master is shown in Fig. 9-45. The programs are in the form of a pair of flowcharts incorporating 8080A assembly language instructions. The block output is given in the top half and block input in the bottom half.

Both programs were started at memory location 0300H, as was the case in Example 1. Either the slave or the master could be started first, with the semaphores and test loops (and the DCX H instruction in the slave) handling the necessary time and memory location synchronization. The 64 data bytes were located starting at memory location 0380H (as was the case in Example 1), and were transferred as a block to a group of memory locations starting at the same address in the slave. The processing of the block was performed by a subroutine located at 0340H in the slave. Once processed, the 64 bytes were transferred back to their original memory locations in the master. The transfer of a single byte from master to slave, and then from slave to master, proceeded along the lines of the description given earlier.

Several measurements of execution times were made. With both microcomputers operating at 0.765 MHz, the master program, in the absence of a slave data processing routine at 0340H, required 15.0 ms, or approximately 117 μs/byte of data transferred from one computer to the other. If both microcomputers were operated at 2 MHz, this data transfer time would decrease to only 44 μs/byte. A 2.43-sec delay, which simulated a data processing routine in the slave, produced a 2.43-sec increase in the time required to execute the master program completely.

DOUBLE-BUFFERED CONDITIONAL I/O

This and several subsequent sections will explore an additional concept, *double-buffered conditional I/O,* that facilitates the discussion of I/O techniques known as the 2-wire handshake and 3-wire handshake. We shall consider two communicating 8080A microcomputers, a master and a slave.

A *buffer,* in the context of data processing and computation, can be defined as follows:

buffer—a device used to compensate for a difference in rate of flow of information or time of occurrence of events when transmitting information from one device to another[16].

The word "storage" is omitted for the original definition, thus permitting the inclusion of latches, which are storage devices, and 3-state buffers, which are not.

In double-buffered conditional I/O, which is so common that the existence of double buffering is rarely given special attention, there are two buffers in series in the data path between the data buses of the master and slave microcomputers. Typically, one of these buffers is associated with the master, and the other with the slave. One buffer is an output port (latch); the other is an input port (3-state buffer). The two buffers compensate for a difference in the time at which data transfer steps occur when data is transmitted between the master and the slave.

Examples of double-buffered conditional I/O have already been given in this chapter. In Example 1, "unidirectional conditional I/O using a semaphore," a 74LS373 buffer/latch integrated circuit is used as the buffer between source and acceptor microcomputers. The 74LS373 contains an 8-bit latch—the output buffer for the source—and an 8-bit three-state buffer—the input buffer for the acceptor. The source microcomputer clocks the latch, and the acceptor microcomputer enables the 3-state buffer.

The bidirectional double-buffered characteristics of port A (mode 2) on the 8255 programmable peripheral interface chip described in Example 2, "bidirectional conditional I/O using two semaphores," are worth emphasizing. When the master microcomputer outputs data to the slave microcomputer, the output instruction OUT 80H clocks data into the 8-bit latch associated with port A. An acknowledge pulse, $\overline{ACKA}$, from the slave enables the 3-state buffers associated with port A and permits data to be input into the slave. When the slave outputs data to the master, the two buffers in series are reversed. An $\overline{STBA}$ pulse from the slave microcomputer clocks the 8-bit latch associated with input port A, and the master microcomputer input instruction IN 80H enables the 3-state buffers. Thus, port A (mode 2) on the 8255 contains four buffers: two for input and two for output.

The utility of the concept of double-buffered conditional I/O becomes evident when two microcomputers are interfaced together via a pair of programmable I/O ports such as those found on peripheral interface chips (6520, 6821, 8255) or on "combo" chips that provide various combinations of CPU, I/O, RAM, ROM, and timer functions (6530, 6532, 6534, 6801, 6803, 6805, 8048, 8049, 8050, 8051, 8155, 8741, 8748, 8751, 8755). Each of these chips has one or more unconditional or conditional I/O ports. As we have shown in the preceding sections, the use of the conditional I/O ports for microcomputer-microcomputer interfacing may be straightforward, but how are two microcomputers interfaced to each other when only unconditional ports exist?

Table 9-4, which summarizes some of the characteristics of flip-flops and programmable I/O ports, provides some answers. In this table, it is assumed that the terms, input and output, refer to a microcomputer, typically a master that can function either as a source or acceptor. With an unconditional port, only a single buffer—either a latch or a 3-state buffer—is present. Unconditional ports need neither a flag nor a semaphore. To create a conditional port from an unconditional port, either a flag or semaphore must be created from unconditional I/O bits available on other ports. To create a unidirectional I/O port between a pair of microcomputers, there must be at least two buffers—one latch and one 3-state buffer—and at least one flag or semaphore. The creation of a bidirectional I/O port requires two latches, two buffers, and at least two flags or semaphores.

Fig. 9-46 demonstrates a simple approach to the interfacing of two microcomputers using only unconditional I/O ports and bits. The master buffer is an 8-bit latch that is clocked by the $\overline{\text{WR X}}$ pulse from the master computer. The slave buffer is a 3-state buffer that is enabled by an $\overline{\text{RD X}}$ pulse from the slave computer. Communication between the master and slave buffers is continuous and is accomplished by a set of eight wire connections.

The interesting aspect of Fig. 9-46 is the way in which the DAV (Data Available) and NDAC (Not Data ACcepted) flags are used to accomplish the conditional I/O. Observe that two flags are required, in contrast to the single semaphore shown in Table 1. DAV is a single output bit on an unconditional output port located on the master buffer. NDAC is a single output bit located on the slave buffer. As shown in Fig. 9-46, the master computer sets and resets the DAV flag, and the slave computer does the same with the NDAC flag. Since the DAC and NDAC flip-flops each communicate with only a single computer, they are clearly flags and not semaphores.

With two flags there must be a total of four different logic conditions, the product of two conditions for DAV and two for NDAC. These conditions are summarized in Fig. 9-47, which provides timing diagrams for the data transfer process between master and slave. The initial conditions—data not available from master and not accepted by slave—are chosen such that DAV is initially logic 1 and NDAC is initially logic 0. Data is first output to the master buffer (latch) by the master computer and given a short time to settle. As shown in the timing diagrams, DAV is then reset, indicating that data is available from the master. The slave computer inputs the DAV flag bit, tests it, detects the logic 0 state, and inputs data from the slave buffer, a 3-state buffer. Once the data is input and stored, the slave sets the NDAC flag, thus indicating that

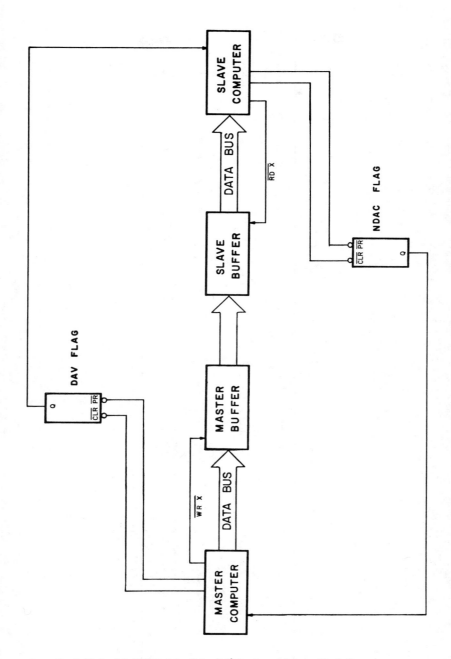

Fig. 9-46. Double-buffered conditional I/O using two flags: block diagram.

Table 9-4. Characteristics of Different Types of I/O Techniques

Type of I/O Technique	Directional Characteristics	Number and Type of Buffers		Sets Flip-Flop	Resets Flip-Flop	Tests Flip-Flop	Minimum Number of Flags or Semaphores
		Latches	3-State Buffers				
unconditional input	unidirectional	0	1	neither	neither	neither	0
unconditional output	unidirectional	1	0	neither	neither	neither	0
conditional input (flag)	unidirectional	1	1	source	acceptor	only acceptor	1
conditional output (flag)	unidirectional	1	1	source	acceptor	only source	1
conditional input (semaphore)	unidirectional	1	1	source	acceptor	both	1
conditional output (semaphore)	unidirectional	1	1	source	acceptor	both	1
condiitional I/O (semaphore)*	bidirectional	2	2	source	acceptor	both	2

*Combination of conditional input (semaphore) plus conditional output (semaphore) data has been accepted. The master computer inputs the NDAC flag, tests it, and determines that data has been accepted. The DAV flag is then set once again, indicating that data is no longer available from the master. The slave computer inputs the DAV flag, tests it, detects the logic 1 condition, and consequently resets the NDAC flag in preparation for the next "handshaking transaction."

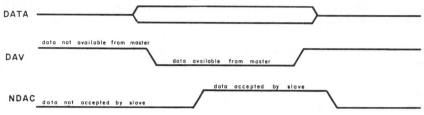

Fig. 9-47. Double-buffered conditional I/O using two flags: timing diagrams.

The 2-wire handshaking process shown in Fig. 9-47 is different from the use of a single semaphore. Fig. 9-48 depicts the difference, in the form of timing diagrams, for the same data transfer process shown in Fig. 9-47. With a semaphore, only a single flip-flop is present so only two different logic conditions exist. When the master computer outputs data to the master buffer, the semaphore is set, indicating that data is available. The slave computer inputs the semaphore bit, tests it, detects

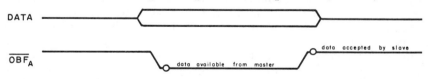

Fig. 9-48. Double-buffered conditional I/O using a semaphore: timing diagrams. OBFA refers to the output-buffer-full semaphore associated with bidirectional port A on the 8255 chip.

the logic 0 state, inputs the data from the slave buffer, and, finally, sets the semaphore. The master computer inputs the semaphore bit, tests it, ultimately detects the logic 1 condition, and concludes that the data byte has been accepted by the slave. From a conceptual point of view, the use of a single semaphore is a simpler type of handshake than the 2-wire handshake scheme shown in Figs. 9-46 and 9-47.

EXAMPLE 3: TWO-WIRE HANDSHAKE
I/O USING FOUR FLAGS

Though the IEEE 488 bus standard employs a 3-wire handshake procedure to synchronize data transfer between a talker (source, transmitter) and a listener (acceptor, receiver), it is instructive to examine experimentally the behavior of a 2-microcomputer system that uses a simple *2-wire interlocked handshake procedure*. The 3-wire handshake is for applications in which a master transfers data to or receives data from many I/O devices, whereas the 2-wire handshake is useful for transferring data between a microcomputer and a single I/O device.

Fig. 9-49 provides a schematic of a double-buffered conditional I/O system consisting of talker and listener 8080A-based microcomputers. The interface between the two microcomputers consists of a pair of 8255 programmable peripheral interface chips, one associated with the talker and the other with the listener. The 8255 chips are each operated in their mode 0 configurations; all the ports exhibit only unconditional I/O behavior. Data transfer occurs between ports A, from talker to listener; several bits from ports B and C are used as flags or flag inputs. The control words for the talker and listener are 82H (output port A, input port B, output port C) and 92H (input port A, input port B, output port C), respectively.

Fig. 9-50 provides versions of the talker and listener flowcharts that are simplified representations of the familiar IEEE 488 handshake flowchart[27-29]. The NRFD (Not Ready For Data) signal is omitted because we are concerned only with a 2-wire (or 2-signal) handshake procedure. The basic characteristics of the flowchart can be discussed with the aid of the timing diagrams for the signal DAV and NDAC, shown in Fig. 9-51. DAV is the mnemonic for the data available signal, and NDAC is the mnemonic for the not data accepted signal. The four edges, shown as ① through ④ in Fig. 9-51, are the basis for understanding the 2-wire handshake procedure. Each edge is tested by a software test loop either in the talker or listener software (two loops are associated with the talker, and two with the listener). The information that these edges convey can be summarized as follows:

① Talker informs listener that data is available;
② Listener acknowledges that it has accepted the data;
③ Talker informs listener that data no longer is valid; and
④ Listener acknowledges that it will not accept data again until DAV = 0.

The talker tests for edges ② and ④, while the listener tests for edges ① and ③. This sequence of tests, along with the associated signal lines, comprises the 2-wire handshake.

The dotted arrows in Fig. 9-50 match the edges shown in Fig. 9-51. As shown in Fig. 9-50, the talker cannot load or output data until NDAC = 0, and the listener cannot input or store data until DAV = 0. After data is transferred from talker to listener, the two devices inform and acknowledge, respectively, that valid data is no longer present be-

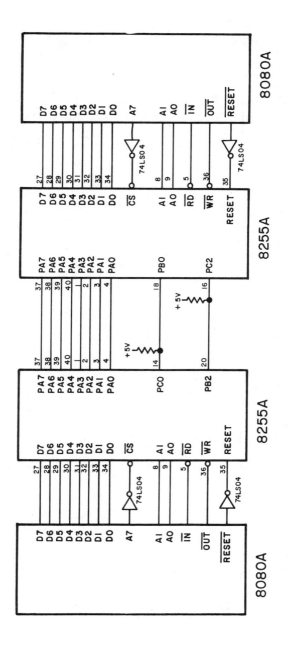

Fig. 9-49. Two-wire handshake protocol: interface circuit diagram. One kilohm pull-up resistors are used for the flag outputs PC0 and PC2.

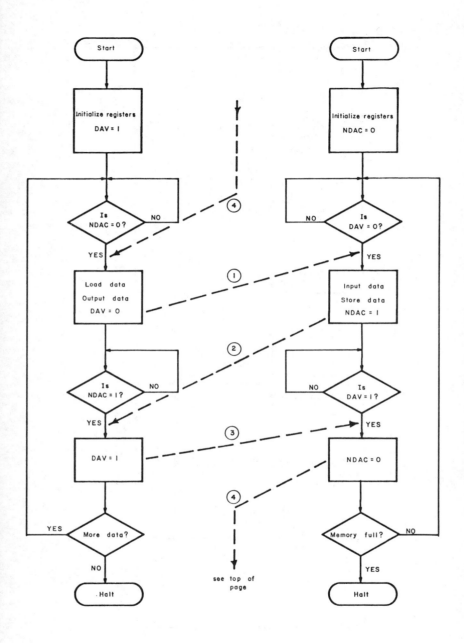

Fig. 9-50. Two-wire handshake protocol: flowcharts for talker and listener. The talker is on the left, and the listener on the right.

tween ports A. Observe the symmetry in the talker and listener flow-charts.

Detailed listings for a pair of 8080A-based microcomputers exchanging a block of data from one memory to the other are provided in Fig. 9-52. A 2-wire handshake protocol is used (compare Fig. 9-52 with Fig. 9-50). Sixty-four data bytes, starting at memory location 0380H (the same data block employed in Examples 1 and 2), are transferred byte

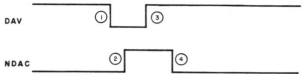

Fig. 9-51. Two-wire handshake protocol: timing diagrams. To understand the basis for the protocol, focus your attention on the four edges, shown as ① through ④. The DAV flag is set and reset by the talker software; the NDAC flag is set and reset by the listener software.

by byte from the talker to the same set of memory locations in the listener. The instruction sequences at the end of the programs—MOV A,L/XRI COR/JNZ 03XXH—test for the completion of the memory-to-memory block-transfer process. For both the talker and listener, the initialization of the stack pointer, memory address pointer, 8255 control register, and output port C occurs in the first fourteen program bytes.

The various input, output, and mask bytes that appear in the software in Fig. 9-52 are summarized in Fig. 9-53. For the talker, the 8255 control register configures the ports as output port A, input port B, and output port C; for the listener, the port configuration is input port A, input port B, and output port C. The talker outputs the DAV flag (bit PC0) and inputs the NDAC flag (bit PB2). For the listener, it is just the opposite: the NDAC flag (bit PC2) is output, and the DAV flag (bit PB0) is input. In the test loops in Fig. 9-52, the mask bytes are 04H for the talker and 01H for the listener. The device codes for the 8255 ports or registers are 80H (port A), 81H (input port B), 82H (output port C), and 83H (control register). The OUT 80H and IN 80H instructions output and input, respectively, the data byte that is being transferred from talker to listener.

Since ports A, B, and C on the 8255 are under software control, the direction of data flow can be changed through modifications in the software. The easiest way to do this is to interchange the bit positions of the DAV and NDAC flags, as shown in Fig. 9-54. Now, the microcomputer on the left in Fig. 9-49 outputs NDAC as bit PC0, and inputs DAV as bit PB2. The microcomputer on the right in Fig. 9-49 inputs NDAC as bit PB0 and outputs DAV as bit PC2. The MOV A,M/OUT 80H and IN 80H/MOV M,A pairs of instructions are interchanged in the software of the two microcomputers, but the mask bytes in the four test loops remain the same. The control words for the 8255 control registers are interchanged as well.

As with Examples 1 and 2, the rate of data transfer has been measured, in this case for the circuit given in Fig. 9-49 plus the software given in Fig. 9-52. For talker and listener microcomputers each operating at 0.75 MHz, 20.37 ms were required to transfer a block of 64 bytes

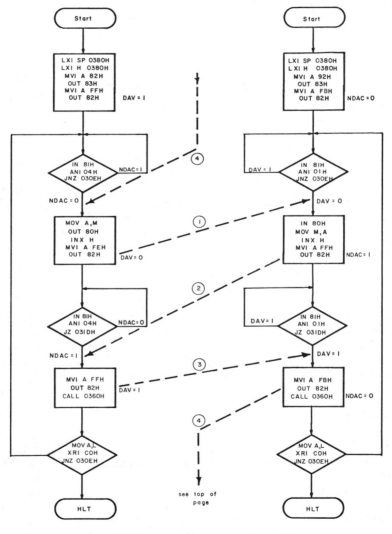

Fig. 9-52. Two-wire handshake protocol: flowcharts and assembly language programs for talker and listener. The talker is on the left, and the listener on the right.

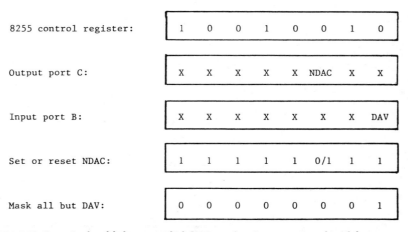

TALKER (microcomputer on left in Fig 9-49)

8255 control register:	1	0	0	0	0	0	1	0

Output port C:	X	X	X	X	X	X	X	DAV

Input port B:	X	X	X	X	X	NDAC	X	X

Set or reset DAV:	1	1	1	1	1	1	1	0/1

Mask all but NDAC:	0	0	0	0	0	1	0	0

LISTENER (microcomputer on right in Fig 9-49)

8255 control register:	1	0	0	1	0	0	1	0

Output port C:	X	X	X	X	X	NDAC	X	X

Input port B:	X	X	X	X	X	X	X	DAV

Set or reset NDAC:	1	1	1	1	1	0/1	1	1

Mask all but DAV:	0	0	0	0	0	0	0	1

Fig. 9-53. Two-wire handshake protocol: definitions of registers, ports, and mask bytes for data flow in Fig. 9-49 from left to right.

of data. This value corresponds to 318.3 μs/byte. The CALL 0360H instruction in each program permits the testing of the effect of time delay loops on the rate of data transfer from the memory of the talker to the memory of the listener. With a 9.53-ms delay in the listener, 617.2 ms, or 9.64 ms/byte, were required to accomplish the same data transfer. A 9.50-ms delay in the talker, but no delay in the listener, resulted in an overall time of 629.6 ms, or 9.84 ms/byte. Finally, when 9.50-ms and 9.53-ms delays were present in the talker and listener, respectively, the rate of data transfer was 9.79 ms/byte.

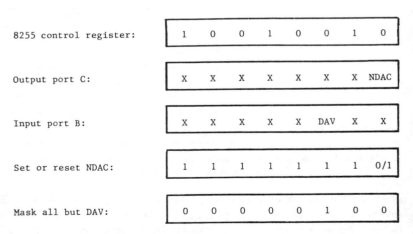

TALKER (microcomputer on right in Fig 9-49)

8255 control register:	1	0	0	0	0	0	1	0

Output port C:	X	X	X	X	X	DAV	X	X

Input port B:	X	X	X	X	X	X	X	NDAC

Set or reset DAV:	1	1	1	1	1	0/1	1	1

Mask all but NDAC:	0	0	0	0	0	0	0	1

LISTENER (microcomputer on left in Fig 9-49)

8255 control register:	1	0	0	1	0	0	1	0

Output port C:	X	X	X	X	X	X	X	NDAC

Input port B:	X	X	X	X	X	DAV	X	X

Set or reset NDAC:	1	1	1	1	1	1	1	0/1

Mask all but DAV:	0	0	0	0	0	1	0	0

Fig. 9-54. Two-wire handshake protocol: definitions of registers, ports, and mask bytes for data flow in Fig. 9-49 from right to left.

BUSED FLAGS: THE IEEE 488 HARDWARE BUS

Synchronization of the transfer of parallel data among many devices is a common problem in microcomputer systems. Parallel data transfer can be achieved using at least two methods. The first method subdivides the system of devices into pairs of communicating devices. Each pair is then interfaced together through eight bidirectional data lines that are synchronized via the use of the address bus, control bus, flags, interrupts, semaphores, or the 2-wire handshake. One example of this method is the interfacing to the 8080A central processing unit of the peripheral interface chips—the 8251 programmable communication interface, 8253 interval timer, 8255 programmable peripheral interface, and 8259 programmable interrupt controller—that are present on the Intel SBC 80/20 single-board computer.

A second method—the IEEE 488 interface bus—is the subject of this section. It uses a single set of eight bused bidirectional data lines that communicate data among all of the devices, plus eight bused flags that synchronize such communication. Fig. 9-55 provides a block diagram for a 3-device system. Only 11 of the 16 bus lines in the IEEE 488 interface bus are shown. The other five IEEE 488 signals—IFC, ATN, SRQ, REN, and EOI—are not essential to this discussion. D101 through D108 are bused bidirectional data lines; there is nothing unusual or special about their behavior. Between each device and the D101 to D108 interface bus lines are eight sets of receivers and drivers, that is, eight IEEE 488 bus transceivers. Either 3-state or open-collector drivers are used. For further details, consult the IEEE Std 488-1978 document[30].

The three bus lines that synchronize the bidirectional data transfer is the interesting aspect of Fig. 9-55. These bus lines participate in the 3-wire handshake protocol, and are called NDAC (Not Data ACcepted), NRFD (Not Ready For Data), and DAV (Data AVailable). All three are based on the principle of the *bused flag*. In most discussions of the IEEE 488 hardware bus, the existence of bused flags is assumed to be understood, and attention is directed instead to hardware (LSI chip sets), to state diagrams, and to the timing diagrams and flowcharts that summarize the characteristics of the 3-wire handshake[27-38]. Since the concept of a bused flag is one of the important ideas contained within the IEEE 488 standard, it is appropriate to discuss the characteristics of such a flag and how it is used.

It is again useful to make the distinction between a flag and a semaphore in the context of a pair of communicating devices. As discussed in the section, "Flag vs Semaphore," the state of a flag is tested by only one of the communicating devices, whereas state of a semaphore is set by one device, reset by the other, and tested by both. According to this distinction, NDAC, NRFD, and DAV appear to possess semaphore characteristics, but it is easy to be misled. In Fig. 9-55, for example,

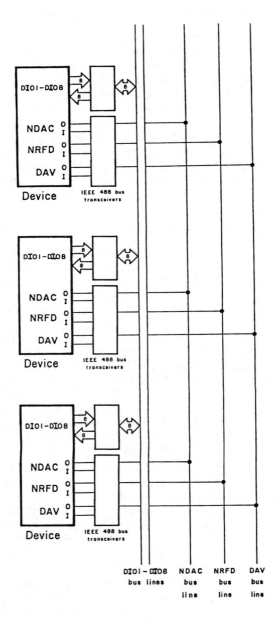

Fig. 9-55. Three-device IEEE 488 bus system. The IEEE 488 bus transceivers provide a critical link between each device and the IEEE 488 hardware bus.

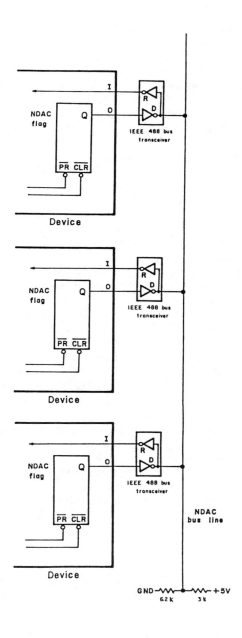

Fig. 9-56. Three-device IEEE 488 NDAC hardware bus line. Each of the three NDAC flags require a separate IEEE 488 transceiver.

when device 1 outputs data to device 2, device 1 sets and resets the DAV signal line, and device 2 tests it. In turn, device 2 sets and resets the NDAC and NRFD lines, and device 1 tests them. The direction of communication can be changed, however, and device 2 can output data to device 1. In such a situation, device 2 now sets and resets the DAV signal line, and device 1 tests it; also, device 1 sets and resets the NDAC and NRFD signal lines, and device 2 tests them. Thus, the DAV, NDAC, and NRFD signal lines may be set, reset, and tested by both devices. Are they semaphores? Our suggested answer is that they are not. Recall that bidirectional data transfer between two devices required two semaphores, one for each direction; for the transfer of data in a given direction, both devices tested the appropriate semaphore (see Example 2). Such is not the case with the IEEE 488 bus system depicted in Fig. 9-55. Thus, for the transfer of a single byte of data in one direction, DAV, NDAC, and NRFD act as flags.

Consider the interface diagram for the NDAC bus line (Fig. 9-56). Open-collector busing is used, as required by the IEEE 488 standard, with a 3-kilohm resistor tied to 5 volts and a 6.2-kilohm resistor tied to ground[30]. Each of the three devices communicates with the NDAC bus line via a single transceiver, which is a combination of an inverter as a receiver (R) and an open-collector inverter as a bus driver (D). Each device outputs (O) its NDAC flag state, and inputs (I) the status of the NDAC bus line. The NDAC bus line possesses the wire-ORed negative-logic convention that is characteristic of open-collector busing.

It is easy to confuse the coded logic state with the electrical signal level on either side of the IEEE 488 bus transceiver shown in Fig. 9-56. Fig. 9-57 assists the interpretation. On the left of the bus transceiver, positive transistor-transistor logic (TTL) is employed for the NDAC flag, with GND potential corresponding to logic 0 (false) and +5 volts corresponding to logic 1 (true). To the right of the transceiver, a negative-logic bus is employed, with the low (L) electrical state (≤ 0.8 volt) corresponding to logic 1* (true), and the high (H) electrical state (≥ 2.0 volts) corresponding to logic 0* (false). The asterisk (*) represents states coded in negative logic. Interconversion between positive TTL logic and the negative-logic bus is accomplished with inverters.

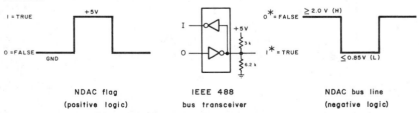

Fig. 9-57. Summary of NDAC flag and hardware bus line logic.

A truth table (Table 9-5) for the NDAC bus line summarizes the logic relationships between the three TTL NDAC flags and the NDAC bus line in Fig. 9-56. The logic states for the NDAC flag for device X have the following meanings:

0 (false)   Device X has accepted current data from DIO1 to DIO8
1 (true)   Device X has not accepted current data from DIO1 to DIO8

The logic states for the NDAC bus line have the following meanings:

0* (false)   All of the devices have accepted current data from DIO1 to DIO8
1* (true)   Not all of the devices have accepted current data from DIO1 to DIO8

If any NDAC flag in Fig. 9-56 is at true, the NDAC bus line is pulled true to indicate that all of the devices have not accepted data from DIO1 to DIO8.

The interface diagram for the NRFD bus line is identical to that for the NDAC bus line in Fig. 9-56; compare the NRFD truth table in Table 9-6. Logic states for the NRFD flag for device X have the following meanings:

0 (false)   Device X is ready for the next data byte from DIO1 to DIO8
1 (true)   Device X is not ready for the next data byte from DIO1 to DIO8

The logic states for the NRFD bus line have the following meanings:

0* (false)   All of the devices are ready for the next data byte from DIO1 to DIO8
1* (true)   All of the devices are not ready for the next data byte from DIO1 to DIO8

Table 9-5. Truth Table for NDAC Hardware Bus Line

NDAC Flag for Device 3	NDAC Flag for Device 2	NDAC Flag for Device 1	NDAC Bus Line
0	0	0	0*
0	0	1	1*
0	1	0	1*
0	1	1	1*
1	0	0	1*
1	0	1	1*
1	1	0	1*
1	1	1	1*

Table 9-6. Truth Table for NRFD Hardware Bus Line

NRFD Flag for Device 3	NRFD Flag for Device 2	NRFD Flag for Device 1	NRFD Bus Line
0	0	0	0*
0	0	1	1*
0	1	0	1*
0	1	1	1*
1	0	0	1*
1	0	1	1*
1	1	0	1*
1	1	1	1*

If any NRFD flag is true, the NRFD bus line is pulled true, thus indicating that all of the devices are not ready for the next data byte from DIO1 to DIO8.

The interface diagram for the DAV signal is identical to that in Fig. 9-56, but the truth table (Table 9-7) for the DAV bus line is different from the NDAC and NRFD tables. Logic states of the DAV flag for device X have the following meanings:

0 (false)	Device X does not have data available for DIO1 to DIO8
1 (true)	Device X has current data available for DIO1 to DIO8

Logic states for the DAV bus line have the following meanings:

0* (false)	None of the devices has data available for DIO1 to DIO8
1* (true)	A single device has current data available for D101 to DIO8

Observe that only one device at a time is permitted to output data to DIO1 to DIO8. Four of the entries in the DAV truth table are not allowed by the IEEE 488 standard.

Table 9-7. Truth Table for DAV Hardware Bus Line

DAV Flag for Device 3	DAV Flag for Device 2	DAV Flag for Device 1	DAV Bus Line	Comments
0	0	0	1*	No output data available
0	0	1	0*	Output data available (from device 1)
0	1	0	0*	Output data available (from device 2)
0	1	1	—	Not allowed
1	0	0	0*	Output data available (from device 3)
1	0	1	—	Not allowed
1	1	0	—	Not allowed
1	1	1	—	Not allowed

To summarize the information provided here for NDAC, NRFD, and DAV, it is appropriate to consider the 3-wire handshake timing diagram (Fig. 9-58). A single device in Fig. 9-55 is assumed to be the source of data, or talker, and one of the other two devices is assumed to be an acceptor of data, or listener. The remaining device is assumed to be inactive. Fig. 9-58 differs from the 3-wire handshake diagrams given in other articles[28, 29, 33-38] in one significant respect: the timing diagrams for the talker and listener TTL flag signals are provided in

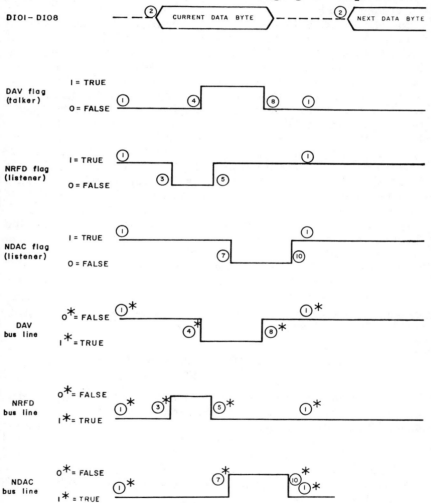

Fig. 9-58. Three-wire handshake protocol: timing diagrams. Positive logic is assumed for flags, and negative logic for hardware bus lines.

addition to the timing diagrams for the DAV, NRFD, and NDAC open-collector bus lines. Defining two types of data aids the discussion of Fig. 9-58: "current" data, which is data being transmitted during the current handshake cycle, and "next" data, which is data to be transmitted during the next handshake cycle. The reason for making such a distinction is that the state of the NRFD bus line, after it has become true (logic 1*), applies to the next data byte, whereas the state of the NDAC bus line, while the DAV bus line is true (logic 1*), applies to the current data byte.

Initially, the talker in Fig. 9-58 is not outputting data (DAV is false) and the listener is not ready for (NRFD is true) and has not accepted (NDAC is true) the next data byte. The talker outputs the current data byte to DIO1 to DIO8; detects the NRFD = logic 0* (false) condition; and sets its DAV flag to logic 1 (true). The listener detects the DAV = logic 1* (true) condition; sets its NRFD flag to logic 0 (true) to indicate that it is not ready for the next data byte; at its own rate, accepts the current data byte from the DIO1 to DIO8 bus; and resets its NDAC flag to logic 0 (false). The talker detects the NDAC = logic 0* (false) condition; resets its DAV flag to logic 0 (false); tests to determine whether more data must be output; outputs the next data byte to DIO1 to DIO8; and waits until NRFD = logic 0* (false), which indicates that the listener is ready for this "next" data byte. The listener detects the DAV = logic 0* (false) condition and sets its NDAC flag to logic 1 (true) to indicate that it has not accepted the next data byte. With the 3-wire handshake protocol, each listener can accept and process data at its own rate. The rate at which output data is transferred from talker to one or more listeners is governed by the slowest listener.

In the next section, we shall provide an experimental example of a 3-wire handshake protocol based upon a pair of 8080A-based microcomputers. A very useful reference on this subject is the introductory text by Fisher and Jensen[35].

EXAMPLE 4: THREE-WIRE HANDSHAKE
I/O USING SIX BUSED FLAGS

The relationship between the flowcharts[29, 30, 32] and timing diagrams[29, 30] for the *IEEE 488 3-wire handshake protocol* can be experimentally demonstrated using two or more microcomputers that are interfaced to each other via the use of 8255 programmable peripheral chips and IEEE 488 bus transceivers or their equivalents. The 3-wire handshake is used for byte-serial data communication applications in which one output port at a time transfers the same data simultaneously to several input ports.

Fig. 9-59 is a schematic diagram of a double-buffered conditional I/O system consisting of talker and listener 8080A-based microcom-

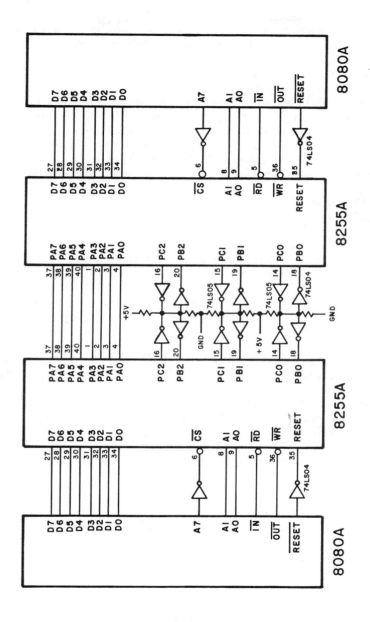

Fig. 9-59. Three-wire handshake protocol: interface circuit diagram.

puters. It is basically the same type of interface circuit used for the 2-wire handshake procedure in Example 3 except that (a) there are three handshaking bus lines between the two microcomputers, (b) each bus line permits additional connections to be made, for example from other microcomputers, (c) three flag outputs from each 8255 chip are required, and (d) three bus line status inputs to each 8255 are also required. As a substitute for the somewhat difficult to obtain IEEE 488 bus transceivers, 74LS05 open-collector bus drivers are employed. Each bus line is pulled up to 5 volts with a 3-kilohm resistor and down to ground with a 6.2-kilohm resistor; these are the values recommended by the IEEE Standard 488-1978[30]. A 74LS04 chip inverts the bus signal back to positive logic before it enters an input port bit on each 8255 chip.

The three IEEE 488 handshake lines are called DAV, NRFD, and NDAC. DAV, or Data Available, corresponds to bits PC0/PB0 in Fig. 9-59; NRFD, or Not Ready For Data, corresponds to bits PC1/PB1; and NDAC, or Not Data ACcepted, corresponds to bits PC2/PB2. The handshake flag and status bytes are shown in Fig. 9-60.

To transfer a data byte from one microcomputer to the other, not all of the flag bits (PC0, PC1, and PC2) or bus line status input bits (PB0, PB1, and PB2) are used on a given 8255 chip. For example, assume that the microcomputer on the left in Fig. 9-59 is the talker, and the one on the right, the listener. The talker outputs the DAV flag and inputs the status of the NRFD and NDAC bus lines. Thus, the microcomputer on the left outputs bit PC0 (DAV) and inputs/tests bits PB1 (NRFD) and PB2 (NDAC). The listener outputs NRFD to bit PC1, NDAC to bit PC2, and inputs/tests bit PB0 (DAV). Now assume that the direction of data transfer is reversed, with the microcomputer on the right talking to the listener on the left. This time, the microcomputer on the right outputs bit PC0 and test bits PB1 and PB2, whereas the microcomputer on the left outputs bits PC1 and PC2 and tests bit PB0. Data transfer can be in only one direction at a time. The use of

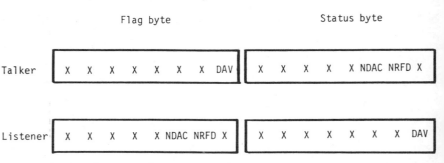

Fig. 9-60. Three-wire handshake protocol: definitions of flag and status bytes.
X indicates that the logic state of the indicated bit is irrelevant.

such bused flags permits bidirectional data transfer between any number of devices that are tied to data lines PA0 to PA7 and to the DAV, NRFD, and NDAC bus lines shown in Fig. 9-59.

Fig. 9-61 is the same as Fig. 9-58, only now a series of circled numbers is assigned to important points on the timing diagrams for the seven signals given. Shown are the data bus, DIO1 to DIO8, which corresponds to data lines PA0 to PA7 in Fig. 9-59; the DAV flag (bits PB0 and PC0 in Fig. 9-59); the NRFD flag (bits PB1 and PC1); the

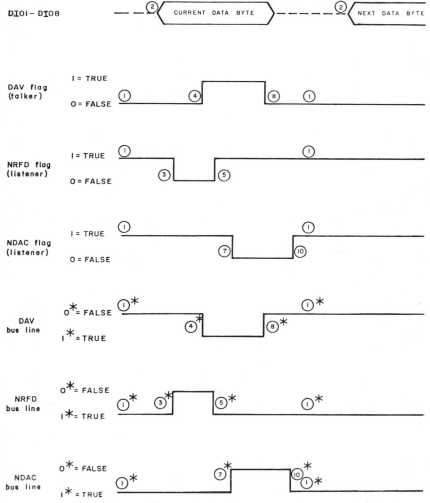

Fig. 9-61. Three-wire handshake protocol: timing diagrams. Diagrams for the three device flags as well as for the three hardware bus lines are shown.

NDAC flag (bits PB2 and PC2); and the DAV, NRFD, and NDAC bus lines, which are located at the intersection of the outputs of the 74LS05 open-collector bus drivers in Fig. 9-59.

The series of circled numbers in Fig. 9-61 corresponds to the circled numbers on the flowchart diagrams in Fig. 9-62 for talker (source) and listener (acceptor) 8080A-based microcomputers participating in the IEEE 488 3-wire handshake data communication protocol. Fig. 9-62 corresponds directly to Fig. B2, "Logical Flow of Events for Source and Acceptor When Transferring Data Using Handshake Process," on page 70 of the IEEE Standard 488-1978. Except for the consolidation of series process blocks, every process block or decision symbol in Fig. 9-62 has a one-to-one correspondence with a similar block or decision symbol in Fig. B2. The only difference between the two figures is the series of circled numbers used; in Fig. 9-62, the numbers correspond to those in Fig. 9-61, whereas in Fig. B2, the numbers correspond to those in Fig. B1, which is also a series of timing diagrams. Transferring 64 bytes of data from the memory of the talker to the same memory locations of the listener is the objective of the programs listed in Fig. 9-62. The memory block for each microcomputer starts at location 0380H and terminates at 03BFH, as it did in Examples 1, 2, and 3.

It is appropriate to discuss here the relationship between the logic states and logic transitions in Fig. 9-61 and the microcomputer instructions in Fig. 9-62. Assume that the talker (source) is on the left and the listener (acceptor) is on the right in Fig. 9-59. In Fig. 9-62, the flowchart for the talker is on the left, and that for the listener is on the right. By location ① both the talker and listener microcomputers have been initialized. This means that port A for the talker 8255 chip is initialized to be an output port, and port A for the listener 8255 chip is initialized to be an input port. (Note that at a later time, the talker and listener roles in Fig. 9-59 could be reversed. This presents no problem since the 8255 chip is programmable. Such a change in roles would not be possible if nonprogrammable chips, such as the 74LS244 3-state octal buffer and the 74LS373 octal D-type latch chips, were used.) Also, PC0 (DAV) is initialized so that the DAV bus line is at logic 0*; PC1 (NRFD) is initialized so that the NRFD bus line is at logic 1*; and PC2 (NDAC) is initialized so that the NDAC bus line is also at logic 1*. Since both the talker and listener 8255 chips contribute to the logic states of the DAV, NRFD, and NDAC bus signals, the correct output bytes to ports C must be picked. In this case, the talker outputs F8H to port C, whereas the listener outputs FEH to its port C. Asterisks (*) are used to distinguish between a positive-logic flag output or status input, and a negative-logic IEEE 488 bus signal.

An attractive feature of the 3-wire handshake protocol is that either talker or listener can be started first. If the talker is started before the listener is ready, NRFD = 0* and NDAC = 0*, and the talker halts.

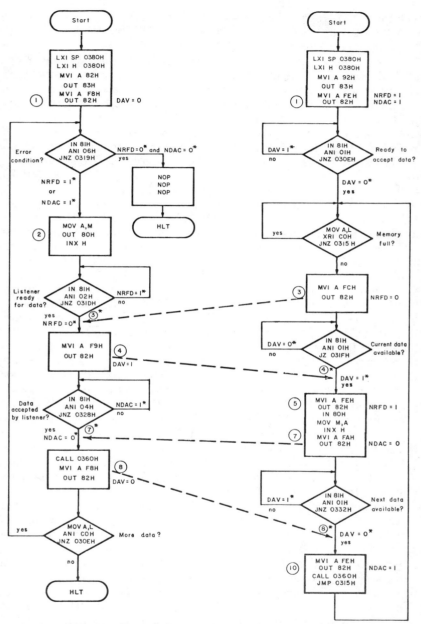

Fig. 9-62. Three-wire handshake protocol: flowchart and assembly language programs for talker and listener. The asterisk (*) indicates the testing of the status of an IEEE 488 hardware bus line signal.

425

The three NOP instructions in the talker flowchart are provided so that a JMP 0319H instruction can be placed to bypass the HLT instruction. If the listener is started before the talker is ready, DAV = 1*, and the listener is trapped in a loop. For the purposes of the experiment described here, we have ignored the situation when either of the 8255 chips has just been reset and port C is no longer an output port; the programs work well, but no attempt has been made to detect the 8255 reset condition.

At location ② the talker outputs a data byte to data lines PA0 to PA7. Prior to location ③, the listener checks whether or not its memory block is full (YES if all 64 bytes have been transferred from talker to listener). If the answer is NO, the listener at point ③ resets NRFD = 0, indicating that it is ready for data, and then waits for DAV = 1*. At point ③ *, the talker detects NRFD = 0* and thus passes to point ④, where it sets DAV = 1 and thus informs the listener that data is available. Finally, the talker proceeds to a loop, where it waits for the NDAC = 0* condition. The listener detects the DAV = 1* condition at point ④ *, sets NRFD = 1 at point ⑤ to indicate that it is not ready for the next data byte, inputs the data from data lines PA0 to PA7, stores the data byte in memory, and increments the memory pointer. At point ⑦, the listener resets NDAC = 0, indicating that it has accepted the data. Finally, the listener proceeds to a loop and waits for the DAV = 0* condition. The talker at point ⑦ * detects the NDAC = 0* condition, calls a subroutine (placed in the program to permit experimentation with a time delay in the talker program), resets DAV = 0 at point ⑧ to indicate to the listener that data is no longer available, tests the memory pointer to determine if more data must be transmitted, and, finally, if the answer is YES, jumps to the loop that tests for an error condition. At point ⑧ *, the listener detects the DAV = 0* condition, and at point ⑩ sets NDAC = 1 to indicate to the talker that it has not accepted the next data byte. The listener then calls a subroutine (also placed in the program to permit experimentation with a time delay in the listener program), and jumps to the loop that tests for the memory full condition.

The time required by the listener to input a single byte of data, that is, the time needed to execute one full pass through its program, was measured for a pair of 8080A-based microcomputers that were both operating at 0.75 MHz. With no delay in either program (a RET instruction at location 0360H), either 379 or 451 μs were required to make a single pass through the listener program. With a 9.53-ms time delay in the talker program, either 9.881 or 9.954 ms were required. With a 9.53-ms time delay in the listener program, 9.891, 9.927, or 9.964 ms were required. Lastly, with 9.53-ms delays in both programs, 19.394 ms, 19.430 ms, or 19.466 ms were required for the transfer of a single data byte from talker to listener. The variations in the preceding figures for a given choice of timing conditions are multiples of 36 μs, which correspond, for microcomputers operating at 0.75 MHz, to 27 machine cycles. Since any of the bit-testing loops consists of IN, ANI, JNZ or JZ instructions that add up to exactly 27 machine cycles, the 36-μs variation is easily understood.

Another example of a software IEEE 488 handshaking protocol is provided by Young[32]. His article helps to develop an understanding of other aspects of the IEEE 488 bus standard by giving bus protocol software listings, reduced state diagrams for the bus controller, and application subroutines.

THE 8255 SEMAPHORES

Since most of the newer microcomputer boards and single-chip microcomputers contain some type of programmable parallel interface port, it is increasingly likely, when interfacing two microcomputers, that you will do it via such a port. One of the more popular programmable parallel interface chips is the Intel 8255, which contains 24 input/output lines and exhibits three different modes of operation: (a) mode 0, unconditional input or output; (b) mode 1, conditional unidirectional input or output; and (c) mode 2, conditional bidirectional input/output. Depending upon how the 8255 is programmed, various combinations of modes 0, 1, and 2 ports can be selected.[26] This section describes the characteristics of the three semaphores present within the chip.

Results presented here were obtained experimentally with two 8080A based microcomputers interfaced to each other via port A of an 8255 chip operated in the mode 2 (port A) and mode 1 (port B) configurations. (The details of the interface circuit and programs have been given in Example 2.) Rather than execute the programs at 2 MHz, each machine cycle on each computer was executed single step using the hardware single-step circuit shown in Fig. 6-21. The logic states of the $\overline{RD}$, $\overline{WR}$, $\overline{ACKA}$, $\overline{STBA}$, $\overline{OBFA}$, and IBFA signals were determined with a logic probe.

The three 8255 semaphores acted identically. Their truth table (Fig. 9-63A) is compared to the truth table (Fig. 9-63B) for a 7474 D-type positive edge triggered flip-flop with preset and clear (Fig. 9-63C). There is one difference between the two tables (Figs. 9-63A and 9-63B): Q is logic 1 for the semaphore and is Q_o for the 7474 flip-flop when PRESET is at logic 1 and CLOCK is at logic 0. This difference in behavior is unexpected. A semaphore that behaves as a 7474 flip-flop should be acceptable.

Shown in Fig. 9-64 is a comparison of the timing diagrams for the 8255 semaphores and the 7474 flip-flop. The asynchronous PRESET input causes output Q to go to a logic 1 state for both flip-flops. Any ad-

PRESET	CLOCK	Q
0	X	1
1	0	1
1	↑	0

(A) Truth table for an 8255 semaphore.

PRESET	CLOCK	Q
0	X	1
1	0	Q_0
1	↑	0

(B) Truth table for a 7474 D-type edge-triggered latch (flip-flop).

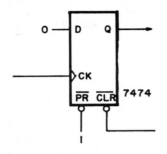

(C) A 7474 D-type edge-triggered latch.

Fig. 9-63. Truth table comparison. The up-arrow symbol (↑) represents a transition from 0 to 1 at the CK input. X indicates that either logic state is acceptable, and Q_0 is the level of Q before the indicated input conditions were established.

ditional negative PRESET pulses that occur while Q is at logic 1 have no effect. The difference in behavior occurs with the synchronous CLOCK input. For the semaphore, the positive edge of the CLOCK

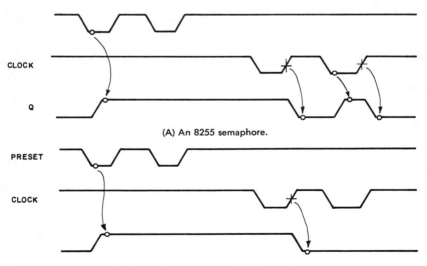

(A) An 8255 semaphore.

(B) A 7474 D-type positive-edge triggered latch.

Fig. 9-64. Timing diagram comparison.

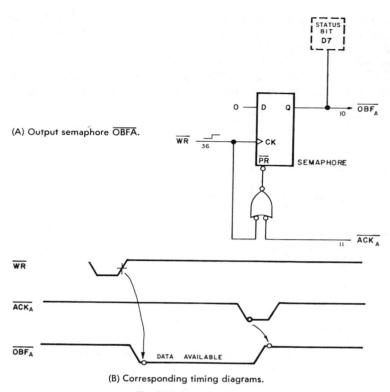

(A) Output semaphore $\overline{\text{OBFA}}$.

(B) Corresponding timing diagrams.

Fig. 9-65. 8255 port A.

input always causes a 1-to-0 transition in Q, whereas for the 7474, the 1-to-0 transition occurs only if Q is at a logic 1.

When operated in the mode 2 configuration, port A on the 8255 chip is an excellent example of bidirectional conditional input/output. The port itself is a bidirectional buffer that has both input and output semaphores associated with it. The two semaphores and the semaphore timing diagrams for I/O operations are summarized in Figs. 9-65 and 9-66. Fig. 9-65A shows the output semaphore for the bidirectional port A. A negative $\overline{\text{WR}}$ pulse at pin 36 on the 8255 clears $\overline{\text{OBFA}}$ and outputs data from the 8080A to port A. An acknowledge signal, $\overline{\text{ACKA}}$, from the I/O device sets $\overline{\text{OBFA}}$ (Fig. 9-65B). The input semaphore is shown in Fig. 9-66A. A negative $\overline{\text{RD}}$ pulse at pin 5 clears IBFA and permits the 8080A to input data from port A. A strobe signal, $\overline{\text{STBA}}$, from the I/O device sets IBFA and causes port A to latch a new data byte (Fig. 9-66B).

The OR gate symbols at the PRESET input of the semaphores in Figs. 9-65A and 9-66A have been added to account for the difference in behavior between the semaphores and the 7474 flip-flop, as discussed previously. Negative logic is used for the OR gate; a logic 0 at either of the two OR gate inputs produces a logic 0 output that presets the semaphore. Thus, if $\overline{WR}$ or $\overline{ACKA}$ is 0, then $\overline{OBFA}$ is set. If $\overline{RD}$ or $\overline{STBA}$ is 0, then IBFA is set. With this OR gate representation, the behavior of these two semaphores is consistent with the truth table in

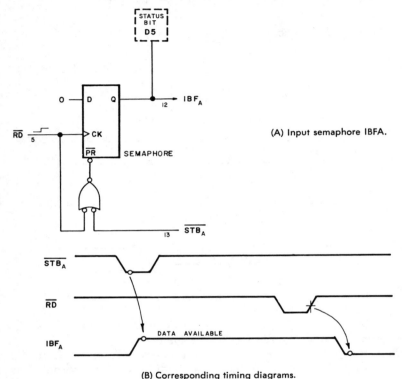

(A) Input semaphore IBFA.

(B) Corresponding timing diagrams.

Fig. 9-66. 8255 port A.

Fig. 9-63A and the timing diagrams in Fig. 9-64. In practice, would negative $\overline{RD}$ or $\overline{WR}$ pulses ever cause IBFA or $\overline{OBFA}$ to be set during the input or output machine cycles, respectively, of the 8080A microcomputer that is interfaced to the 8255? This situation is unlikely because there would never be an attempt to read data from an empty input buffer (IBFA at logic 0) or to output data to a full output buffer ($\overline{OBFA}$ at logic 0).

Port B on the 8255 chip can be operated as a conditional input or output port with semaphore, but not as a bidirectional conditional I/O port. Bit D1 in the control word determines the I/O characteristics of this port, with logic 1 selecting input and logic 0 selecting output. The port B semaphore has the same truth table, timing characteristics, and configuration as shown for the port A semaphores in Figs. 9-63 to 9-66. The difference is that the clock input (CK) to the semaphore is more complex than simply $CK = \overline{RD}$ or $CK = \overline{WR}$, which is the case for the port A semaphores. For the port B semaphore, the CK input exhibits the following logic, $CK = \overline{CD1} \cdot \overline{WR} + CD1 \cdot \overline{RD} + \overline{CD1} \cdot \overline{RD}$, where CD1 represents the logic 1 state of the D1 control bit, $\overline{CD1}$ represents the logic 0 state, and $\cdot$ and $+$ represent the AND and OR logic operations, respectively. A negative $\overline{WR}$ pulse produces a negative CK pulse only if control bit D1 is logic 0. A negative $\overline{RD}$ pulse produces a negative CK pulse no matter whether control bit D1 is logic 0 or logic 1. Consequently, the logic for CK can be simplified to $CK = \overline{CD1} \cdot \overline{WR} + \overline{RD}$, an expression that can be verified experimentally.

References

The references that are cited by superscripts in this book are as follows:

1. Charles L. Garfinkel, of Keithley Instruments, Inc., is the originator of this definition.
2. Donald Eadie, *Introduction to the Basic Computer,* Prentice-Hall, Inc., Englewood Cliffs, New Jersey, 1973.
3. Texas Instruments, Inc., *Microprocessor Handbook,* Dallas, Texas, 1975.
4. Rudolf F. Graf, *Modern Dictionary of Electronics,* Howard W. Sams & Company, Inc., Indianapolis, 1977.
5. Microdata Corp., *Microprogramming Handbook,* Santa Ana, California, 1971.
6. Abraham Marcus and John D. Lenk, *Computers for Technicians,* Prentice-Hall, Inc., Englewood Cliffs, New Jersey, 1973.
7. Intel Corp., *Intel 8080 Assembly Language Programming Manual,* Santa Clara, California, 1974.
8. Intel Corp., *Intel Intellec 8/Mod 80 Microcomputer Development System Reference Manual,* Santa Clara, California, 1975.
9. Intel Corp., *Intel 8080 Microcomputer Systems User's Manual,* Santa Clara, California, July, 1975.
10. J. Blukis and M. Baker, *Practical Digital Electronics,* Hewlett-Packard Company, Santa Clara, California, 1974.
11. *An Introduction to Microcomputers,* Adam Osborne and Associates, Inc., Berkeley, California, 1975.
12. The Intel literature is available from Intel Corporation, 3065 Bowers Avenue, Santa Clara, California 95051 [telephone: (408) 246-7051], or from their dealers, representatives, and distributors.

13. A. Osborne and J. Kane, *An Introduction to Microcomputers, Volume 2, Some Real Products*, Osborne/McGraw-Hill, Berkeley, CA, 1978, p. xlvii.
14. Charles J. Sippl and David A. Kidd, *Microcomputer Dictionary and Guide*, Matrix Publishers, Inc., Champaign, Illinois 1976.
15. J. D. Nicoud, *MicroScope* 1, April 1977.
16. *IEEE Standard Dictionary of Electrical and Electronics Terms*, Wiley-Interscience, New York, New York, 1972.
17. William I. Fletcher, *An Engineering Approach to Digital Design*, Prentice-Hall, Englewood Cliffs, New Jersey, 1980.
18. C. A. Ogdin, *Software Design for Microcomputers*, Prentice-Hall, Inc., Englewood Cliffs, New Jersey, 1978, p. 77.
19. R. C. Turner, *Real-Time Programming With Microcomputers*, D. C. Heath and Co., Lexington, Maine, 1978, p. 97.
20. R. Dowsing, "Structured Programming," *Introduction to Microprocessors*, Pitman Publishing/Academic Press, New York, New York, 1977, p. 97.
21. E. W. Dijkstra, "Structured Programming," *Classics in Software Engineering*, E. N. Yourdon, Ed., Yourdon Press, New York, New York, pp. 43-50. (Article originally appeared in a conference sponsored by the NATO Science Committee, Rome, Italy, October 1969 and was printed in *Software Engineering Concepts and Techniques*, Litton Educational Publishing, 1976.)
22. E. W. Dijkstra, "Go-To-Statement Considered Harmful," Letter to the Editor, *Communications of the ACM*, Volume 11 (3), March 1968, pp. 147-148.
23. E. Yourdon, Ed., *Classics in Software Engineering*, Yourdon Press, New York, New York, 1979.
24. R. Baumann, "Software-Entwicklung," *Elektroniker*, October 1977.
25. P. F. Goldsborough and P. R. Rony, *Microcomputer Interfacing with the 8255 PPI Chip*, Howard W. Sams & Co., Inc., Indianapolis, 1979, p. 52.
26. *Intel Peripheral Design Handbook*, Intel Corp., Santa Clara, California, 1979, pp. 1-52 to 1-72 and 2-114 to 2-144.
27. G. R. Samsen and R. D. Hudson, "Bus Adapter Simplifies Interprocessor Communication," *Computer Design*, December 1980, pp. 119-124.
28. R. M. Williams, "LSI Chips Ease Standard 488 Bus Interfacing," *Computer Design*, October 1979, pp. 123-131.
29. J. Pieper and R. J. Grossi, "LSI Streamlines Instrument Interface with Standard IEEE-488 Bus," *Electronics*, April 26, 1979, pp. 145-150.
30. *IEEE Standard Digital Interface for Programmable Instrumentation*, IEEE, Inc., New York, New York, November 30, 1978.

31. D. W. Ricci and G. E. Nelson, "Standard Instrument Interface Simplifies System Design," *Electronics,* November 14, 1974, pp. 95-106.
32. R. Young, "Implementing an IEEE-488 Bus Controller with Microprocessor Software," *IEEE Trans. on IECI,* IECI-27 (1), February 1980, pp. 10-15.
33. *Condensed Description of the Hewlett-Packard Interface Bus,* Hewlett-Packard Co., Loveland, Colorado, March 1975, p. 9.
34. *Getting Aboard the 488-1975 Bus,* Motorola Semiconductor Products Inc., Phoenix, Arizona, p. 14.
35. E. Fisher and C. W. Jensen, *PET and the IEEE 488 Bus (GPIB),* Osborne/McGraw Hill, Berkeley, California, 1980.
36. J. Kane and A. Osborne, *An Introduction to Microcomputers, Volume 3: Some Real Support Devices,* Osborne/McGraw-Hill, Berkeley, California, 1978-9, pp. J5-1 to J5-9.
37. S. Leibson, "The Standard Interface," *Keyboard,* Hewlett-Packard Desktop Computer Div., Fort Collins, Colorado, July 1979, pp. 8-11.
38. *Intel Peripheral Design Handbook,* Intel Corp., Santa Clara, CA, 1979, pp. 1-231.

The 8080A Instruction Set

This appendix summarizes all of the important characteristics of each instruction in the 8080A instruction set: the number of machine cycles, the number of states, the type of memory addressing, and the flags that are influenced upon execution of the instruction. In addition, the available literature on 8080A microcomputer programming and interfacing is briefly reviewed.

MICROCOMPUTER PROGRAMMING

Unless you have a background in computer science or possess a special knack for computer programming, you will probably find machine level and assembly language programming somewhat tedious and difficult initially. In time, you will become sufficiently familiar with the 8080 instruction set, available software, and programming tricks to be able to write programs of modest size with little effort. You will be able to apply skills that you have learned with the 8080 instruction set to other instruction sets.

So much has happened since the first introduction to Appendix 2 was written in 1976 (see the first edition of this book if you can find a copy) that it is difficult to know where to begin. Five years ago, there were few available books on microcomputers, the manufacturer's literature was very important, and the first hobby microcomputer magazine—*Byte*—had just been introduced. FORTRAN, COBOL, and PASCAL were not available in 8080 code. Hobby computing was in its infancy.

How the situation has changed. There are now a multitude of magazines devoted exclusively to microcomputers and personal computers, including *Byte, Kilobaud, 80 Microcomputing, Micro, Compute, Personal Computing, IEEE Micro, Microprocessors and Microsystems, Microprocessing and Microprogramming, Dr. Dobb's Journal,* and *Interface Age.* Microcomputer textbooks represent a growth industry; new microcomputer or personal computer books are being published at the rate of one every two weeks. Library shelves are overflowing, and it is difficult to keep up with the tide of new texts.

What actions can be recommended to you? First, as was pointed out in the first edition, you probably will need to learn some assembly language programming. Simple programs—especially programs known as "device drivers," which handle the I/O operations between a personal computer and a printer—often can be written as easily and quickly in assembly language as they can in a high-level language. More important, however, is the fact that such programs are executed more quickly, require less memory, and often are absolutely necessary if high-speed data transfer is required. It is difficult to transfer data between a personal computer and another computer at 9600 baud using a BASIC interpreter program as your driver. You will need to learn assembly language programming in order to understand other assembly language programs that receive widespread distribution. A knowledge of assembly language programming provides a basis both for understanding how a microprocessor works and for comparing instruction sets.

SOURCES OF 8080 PROGRAMMING AND INTERFACING INFORMATION

There are so many magazines, books, and software packages available today that it is difficult to know where to start. Perhaps the best that can be done is to list some of the available sources of information.

INTEL CORPORATION

Several of the Intel Corporation manuals should be in your library if you plan to develop interface circuits. Consider the following:

1. *Intel Component Data Catalog,* Intel Corporation, 3065 Bowers Avenue, Santa Clara, California 95051, January 1981.
2. *Intel Peripheral Design Handbook,* August 1980.
3. *Intel Memory Design Handbook,* 1977 (or more recent manual).
4. *Intel E2Prom Family Applications Handbook,* April 1981.
5. *Intel MCS-85 User's Manual,* June 1977 (or more recent manual).
6. *Intel 8080 Microcomputer Systems User's Manual,* September 1975 (or more recent manual; I like the 1975 edition).

7. *Intel 8080/8085 Assembly Language Programming,* 1979.
8. *Intel Systems Data Catalog,* 1980.

OSBORNE/McGRAW-HILL

Some of the best reference books on microcomputers have been published by Osborne, who sold his company to McGraw-Hill in the early 1980s. The assembly language programming volumes written by Lance Leventhal are special favorites.

1. Lance A. Leventhal, *8080A/8085 Assembly Language Programming,* Osborne/McGraw-Hill, 630 Bancroft Way, Berkeley, California 94710, 1978.
2. Lance A. Leventhal, *Z80 Assembly Language Programming,* 1979.
3. Adam Osborne and Gerry Kane, *Osborne 4 & 8-Bit Microprocessor Handbook,* 1981.
4. Jerry Kane and Adam Osborne, *An Introduction to Microcomputers: Volume 3—Some Real Support Devices,* 1978.
5. Gerry Kane, *CRT Controller Handbook,* 1980.
6. Thom Hogan, *Osborne CP/M User Guide,* 1981.
7. Adam Osborne, *An Introduction to Microcomputers: Volume 1— Basic Concepts, Second Edition,* 1980.
8. David M. Auslander and Paul Sagues, *Microprocessors for Measurement and Control,* 1981.

ZENITH

An excellent personal computer is the Zenith Z-89. The available software from Zenith is particularly interesting: the entire source listing for HDOS can be purchased. If you have time and funds, this is one way to learn the basic principles behind the development of an operating system. Summarized below are the 8080 listings—in source code and assembled octal code—and other information that are available from Zenith.

1. *How to Program Your Microcomputer in Assembly Language* (Separate text, Student Workbook, and Instructor's Guide), Heath Company, Benton Harbor, Michigan 49022, 1980.
2. *Model Z19 Video Terminal Operation Manual,* 1980.
3. *H19 ROM Source Code* (For Z19 Videl Terminal), 1980.
4. *Model Z89 Digital Computer Operation Manual,* 1980.
5. *Monitor MTR-88 Operation Manual and Source Code* (For HDOS 1.6), 1980.
6. *Monitor MTR-89 Operation Manual and Source Code* (For HDOS 2.0), 1980.
7. *HDOS System Programmer's Guide:* (1) Software Reference Manual, (2) General Operations and H17 ROM Code Listing, (3) DBUG, Console Debugger, (4) EDIT, Heath Text Editor, (5)

ASM, Heath Assembly Language, (6) Extended Benton Harbor BASIC, 1980.

8. *HDOS Source Listing, Volume 1:* (1) System I/O Handler, (2) HDOSOVL2, Mount/Dismount Overlay, (3) SYSCMD, System Command Processor, (4) PIP, Peripheral Interchange Program, 1980.

9. *HDOS Source Listing, Volume 2:* (1) NDDVD, No Device Driver, (2) ATDVD, AT: Device Driver, (3) LPDVD, Line Printer Device Driver, (4) DBDVD, Diablo Device Driver, (5) SYDD, H17 Mini-Floppy Device Driver, 1980.

10. *HDOS Source Listing, Volume 3:* (1) SET, Set System Parameters, (2) FLAGS, Set and Clear Program Flags, (3) NECOPY, Transfer Disk File, (4) PATCH, Patch System and User Files, (5) INIT, Initialize Disk, (6) SYSGEN, System Generation, (7) TEST, Floppy Disk Diagnostic, 1980.

11. *HDOS Source Listing, Volume 4:* (1) EDIT, Heath HDOS Text Editor, (2) ASM, Assembler, (3) DBUG, Heath/Wintek Terminal Debugger, (4) BASIC, Wintek BASIC Interpreter, 1980.

12. *Full Screen Editor* (PIE: Programma Improved Editor, by Thomas Crosley and Walt Bilofsky), 1980 (available from the Software Toolworks, 14478 Glorietta Drive, Sherman Oaks, CA 91423.

Additional software packages and occasional software listings are available through (a) Heath User's Group, Hilltop Road, St. Joseph, Michigan 49085, and (b) BUSS, 325 Pennsylvania Avenue, S.E., Washington, D.C. 20003.

PRENTICE-HALL

Prentice-Hall is probably the most active publisher of microcomputer textbooks among the established publishers (Wiley, McGraw-Hill, Prentice-Hall, Addison Wesley, Harper and Row, etc.). It is interesting to note how effective the newcomers—such as Osborne, Sybex, and even E&L Instruments—to the publishing industry have been. There is a lesson to be learned regarding the inability of major publishers to respond in the mid-1970s to the enormous demand for books on microcomputers. There are some outstanding books in the following list:

1. William I. Fletcher, *An Engineering Approach to Digital Design,* Prentice-Hall, Inc., Englewood Cliffs, New Jersey 07632, 1980.
2. Lance A. Leventhal, *Introduction to Microprocessors: Software, Hardware, Programming,* 1978.
3. Edwin E. Klingman, *Microprocessor Systems Design,* 1977.
4. Lance Leventhal and Colin Walsh, *Microcomputer Experimentation With the Intel SDK-85,* 1980.
5. F. G. Duncan, *Microprocessor Programming and Software Devel-*

opment, Prentice-Hall International Series in Computer Science (C.A.R. Hoare, Series Editor), 1979.

6. Kenneth L. Short, *Microprocessors and Programmed Logic,* 1981.
7. Bruce A. Artwick, *Microcomputer Interfacing,* 1980.
8. George D. Kraft and Wing N. Toy, *Mini/Microcomputer Hardware Design,* 1979.
9. Carol Anne Ogdin, *Microcomputer Design,* 1978.
10. Carol Anne Ogdin, *Software Design for Microcomputers,* 1978.
11. John L. Hilburn and Paul M. Julich, *Microcomputers/Microprocessors: Hardware, Software, and Applications,* 1976.

McGRAW-HILL

1. John B. Peatman, *Microcomputer-Based Design,* McGraw-Hill Book Company, New York, New York, 1977.
2. Richard S. Sandige, *Digital Concepts Using Standard Integrated Circuits,* 1978.
3. Douglas V. Hall, *Microprocessors and Digital Systems,* 1980.
4. Harry Garland, *Introduction to Microprocessor System Design,* 1979.

HOWARD W. SAMS & CO., INC.

Thanks are extended to Howard W. Sams & Co., Inc. for publishing the first edition of this book way back in 1977. Since then, as you know, they have added many other microcomputer books to their series. The 8080/8085 Software Design books have a large number of interesting and useful programs. Insider information has been employed to indicate who actually wrote the listed books.

1. Peter R. Rony, *Introductory Experiments in Digital Electronics and 8080A Microcomputer Programming and Interfacing, Books 1 and 2,* Howard W. Sams & Co., Inc., 4300 W. 62nd Street, P. O. Box 7092, Indianapolis, Indiana 46206, 1977.
2. Elizabeth A. Nichols, Joseph C. Nichols, and Peter R. Rony, *Z-80 Microprocessor Programming and Interfacing, Books 1 and 2,* 1979.
3. Christopher A. Titus, *8080/8085 Software Design, Books 1 and 2,* 1978.
4. Jonathan A. Titus, *Microcomputer-Analog Converter Software and Hardware Interfacing,* 1978.
5. William Barden, Jr., *The Z-80 Microcomputer Handbook,* 1978.
6. Peter R. Rony, *Interfacing & Scientific Data Communications Experiments,* 1979.

DILITHIUM PRESS

1. Howard Boyet, *8080 Microcomputer Experiments,* dilithium Press, 30 N.W. 23d Place, Portland, Oregon 97210, 1978.

2. Ron Santore, *8080 Machine Language Programming for Beginners*, 1978.

E&L INSTRUMENTS

Thanks are extended to E&L Instruments, Inc. for publishing *Microcomputer Interfacing Experiments Using the Mark 80 Microcomputer, an 8080 System*, the predecessor manuscript to this book, in 1975. E&L markets private-label editions—called *Technibooks*—of a number of Howard W. Sams books, including books 1, 3, 4, and 6 in the Howard W. Sams listing above, as well as the experimental hardware described in Chapter 2 of this book.

1. Howard Boyet and Ron Katz, *Applications Experiments with an 8080/8085 Microprocessor-Microcontroller, Volumes 1 and 2*, E&L Instruments, Inc., 61 First Street, Derby, Connecticut 06418, 1979.

SYBEX

1. Rodnay Zaks, *How to Program the Z80*, Sybex, 2344 Sixth Street, Berkeley, California 94710, 1980.
2. Rodnay Zaks, *The CP/M Handbook*, 1980.

OTHER PUBLISHERS

1. William S. Bennett and Carl F. Evert, Jr., *What Every Engineer Should Know about Microcomputers*, Marcel Dekker, Inc., New York, New York, 1980.
2. Michael Slater and Barry Bronson, *Practical Microprocessors*, Hewlett-Packard Company, 5301 Stevens Creek Blvd., Santa Clara, California, 95050, 1980.
3. John F. Wakerly, *Logic Design Projects Using Standard Integrated Circuits*, John Wiley & Sons, New York, New York, 1976.
4. W. J. Weller, A. V. Shatzel, and H. Y. Nice, *Practical Microcomputer Programming: The Intel 8080*, Northern Technology Books, P. O. Box 62, Evanston, Illinois 60204, 1976.
5. Guthikonda V. Rao, *Microprocessors and Microcomputer Systems*, Van Nostrand Reinhold Company, New York, New York, 1978.
1. Rodnay Zaks, *How to Program the Z80*, Sybex, 2344 Sixth Street,
6. Don L. Cannon and Gerald Luecke, *Understanding Microcomputers*, Texas Instruments Learning Center, P. O. Box 225012 MS-54, Dallas, Texas 75265 (book available also from Radio Shack).
7. John G. Wester and William D. Simpson, *Software Design for Microprocessors*, Texas Instruments Learning Center, 1976.
8. Kathe Spracklen, *Z-80 and 8080 Assembly Language Programming*, Hayden Book Company, Inc., Rochelle Park, New Jersey, 1979.
9. Microelectronics, *Scientific American 237* (3), September 1977.
10. Electronics Revolution, *Science 195*, No. 4283 (March 18, 1977).

11. M. Rafiquzzaman, *Microcomputer Theory and Applications With the Intel SDK-85,* John Wiley & Sons, New York, NY, 1982.

MAGAZINES

1. *BYTE,* BYTE Publications, Inc., 70 Main St., Peterborough, NH 03458.
2. *Computer Design,* 11 Goldsmith Street, Littleton, MA 01460.
3. *Dr. Dobb's Journal,* People's Computer Company, Box E, 1263 El Camino Real, Menlo Park, CA 94025.
4. *EDN,* Cahners Publishing Company, 221 Columbus Avenue, Boston, MA 02116.
5. *Electronics,* McGraw-Hill, Inc., 1221 Avenue of the Americas, New York, NY 10020.
6. *Elektor,* Elektor Publishers Ltd., File No. 1504, 1000 W. Temple, Los Angeles, CA 90074.
7. *Interface Age,* McPheters, Wolfe & Jones, 16704 Marquardt Avenue, Cerritos, CA 90701.
8. *80 Microcomputing,* 1001001 Inc., 80 Pine Street, Peterborough, NH 03458.
9. *Popular Computing,* 70 Main St., Peterborough, NH 03458.
10. *Radio-Electronics,* Gernsback Publications, Inc., 200 Park Avenue South, New York, NY 10003.
11. *IEEE MICRO,* IEEE Computer Society, 10662 Los Vaqueros Circle, Los Alamitos, CA 90720.

DESCRIPTION OF INDIVIDUAL 8080 INSTRUCTIONS

We now shall proceed to describe the 8080 instruction set in detail. We shall use material from both the *Intel 8080 Microcomputer Systems User's Manual* and the *μCOM-8 Software Manual,* courtesy of Intel Corporation and NEC Microcomputers, Inc., respectively. For your use, several pages are provided from the Intel manual to help you understand the significance of the terms, symbols, and abbreviations used in the description of each instruction. Intel groups the 8080 instructions as:

- DATA TRANSFER GROUP: Move data between registers or between memory and registers
- ARITHMETIC GROUP: Add, subtract, increment, or decrement data in registers or in memory
- LOGICAL GROUPS: AND, OR, exclusive-OR, compare, rotate, or complement data in registers in memory.
- BRANCH GROUP: Conditional and unconditional jump instructions, subroutine call instructions, and return instructions.

- STACK, I/O, AND MACHINE CONTROL GROUP: Includes I/O instructions, as well as instructions for maintaining the stack and internal control flags.

INSTRUCTION SET

A computer, no matter how sophisticated, can only do what it is "told" to do. One "tells" the computer what to do via a series of coded instructions referred to as a **Program**. The realm of the programmer is referred to as **Software**, in contrast to the **Hardware** that comprises the actual computer equipment. A computer's software refers to all of the programs that have been written for that computer.

When a computer is designed, the engineers provide the Central Processing Unit (CPU) with the ability to perform a particular set of operations. The CPU is designed such that a specific operation is performed when the CPU control logic decodes a particular instruction. Consequently, the operations that can be performed by a CPU define the computer's **Instruction Set**.

Each computer instruction allows the programmer to initiate the performance of a specific operation. All computers implement certain arithmetic operations in their instruction set, such as an instruction to add the contents of two registers. Often logical operations (e.g., OR the contents of two registers) and register operate instructions (e.g., increment a register) are included in the instruction set. A computer's instruction set will also have instructions that move data between registers, between a register and memory, and between a register and an I/O device. Most instruction sets also provide **Conditional Instructions**. A conditional instruction specifies an operation to be performed only if certain conditions have been met; for example, jump to a particular instruction if the result of the last operation was zero. Conditional instructions provide a program with a decision-making capability.

By logically organizing a sequence of instructions into a coherent program, the programmer can "tell" the computer to perform a very specific and useful function.

The computer, however, can only execute programs whose instructions are in a binary coded form (i.e., a series of 1's and 0's), that is called **Machine Code**. Because it would be extremely cumbersome to program in machine code, programming languages have been developed. There are programs available which convert the programming language instructions into machine code that can be interpreted by the processor.

One type of programming language is **Assembly Language**. A unique assembly language mnemonic is assigned to each of the computer's instructions. The programmer can write a program (called the **Source Program**) using these mnemonics and certain operands; the source program is then converted into machine instructions (called the **Object Code**). Each assembly language instruction is converted into one machine code instruction (1 or more bytes) by an **Assembler** program. Assembly languages are usually machine dependent (i.e., they are usually able to run on only one type of computer).

THE 8080 INSTRUCTION SET

The 8080 instruction set includes five different types of instructions:

- **Data Transfer Group** — move data between registers or between memory and registers
- **Arithmetic Group** — add, subtract, increment or decrement data in registers or in memory
- **Logical Group** — AND, OR, EXCLUSIVE-OR, compare, rotate or complement data in registers or in memory
- **Branch Group** — conditional and unconditional jump instructions, subroutine call instructions and return instructions
- **Stack, I/O and Machine Control Group** — includes I/O instructions, as well as instructions for maintaining the stack and internal control flags.

Instruction and Data Formats:

Memory for the 8080 is organized into 8-bit quantities, called Bytes. Each byte has a unique 16-bit binary address corresponding to its sequential position in memory.

The 8080 can directly address up to 65,536 bytes of memory, which may consist of both read-only memory (ROM) elements and random-access memory (RAM) elements (read/write memory).

Data in the 8080 is stored in the form of 8-bit binary integers:

DATA WORD

D_7	D_6	D_5	D_4	D_3	D_2	D_1	D_0

MSB   LSB

When a register or data word contains a binary number, it is necessary to establish the order in which the bits of the number are written. In the Intel 8080, BIT 0 is referred to as the **Least Significant Bit (LSB)**, and BIT 7 (of an 8 bit number) is referred to as the **Most Significant Bit (MSB)**.

The 8080 program instructions may be one, two or three bytes in length. Multiple byte instructions must be stored in successive memory locations; the address of the first byte is always used as the address of the instructions. The exact instruction format will depend on the particular operation to be executed.

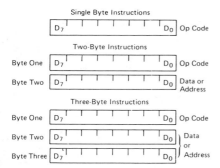

Addressing Modes:

Often the data that is to be operated on is stored in memory. When multi-byte numeric data is used, the data, like instructions, is stored in successive memory locations, with the least significant byte first, followed by increasingly significant bytes. The 8080 has four different modes for addressing data stored in memory or in registers:

- Direct — Bytes 2 and 3 of the instruction contain the exact memory address of the data item (the low-order bits of the address are in byte 2, the high-order bits in byte 3).

- Register — The instruction specifies the register or register-pair in which the data is located.

- Register Indirect — The instruction specifies a register-pair which contains the memory

address where the data is located (the high-order bits of the address are in the first register of the pair, the low-order bits in the second).

- Immediate — The instruction contains the data itself. This is either an 8-bit quantity or a 16-bit quantity (least significant byte first, most significant byte second).

Unless directed by an interrupt or branch instruction, the execution of instructions proceeds through consecutively increasing memory locations. A branch instruction can specify the address of the next instruction to be executed in one of two ways:

- Direct — The branch instruction contains the address of the next instruction to be executed. (Except for the 'RST' instruction, byte 2 contains the low-order address and byte 3 the high-order address.)

- Register indirect — The branch instruction indicates a register-pair which contains the address of the next instruction to be executed. (The high-order bits of the address are in the first register of the pair, the low-order bits in the second.)

The RST instruction is a special one-byte call instruction (usually used during interrupt sequences). RST includes a three-bit field; program control is transferred to the instruction whose address is eight times the contents of this three-bit field.

Condition Flags:

There are five condition flags associated with the execution of instructions on the 8080. They are Zero, Sign, Parity, Carry, and Auxiliary Carry, and are each represented by a 1-bit register in the CPU. A flag is "set" by forcing the bit to 1; "reset" by forcing the bit to 0.

Unless indicated otherwise, when an instruction affects a flag, it affects it in the following manner:

Zero: If the result of an instruction has the value 0, this flag is set; otherwise it is reset.

Sign: If the most significant bit of the result of the operation has the value 1, this flag is set; otherwise it is reset.

Parity: If the modulo 2 sum of the bits of the result of the operation is 0, (i.e., if the result has even parity), this flag is set; otherwise it is reset (i.e., if the result has odd parity).

Carry: If the instruction resulted in a carry (from addition), or a borrow (from subtraction or a comparison) out of the high-order bit, this flag is set; otherwise it is reset.

Auxiliary Carry: If the instruction caused a carry out of bit 3 and into bit 4 of the resulting value, the auxiliary carry is set; otherwise it is reset. This flag is affected by single precision additions, subtractions, increments, decrements, comparisons, and logical operations, but is principally used with additions and increments preceding a DAA (Decimal Adjust Accumulator) instruction.

Symbols and Abbreviations:

The following symbols and abbreviations are used in the subsequent description of the 8080 instructions:

SYMBOLS	MEANING
accumulator	Register A
addr	16-bit address quantity
data	8-bit data quantity
data 16	16-bit data quantity
byte 2	The second byte of the instruction
byte 3	The third byte of the instruction
port	8-bit address of an I/O device
r,r1,r2	One of the registers A,B,C,D,E,H,L
DDD,SSS	The bit pattern designating one of the registers A,B,C,D,E,H,L (DDD=destination, SSS= source):

DDD or SSS	REGISTER NAME
111	A
000	B
001	C
010	D
011	E
100	H
101	L

rp	One of the register pairs:

B represents the B,C pair with B as the high-order register and C as the low-order register;

D represents the D,E pair with D as the high-order register and E as the low-order register;

H represents the H,L pair with H as the high-order register and L as the low-order register;

SP represents the 16-bit stack pointer.

RP	The bit pattern designating one of the registers pair B,D,H,SP:

RP	REGISTER PAIR
00	B-C
01	D-E
10	H-L
11	SP

rh	The first (high-order) register of a designated register pair.
rl	The second (low-order) register of a designated register pair.
PC	16-bit program counter register (PCH and PCL are used to refer to the high-order and low-order 8 bits respectively).
SP	16-bit stack pointer register (SPH and SPL are used to refer to the high-order and low-order 8 bits respectively).
r_m	Bit m of the register r (bits are number 7 through 0 from left to right).
Z,S,P,CY,AC	The condition flags: Zero, Sign, Parity, Carry, and Auxiliary Carry, respectively.
( )	The contents of the memory location or registers enclosed in the parentheses.
←	"Is transferred to"
∧	Logical AND
∀	Exclusive OR
∨	Inclusive OR
+	Addition
−	Two's complement subtraction
*	Multiplication
←→	"Is exchanged with"
‾	The one's complement (e.g., $(\overline{A})$)
n	The restart number 0 through 7
NNN	The binary representation 000 through 111 for restart number 0 through 7 respectively.

Description Format:

The following pages provide a detailed description of the instruction set of the 8080. Each instruction is described in the following manner:

1. The MAC 80 assembler format, consisting of the instruction mnemonic and operand fields, is printed in **BOLDFACE** on left side of first line.

2. The name of the instruction is enclosed in parenthesis on the right side of the first line.

3. The next line(s) contain a symbolic description of the operation of the instruction.

4. This is followed by a narative description of the operation of the instruction.

5. The following line(s) contain the binary fields and patterns that comprise the machine instruction.

6. The last four lines contain incidental information about the execution of the instruction. The number of machine cycles and states required to execute the instruction are listed first. If the instruction has two possible execution times, as in a Conditional Jump, both times will be listed, separated by a slash. Next, any significant data addressing modes are listed. The last line lists any of the five Flags that are affected by the execution of the instruction.

DATA TRANSFER GROUP

This group of instructions transfers data to and from registers and memory. *Condition flags are not affected* by any instruction in this group.*

MOV r1, r2

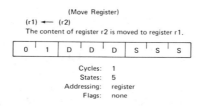

(Move Register)

(r1) ◄── (r2)

The content of register r2 is moved to register r1.

| 0 | 1 | D | D | D | S | S | S |

Cycles: 1
States: 5
Addressing: register
Flags: none

The MOV r1, r2 instruction transfers data from the specified source register S (or r2) to the specified destination register D (or r1). The source or destination may be any of the single registers B, C, D, H, or L, the accumulator A, and M (the contents of the memory address specified by the register pair H, L). In the three-octal-digit byte, the first digit is always a 1. The second and third octal digits vary depending upon the source and destination. The octal instruction, 166, is a halt rather than a MOV instruction. The contents of the source register are not changed during a MOV instruction; you are copying the register contents to some other location.

MOV r,M

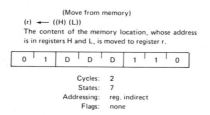

(Move from memory)

(r) ◄── ((H) (L))

The content of the memory location, whose address is in registers H and L, is moved to register r.

| 0 | 1 | D | D | D | 1 | 1 | 0 |

Cycles: 2
States: 7
Addressing: reg. indirect
Flags: none

The MOV r,M instruction transfers data from M (the contents of the memory address specified by the register pair H,L) to the specified destination register *r*, which may be any of the single registers B, C, D, H, or L, or the accumulator, A. You copy the contents of the memory address into a register; the contents of memory remain unchanged.

The following description of an 8080A instruction, and others like it in the following pages, appears in the Intel 8080 Microcomputer Systems User's Manual *and is reprinted in this text through the courtesy of the Intel Corporation, Santa Clara, California 95051. All rights reserved.*

MOV M,r

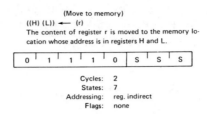

(Move to memory)

((H) (L)) ◄── (r)

The content of register r is moved to the memory location whose address is in registers H and L.

| 0 | 1 | 1 | 1 | 0 | S | S | S |

Cycles: 2
States: 7
Addressing: reg. indirect
Flags: none

The MOV M,r instruction transfers data from the specified source register *r* to M (the memory address specified by the register pair H,L). The source register may be any of the single registers B, C, D, E, H, or L, or the accumulator, A. The register contents are copied in memory; the contents of the register remain unchanged.

MVI r,data

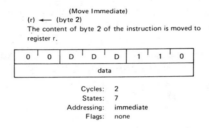

(Move Immediate)

(r) ◄── (byte 2)

The content of byte 2 of the instruction is moved to register r.

| 0 | 0 | D | D | D | 1 | 1 | 0 |
| data |

Cycles: 2
States: 7
Addressing: immediate
Flags: none

The MVI r,data instruction transfers data from the second byte of the two-byte instruction to the specified destination register r. The term *immediate* refers to the fact that the data byte is contained within the multibyte instruction. The specified destination register may be any of the single registers B, C, D, E, H, or L, the accumulator, A, and M (the contents of the memory address specified by the register pair H,L). When the destination is M, you have the instruction MVI M, data, which is discussed in the following paragraph. The data can be any 8-bit binary number between 00000000 and 11111111.

MVI M,data

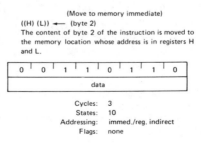

(Move to memory immediate)

((H) (L)) ◄── (byte 2)

The content of byte 2 of the instruction is moved to the memory location whose address is in registers H and L.

| 0 | 0 | 1 | 1 | 0 | 1 | 1 | 0 |
| data |

Cycles: 3
States: 10
Addressing: immed./reg. indirect
Flags: none

The MVI M,data instruction transfers data from the second byte of the instruction to M (the memory address specified by the register pair H,L). The data can be any 8-bit binary number between 00000000 and 11111111.

LXI rp,data 16

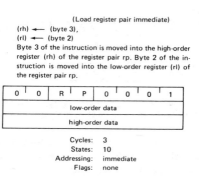

(Load register pair immediate)

(rh) ⟵ (byte 3),

(rl) ⟵ (byte 2)

Byte 3 of the instruction is moved into the high-order register (rh) of the register pair rp. Byte 2 of the instruction is moved into the low-order register (rl) of the register pair rp.

0	0	R	P	0	0	0	1
low-order data
high-order data

Cycles:	3
States:	10
Addressing:	immediate
Flags:	none

The LXI rp,data instruction causes a 16-bit quantity contained in the second and third bytes of the instruction to be loaded into the register pair specified by rp. Register pair rp can be any of the double registers HL, DE, or BC or the stack pointer, which are represented by the mnemonics H, D, B, and SP, respectively. The second instruction byte is loaded into the LO registers L, E, C, or the LO eight bits of the stack pointer; the third instruction byte is loaded into the HI registers H, D, B, or the HI eight bits of the stack pointer. The 16-bit data word can vary from 0000000000000000 to 1111111111111111, in binary notation.

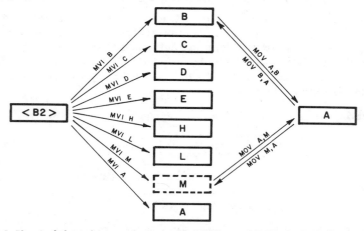

Fig. A-1. The single-byte data transfer instructions MVI r and MOV r1, r2. Only two sets of MOV r1, r2 instructions are shown.

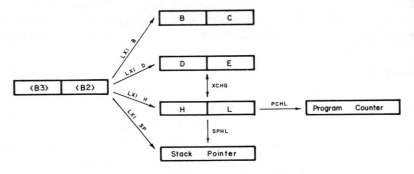

Fig. A-2. The two-byte data transfer instructions LXI rp, PCHL, SPHL, and XCHG. PCHL causes a branch to the location initially contained in register pair H.

Figs. A-1 and A-2 illustrate some of the characteristics of the MOV, MVI, and LXI instructions. Only two sets of MOV r1,r2 instructions are shown. Note that LXI rp,data is equivalent to two MVI r,data instructions. Thus:

>LXI B
><B2>
><B3>

is equivalent to:

>MVI B
><B2> (*corresponds to <B3> in the LXI B instruction*)
>MVI C
><B2> (*corresponds to <B2> in the LXI B instruction*)

The second byte in a two-byte instruction is always referred to as <B2>. A single LXI rp,data instruction requires ten states for its execution, whereas two MVI r,data instructions require a total of fourteen states of execution time. Thus, by using the LXI rp,data instruction, you save four states of execution time. In many cases, however, such a saving is unimportant.

STA addr

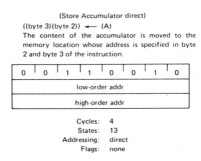

(Store Accumulator direct)

((byte 3)(byte 2)) ◄— (A)

The content of the accumulator is moved to the memory location whose address is specified in byte 2 and byte 3 of the instruction.

0	0	1	1	0	0	1	0

low-order addr

high-order addr

Cycles:	4
States:	13
Addressing:	direct
Flags:	none

The STA addr instruction permits you to store the contents of the accumulator directly into a memory location without the use of the register pair H,L. The address of the memory location is specified in the second and third bytes of the instruction. The LO address byte is byte 2 and the HI address byte is byte 3. The STA addr instruction performs an operation similar to the two-instruction sequence:

$$\text{LXI H}$$
$$<\text{B2}>$$
$$<\text{B3}>$$
$$\text{MOV M,A}$$

LDA addr

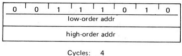

(Load Accumulator direct)

(A) ◄— ((byte 3)(byte 2))

The content of the memory location, whose address is specified in byte 2 and byte 3 of the instruction, is moved to register A.

0	0	1	1	1	0	1	0
low-order addr							
high-order addr							

Cycles: 4
States: 13
Addressing: direct
Flags: none

The LDA addr instruction permits you to load the accumulator with the contents of the memory location specified by bytes B2 and B3 in the instruction. You need not use the H,L register pair. The LO address byte is <B2> and the HI address byte is <B3>. The LDA addr instruction operation is similar to the two-instruction sequence:

$$\text{LXI H}$$
$$<\text{B2}>$$
$$<\text{B3}>$$
$$\text{MOV A,M}$$

LHLD addr

(Load H and L direct)

(L) ◄— ((byte 3)(byte 2))

(H) ◄— ((byte 3)(byte 2) + 1)

The content of the memory location, whose address is specified in byte 2 and byte 3 of the instruction, is moved to register L. The content of the memory location at the succeeding address is moved to register H.

0	0	1	0	1	0	1	0
low-order addr							
high-order addr							

Cycles: 5
States: 16
Addressing: direct
Flags: none

This instruction is useful when memory locations contain address information. Thus, LHLD addr causes the L register to be loaded with the memory byte addressed by bytes B2 and B3 in the instruction, *i.e.,* addr. The H register is loaded with the memory byte located at addr + 1. Thus, you perform a 16-bit transfer of a memory address to the register pair H,L. Once you learn XCHG, you will observe that the section of code:

LHLD
<B2>
<B3>
XCHG

performs in a manner similar to:

LXI H
<B2>
<B3>
MOV E,M
INX H
MOV D,M

The first section of code requires 20 states for execution; the second section of code requires 29 states.

XCHG

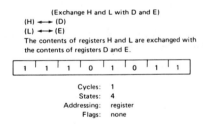

(Exchange H and L with D and E)
(H) ⟷ (D)
(L) ⟷ (E)
The contents of registers H and L are exchanged with
the contents of registers D and E.

1	1	1	0	1	0	1	1

Cycles: 1
States: 4
Addressing: register
Flags: none

The XCHG instruction causes the contents of the register pairs D,E and H,L to be exchanged. To be specific, the contents of registers D and H are exchanged, and the contents of registers E and L are exchanged. This instruction permits you to use register pair H,L as a memory address while another address is held in register pair D,E. You can modify the contents of register pair D,E, without changing register pair H,L. For example, register pair H,L may specify a memory location that you use to modify register pair D,E. Two XCHG instructions in sequence:

XCHG
XCHG

are equivalent to a no operation.

SHLD addr

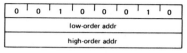

(Store H and L direct)

$((\text{byte 3})(\text{byte 2})) \leftarrow (L)$

$((\text{byte 3})(\text{byte 2}) + 1) \leftarrow (H)$

The content of register L is moved to the memory location whose address is specified in byte 2 and byte 3. The content of register H is moved to the succeeding memory location.

0	0	1	0	0	0	1	0
low-order addr							
high-order addr							

Cycles: 5
States: 16
Addressing: direct
Flags: none

The SHLD addr instruction causes the contents of the L register to be stored at the memory location given by bytes B2 and B3 in the instruction, *i.e.*, addr. The contents of the H register are stored in the memory location, addr + 1. In other words, you perform a 16-bit transfer of an address byte in register pair H,L to two successive memory locations, addr and addr + 1. This instruction is useful in creating a group of memory locations that contain address information rather than data. As for most 8080A instructions, byte B2 is the LO address byte and byte B3 is the HI address byte of addr. The section of code:

XCHG
SHLD
\<B2>
\<B3>

performs in a manner similar to the section of code:

LXI H
\<B2>
\<B3>
MOV M,E
INX H
MOV M,D

LDAX rp

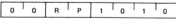

(Load accumulator indirect)

$(A) \leftarrow ((rp))$

The content of the memory location, whose address is in the register pair rp, is moved to register A. Note: only register pairs rp=B (registers B and C) or rp=D (registers D and E) may be specified.

0	0	R	P	1	0	1	0

Cycles: '2
States: 7
Addressing: reg. indirect
Flags: none

The LDAX rp instruction permits you to load the accumulator with the contents of the memory location addressed by a register pair other than register pair H,L. Thus, with LDAX B, you use register pair B,C to supply the 16-bit memory address; with LDAX D, you use register pair D,E to supply the address. The section of code:

LXI D
<B2>
<B3>
LDAX D

is functionally identical with:

LXI H
<B2>
<B3>
MOV A,M

STAX rp

(Store accumulator indirect)

((rp)) ← (A)

The content of register A is moved to the memory location whose address is in the register pair rp. Note: only register pairs rp=B (registers B and C) or rp=D (registers D and E) may be specified.

0	0	R	P	0	0	1	0

Cycles: 2
States: 7
Addressing: reg. indirect
Flags: none

The STAX rp instruction permits you to store the contents of the accumulator in the memory location addressed by either register pair B,D or register pair D,E. The section of code:

LXI B
<B2>
<B3>
STAX B

is identical with:

LXI H
<B2>
<B3>
MOV M,A

The significance of the STAX rp and LDAX rp instructions is that you can have three independent 16-bit memory addresses stored in the general-purpose registers inside the 8080A microprocessor chip. Enough instructions are available to permit you to use all three addresses.

The condition flags are not affected by any of the instructions in the following list:

MOV rl,r2
MOV r,M
MOV M,r
MVI r, data
MVI M, data
LXI rp, data 16
STA addr
LDA addr
XCHG
LHLD addr
SHLD addr
LDAX rp
STAX rp

These instructions comprise the data transfer group in the 8080A microprocessor.

ARITHMETIC GROUP

This group of instructions performs arithmetic operations on data in registers and memory. *Unless indicated otherwise, all instructions in this group affect the zero, sign, parity, carry, and auxiliary carry flags according to standard rules.* All subtraction operations are performed via two's complement arithmetic and set the carry flag to one to indicate a borrow and clear it to indicate no borrow.

ADD r

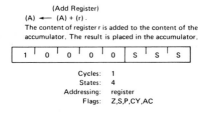

(Add Register)
(A) ◄— (A) + (r) .
The content of register r is added to the content of the accumulator. The result is placed in the accumulator.

| 1 | 0 | 0 | 0 | 0 | S | S | S |

Cycles: 1
States: 4
Addressing: register
Flags: Z,S,P,CY,AC

The ADD r instruction causes the contents of the source register S to be added to the contents of the accumulator. The source register can be any of the general-purpose registers B, C, D, E, H, L, the accumulator A, or M (the contents of memory as addressed by register pair H,L). The ADD M instruction is described below. The instruction

455

affects all four of the testable flag bits: carry, parity, zero, and sign. The auxiliary carry flag is also affected.

ADD M

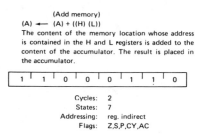

(Add memory)

(A) ⟵ (A) + ((H) (L))

The content of the memory location whose address is contained in the H and L registers is added to the content of the accumulator. The result is placed in the accumulator.

1	1	0	0	0	1	1	0

Cycles: 2
States: 7
Addressing: reg. indirect
Flags: Z,S,P,CY,AC

The ADD M instruction causes the contents of the memory location M, which is addressed by register pair H,L, to be added to the contents of the accumulator. The memory contents remain unchanged after the addition. The instruction affects all five flags and requires two machine cycles.

ADI data

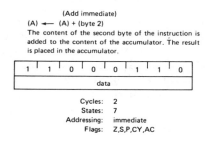

(Add immediate)

(A) ⟵ (A) + (byte 2)

The content of the second byte of the instruction is added to the content of the accumulator. The result is placed in the accumulator.

1	1	0	0	0	1	1	0
data

Cycles: 2
States: 7
Addressing: immediate
Flags: Z,S,P,CY,AC

The ADI data instruction causes the data present in the second byte of the instruction to be added to the contents of the accumulator. The instruction affects all five flags.

ADC r and ADC M

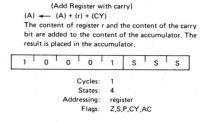

(Add Register with carry)

(A) ⟵ (A) + (r) + (CY)

The content of register r and the content of the carry bit are added to the content of the accumulator. The result is placed in the accumulator.

1	0	0	0	1	S	S	S

Cycles: 1
States: 4
Addressing: register
Flags: Z,S,P,CY,AC

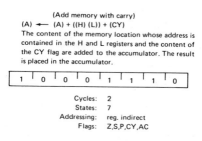

(Add memory with carry)

(A) ◂— (A) + ((H) (L)) + (CY)

The content of the memory location whose address is contained in the H and L registers and the content of the CY flag are added to the accumulator. The result is placed in the accumulator.

1	0	0	0	1	1	1	0

Cycles: 2
States: 7
Addressing: reg. indirect
Flags: Z,S,P,CY,AC

To quote the *μCOM-8 Software Manual*: "In order to perform add and subtract operations, some special arithmetic instructions are required. Multiple-digit arithmetic requires that two items be monitored and saved somewhere. These two items are the sum of the digits as they are added, and the presence or absence of a carry bit. When a carry bit is produced, it must be added to the sum of the next digits. Similarly, with subtract operations, the existence of a borrow must be detected so it can be deducted from the difference of the next digits. The Add with Carry and Subtract with Borrow instructions provide simple monitoring and saving of carry bits, making multidigit addition and subtraction quite straightforward. ADC r, ADC M, and ACI data are the Add with Carry instructions. ADC r causes the contents of the source S to be added to the sum of the accumulator contents and the carry bit."

The ADC r and ADC M instructions are similar to the ADD r and ADD M instructions; the only difference is that the carry bit is added to the least-significant bit in the 8-bit accumulator byte. All flags are affected by these instructions. Memory location M is addressed by the contents of register pair H,L.

ACI data

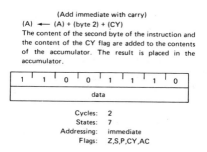

(Add immediate with carry)

(A) ◂— (A) + (byte 2) + (CY)

The content of the second byte of the instruction and the content of the CY flag are added to the contents of the accumulator. The result is placed in the accumulator.

1	1	0	0	1	1	1	0
data							

Cycles: 2
States: 7
Addressing: immediate
Flags: Z,S,P,CY,AC

The ACI data instruction causes the 8-bit data quantity present in the second byte of the instruction to be added to the sum of the accumulator contents and the carry bit. The instruction affects all five flags.

457

SUB r and SUB M

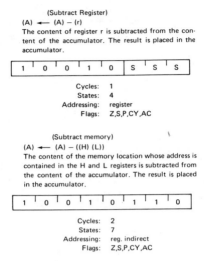

(Subtract Register)

(A) ← (A) − (r)

The content of register r is subtracted from the content of the accumulator. The result is placed in the accumulator.

| 1 | 0 | 0 | 1 | 0 | S | S | S |

Cycles: 1
States: 4
Addressing: register
Flags: Z,S,P,CY,AC

(Subtract memory)

(A) ← (A) − ((H) (L))

The content of the memory location whose address is contained in the H and L registers is subtracted from the content of the accumulator. The result is placed in the accumulator.

| 1 | 0 | 0 | 1 | 0 | 1 | 1 | 0 |

Cycles: 2
States: 7
Addressing: reg. indirect
Flags: Z,S,P,CY,AC

The SUB r instruction causes the contents of the source register S to be subtracted from the accumulator. The source register can be any of the general-purpose registers B, C, D, E, H, and L, the accumulator, A, or M (the contents of memory as addressed by register pair H,L). All five flags are affected by the execution of this instruction. If you wish to clear the accumulator, the single instruction:

SUB A

which has an instruction code of **227**, will do it.

SUI data

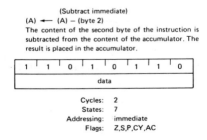

(Subtract immediate)

(A) ← (A) − (byte 2)

The content of the second byte of the instruction is subtracted from the content of the accumulator. The result is placed in the accumulator.

| 1 | 1 | 0 | 1 | 0 | 1 | 1 | 0 |
| data |

Cycles: 2
States: 7
Addressing: immediate
Flags: Z,S,P,CY,AC

The SUI data instruction causes the 8-bit data quantity specified in the second instruction byte to be subtracted from the accumulator. All five flags are affected.

SBB r and SBB M

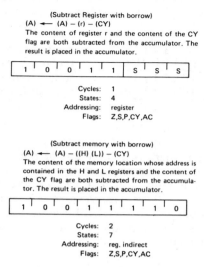

(Subtract Register with borrow)

$(A) \leftarrow (A) - (r) - (CY)$

The content of register r and the content of the CY flag are both subtracted from the accumulator. The result is placed in the accumulator.

1	0	0	1	1	S	S	S

Cycles: 1
States: 4
Addressing: register
Flags: Z,S,P,CY,AC

(Subtract memory with borrow)

$(A) \leftarrow (A) - ((H) (L)) - (CY)$

The content of the memory location whose address is contained in the H and L registers and the content of the CY flag are both subtracted from the accumulator. The result is placed in the accumulator.

1	0	0	1	1	1	1	0

Cycles: 2
States: 7
Addressing: reg. indirect
Flags: Z,S,P,CY,AC

The SBB r instruction causes the contents of the source S to be subtracted from the difference of the accumulator contents and the borrow bit. The source register can be any of the general-purpose registers B, C, D, E, H, and L; the accumulator, A; or M, the contents of memory addressed by register pair H,L. All five flags are affected by the SBB r and SBB M instructions.

SBI data

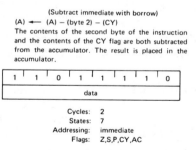

(Subtract immediate with borrow)

$(A) \leftarrow (A) - (byte 2) - (CY)$

The contents of the second byte of the instruction and the contents of the CY flag are both subtracted from the accumulator. The result is placed in the accumulator.

1	1	0	1	1	1	1	0
			data				

Cycles: 2
States: 7
Addressing: immediate
Flags: Z,S,P,CY,AC

The SBI data instruction causes the 8-bit data quantity specified in the second instruction byte to be subtracted from the difference of the accumulator contents and the borrow bit. All five flags are affected.

Some examples of the various addition and subtraction operations would be appropriate. Consider the following program:

ADD B
ADD C

If the initial register contents are $A = 00111110$, $B = 11100000$, and $C = 00101111$, and if the carry bit were initially zero, then the above section of code would yield the following result in the accumulator:

Carry Bit

0	00111110	accumulator contents
	+11100000	register B contents
1	00011110	sum stored in accumulator
	+00101111	register C contents
0	01001101	sum' stored in accumulator

Note carefully the behavior of the carry bit in this situation. If there is no carry out of the most significant bit (MSB) in the accumulator, the carry bit is cleared; if there is a carry out of the most significant bit in the accumulator during the addition, the carry bit is set. When you added B to the accumulator, you had a carry. When you added the contents of C to the sum, there was no carry. The carry from previous operations is not preserved, or "carried forward."

Now let us contrast the preceding results with the behavior of the following section of code:

ADC B
ADC C

Assume the same initial values for registers A, B, C, and the carry bit. You would obtain the following results:

Carry Bit

0	00111110	accumulator contents
	+11100000	register B contents
1	00011110	sum stored in accumulator

So far, there is no difference. However, when we add the contents of register C to the above sum, we do observe a difference:

Carry Bit

	00011110	sum stored in accumulator
	+ 1	carry bit
	+00101111	register C contents
0	01001110	sum'

Now consider the following section of code:

SUB B
SUB C

for the same initial values of registers A, B, C, and the carry bit. Note that if you perform a borrow out of the MSB of the accumulator, the carry bit is set; if no borrow occurs, the carry bit is cleared. Thus you should observe the following:

Carry Bit

0	00111110	accumulator contents
	−11100000	register B contents
1	01011110	difference stored in accumulator
	−00101111	register C contents
0	00101111	difference' stored in accumulator

Now let us perform subtraction operations using the SBB r instructions:

SBB B

SBB C

We have the following results:

Carry Bit

0	00111110	accumulator contents
	−11100000	register B contents
1	01011110	difference stored in accumulator

When we perform the SBB C operation, we subtract the contents of register C from the difference between the borrow bit and the contents of the accumulator:

	01011110	difference stored in accumulator
	− 1	
	−00101111	register C contents
0	00101110	difference' stored in accumulator

The ADC r and SBB r instructions are used whenever you perform double- or triple-precision arithmetic operations. A *double-precision* arithmetic operation is one which is performed on two 16-bit quantities to yield a 16-bit result. A *triple-precision* operation is one which is performed on two 24-bit quantities to yield a 24-bit result. The preceding examples of addition and subtraction operations are provided courtesy of NEC Microcomputers, Inc., from their *μCOM-8 Software Manual*.

DAA

(Decimal Adjust Accumulator)

The eight-bit number in the accumulator is adjusted to form two four-bit Binary-Coded-Decimal digits by the following process:

1. If the value of the least significant 4 bits of the accumulator is greater than 9 **or** if the AC flag is set, 6 is added to the accumulator.

2. If the value of the most significant 4 bits of the accumulator is now greater than 9, **or** if the CY flag is set, 6 is added to the most significant 4 bits of the accumulator.

NOTE: All flags are affected.

0	0	1	0	0	1	1	1

Cycles: 1
States: 4
Flags: Z,S,P,CY,AC

To quote the *μCOM-8 Software Manual*: "In order to perform operations in binary coded decimal (bcd), one special instruction is needed. When the 8080A CPU performs an arithmetic operation, it produces the result in binary. When working in bcd this does not produce the correct result. To remedy this, a DAA instruction is used. DAA stands for Decimal Adjust Accumulator, which is exactly what DAA does. The DAA instruction treats the 8-bit Accumulator as two 4-bit Accumulators. Through the use of a nontestable flag known as the Auxiliary Carry, the DAA operation adjusts the result of a binary addition operation to packed bcd.

"For example, the DAA instruction causes the following operation. If the Auxiliary Carry is set to one or the least significant *nibble* (LSN) is greater than 9, six is added to the least significant nibble. Then, if the Carry flag is set to one or the most significant nibble is greater than 9, six is added to the most significant nibble (MSN)."

The term *nibble* is defined as follows:

nibble—A group of four contiguous bits that usually represent a bcd digit.

The least significant nibble (LSN), most significant nibble (MSN), accumulator, auxiliary carry flag (ACy), and carry flag (Cy) can be represented as shown in Fig. A-3. Assume, as is done in an example in the *μCOM-8 Software Manual*, that the accumulator contains the bcd representation for 75 (MSN = 0111 and LSN = 0101), that the B register contains the bcd representation for 38 (MSN = 0011 and LSN = 1000), and the carry flag is logic zero. The instruction ADC B produces the following result in the accumulator:

Carry Bit	Auxiliary Carry Bit		
0		01110101	accumulator contents
		+ 00111000	register B contents
0	0	10101101	sum stored in the accumulator

With the auxiliary carry, if the instruction causes a carry out of bit 3 and into bit 4 of the resulting value, the auxiliary carry flag is set; other-

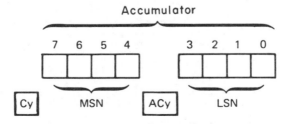

Fig. A-3. Identification of the most significant and least significant nibbles.

wise it is reset. In the preceding example, there is no carry out of bit 3 and into bit 4, so the auxiliary carry bit is zero after the operation.

The DAA command finds ACy reset to 0 and LSN = 1101. Because the LSN is greater than nine, six is added to it and the result is 0011. Because the MSN is greater than nine, six is also added to it and the result is 0000. The final result after the DAA operation is:

1   0   0 0 0 0 0 0 1 1   decimal adjusted sum

which is equivalent to the decimal number 103. The DAA operation can be written as follows:

Carry Bit	Auxiliary Carry Bit			
0	0	1 0 1 0	1 1 0 1	sum
		+ 0 1 1 0	+ 0 1 1 0	DAA Operation
1	1	0 0 0 0	0 0 1 1	result of DAA Operation
1		0 0 0 0	0 0 1 1	bcd
1		0	3	decimal number

Thus, $75 + 38 = 103$.

In actual operation, the DAA adjustment is done in parallel, rather than in the serial manner illustrated. However, this serial explanation, courtesy of the *μCOM-8 Software Manual* of NEC Microcomputers, Inc., is easier to understand and illustrates the adjustment better. *The DAA instruction should immediately follow an addition operation, as certain 8080A instructions alter the state of the auxiliary carry flag. Such an alteration could result in incorrect results.*

There is an important difference between the Intel 8080A microprocessor chip and the equivalent chip, the μCOM-8 chip of NEC Microcomputers, Inc. The μCOM-8 chip has an extra nontestable flag called Subtract. To quote from the NEC Manual: "For addition, the Sub flag is set to zero. . . For subtraction, Sub is set to one causing the following DAA operation. If ACy is set to one (a borrow occurred) six is subtracted from the LSN. Then if the Cy is set to one (a borrow occurred) six is subtracted from the MSN. The use of a DAA instruction immediately after an operation on two bytes in packed bcd format adjusts the result to two bcd digits and a carry or borrow in packed bcd format. Note that the DAA operations performs directly after subtraction, *eliminating the need for 100's complement arithmetic for subtraction.*"

If you are doing considerable amounts of bcd manipulation, you would be interested in the μCOM-8 chip in preference to the 8080A. However, such would only be the case if you require the full speed of the microcomputer. With additional instructions, the 8080A can easily accomplish the same task of producing a packed bcd format after a subtraction.

INR r and INR M

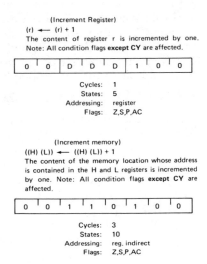

(Increment Register)

$(r) \leftarrow (r) + 1$

The content of register r is incremented by one. Note: All condition flags **except CY** are affected.

0	0	D	D	D	1	0	0

Cycles: 1
States: 5
Addressing: register
Flags: Z,S,P,AC

(Increment memory)

$((H) (L)) \leftarrow ((H) (L)) + 1$

The content of the memory location whose address is contained in the H and L registers is incremented by one. Note: All condition flags **except CY** are affected.

0	0	1	1	0	1	0	0

Cycles: 3
States: 10
Addressing: reg. indirect
Flags: Z,S,P,AC

The INR r instruction causes a one to be added to the destination register D. The destination register can be any of the general-purpose registers B, C, D, E, H, and L; the accumulator, A; or M, the contents of memory as addressed by register pair H,L. All flags are affected except the carry flag.

DCR r and DCR M

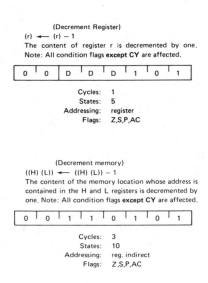

(Decrement Register)

$(r) \leftarrow (r) - 1$

The content of register r is decremented by one. Note: All condition flags **except CY** are affected.

0	0	D	D	D	1	0	1

Cycles: 1
States: 5
Addressing: register
Flags: Z,S,P,AC

(Decrement memory)

$((H) (L)) \leftarrow ((H) (L)) - 1$

The content of the memory location whose address is contained in the H and L registers is decremented by one. Note: All condition flags **except CY** are affected.

0	0	1	1	0	1	0	1

Cycles: 3
States: 10
Addressing: reg. indirect
Flags: Z,S,P,AC

The DCR r instruction causes a one to be subtracted from the destination register D. The destination register can be any of the general-purpose registers B, C, D, E, H, and L; the accumulator, A; or M, the contents of memory as addressed by register pair H,L. Only four of the five flags are affected; the carry flag remains unchanged.

INX rp and DCX rp

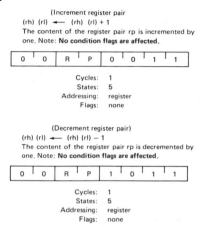

(Increment register pair
(rh) (rl) ◄── (rh) (rl) + 1
The content of the register pair rp is incremented by one. Note: **No condition flags are affected.**

0	0	R	P	0	0	1	1

Cycles: 1
States: 5
Addressing: register
Flags: none

(Decrement register pair)
(rh) (rl) ◄── (rh) (rl) − 1
The content of the register pair rp is decremented by one. Note: **No condition flags are affected.**

0	0	R	P	1	0	1	1

Cycles: 1
States: 5
Addressing: register
Flags: none

The INX rp causes the register pair specified by rp to be incremented by one; the DCX rp causes the register pair specified by rp to be decremented by one. RP can be the register pair specified by B, D, or H (corresponding to BC, DE, or HL) or the 16-bit stack pointer specified by SP. INX and DCX do not affect any flag bits; they are usually not used in arithmetic operations, their main use being to increment or decrement 16-bit memory addresses.

DAD rp

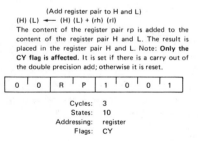

(Add register pair to H and L)
(H) (L) ◄── (H) (L) + (rh) (rl)
The content of the register pair rp is added to the content of the register pair H and L. The result is placed in the register pair H and L. Note: **Only the CY flag is affected.** It is set if there is a carry out of the double precision add; otherwise it is reset.

0	0	R	P	1	0	0	1

Cycles: 3
States: 10
Addressing: register
Flags: CY

According to the NEC manual: "While the INX and DCX instructions allow incrementing and decrementing register pairs, the DAD, Double

Add, instruction allows adding register pairs together. DAD rp causes the register pair specified by rp to be added to the contents of the H,L register pair, with the result remaining in the H,L pair. The Carry Flag is the only status flag affected by the DAD instruction. The instructions INX, DCX, and DAD allow the calculation of table lookup." Also used for indexed addressing and file data manipulation.

CMP r and CMP M

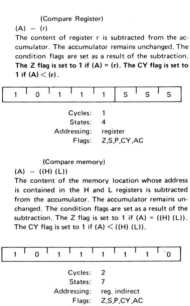

(Compare Register)

(A) − (r)

The content of register r is subtracted from the accumulator. The accumulator remains unchanged. The condition flags are set as a result of the subtraction. **The Z flag is set to 1 if (A) = (r). The CY flag is set to 1 if (A) < (r).**

1	0	1	1	1	S	S	S

Cycles: 1
States: 4
Addressing: register
Flags: Z,S,P,CY,AC

(Compare memory)

(A) − ((H) (L))

The content of the memory location whose address is contained in the H and L registers is subtracted from the accumulator. The accumulator remains unchanged. The condition flags are set as a result of the subtraction. The Z flag is set to 1 if (A) = ((H) (L)). The CY flag is set to 1 if (A) < ((H) (L)).

1	0	1	1	1	1	1	0

Cycles: 2
States: 7
Addressing: reg. indirect
Flags: Z,S,P,CY,AC

To quote the μCOM-8 Software Manual: "CMP r and CMP M are used to compare two data quantities *without altering them*. CMP r compares the contents of the accumulator with one of the single registers B, C, D, E, H, and L; the accumulator, A; or M, the memory location addressed by the H,L register pair. The instruction does not affect any of the data registers, but affects the four flag bits Carry, Zero, Sign, and Parity. The compare instructions actually perform an internal subtraction of the source S from the accumulator. The flags are set on the basis of what would have been the result of the subtraction. Thus Zero is set if the quantities were equal, Sign is set if the result was negative (the most significant bit is logic 1), Parity is set if the result has even parity, and Carry is set if there is a borrow out of bit 7 (source data greater than Accumulator data).

"Thus, in every case:

Carry is set if a borrow occurs; else reset;
Sign is set equal to the MSB of the result;

Zero is set if the result is zero; else reset;
Parity is set if the parity of the result is even; else reset."

The compare instructions are best used for unsigned arithmetic comparison (numbers in the range of 0 to 255_{10}), also called logical or character comparisons. For this case, the results for the zero and carry flags may be interpreted as follows:

Result of Compare Operation

Zero Flag	Carry Flag	Relationship Between Accumulator and Register
1	X	accumulator = register
X	1	accumulator < register
1	1	accumulator ≤ register
0	0	accumulator > register
X	0	accumulator ≥ register

NOTE: X = don't care

Thus, the relations =, <, ≥ may be tested using a single jump instruction, while ≤, > require two. Note that if the operands are reversed, > replaces ≤ and < replaces ≥.

CPI data

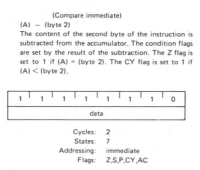

(Compare immediate)

(A) − (byte 2)

The content of the second byte of the instruction is subtracted from the accumulator. The condition flags are set by the result of the subtraction. The Z flag is set to 1 if (A) = (byte 2). The CY flag is set to 1 if (A) < (byte 2).

1	1	1	1	1	1	1	0
			data				

Cycles: 2
States: 7
Addressing: immediate
Flags: Z,S,P,CY,AC

The CPI data instruction is an immediate operation which compares the contents of the accumulator with the 8-bit quantity in the second byte of the instruction. The instruction affects all five flags, but only four of the flags produce useful results. The flags are set or cleared on the basis of what would have been the result of the subtraction. *The contents of the accumulator remain unchanged.* See the preceding discussion of the CMP r instruction for additional details.

It can be argued that the CMP r and CPI data instructions are logical rather than arithmetic operations. In view of the fact that an arithmetic operation—subtraction—is performed, we include it in the group of arithmetic operations. The objective of the compare instructions is to produce decisions that are reflected in the logic states of the flag bits.

LOGICAL GROUP

This group of instructions performs logical, i.e., Boolean, operations on data in registers and memory and on condition flags. Unless indicated otherwise, all instructions in this group affect the zero, sign, parity, auxiliary carry, and carry flags according to the standard rules.

ANA r and ANA M

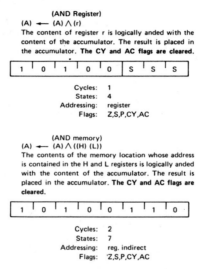

(AND Register)

$(A) \leftarrow (A) \wedge (r)$

The content of register r is logically anded with the content of the accumulator. The result is placed in the accumulator. **The CY and AC flags are cleared.**

| 1 | 0 | 1 | 0 | 0 | S | S | S |

Cycles: 1
States: 4
Addressing: register
Flags: Z,S,P,CY,AC

(AND memory)

$(A) \leftarrow (A) \wedge ((H) (L))$

The contents of the memory location whose address is contained in the H and L registers is logically anded with the content of the accumulator. The result is placed in the accumulator. **The CY and AC flags are cleared.**

| 1 | 0 | 1 | 0 | 0 | 1 | 1 | 0 |

Cycles: 2
States: 7
Addressing: reg. indirect
Flags: Z,S,P,CY,AC

The ANA r instruction performs a parallel bit-by-bit logical AND of the contents of the accumulator and the contents of the source register S. The source register can be any of the general-purpose registers B, C, D, E, H, and L; the accumulator, A; or M, the contents of the memory location addressed by the register pair H,L. For example, the ANA B operation performs a bit-by-bit logic AND operation with the contents of register B and the contents of the accumulator. The special case of

ANA A

clears the carry flag and causes the zero flag to be set if the result is zero, cleared if the result is not zero. All of the flags are affected by the ANA r instruction. Since A • A = A, the data in the accumulator is not changed. This is a "trick" to clear the carry flag or simply test for zero in the accumulator.

ANI data

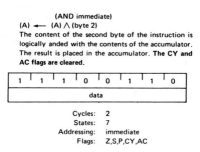

(AND immediate)

(A) ← (A) ∧ (byte 2)

The content of the second byte of the instruction is logically anded with the contents of the accumulator. The result is placed in the accumulator. **The CY and AC flags are cleared.**

1	1	1	0	0	1	1	0
data							

Cycles: 2
States: 7
Addressing: immediate
Flags: Z,S,P,CY,AC

The ANI data instruction performs a bit-by-bit logical AND of the contents of the accumulator with the contents of the second byte of the instruction. All flags are affected by the instruction.

ORA r and ORA M

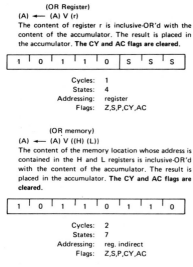

(OR Register)

(A) ← (A) V (r)

The content of register r is inclusive-OR'd with the content of the accumulator. The result is placed in the accumulator. **The CY and AC flags are cleared.**

1	0	1	1	0	S	S	S

Cycles: 1
States: 4
Addressing: register
Flags: Z,S,P,CY,AC

(OR memory)

(A) ← (A) V ((H) (L))

The content of the memory location whose address is contained in the H and L registers is inclusive-OR'd with the content of the accumulator. The result is placed in the accumulator. **The CY and AC flags are cleared.**

1	0	1	1	0	1	1	0

Cycles: 2
States: 7
Addressing: reg. indirect
Flags: Z,S,P,CY,AC

The ORA r instruction performs a parallel bit-by-bit logical OR of the contents of the accumulator and the contents of the source register S. The source register can be any of the general-purpose registers B, C, D, E, H, and L; the accumulator, A; or M, the contents of the memory location addressed by the register pair H,L. The command

ORA A

which has the octal instruction code **267,** is a convenient way to clear the carry flag without affecting anything else. Both ORA r and a related

469

two-byte instruction, ORI data, clear the carry flag and cause the zero
flag to be set if the result is zero, or cleared if the result is not zero.

ORI data

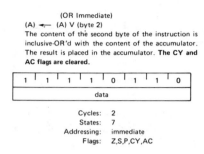

(OR Immediate)

(A) ◄── (A) V (byte 2)

The content of the second byte of the instruction is
inclusive-OR'd with the content of the accumulator.
The result is placed in the accumulator. **The CY and
AC flags are cleared.**

1	1	1	1	0	1	1	0
data

Cycles:	2
States:	7
Addressing:	immediate
Flags:	Z,S,P,CY,AC

The ORI data instruction performs a bit-by-bit logical OR of the contents of the accumulator with the contents of the second byte of the
instruction. All flags are affected by the instruction.

XRA r and XRA M

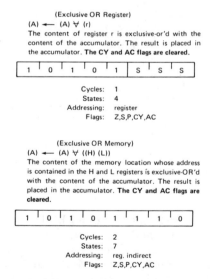

(Exclusive OR Register)

(A) ◄── (A) ⊻ (r)

The content of register r is exclusive-or'd with the
content of the accumulator. The result is placed in
the accumulator. **The CY and AC flags are cleared.**

1	0	1	0	1	S	S	S

Cycles:	1
States:	4
Addressing:	register
Flags:	Z,S,P,CY,AC

(Exclusive OR Memory)

(A) ◄── (A) ⊻ ((H) (L))

The content of the memory location whose address
is contained in the H and L registers is exclusive-OR'd
with the content of the accumulator. The result is
placed in the accumulator. **The CY and AC flags are
cleared.**

1	0	1	0	1	1	1	0

Cycles:	2
States:	7
Addressing:	reg. indirect
Flags:	Z,S,P,CY,AC

The XRA r instruction performs a bit-by-bit logical exclusive-OR of the
contents of the accumulator and the contents of the source register S.
The source register can be any of the general-purpose registers B, C,
D, E, H, and L; the accumulator, A; or M, the memory location addressed by the register pair H,L. All flags are affected by the instruction.

XRI data

(Exclusive OR immediate)

$(A) \leftarrow (A) \veebar (byte\ 2)$

The content of the second byte of the instruction is exclusive-OR'd with the content of the accumulator. The result is placed in the accumulator. **The CY and AC flags are cleared.**

1	1	1	0	1	1	1	0
			data				

Cycles:	2
States:	7
Addressing:	immediate
Flags:	Z,S,P,CY,AC

The XRI data instruction performs a bit-by-bit logical exclusive-OR of the contents of the accumulator with the contents of the second byte of the instruction. All flags are affected by the instruction.

To quote the NEC Microcomputers, Inc., *μCOM-8 Software Manual*:

"The above logic instructions will be used to implement a programming technique known as *masking*. Masking is a technique by which bits of an operand are selectively modified for use in a later operation. There are three general types of masking:

* Clear all bits not operated upon.
* Set all bits not operated upon (seldom used).
* Leave unaltered all bits not operated upon."

"The first two approaches are called *exclusive masking* and the third approach is called *inclusive masking*. For example, assume that the accumulator contains the following value:

Bit: $\quad\begin{smallmatrix}7&6&5&4&3&2&1&0\end{smallmatrix}$
$1\ 1\ 0\ 1\ {}^1/_0\ 1\ 1\ 0$ accumulator contents

To test bit 3 for a zero or one and simultaneously clear the other bits, the accumulator is masked with 00001000. By using the instruction

ANI
010

the accumulator will contain zeros with the zero flag set if bit 3 had been a zero, and it will contain 010, in octal code, with the zero flag cleared if bit 3 had been one.

"In order to set bit 3 to one and leave the other bits alone, the same bit pattern is used and the instruction

ORI
010

is used. The result in this case is 11011110 in the accumulator.

"In order to set bit 3 to zero and leave the other bits alone, the accumulator is ANDed with 1111011, the complement of the mask of the first example. With the instruction

ANI
367

the accumulator result is 11010110. These are the most commonly used bit manipulation operations, since masking is accomplished in one step. Many others are possible, but they often require more than one instruction for implementation."

RAL and RAR

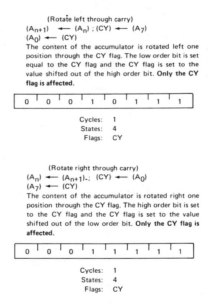

(Rotate left through carry)
$(A_{n+1}) \leftarrow (A_n) ; (CY) \leftarrow (A_7)$
$(A_0) \leftarrow (CY)$
The content of the accumulator is rotated left one position through the CY flag. The low order bit is set equal to the CY flag and the CY flag is set to the value shifted out of the high order bit. **Only the CY flag is affected.**

0	0	0	1	0	1	1	1

Cycles: 1
States: 4
Flags: CY

(Rotate right through carry)
$(A_n) \leftarrow (A_{n+1})$-; $(CY) \leftarrow (A_0)$
$(A_7) \leftarrow (CY)$
The content of the accumulator is rotated right one position through the CY flag. The high order bit is set to the CY flag and the CY flag is set to the value shifted out of the low order bit. **Only the CY flag is affected.**

0	0	0	1	1	1	1	1

Cycles: 1
States: 4
Flags: CY

The RAL instruction, or rotate accumulator left, causes the accumulator to rotate all bits one position to the left through the carry bit, i.e., a 9-bit rotate. Bit 7 transfers to the carry flag, the carry bit transfers to bit 0, bit 0 transfers to bit 1, bit 1 transfers to bit 2, and so on, as shown in Fig. A-4.

The RAR instruction, or rotate accumulator right, causes the accumulator to rotate all bits one position to the right through the carry bit, i.e., a 9-bit rotate. Bit 0 transfers to the carry flag, the carry bit transfers to bit 7, bit 7 transfers to bit 6, bit 6 transfers to bit 5, and so on, as shown in Fig. A-4.

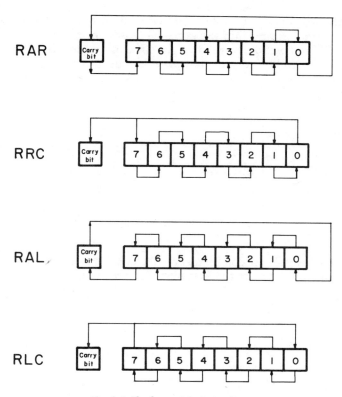

RAR

RRC

RAL

RLC

Fig. A-4. The four rotate instructions.

RLC and RRC

(Rotate left)

$(A_{n+1}) \leftarrow (A_n) ; (A_0) \leftarrow (A_7)$
$(CY) \leftarrow (A_7)$

The content of the accumulator is rotated left one position. The low order bit and the CY flag are both set to the value shifted out of the high order bit position. **Only the CY flag is affected.**

| 0 | 0 | 0 | 0 | 0 | 1 | 1 | 1 |

Cycles: 1
States: 1
Flags: CY

(Rotate right)

$(A_n) \leftarrow (A_{n-1}) ; (A_7) \leftarrow (A_0)$
$(CY) \leftarrow (A_0)$

The content of the accumulator is rotated right one position. The high order bit and the CY flag are both set to the value shifted out of the low order bit position. **Only the CY flag is affected.**

| 0 | 0 | 0 | 0 | 1 | 1 | 1 | 1 |

Cycles: 1
States: 4
Flags: CY

The RLC instruction, or rotate left circular, rotates the accumulator one bit to the left and into the carry flag, as shown in Fig. A-4.

The RRC instruction, or rotate right circular, rotates the accumulator one bit to the right and into the carry flag, as also shown in Fig. A-4.

In both of these instructions, the original information appearing in the carry flag is lost.

CMA

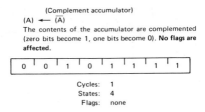

(Complement accumulator)

(A) ← (A̅)

The contents of the accumulator are complemented (zero bits become 1, one bits become 0). **No flags are affected.**

| 0 | 0 | 1 | 0 | 1 | 1 | 1 | 1 |

Cycles: 1
States: 4
Flags: none

The CMA instruction complements the contents of the accumulator without affecting any of the flag bits. For example, if the accumulator contained 11010001, the CMA instruction would convert it to 00101110. Each individual bit is complemented.

STC and CMC

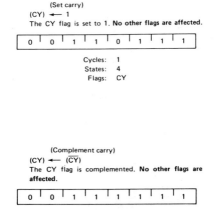

(Set carry)

(CY) ← 1

The CY flag is set to 1. **No other flags are affected.**

| 0 | 0 | 1 | 1 | 0 | 1 | 1 | 1 |

Cycles: 1
States: 4
Flags: CY

(Complement carry)

(CY) ← (C̅Y̅)

The CY flag is complemented. **No other flags are affected.**

| 0 | 0 | 1 | 1 | 1 | 1 | 1 | 1 |

Cycles: 1
States: 4
Flags: CY

The STC instruction sets the carry flag to logic 1; the CMC instruction complements the carry flag. No other flag bits are affected.

BRANCH GROUP

This group of instructions alters normal sequential program flow. *Condition flags are not affected by any instruction in this group.* The two types of branch instructions are unconditional and conditional. Unconditional transfers simply perform the specified operation on register PC, the program counter. Conditional transfers examine the status of one of the four process flags—zero, sign, parity, or carry—to determine if the specified branch operation is to be executed. The conditions that may be specified are as follows:

	Condition	CCC
NZ	not zero ($Z = 0$)	000
Z	zero ($Z = 1$)	001
NC	no carry ($CY = 0$)	010
C	carry ($CY = 1$)	011
PO	parity odd ($P = 0$)	100
PE	parity even ($P = 1$)	101
P	plus ($S = 0$)	110
M	minus ($S = 1$)	111

NOTE: CCC is the three-bit code for the condition of the flags

JMP addr

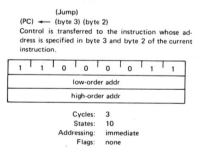

```
                    (Jump)
(PC) ◄— (byte 3) (byte 2)
Control is transferred to the instruction whose ad-
dress is specified in byte 3 and byte 2 of the current
instruction.
```

1	1	0	0	0	0	1	1

low-order addr
high-order addr

```
    Cycles:   3
    States:   10
Addressing:   immediate
     Flags:   none
```

The *program counter* is the 16-bit register in the 8080A microprocessor chip that contains the memory address of the next instruction byte that must be executed in a computer program. The JMP addr instruction is simply a byte transfer instruction, in which the second and third instruction bytes are transferred directly to the program counter. No arithmetic or logical operations are involved, and no flag bits are affected. The JMP instruction is a three-byte instruction that contains the

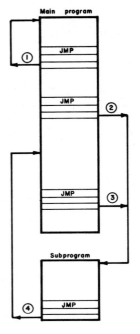

Fig. A-5. Diagram that illustrates the branching characteristics of the JMP instruction.

16-bit memory address to which program control is transferred. You can jump forwards or backwards to any of the 65,536 possible memory locations. The microprocessor chip does not remember the point from which it jumped, in distinct contrast to the behavior of the CALL and RET instructions discussed in the following.

The behavior of the JMP instruction can be understood with the aid of Fig. A-5. The first JMP instruction, ①, is a backwards jump that creates a loop. JMP ② and JMP ③ transfer program control to the subprogram. The exit from the subprogram is to the same place, that designated by the JMP ④ instruction.

CALL addr and RET

Many times you may want to branch out of a main program but return to it later. To do so, you must not only know your new destination, but you must somehow also remember your original location. To accomplish this, you have two types of instructions: call subroutine and return from subroutine. Here we shall discuss the unconditional instructions CALL addr and RET. To quote the NEC Microcomputers, Inc., manual: "The call instruction transfers control to a subroutine. The instruction CALL addr saves the incremented program counter on the pushdown *stack* and places the address in the program counter. The pushdown stack is a block of read/write memory addressed by a

(Call)

$((SP) - 1) \leftarrow (PCH)$
$((SP) - 2) \leftarrow (PCL)$
$(SP) \leftarrow (SP) - 2$
$(PC) \leftarrow (byte\ 3)\ (byte\ 2)$

The high-order eight bits of the next instruction address are moved to the memory location whose address is one less than the content of register SP. The low-order eight bits of the next instruction address are moved to the memory location whose address is two less than the content of register SP. The content of register SP is decremented by 2. Control is transferred to the instruction whose address is specified in byte 3 and byte 2 of the current instruction.

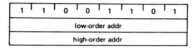

1	1	0	0	1	1	0	1
low-order addr							
high-order addr							

Cycles: 5
States: 17
Addressing: immediate/reg. indirect
Flags: none

special 16-bit register known as the Stack Pointer which can be loaded by the user (LXI H, data 16). The stack operates as a last-in first-out memory (LIFO), with the Stack Pointer register addressing the most recent entry into the stack. The Return instruction causes the entry at the top of the stack to be placed into the Program Counter. Thus a

(Return)

$(PCL) \leftarrow ((SP));$
$(PCH) \leftarrow ((SP) + 1);$
$(SP) \leftarrow (SP) + 2;$

The content of the memory location whose address is specified in register SP is moved to the low-order eight bits of register PC. The content of the memory location whose address is one more than the content of register SP is moved to the high-order eight bits of register PC. The content of register SP is incremented by 2.

1	1	0	0	1	0	0	1

Cycles: 3
States: 10
Addressing: reg. indirect
Flags: none

CALL instruction transfers program control from the main program into the subroutine and a RET instruction transfers control back to the main program." See Fig. A-6.

The location of the *stack* is usually at the higher memory addresses in the available memory of an 8080A-based microcomputer. In Fig. A-7, the stack is some distance from the main program and subroutines.

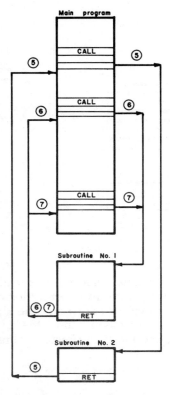

Fig. A-6. Diagram that demonstrates the branching characteristics of the CALL and RET instructions. Note that the return is always to the instruction byte immediately following the CALL instruction.

JNZ, JZ, JNC, JC, JPO, JPE, JP, and JM addr

(Conditional jump)

If (CCC),
  (PC) ◄— (byte 3) (byte 2)

If the specified condition is true, control is transferred to the instruction whose address is specified in byte 3 and byte 2 of the current instruction; otherwise, control continues sequentially.

1	1	C	C	C	0	1	0
low-order addr							
high-order addr							

Cycles:	3
States:	10
Addressing:	immediate
Flags:	none

In a conditional jump instruction, if the condition is satisfied, the second and third bytes of the instruction are transferred to the program counter and a jump occurs. If the condition is not satisfied, no changes occur to the program counter; program control passes to the instruction immediately following the jump.

```
           Memory  address

              H    L
             000  000  ┌──────────────────┐
                       │  Interrupt       │
                       │  service         │
                       │  routines        │
                       ├──────────────────┤
             000  100  │                  │
                       │  Main            │
                       │  program         │
                       ├──────────────────┤
             001  300  │                  │
                       │  Subroutines     │
                       │                  │
                       ├──────────────────┤
                       │                  │
             003  300  │                  │
                       │  Stack           │
                       │                  │
                       │                  │
                       └──────────────────┘
```

Fig. A-7. Memory map for a typical 8080-based microcomputer. Observe that the stack is located near the end of memory.

The various conditions can be summarized as follows:

NZ: The 8-bit result of the immediately preceding arithmetic or logical operation is Not equal to Zero, i.e., the zero flag is cleared.

Z: The 8-bit result of the immediately preceding arithmetic or logical operation is equal to Zero, i.e., the zero flag is set.

NC: The 8-bit result of the immediately preceding arithmetic or logical operations produces No Carry out of the most significant bit; or, the carry flag is cleared.

C: The 8-bit result of the immediately preceding arithmetic or logical operation produces a Carry out of the most significant bit; or, the carry flag is set.

PO: The 8-bit result of the immediately preceding arithmetic or logical operation has a Parity that is Odd, i.e., the parity flag is cleared.

PE: The 8-bit result of the immediately preceding arithmetic or logical operation has a Parity that is Even, i.e., the parity flag is set.

P: The 8-bit result of the immediately preceding arithmetic or logical operation produces a MSB that has a Plus sign, i.e., the sign flag is cleared.

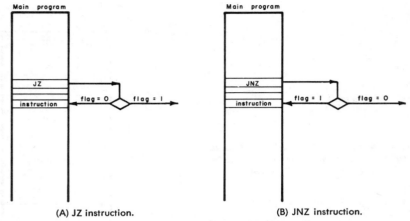

(A) JZ instruction.   (B) JNZ instruction.

Fig. A-8. The characteristics of JZ and JNZ instructions.

M: The 8-bit result of the immediately preceding arithmetic or logical operation produces a MSB that has a Minus sign, i.e., the sign flag is set.

The value of CCC that corresponds to each of the conditions has been shown several pages previously. The behavior of two of the conditional instructions, JNZ and JZ, can be understood with the aid of Fig. A-8.

In the JNZ instruction, the jump occurs only if the 8-bit result or an arithmetic or logical operation is Not Zero. The decision symbol

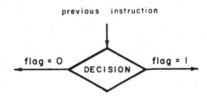

which is used in flowcharting, indicates that what happens next depends upon the state of the zero flag. For JNZ, a jump occurs only if the zero flag is cleared, i.e., at logic 0. For JZ, a jump occurs if the 8-bit result is equal to zero; in such a case the zero flag is at logic 1.

It is possible to become confused concerning the conditions NZ and Z. Note that NZ and Z refer to the 8-bit result of an operation, not to the logic state of the zero flag. NZ means that the 8-bit result of an operation is not zero; Z means that the 8-bit result of an operation is zero (though the zero flag is at logic 1). This discussion has tried to demonstrate that a condition can be viewed in terms of the 8-bit result of an arithmetic/logic operation (NZ, Z, NC, C, PO, PE, P, or M) *or* in terms of the logic state of the individual flags that test the result of an arithmetic/logic operation. The authors prefer the use of the 8-bit result of an ALU operation, including the letter symbols NZ, Z, NC, etc.

CNZ, CZ, CNC, CC, CPO, CPE, CP, and CM addr

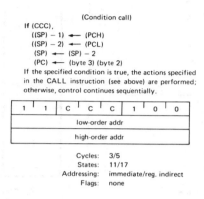

(Condition call)

If (CCC),

((SP) − 1) ←— (PCH)
((SP) − 2) ←— (PCL)
(SP) ←— (SP) − 2
(PC) ←— (byte 3) (byte 2)

If the specified condition is true, the actions specified in the CALL instruction (see above) are performed; otherwise, control continues sequentially.

1	1	C	C	C	1	0	0
low-order addr							
high-order addr							

Cycles: 3/5
States: 11/17
Addressing: immediate/reg. indirect
Flags: none

In a conditional call instruction, if the condition is satisfied, the subroutine at the memory location given in the second and third instruction bytes is called. The contents of the program counter are placed on the stack, so that a return instruction can return program control to the instruction immediately following the conditional call instruction.

If the condition is not satisfied, program execution passes to the instruction immediately following the conditional call instruction.

RNZ, RZ, RNC, RC, RPO, RPE, RP, and RM

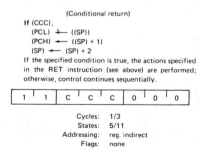

(Conditional return)

If (CCC),

(PCL) ←— ((SP))
(PCH) ←— ((SP) + 1)
(SP) ←— (SP) + 2

If the specified condition is true, the actions specified in the RET instruction (see above) are performed; otherwise, control continues sequentially.

1	1	C	C	C	0	0	0

Cycles: 1/3
States: 5/11
Addressing: reg. indirect
Flags: none

In a conditional return instruction, if the condition is satisfied, a return occurs from the subroutine; the program counter contents on the stack are transferred to the program counter and program execution resumes at the instruction immediately after the subroutine call instruction.

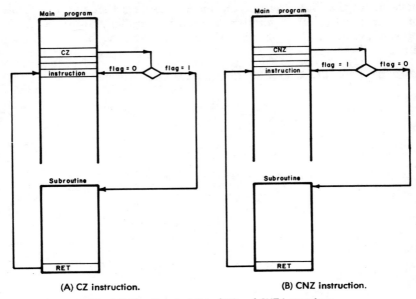

(A) CZ instruction.   (B) CNZ instruction.

Fig. A-9. The characteristics of CZ and CNZ instructions.

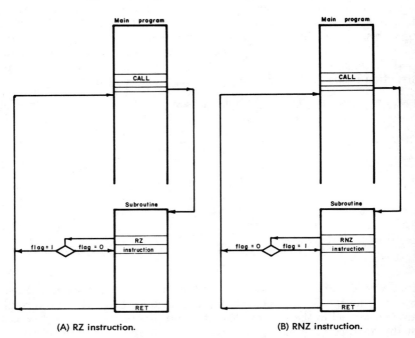

(A) RZ instruction.   (B) RNZ instruction.

Fig. A-10. The characteristics of RZ and RNZ instructions.

If the condition is not satisfied, the program execution passes to the instruction that immediately follows the conditional return instruction.

The conditional instructions CZ, CNZ, RZ, and RNZ are depicted schematically in Figs. A-9 and A-10. Remember, Z means that the zero flag must be at logic 1 for a call or return to occur; otherwise, program control passes to the next instruction. NZ means that the zero flag must be at logic 0 for a call or return to occur; otherwise, program control passes to the next instruction.

RST n

((SP) − 1) ◄— (PCH)
((SP) − 2) ◄— (PCL)
(SP) ◄— (SP) − 2
(PC) ◄— 8 · (NNN)

The high-order eight bits of the next instruction address are moved to the memory location whose address is one less than the content of register SP. The low-order eight bits of the next instruction address are moved to the memory location whose address is two less than the content of register SP. The content of register SP is decremented by two. Control is transferred to the instruction whose address is eight times the content of NNN.

1	1	N	N	N	1	1	1

Cycles: 3
States: 11
Addressing: reg. indirect
Flags: none

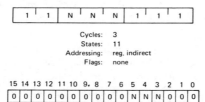

15	14	13	12	11	10	9.	8	7	6	5	4	3	2	1	0
0	0	0	0	0	0	0	0	0	0	N	N	N	0	0	0

Program Counter After Restart

To quote the *μCOM-8 Software Manual*: "The EI (Enable interrupt) and DI (disable interrupt) instructions provide control over the acceptance of an interrupt request. With this control established, the next problem to be resolved is how does the external device indicate to the processor where the desired interrupt routine is located. The 8080A accomplishes this identification by allowing the device to supply one instruction when the interrupt is acknowledged. Although any 8080A instruction can be specified, only two are of practical value: a Call instruction, CALL, and a Restart instruction, RST. . . A RST instruction is actually a specialized type of CALL. The instruction RST N is a call to one of eight locations in memory specified by an integer expression in the range, 0 through 7 in octal code, indicated by N. The locations specified by the integers 0 through 7 are listed below.

Value of N	Location Called
0	HI = 000 and LO = 000
1	HI = 000 and LO = 010
2	HI = 000 and LO = 020
3	HI = 000 and LO = 030
4	HI = 000 and LO = 040
5	HI = 000 and LO = 050
6	HI = 000 and LO = 060
7	HI = 000 and LO = 070

"A RST instruction causes the incremented program counter to be pushed onto the stack exactly as a CALL instruction does. It then loads the program counter with HI = 000 and LO = 0N0, where N is 0 through 7. Thus, RST 4 causes the program counter to be pushed onto the stack and HI = 000 and LO = 040 to be entered into the program counter.

"Program execution then continues from the restart location. If the device service routine requires more than eight bytes to service (as most do), the instruction placed at the Restart point must jump to the interrupt service subroutine. Since RST is actually a specialized subroutine call, the interrupt service subroutine *must end with a return instruction,* to return control to the interrupted program by popping the return address.

"Since the 8080A has only eight RST instructions, any additional levels of interrupt must be implemented using CALL instructions. This means a CALL addr instruction must be supplied by the interrupting device, which is somewhat more difficult to implement in hardware because CALL is a three-byte instruction. However, once implemented, a direct call to a routine is slightly faster than a Restart and subsequent jump operation. Although this is not a major factor, this difference in response speed should be considered when determining how to implement interrupt service routines. The primary benefit realized by using the CALL approach is that n-way interrupt vectoring is achieved in hardware, eliminating the need for software in low order memory (for RST processing). This frees those memory locations for use by user programs and removes a constraint from the system memory design."

PCHL

The PCHL instruction causes the program counter to be loaded with the contents of the H,L register pair. Program execution then continues at the point designated by the content of H,L. In effect, this is a jump instruction, but since the H,L register pair can be operated upon arithmetically, it allows the implementation of a variety of calculated jumps. The instruction sequence:

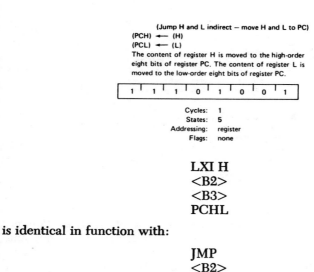

(Jump H and L indirect — move H and L to PC)

(PCH) ◄— (H)

(PCL) ◄— (L)

The content of register H is moved to the high-order eight bits of register PC. The content of register L is moved to the low-order eight bits of register PC.

1	1	1	0	1	0	0	1

Cycles: 1
States: 5
Addressing: register
Flags: none

LXI H
\<B2\>
\<B3\>
PCHL

is identical in function with:

JMP
\<B2\>
\<B3\>

STACK, I/O, AND MACHINE CONTROL GROUP

This group of instructions performs I/O, manipulates the stack, and alters internal control flags. Unless otherwise specified, *condition flags are not affected by any instructions in this group.*

PUSH rp and POP rp

To quote the *µCOM-8 Software Manual*: "Two special instructions enable programmers to save and restore the registers using the stack, PUSH and POP. PUSH rp causes the register pair specified by rp to be placed at the top of the stack. The stack is a special portion of read/write memory designated by the user and treated as a last-in

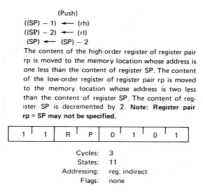

(Push)

((SP) − 1) ◄— (rh)

((SP) − 2) ◄— (rl)

(SP) ◄— (SP) − 2

The content of the high-order register of register pair rp is moved to the memory location whose address is one less than the content of register SP. The content of the low-order register of register pair rp is moved to the memory location whose address is two less than the content of register SP. The content of register SP is decremented by 2. **Note: Register pair rp = SP may not be specified.**

1	1	R	P	0	1	0	1

Cycles: 3
States: 11
Addressing: reg. indirect
Flags: none

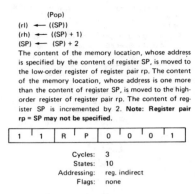

(Pop)

$(rl) \leftarrow ((SP))$

$(rh) \leftarrow ((SP) + 1)$

$(SP) \leftarrow (SP) + 2$

The content of the memory location, whose address is specified by the content of register SP, is moved to the low-order register of register pair rp. The content of the memory location, whose address is one more than the content of register SP, is moved to the high-order register of register pair rp. The content of register SP is incremented by 2. **Note: Register pair rp = SP may not be specified.**

1	1	R	P	0	0	0	1

Cycles: 3
States: 10
Addressing: reg. indirect
Flags: none

first-out (LIFO) memory through the use of a 16-bit Stack Pointer. A PUSH operation causes the Stack Pointer to decrement by one and store the most significant register (the HI register) in memory at this new location specified by the Stack Pointer. The Stack Pointer is then decremented again and the least significant register (the LO register) is then stored in memory at that address. For a POP operation, the data at the memory location addressed by the Stack Pointer is moved into the least significant register (the LO register, which can be C, E, or L); the Stack Pointer is incremented and the data at the new memory location is loaded into the most significant register (the HI register, which can be B, D, or H). The Stack Pointer is then incremented again.

"For both PUSH and POP operations, the register pair, rp, may be one of the three double registers BC, DE, or HL (identified as B, D,

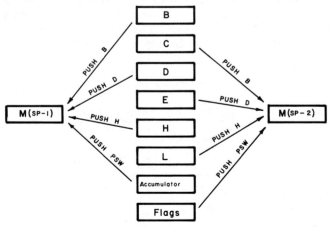

Fig. A-11. The four different PUSH instructions. Observe that the HI byte is pushed first on the stack.

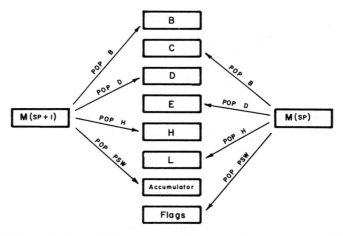

Fig. A-12. The four different POP instructions. Observe that the LO byte is popped first.

and H, respectively) or the contents of the Flag register and the Accumulator, indicated by PSW which stands for program status word)."

The PUSH and POP instructions are represented schematically in Figs. A-11 and A-12. In these diagrams, SP is the stack pointer location before the PUSH or POP instruction.

PUSH psw and POP psw

(Push processor status word)

$((SP) - 1) \leftarrow (A)$

$((SP) - 2)_0 \leftarrow (CY)$, $((SP) - 2)_1 \leftarrow 1$

$((SP) - 2)_2 \leftarrow (P)$, $((SP) - 2)_3 \leftarrow 0$

$((SP) - 2)_4 \leftarrow (AC)$, $((SP) - 2)_5 \leftarrow 0$

$((SP) - 2)_6 \leftarrow (Z)$, $((SP) - 2)_7 \leftarrow (S)$

$(SP) \leftarrow (SP) - 2$

The content of register A is moved to the memory location whose address is one less than register SP. The contents of the condition flags are assembled into a processor status word and the word is moved to the memory location whose address is two less than the content of register SP. The content of register SP is decremented by two.

1	1	1	1	1	0	1	0	1

Cycles: 3
States: 11
Addressing: reg. indirect
Flags: none

The letters PSW stand for *processor status word*, which is the contents of the accumulator and the five status flags. Refer to the preceding description of the PUSH rp and POP rp instructions. The flag register, F, is regarded as the least significant register and the accumulator, A,

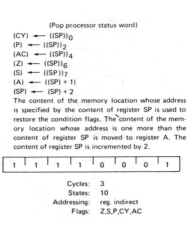

(Pop processor status word)

$(CY) \leftarrow ((SP))_0$
$(P) \leftarrow ((SP))_2$
$(AC) \leftarrow ((SP))_4$
$(Z) \leftarrow ((SP))_6$
$(S) \leftarrow ((SP))_7$
$(A) \leftarrow ((SP) + 1)$
$(SP) \leftarrow (SP) + 2$

The content of the memory location whose address is specified by the content of register SP is used to restore the condition flags. The content of the memory location whose address is one more than the content of register SP is moved to register A. The content of register SP is incremented by 2.

1	1	1	1	0	0	0	1

Cycles:	3
States:	10
Addressing:	reg. indirect
Flags:	Z,S,P,CY,AC

is regarded as the most significant register. The program status word is important because it saves the actual machine status as determined by the five flag bits. When it is restored, machine operation can resume in the correct state, regardless of how the interrupting subroutine affected the flags.

FLAG WORD

D_7	D_6	D_5	D_4	D_3	D_2	D_1	D_0
S	Z	0	AC	0	P	1	CY

In the μCOM-8 integrated-circuit chip, which is essentially identical in function with the 8080A microprocessor chip, there is an extra status flag, SUB. In the flag register, SUB occupies the D_5 bit position. In addition, the D_3 bit position is at logic 1 rather than at logic 0 (which is the case for the 8080A chip). The authors consider the SUB flag to be a useful feature of 8080A-type microprocessors, and hope that it becomes incorporated in future versions of the chip by manufacturers such as Texas Instruments, National Semiconductor, Intel, etc.

An example of the operation of the stack is given in Fig. A-13. The section of code employed is

Main Task	Subroutine
LXI SP	PUSH B
303	PUSH D
003	PUSH H
CALL	PUSH PSW
<B2>	
<B3>	

The stack pointer originally was located at HI = 003 and LO = 303. After the CALL subroutine instruction, the two program counter bytes are pushed onto the stack and the stack pointer moves to HI = 003 and LO = 301. Note that the HI program counter byte goes on the stack first, but comes off the stack last. A succession of four push instructions load the stack with the contents of the six general-purpose registers, the accumulator, and the flag register. After all of this, the stack pointer (SP) location is HI = 003 and LO = 271, the top filled location on the stack.

Once the subroutine has been executed, there is the problem of removing the contents of the stack and placing them back into the 8080A microprocessor chip. The section of code, located at the end of the subroutine, that accomplishes this is:

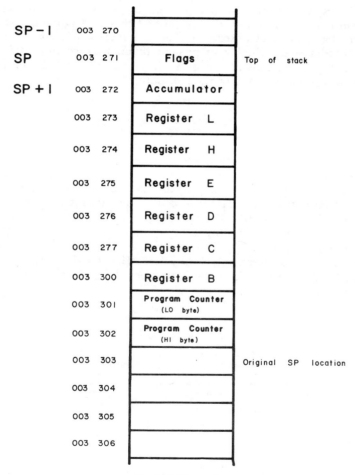

Fig. A-13. The stack.

POP PSW
POP H
POP D
POP B
RET

In each case, the LO byte comes off the stack first. Recall that in three-byte instructions, the LO byte is always the second byte of the instruction. Thus, the 8080A chip is consistent in its handling of 16-bit address words. Once the contents of the stack have been popped off, the stack pointer returns to its original location of HI = 003 and LO = 303.

Registers can be pushed and popped in any order. However, the program counter is almost always pushed first and popped last. The caution that you must observe is that you must pop registers in the reverse order with which you pushed them. For example, with the stack configuration shown in Fig. A-13, if you executed the following section of code at the end of the subroutine

POP PSW
POP B
POP H
POP D
RET

you would encounter problems with the execution of the main program. The original register contents would not be returned to their original locations. The chip would attempt to execute the program, but there is not much chance of a useful result.

If you do not need to push registers on a stack during a subroutine call, do not do so. Store only that information on the stack which is needed by the 8080A chip when it resumes the main program.

XTHL

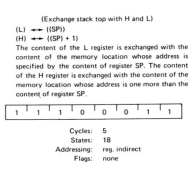

(Exchange stack top with H and L)

(L) ←→ ((SP))
(H) ←→ ((SP) + 1)

The content of the L register is exchanged with the content of the memory location whose address is specified by the content of register SP. The content of the H register is exchanged with the content of the memory location whose address is one more than the content of register SP.

1	1	1	0	0	0	1	1

Cycles: 5
States: 18
Addressing: reg. indirect
Flags: none

The XTHL instruction is used to exchange the contents of the H,L register pair with the top pair of items on the stack. The contents of the top location, the one addressed by the stack pointer SP, are exchanged with the contents of register L. The stack pointer is incremented, and the contents of memory addressed by this new value of SP are exchanged with the contents of register H.

SPHL

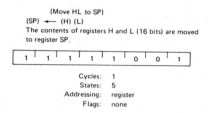

(Move HL to SP)

(SP) ◄— (H) (L)

The contents of registers H and L (16 bits) are moved to register SP.

| 1 | 1 | 1 | 1 | 1 | 0 | 0 | 1 |

Cycles: 1
States: 5
Addressing: register
Flags: none

The SPHL instruction is used to load the stack pointer register with the contents of the register pair H,L. The contents of L are placed in the LO eight bits of the stack pointer, and the contents of H are placed in the HI eight bits of the stack pointer. As pointed out in the NEC Microcomputers, Inc., manual: "The SPHL instruction can be used to load the stack pointer with a value which has been computed using the double register arithmetic operations available with the HL register pair. This should always be done with care, since it is easy to lose track of where the stack pointer is pointing, with subsequent loss of stack content."

OUT port

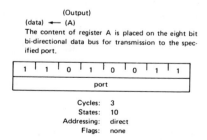

(Output)

(data) ◄— (A)

The content of register A is placed on the eight bit bi-directional data bus for transmission to the specified port.

| 1 | 1 | 0 | 1 | 0 | 0 | 1 | 1 |
| port |

Cycles: 3
States: 10
Addressing: direct
Flags: none

The OUT port instruction moves the 8-bit contents of the accumulator to the output port specified by the second byte of the instruction. Two-hundred fifty-six unique output ports can be selected. During the third machine cycle of the instruction, the device code appears on the ad-of an interrupt. Both operations clear INTE and thus disable the interrupt facility. If further interrupts are to be acknowledged after a Reset or Acknowledge Interrupt, the program must re-enable the flip-flop. Two instructions, EI, Enable Interrupt, and DI, Disable Interrupt, provide programmed control of the INTE flip-flop. The EI instruction sets the INTE flip-flop to one, enabling the interrupt facility, while the DI instruction clears the INTE flip-flop to zero, disabling the interrupt facility. Thus if it is desired that a section of the program be executed with high speed and without the possibility of being interrupted, the DI instruction may be used to disable interrupts for that section of code. After the section is complete, EI re-enables the interrupt facility. Since the acknowledgement of an interrupt request resets the INTE flip-flop to zero, an EI should be the first instruction in any routine that services interrupts. (This assumes that the interrupt acknowledge resets the interrupt request. This must be done to prevent hanging up the 8080A processor.) An exception should be made when servicing the fastest I/O device. To avoid disturbing service to this I/O unit, the INTE flip-flop should be enabled at the end of the routine."

HLT

(Halt)
The processor is stopped. The registers and flags are unaffected.

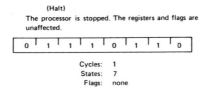

Cycles: 1
States: 7
Flags: none

The HLT instruction causes the processor to suspend operation until the 8080A chip receives a reset signal or receives an interrupt request signal (INT). The processor accepts the INT request regardless of the condition of the internal interrupt flip-flop. After processing the interrupt, instruction execution continues at the next location after the halt command.

NOP

(No op)
No operation is performed. The registers and flags are unaffected.

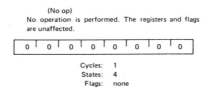

Cycles: 1
States: 4
Flags: none

dress bus, an $\overline{\text{OUT}}$ control pulse is generated, and the contents of the accumulator appear on the external bidirectional data bus.

IN port

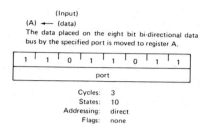

(Input)

(A) ◄— (data)

The data placed on the eight bit bi-directional data bus by the specified port is moved to register A.

| 1 | 1 | 0 | 1 | 1 | 0 | 1 | 1 |

port

Cycles: 3
States: 10
Addressing: direct
Flags: none

The IN port instruction permits the 8080A chip to read the data present at the input port given by the second byte of the instruction. Two-hundred fifty-six unique input ports can be addressed. During the third machine cycle of the instruction, the device code for the input device appears on the address bus, an $\overline{\text{IN}}$ control signal appears on the control bus, and information appearing on the bidirectional data bus also appears in the accumulator.

EI and DI

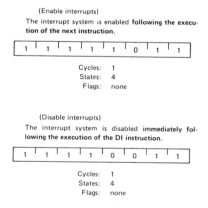

(Enable interrupts)

The interrupt system is enabled following the execution of the next instruction.

| 1 | 1 | 1 | 1 | 1 | 0 | 1 | 1 |

Cycles: 1
States: 4
Flags: none

(Disable interrupts)

The interrupt system is disabled immediately following the execution of the DI instruction.

| 1 | 1 | 1 | 1 | 0 | 0 | 1 | 1 |

Cycles: 1
States: 4
Flags: none

To quote the NEC Microcomputers, Inc., *μCOM-8 Software Manual*: "Whether the 8080A responds to an interrupt request is determined by the state of an internal interrupt flip-flop, INTE. When this flip-flop is set to one, the processor responds to interrupts. When it is reset to zero, the processor ignores interrupt requests. The INTE flip-flop is affected by both program control and system operation. System operations which affect INTE are a system reset and the acknowledgement

The NOP instruction does absolutely nothing except occupy a location in memory and take up four states during program execution. It is used for program debugging, in which extra NOP instructions are placed in a program for subsequent modification. When deletions are made to a program, NOPs should be inserted in their place.

With the aid of material in the *Intel 8080 Microcomputer Systems User's Manual* and the NEC Microcomputers, Inc., *μCOM-8 Software Manual*, a detailed description of the individual instructions of the 8080A microprocessor chip has been provided. The authors are grateful to both Intel Corporation and NEC Microcomputers, Inc., for their kind permission to use information in their manuals. If you are a serious user of the 8080A chip, you should have both manuals in your possession.

8080 Instruction Set (Intel Corp. Summary)

Mnemonic	Description	D7	D6	D5	D4	D3	D2	D1	D0	Clock[2] Cycles
MOV r1,r2	Move register to register	0	1	D	D	D	S	S	S	5
MOV M,r	Move register to memory	0	1	1	1	0	S	S	S	7
MOV r,M	Move memory to register	0	1	D	D	D	1	1	0	7
HLT	Halt	0	1	1	1	0	1	1	0	7
MVI r	Move immediate register	0	0	D	D	D	1	1	0	7
MVI M	Move immediate memory	0	0	1	1	0	1	1	0	10
INR r	Increment register	0	0	D	D	D	1	0	0	5
DCR r	Decrement register	0	0	D	D	D	1	0	1	5
INR M	Increment memory	0	0	1	1	0	1	0	0	10
DCR M	Decrement memory	0	0	1	1	0	1	0	1	10
ADD r	Add register to A	1	0	0	0	0	S	S	S	4
ADC r	Add register to A with carry	1	0	0	0	1	S	S	S	4
SUB r	Subtract register from A	1	0	0	1	0	S	S	S	4
SBB r	Subtract register from A with borrow	1	0	0	1	1	S	S	S	4
ANA r	And register with A	1	0	1	0	0	S	S	S	4
XRA r	Exclusive Or register with A	1	0	1	0	1	S	S	S	4
ORA r	Or register with A	1	0	1	1	0	S	S	S	4
CMP r	Compare register with A	1	0	1	1	1	S	S	S	4
ADD M	Add memory to A	1	0	0	0	0	1	1	0	7
ADC M	Add memory to A with carry	1	0	0	0	1	1	1	0	7
SUB M	Subtract memory from A	1	0	0	1	0	1	1	0	7
SBB M	Subtract memory from A with borrow	1	0	0	1	1	1	1	0	7
ANA M	And memory with A	1	0	1	0	0	1	1	0	7
XRA M	Exclusive Or memory with A	1	0	1	0	1	1	1	0	7
ORA M	Or memory with A	1	0	1	1	0	1	1	0	7
CMP M	Compare memory with A	1	0	1	1	1	1	1	0	7
ADI	Add immediate to A	1	1	0	0	0	1	1	0	7
ACI	Add immediate to A with carry	1	1	0	0	1	1	1	0	7
SUI	Subtract immediate from A	1	1	0	1	0	1	1	0	7
SBI	Subtract immediate from A with borrow	1	1	0	1	1	1	1	0	7
ANI	And immediate with A	1	1	1	0	0	1	1	0	7
XRI	Exclusive Or immediate with A	1	1	1	0	T	1	1	0	7
ORI	Or immediate with A	1	1	1	1	0	1	1	0	7
CPI	Compare immediate with A	1	1	1	1	1	1	1	0	7
RLC	Rotate A left	0	0	0	0	0	1	1	1	4
RRC	Rotate A right	0	0	0	0	1	1	1	1	4
RAL	Rotate A left through carry	0	0	0	1	0	1	1	1	4
RAR	Rotate A right through carry	0	0	0	1	1	1	1	1	4
JMP	Jump unconditional	1	1	0	0	0	0	1	1	10
JC	Jump on carry	1	1	0	1	1	0	1	0	10
JNC	Jump on no carry	1	1	0	1	0	0	1	0	10
JZ	Jump on zero	1	1	0	0	1	0	1	0	10
JNZ	Jump on no zero	1	1	0	0	0	0	1	0	10
JP	Jump on positive	1	1	1	1	0	0	1	0	10
JM	Jump on minus	1	1	1	1	1	0	1	0	10
JPE	Jump on parity even	1	1	1	0	1	0	1	0	10
JPO	Jump on parity odd	1	1	1	0	0	0	1	0	10
CALL	Call unconditional	1	1	0	0	1	1	0	1	17
CC	Call on carry	1	1	0	1	1	1	0	0	11/17
CNC	Call on no carry	1	1	0	1	0	1	0	0	11/17
CZ	Call on zero	1	1	0	0	1	1	0	0	11/17
CNZ	Call on no zero	1	1	0	0	0	1	0	0	11/17
CP	Call on positive	1	1	1	1	0	1	0	0	11/17
CM	Call on minus	1	1	1	1	1	1	0	0	11/17
CPE	Call on parity even	1	1	1	0	1	1	0	0	11/17
CPO	Call on parity odd	1	1	1	0	0	1	0	0	11/17
RET	Return	1	1	0	0	1	0	0	1	10
RC	Return on carry	1	1	0	1	1	0	0	0	5/11
RNC	Return on no carry	1	1	0	1	0	0	0	0	5/11
RZ	Return on zero	1	1	0	0	1	0	0	0	5/11
RNZ	Return on no zero	1	1	0	0	0	0	C	0	5/11
RP	Return on positive	1	1	1	1	0	0	0	0	5/11
RM	Return on minus	1	1	1	1	1	0	0	0	5/11
RPE	Return on parity even	1	1	1	0	1	0	0	0	5/11
RPO	Return on parity odd	1	1	1	0	0	0	0	0	5/11
RST	Restart	1	1	A	A	A	1	1	1	11
IN	Input	1	1	0	1	1	0	1	1	10
OUT	Output	1	1	0	1	0	0	1	1	10
LXI B	Load immediate register Pair B & C	0	0	0	0	0	0	0	1	10
LXI D	Load immediate register Pair D & E	0	0	0	1	0	0	0	1	10
LXI H	Load immediate register Pair H & L	0	0	1	0	0	0	0	1	10
LXI SP	Load immediate stack pointer	0	0	1	1	0	0	0	1	10
PUSH B	Push register Pair B & C on stack	1	1	0	0	0	1	0	1	11
PUSH D	Push register Pair D & E on stack	1	1	0	1	0	1	0	1	11
PUSH H	Push register Pair H & L on stack	1	1	1	0	0	1	0	1	11
PUSH PSW	Push A and Flags on stack	1	1	1	1	0	1	0	1	11
POP B	Pop register Pair B & C off stack	1	1	0	0	0	0	0	1	10
POP D	Pop register Pair D & E off stack	1	1	0	1	0	0	0	1	10
POP H	Pop register Pair H & L off stack	1	1	1	0	0	0	0	1	10
POP PSW	Pop A and Flags off stack	1	1	1	1	0	0	0	1	10
STA	Store A direct	0	0	1	1	0	0	1	0	13
LDA	Load A direct	0	0	1	1	1	0	1	0	13
XCHG	Exchange D & E, H & L Registers	1	1	1	0	1	0	1	1	4
XTHL	Exchange top of stack, H & L	1	1	1	0	0	0	1	1	18
SPHL	H & L to stack pointer	1	1	1	1	1	0	0	1	5
PCHL	H & L to program counter	1	1	1	0	1	0	0	1	5
DAD B	Add B & C to H & L	0	0	0	0	1	0	0	1	10
DAD D	Add D & E to H & L	0	0	0	1	1	0	0	1	10
DAD H	Add H & L to H & L	0	0	1	0	1	0	0	1	10
DAD SP	Add stack pointer to H & L	0	0	1	1	1	0	0	1	10
STAX B	Store A indirect	0	0	0	0	0	0	1	0	7
STAX D	Store A indirect	0	0	0	1	0	0	1	0	7
LDAX B	Load A indirect	0	0	0	0	1	0	1	0	7
LDAX D	Load A indirect	0	0	0	1	1	0	1	0	7
INX B	Increment B & C registers	0	0	0	0	0	0	1	1	5
INX D	Increment D & E registers	0	0	0	1	0	0	1	1	5
INX H	Increment H & L registers	0	0	1	0	0	0	1	1	5
INX SP	Increment stack pointer	0	0	1	1	0	0	1	1	5
DCX B	Decrement B & C	0	0	0	0	1	0	1	1	5
DCX D	Decrement D & E	0	0	0	1	1	0	1	1	5
DCX H	Decrement H & L	0	0	1	0	1	0	1	1	5
DCX SP	Decrement stack pointer	0	0	1	1	1	0	1	1	5
CMA	Complement A	0	0	1	0	1	1	1	1	4
STC	Set carry	0	0	1	1	0	1	1	1	4
CMC	Complement carry	0	0	1	1	1	1	1	1	4
DAA	Decimal adjust A	0	0	1	0	0	1	1	1	4
SHLD	Store H & L direct	0	0	1	0	0	0	1	0	16
LHLD	Load H & L direct	0	0	1	0	1	0	1	0	16
EI	Enable Interrupts	1	1	1	1	1	0	1	1	4
DI	Disable interrupt	1	1	1	1	0	0	1	1	4
NOP	No-operation	0	0	0	0	0	0	0	0	4

NOTES: 1. DDD or SSS — 000 B — 001 C — 010 D — 011 E — 100 H — 101 L — 110 Memory — 111 A.

2. Two possible cycle times, (5/11) indicate instruction cycles dependent on condition flags.

Index

MW, 59